JUDITH ANDERSON

Desley Deacon is a writer and prize-winning historian living in Sydney. Her experience of living and working in many countries, including a long period in the United States, has stimulated her interest in transnational lives and careers. She is currently Emeritus Professor at the Australian National University and was Director of Women's and Gender Studies at the University of Texas at Austin. Her work has been reviewed in the *New York Times Review of Books*, the *New Yorker* and the *Washington Post*. She reviewed regularly for the *Women's Review of Books* and now writes for the *Australian Book Review*.

Also by Desley Deacon:

Elsie Clews Parsons: Inventing Modern Life
University of Chicago Press, 1997

Managing Gender: The State, the New Middle Class and Women Workers 1830–1930
Oxford University Press, 1989

Elites in Australia
With John Higley and Don Smart. Routledge and Kegan Paul, 1979

Talking and Listening in the Age of Modernity
Edited with Joy Damousi. ANU Press, 2007

Transnational Ties: Australian Lives in the World
Edited with Penny Russell and Angela Woollacott. ANU Press, 2008

Transnational Lives: Biographies of Global Modernity
Edited with Penny Russell and Angela Woollacott.
Palgrave Macmillan, 2010

JUDITH ANDERSON

**Australian Star
First Lady of the American Stage**

DESLEY DEACON

Melbourne, Victoria

First published 2019
Kerr Publishing Pty Ltd
Melbourne, Victoria
ABN 64 124 219 638

© 2019 Desley Deacon. All rights reserved.

This book is copyright. Apart from fair dealing for the purpose of private study, research, criticism or review, or under Copyright Agency Ltd rules of recording, no part may be reproduced by any means.
The moral right of the author has been asserted.

All efforts have been made to contact copyright owners and controllers for permission to reproduce herein. If you believe your copyright material has been infringed, please contact the author or publisher.

ISBN 978-1-875703-18-0 (eBook)
ISBN 978-1-875703-06-7 (Print on Demand, PoD)

BIC Category:	Biography & Autobiography
BISAC Category 1:	BIO005000 BIOGRAPHY & AUTOBIOGRAPHY / Entertainment & Performing Arts
	BIO006000 BIOGRAPHY & AUTOBIOGRAPHY / Historical
	BIO022000 BIOGRAPHY & AUTOBIOGRAPHY / Women
BISAC Category 2:	DRA01000 Shakespeare; 001000 / American / General; DRA012000 Australian & Oceanian
BISAC Category 3:	HIS038000 / Americas; HIS004000 / Australia & New Zealand
	HIS036060 HISTORY / United States / 20th Century
	HIS058000 / Women

Cover photograph: © 1927 Judith Anderson, by Nickolas Muray, 1927. Eastman Museum / Mimi Muray Levitt
Cover design: Paul Taylder
Book design: Paul Taylder of Xigrafix Media & Design
Typeset in Palatino 11/15pt

Print-on-Demand and eBook distribution: ebookalchemy.com.au

National Library of Australia PrePublication Data Service:

A catalogue record for this book is available from the National Library of Australia

*To my darling grandchildren
Inez and Raphy*

Contents

ACT I	Beginnings	
Scene 1	Adelaide	2
Chapter 1	The Silver King 1870s–1903	3
Chapter 2	Outlaw Fan 1903–1912	9
Scene 2	Sydney	20
Chapter 3	Frantic 1913–14	21
Chapter 4	Francee 1915	31
Chapter 5	Marking Time 1915–17	43
ACT II	Sensation	
Scene 3	New York	54
Chapter 6	Godzone Country 1918–22	55
Chapter 7	Judith 1923–4	67
Chapter 8	Star 1925–6	79
Interlude	Australia	92
Chapter 9	Failure 1927	93
ACT III	Greatness	
Scene 4	California Dreaming	118
Chapter 10	New Beginnings	119
Chapter 11	Love and Ambition 1929	129
Chapter 12	Sophisticated Lady 1930–33	139
Chapter 13	Hollywood Calling 1933	149
Scene 5	London Calling	158
Chapter 14	The Quality of Greatness 1934	159
Chapter 15	Directed by Guthrie McClintic 1934–5	165
Chapter 16	Co-starring John Gielgud 1936–7	177
Chapter 17	Marriage and Olivier 1937–8	187
Interlude	Marriage and Career	196
Chapter 18	Faculty Wife 1938	197
Chapter 19	*Family Portrait* 1939	209
Scene 6	Hollywood	216
Chapter 20	Directed by Alfred Hitchcock 1939–40	217
Chapter 21	*Macbeth* 1941–2	235

Chapter 22	*Three Sisters* 1942–3	241
Chapter 23	In the Pacific 1943–4	249
Chapter 24	Character Actress 1944–7	263

ACT IV	Climax	
Scene 7	*Medea*	278
Chapter 25	Judith the Great 1947–8	279
Chapter 26	*Medea* and Friends 1948–9	293

ACT V	Anti-climax	
Scene 8	Santa Barbara	308
Chapter 27	Families, Professional and Personal 1950	309
Chapter 28	Changes, Professional and Personal 1951–9	321
Chapter 29	A New Career: Television Star 1950–59	343
Interlude	Paris and Canberra	360
Chapter 30	International Icon 1955–60	361
Scene 9	Grande Dame	382
Chapter 31	Dear Darling Dame 1960–63	383
Chapter 32	Dame Judith the Great, in Tennis Shoes 1963–9	399
Chapter 33	*Hamlet* 1969–71	417
Chapter 34	*Medea* Recidiva 1982–92	427

| **ACT VI** | Finis | |
| Chapter 35 | The (Almost) Last First Lady | 443 |

ACT VII	Afterlife	
Chapter 36	Popular Culture Icon	453
	Judith Anderson Performances	463
	Recordings	481
	Sources	482
	Reference	484
	Frequently Consulted Newspapers and Journals	484
	Published Material	486
	Documentary	498
	Acknowledgements	499
	List of Illustrations	501
	Index	505

A personality – real or manufactured – produces its share of applause on sight. The real kind, the indefinable, individual, unique, magnetic something that is radiated by a particular human being, has the special power of creating wild excitement when he simply appears... whatever it is, it is obviously present on sight. Arturo Toscanini, Leonard Bernstein, Lotte Lehmann, Laurette Taylor, Ezio Pinza, Leopold Stokowski, Judith Anderson, President Kennedy, Greta Garbo, Marlene Dietrich, Alla Nazimova, and a few others... had this 'something.' What I refer to is not accomplishment but personality – what they stir on sight in audiences before they have performed: animal magnetism, if you like.

Lehman Engel, 1971

ACT I
Beginnings

Scene One
Adelaide

View from Mount Lofty, looking towards the Port, across the Adelaide Plains ca 1846 by George French Angas and J W Giles.

State Library of South Australia

Chapter One
The Silver King 1870s–1903

Sometime in the late 1870s two young men set out for the Antipodes from the family farm outside the Scottish town of Arbroath. Like many Scots adventurers before and after them, they were determined to make their fortune wherever it could be made. They were joining a kinsman in New Zealand, the latest outpost of the British Empire, literally half a world away. Not only was there the prospect of land, but more enticing to the young adventurers, there was the glittering lure of gold.

One of these young men was Judith Anderson's father, James Anderson Anderson, and his companion was his younger brother George Batchelor Anderson.[1] Even if they had set off from home with the intention of settling on the rich farming lands west of Dunedin in New Zealand's South Island, they couldn't resist trying their luck on the nearby goldfields, and gold – and silver – were the sirens that led James a merry dance till his death, alone and indigent, in Kalgoorlie sixty years later.

James and George crossed the Tasman sometime in the early 1880s, when rumours of gold sent thousands of men tramping a thousand miles north of Melbourne to the dry, dusty Mount Browne, then south to the Barrier Ranges, where silver had been mined in small quantities for several years.

---
1 James 1858–1939 and George 1861–1924 were the sons of David Anderson and Elizabeth Anderson Batchelor.

Young and healthy enough to avoid the death by thirst, starvation, sunstroke, exhaustion or typhoid that claimed many of these fortune seekers, James ended up in the vicinity of Broken Hill, in the dry far west of New South Wales, when Australia's greatest mining field was discovered. He may have been one of the many small prospectors around Silverton, 50 kilometres west of the ranges; or he could well have been one of the shepherds or well-sinkers who were the first to spot signs of precious minerals on the huge sheep stations bordering the range – the Mount Gipps station managed by Scot George McCulloch, and Kinchega owned by the Hughes brothers. Indeed, it was Mount Gibbs boundary rider, Charles Rasp, and two dam-sinkers, David James and James Poole, who, in September 1883, first pegged a 40-acre mineral lease on the centre of the rocky outcrop known as Broken Hill; and a group of workers on the station, including manager McCulloch, who formed a syndicate to peg six more claims and explore them more fully. The Broken Hill Proprietary Limited was formed in June 1885.

Among the first to follow up on the claims of this syndicate was the 25-year-old James Anderson. In December 1883, with Julius Nickel and Otto Fischer of Silverton, Anderson pegged out the Cosmopolitan claim on Block 17, immediately to the north of the syndicate's Blocks 10–16. When they sold the claim two years later he was a wealthy man.

Although Broken Hill was rich, it was, however, unhealthy. The residents pleaded with the New South Wales government to supply pure water to the parched town, but before they did so, it experienced a major typhus epidemic. In early 1888, at the peak of his prosperity, James Anderson became so ill he had to be evacuated to Adelaide, South Australia's capital and the closest and most accessible large town. There he was nursed by Jessie Margaret Saltmarsh, whom he married on 10 May 1888 at the residence of her brother William in the rapidly growing suburb of Parkside. Over the next nine years they had four children, Elizabeth Jessie (Diddie) born in 1889, Jack (1891), Frank Batchelor (1895), and finally, Frances Margaret (Fanny, later Judith) in 1897.

Judith Anderson's parents could be seen as representing two sides of the young colony of South Australia. Established as a free settlement a little more than 50 years before to the idealistic but systematic plans of Edward Gibbon Wakefield, it had a small fertile fringe on the coast and a vast area of mineral-rich arid and semi-arid land in the interior. Almost half of the tiny population of 300,000 lived in Adelaide. Among them were Jessie Saltmarsh's family, worthy townspeople active in the Parkside Baptist Church and the trade union and musical communities. She herself was a trained nurse, recently graduated from the Adelaide Children's Hospital. James Anderson, on the other hand, was a risk-taker, at home in the dusty, sparsely-populated inland, in brawling pubs, and on racecourses from Silverton to Adelaide's Victoria Park.

In the early days of the marriage he continued to prosper. As his eldest daughter Elizabeth put it many years later, 'Everything Father turned his hand to he made money... He became a millionaire and they used to call him "The Silver King"'(from the enormously popular play of the period).[2]

But his luck did not last. 'Father made money but did not keep it for long,' Elizabeth wrote. 'He had race horses... He gambled so much, [and] was known to take the biggest doubles in big races... He also played cards... [he] took no

---

2   Elizabeth Anderson wrote a series of brief autobiographical memoirs held by the family. I do not provide footnotes where it is clear that this is the source.

interest in anything but races and gambling.' His rise and fall in the Adelaide racing fraternity can be traced in the newspapers and city directories of the time. In 1891 the family moved to the seaside suburb of Glenelg, close to the Morphettville Racecourse, and his name began to appear in accounts of the races, along with his horse Herod. As he joined the committee of the Tattersalls Club and acted as racing steward, they moved to the spacious house at 6 Angas Street, Kent Town, where Fanny was born. Close to the Victoria Park Racecourse, it was next door to the home of his friend Henry Hughes, the veteran racing handicapper.

Sometime around the time of Fanny's birth in 1897 something disastrous happened. Elizabeth remembered simply that her father 'lost his Broken Hill Silver Mine.' They moved to a smaller home in nearby Rose Park, and then to an even smaller one. Appointed judge by the Port Adelaide Racing Club at their recently opened Cheltenham Racecourse, James became even more involved in the racing world, drinking heavily and gambling recklessly. In September 1903 he made an unpopular decision that, according to the Adelaide *Advertiser*, 'put in peril his reputation as a good judge.'

Born into this disintegrating family, Judith Anderson was always haunted by the sense that she was an unwanted baby. 'It was a great shock to mother when she found out she had married a gambler,' she wrote in a memoir.[3] When James finally terrified his family with his drunken rages, Jessie Anderson sued for a separation. Around 1903, when Fanny was about six years old, James Anderson left the family to join his brother on the Western Australian goldfields. She never saw her father again, but, too young to have understood the

---

3 Judith Anderson's unpublished memoir, written with Robert Wallsten, is in the Wallsten Papers in the Special Research Collections of the University of California Santa Barbara Library. I do not provide footnotes where it is clear that this is the source.

depth of his decline, she continued to think of him as the golden Adonis who had carried her on his shoulders as a little girl.[4]

---

[4] Elizabeth Anderson gives an affectionate picture of James Anderson before his final deterioration in 'John Anderson', 1–2.

My Pretty Maid. *Fanny Anderson and Nancy Sack. Winners of the Humorous Duet at the Recent Unley Competitions.*

Thelma Photos / *Critic* (Adelaide) 2 August 1911: 16

Chapter Two
Outlaw Fan 1903–1912

Jessie Anderson was for all intents and purposes a widow from 1903, and Fanny Anderson was one of several high achieving daughters of the period who were brought up by widowed mothers. In the case of the artist Stella Bowen, born four years before Fanny, her mother had sufficient financial resources to maintain, even if precariously, their social position.[5] Fanny's mother had to support herself. The last of the fortune had disappeared, so family lore has it, on a horse race. She sold everything that was left and rented a grocery store on Watson Avenue, Rose Park, close to the Rose Park Primary School, with living quarters behind.

Stella Bowen describes a middle-class childhood in a 'sizable' house, 'at a sufficiently good but not fashionable address,' with a summer-house in front and a stable and a coach house behind. She played 'decorous games' in the garden of Bishop's Court, went to dancing classes at Government House, and whiled away her days reading through the family library.

This is the sort of childhood Fanny Anderson might have had – although the family's social milieu would have revolved more around the Jockey Club and Tattersalls. But from the age of six, her world was the little shop, with its bags of sugar and other staples, its tins of biscuits, its penny sweets, its school supplies, chemist items, and haberdashery,

---

5 Stella Bowen, *Drawn from Life: A Memoir*, 1999, 11-12, 15, 16, 17.

its homemade ice cream, cakes and pies, and the living room, two bedrooms and kitchen at the back, her mother busy with the shop, the housework, the cooking, the sewing, and the four children, who helped in the shop before and after school. Elizabeth had gone to a private school; now they attended the state school on their doorstep.

Nevertheless, Judith Anderson recalled in her memoirs, they were extremely happy. Their backyard had its poultry run and its patch of vegetables and flowers; they were free to pick fruit from their neighbour's fruit trees; and they had a grape arbour that provided a cool escape from the summer heat. Elizabeth remembered the profusion of roses that flourished in the black, lime-rich soil; and Judith recollected the flurry of jamming and preserving when oranges, lemons, peaches, apricots and nectarines were ripe. And, importantly, they still lived in a desirable part of the city. Anderson quotes her former teacher Miss Lona 'Biddy' Nation on the 'nice homes, lovely gardens, tree-lined avenues, very "select" neighbours' of Rose Park that ensured that the Anderson children had grown up 'in the right environment.' Part of this 'right environment' was attendance at the local Church of England, where Jessie Anderson's old friend, Matthew Williams, officiated.

Stella Bowen recalled her mother as 'a gentle and loving saint.' 'No compromise, and no lapse from her own standard of conduct can ever have clouded my mother's conscience,' she wrote. Her life was 'a simple and perfect demonstration of all that [she] believe[d].'[6] Anderson saw her mother in the same light, although her sainthood had to express itself differently. 'She never for a moment regarded [the move to the shop] as a disaster,' she wrote. 'It was just something that had to be done... Without self-pity or false dramatics, she

---

6 Bowen, 14.

merely adapted herself to circumstances as they were. And the community respected her for it.'

The children helped, of course – Frank and Fanny delivering orders, first with a handcart, then by bicycle, then, to Fanny's delight, in a spring-cart with a beloved pony named Dolly. 'She used to stand with feet wide apart, in an old-fashioned cart drawn by a large and hairy horse, with whom she appeared to be on very good terms,' a former playmate remembered, 'for she held the reins lightly in her small hands.' 'I remember seeing her delivering parcels,' another recalled, 'riding bareback on their horse, with a basket over her arm… She was so fearless and frank and gay.'

Anderson recalled a childhood where 'boys existed for only one purpose: to compete with, and to win from. I out-shouted, outran, outfought them all. It was not enough to be good, or better. I must be best, and never bested. I was a tom-boy. I was known – and gloried in the name – as Outlaw Fan from the Anderson Gang.'

This busy life was probably the best thing that could have happened to young Fanny. A friend remembered 'a bright alert face with an imp of mischief lurking somewhere in it, and her own special husky chuckle and voice. Always busy going somewhere, doing something… Movement is the first thing I associate with her, not restless movement, but aliveness.' But as she said herself, 'I was noisy, self-willed, temperamental, given to screaming scenes on any pretext.'

Stella Bowen's younger brother had similar 'childish rages of a spectacular sort', but as she discovered when she grew older, 'these small unmanageables generally turn into the most valuable adults.'[7] From an early age it was clear that Fanny, this particular 'small unmanageable,' was very talented, as a singer and as a reciter. And it was also clear

---
7   Bowen, 19.

that she had character. Her former teacher, 'Biddy' Nation, remembered in the 1950s that her little pupil was 'a very *individual* individual.' She hated school and wagged it whenever she could. She wrote a friend in the 1950s that she had been 'queen dunce – practically expelled.' But she loved the opportunity to perform that school provided at the monthly Friday afternoon Penny Concerts, when the principal, August Wittber, played the fiddle and pupils entertained each other and the teachers.

Fanny had already established herself as a performer at the home entertainments that were a feature of many homes, rich or poor, at that time. Anderson recalled that 'some of the happiest memories of this time are of the evening concerts, at our own house or at one of the neighbours.' When Mrs Anderson sold her furniture, she retained her piano, and home entertainments revolved around it in their tiny dining-living room. Elizabeth had a lovely contralto voice, and Frank played the mandolin; but Fanny took centre stage. As she recalls, she had learned at an early age that she could use her talents for barter – to 'get something for it.'

She was soon absorbed into the larger world of amateur entertainments that was an important part of the life of Adelaide, and no doubt of every Australian town, at that time. Mrs Anderson was determined that her children take part in community cultural activities and develop their talents. Shy Elizabeth reported that her mother had tried, in vain, to get her to join a literary debating society. Fanny had no such reticence. At first, like her older sister, she followed her mother's family into the world of music. Her grandfather, William Henry Saltmarsh, had been the music critic of the Melbourne *Argus* before he died and the family moved to Adelaide. Her aunt Fanny, after whom she was named, was extremely talented as a pianist, harpist, contralto, and poet; unfortunately she had died young, in 1884, at the age of 23. Her uncle William was a tenor who conducted the choir at the Parkside Baptist Church Sunday School and was a member of the Adelaide Choral Society; and another uncle, Frederick, was a trombonist who led the band of the Adelaide *Register* employees.[8]

It is no doubt this family connection that found her in 1905, at eight years old, singing Tosti's 'Goodbye' at the Adelaide Town Hall. She had started music lessons the year before with well-known Rose Park teacher, Katherine Cook. 'She showed brilliance from the start,' a 1932 article in the Adelaide *News* recalled, 'but in her four years of training would not devote the proper time to practising. Her interests lay with elocution.'[9]

A young elocution and voice production teacher and performer, Miss Mabel Best (from 1906 Mrs S D Kerr), heard Fanny singing 'Tosti' and offered to give her free lessons. When it became clear, in 1908, that the self-willed young Fanny was not going to persevere with her musical studies, Mrs Anderson put her to work with Mrs Kerr. 'She was a pretty little thing,' Mrs Kerr recalled in the 1932 article, 'with regular features, and an air of self-possession.' Fanny could not have fallen into better hands. Mabel Kerr was a rising star in her profession. She had studied with Edward Reeves, the elocution teacher at Prince Alfred College and the Elder Conservatorium of Music, whose most famous pupil was Lionel Logue, of *The King's Speech* fame.[10]

This was a period of major enthusiasm for elocution in Australia and elsewhere in the English-speaking world. Elocution lessons were considered an essential part of the 'accomplishments' middle class girls were expected to acquire;

---

8   For Frances Sarah (Fanny) (1861–84), William H. (b.1855) and Frederick Saltmarsh (b.1862) see Adelaide newspapers; Anderson to Miss Ahrens, 14 Sep 1990, UCSB.
9   *News* 24 Nov 1932. See also clippings 1955 and 1956, PAC.
10 *Mail* 4 Mar 1916:13.

but they also opened up new opportunities – as teachers, actresses, and public speakers – for those with talent, ambition and, as in Fanny Anderson's case, the need to make a living.[11] Mabel Kerr was one of these.

Elocution also introduced girls to a new competitive culture fostered by the introduction of the eisteddfod system to Australia in the early 1890s.[12] The young Mabel Kerr had developed her career through the numerous elocutionary competitions run by the Woman's Christian Temperance Union (WCTU) and local literary societies, and, further afield, the Australian Natives Association (ANA) and the prestigious Ballarat South Street Eisteddfod in Victoria. By 1906, when she married, she had established herself as the teacher of elocution at the YWCA on Hindmarsh Square, the counterpart of Edward Reeves at the YMCA, and her students were winning the prizes she had formerly won. Chief among these was Jean Robertson, who later played with the then Francee Anderson in Julius Knight's Company and preceded her to the United States stage.[13] Mrs Kerr and her students had a busy life performing at the numerous amateur entertainments held throughout the city, and, as the Willing Workers Society, performing for charities.

Mabel Kerr's teaching style and competitive performance activities proved ideal for the young Fanny. As an account of her career pointed out, '[Mabel Kerr] believes… that in order to stimulate and maintain interest in juvenile students… the dramatic class of work plays an important part, for while

---

11   Joy Damousi, *Colonial Voices: a Cultural History of English in Australia, 1840–1940*, 2010; Jill Matthews, 'Education for Femininity: Domestic Arts Education in South Australia,' *Labour History* Nov 1983: 30–53.
12   Desley Deacon, 'From Victorian Accomplishment to Modern Profession: Elocution Takes Judith Anderson, Sylvia Bremer and Dorothy Cumming to Hollywood, 1912–1918,' *Australasian Journal of Victorian Studies* 18.1, 2013: 40–65.
13   Jean Robertson (1894–1967) married Henry Brose in 1927.

it encourages naturalness of style and easy deportment it furnishes the student with excellent material to develop latent talents and early ambition. It also encourages individuality, and a sense of self-dependence which is most admirable in formative training.'[14]

As Anderson remembers, 'For once… there was no more hookey, no more refusal to study, no more impertinence in class. I was doing something I cared terribly about and I applied myself.' Soon after she began work with Mabel Kerr, she was winning medals of her own for both recitation and singing. Nineteen hundred and nine, when she was 12, was an especially busy year, with prizes at a number of local competitions, where 'A humorous song, in character, was given by the clever little stage artists, Misses Vera Coffey and Fanny Anderson,' all of which seemed to be practice for the prestigious national competition, the South Street Competitions at Ballarat, where she won first prize for her duet with Vera Coffey, and some lesser prizes. In her first taste of fame, her portrait was published in the weekly Adelaide *Chronicle*.[15]

The following year, when her determined mother made sure her unwilling daughter was among the few girls who attended the new Norwood District High School, Fanny's focus was still on excelling as a performer. She won the South Australian WCTU's silver, gold and diamond medals; and at the High School's first speech day – that institution that emerged from the craze for elocution – Fanny Anderson, despite her poor school record, was featured reciting the harrowing 'Prince Arthur to Hubert' from Shakespeare's *King John*.

Looking back from the perspective of a successful career,

---

14 *Mail* 4 Mar 1916: 13.
15 *Chronicle* 13 Nov 1909: 30.

Judith Anderson remembered these achievements as more than they were, with a gathering drama, in her accounts, over several years of silver medal, gold medal and a specially devised diamond medal at the national Ballarat competitions rather than those of the state WCTU. But if this was a somewhat inflated memory, it was true to the growing self-confidence and ambition of the young Fanny. Part of this was discovering that her gifts, which could be seen just as showing off, had a wonderful power. 'I knew now,' she wrote, 'that this curious impulsion to perform was not unique to me. Grown-ups had it too – and wrought magic with it.'

In her memoirs Anderson attributed this discovery to Dame Nellie Melba and Peter Pan. Melba gave two concerts in Adelaide in February 1908, when Anderson was 11 years old. In later life she often recalled sitting in Madame Melba's audience by the good offices of her mother's old friend Jack Lemmone, who was the prima donna's flautist and tour organiser. 'This was when I first felt that quite indescribable sense of miracle that a great talent can produce,' she wrote. 'It was the moment when I knew that I, too, must do something in public; that I too must try in my own way to do to people what she, standing by a piano, was doing to me and to everyone else in that theatre.' A few months later she attended a matinee of *Peter Pan*, a production of the leading theatrical organisation, J C Williamson, featuring the charismatic American actress Minnie Tittell Brune as Peter Pan. As Brune flew out on her wire over the audience and up to the gallery where Fanny sat, 'she hovered there [and] sprinkled star-dust on me,' Anderson recollected sixty years later.[16]

---

16   For Brune see Veronica Kelly, 'Minnie Tittell Brune and the Gallery Girls: an Australian idol of modernist consumerism,' *Theatre Research International* 31.1, 2006:

Fanny Anderson had plenty of opportunity to experience good theatre during her childhood in Adelaide. Australians were enthusiastic theatregoers, and theatre had flourished in Adelaide at least since the great George Coppin opened the New Queen's Theatre in 1846. Mrs Anderson had enjoyed going to the theatre when younger, and Fanny's sister, Elizabeth, took her to the J C Williamson production of *The Pirates of Penzance* in 1905, when she was 8 years old. She does not tell us what else she saw before she left for Sydney in 1913, but during 1909, which seems to have been a year of awakening ambition for her, she could have seen the Harcourt Beatty-Madge McIntosh Company in *She Stoops to Conquer*, *Camille*, and *Fedora*, featuring the actor, Gaston Mervale, who was important in her future career;[17] she could also have seen Minnie Tittell Brune again, this time in *The Girl of the Golden West*, *Diana of Dobson's* and *Sunday*; the William Anderson Dramatic Company with the Australian *For the Term of His Natural Life*; Australia's sweetheart, Nellie Stewart, in her signature performance as *Sweet Nell of Old Drury*; Walter Bentley in *The Silver King*; Maggie Moore (J C Williamson's former wife) in their famous comedy, *Struck Oil*; Roy Redgrave – grandfather of Vanessa – in *The Man from Outback*; and above all, J C Williamson's *The Duke's Motto*, *The Sign of the Cross*, and *Monsieur Beaucaire*, presented by the company led by the universal favourite, Julius Knight, with whom, as Francee Anderson, she made her professional debut in 1915.[18]

By 1912, although she was nominally still at high school,

17–36.
17 See Veronica Kelly, 'Australia's Svengali: Gaston Mervale in Theatre and Film,' *Australasian Drama Studies* 5, 2011: 107–25.
18 See Veronica Kelly, 'Julius Knight, Australian Matinee Idol: Costume Drama as Historical Re-presentation,' *Australasian Victorian Studies Journal* 9, 2003: 128–44.

the 15-year-old Fanny Anderson was what could be called a professional amateur, performing regularly with Mabel Kerr and her fellow students for charity and in local entertainments. She might have continued along this path, becoming a teacher and local celebrity like her mentor. But she had been sprinkled with that stardust by Peter Pan, and she had a mother with a will of iron. Jessie Anderson, recognising her daughter's gifts and dedication, and no doubt feeling the family could do with the money, made use of every opportunity to develop these talents as a profession. When the Tasmanian-born singer Amy Sherwin visited Adelaide in 1906, Jessie had asked the international star to assess the 9-year-old Fanny's singing voice, which had, apparently 'great contralto "fullness" and "soul"' unusual in such a young child. And at some stage, probably in 1908, she did the same with John Lemmone, who told her, in a vivid phrase, that she had tears in her voice. This was when she, or rather her mother, was still thinking of a singing career and the possibility of training overseas under the patronage of someone like Amy Sherwin or Nellie Melba. Amy Sherwin advised her to rest her voice until she was older.[19] Anderson remained a passionate music lover throughout her life, enjoying close friendships with some of the world's greatest musicians; and she actually sang in her 1925 Broadway hit under David Belasco, *The Dove*. But by 1912, under the guidance of Mabel Kerr and the firm hand of her mother, Fanny was set on a future in the theatre. When one of her exasperated teachers at Norwood District High School asked her, 'Fanny Anderson, whatever do you think will happen to you when you grow up?' she answered calmly, 'Mr Paynter, I am going on the stage.'

---

19   Elizabeth Anderson recollected that her own aim in life was to go to Germany to study music. As the shy eldest sister she seems to have suffered more than her siblings from the family's change of status. She had a nervous breakdown in the US in 1932 and spent a number of years in a sheltered facility in Vermont.

Scene Two
Sydney

With its beautiful harbour opening out to the Pacific, its glistening beaches and its subtropical gardens, this small port city was at the same time an exciting cosmopolitan meeting-place and a familiar playground where a swim or a picnic was just a few minutes away.

Picnickers at Watson's Bay, Looking Towards North Head

Arthur Streeton

Chapter Three
Frantic 1913–14

At the end of 1912 Fanny Anderson had to decide whether to follow her fellow elocution pupil Jean Robertson into the Adelaide Repertory or to take her chance in the larger theatrical world of Sydney. Ever keen to 'give Fanny her chance,' Mrs Anderson decided it was the right moment to move. Jack, now aged 22, was in Norseman in the goldfields of Western Australia, working in the butcher shop of his Uncle George. Frank, at 18, was a telegraphist with the Eastern Establishment Cable Company. He would board in Adelaide until he could get a transfer. 'Did,' Fanny's beautiful, shy, older sister, would come with them to Sydney.

As Anderson recalled in her memoirs, 'Mother burned our Adelaide bridges quickly and thoroughly – the way she did everything once she'd made up her mind':

Fanny Anderson at 15
Mail (Adelaide)
14 September 1912
National Library of Australia

> She sold the shop. Lock, stock, and barrel – all the barrels, every bit of stock. She sold Dolly, the pony, and Dolly's spring-cart. She sold all the furniture, including the piano. She was used to wiping the slate clean and starting fresh from nothing, nor was this the last time she would have to do it.

When she arrived in Sydney early in 1913, 'a teenage ego spoiling to test [herself] against a new environment,' Fanny was just 16 years old. Small and slight, with a cloud of dark, curly hair, an infectious giggle, and a load of determination, she was still a child physically and mentally. Excitable, never still, and ready for any adventure, her new friend, the much older Oliver Hogue, nicknamed her 'Frantic.'

Sydney in 1913 suited the impetuous and ambitious Fanny. It was, in the words of one of its leading writers, 'a sailors' town; a free trade port where sailors from all nations jostled in the crowd at Circular Quay.' The lively port was, in turn, 'the nucleus of the crowded city, pulsing with vitality as the core of its prosperity.'[20] With a population of close to 650,000, Sydney had recently become Australia's largest and fastest-growing city.

In this vital city Fanny found the perfect place to develop her talents, her gift for friendship and the remarkable control over her body and her voice that was a striking part of her later abilities as an actress. With its beautiful harbour opening out to the Pacific, its glistening beaches and its subtropical gardens, this small port city was at the same time an exciting cosmopolitan meeting-place and a familiar playground where a swim or a picnic was just a few minutes away.

Fanny's strong-minded and competent mother quickly found 'Elleroy', 'a house of charm and dignity' at 121 Macleay Street, Potts Point, one of the city's most beautiful suburbs, on a finger of land high above the water and within walking distance of the Botanic Gardens, the bustling quay and city centre. There she established a 'residential' – an upscale rooming house whose residents, often from faraway places,

---

20 Norman Lindsay, *Bohemians of the Bulletin*, 1965.

became extensions of their three-woman family. Surrounded by mansions in spacious gardens (novelist Patrick White was a small boy in nearby 'Lulworth' from 1916), 'Elleroy' was on the border of the more bohemian Kings Cross, and across the road from 'Maramanah,' the sprawling stately home etched on the Australian memory by Robin Eakin in her classic *Aunts Up the Cross*.[21]

In Sydney 'Did' found work colouring postcards – a distant expression of her artistic yearnings – and Fanny was set to learn typing – an insurance against failure on the stage. But she was never called upon to apply this new skill, if she ever acquired it. She and her Adelaide friend Pom Carlyle had enrolled with Sydney's leading elocution and drama teacher, Lawrence Campbell. A fat, rubicund man dubbed 'Lolly' by his students, Campbell immediately recognised Fanny's potential and urged her mother to allow her to devote all her energies to her professional development. That was the end of any thoughts of what was then called a 'business career.' Fanny adored Lolly Campbell's classes, and, as she had with Mrs Kerr, she applied herself to them.

From the start, Fanny Anderson loved her new home. 'To this day I have never seen a harbor more beautiful,' she wrote 50 years later. And its names caused her vivid imagination to race – 'Botany Bay, Frenchman's Bay, Rushcutter's Bay' recalling early voyages of discovery – 'Maroubra, Kogarah, Woolloomooloo,' recording the language of the Aboriginal inhabitants. 'The constant steaming, hooting traffic fascinated me,' she remembered, 'the ponderous liners standing in from the Orient or Europe or America, with their long wakes crisscrossed by barges and tugs and other small harbor craft

---

21 Robin Eakin, *Aunts Up the Cross*, 1997; David Marr, *Patrick White, a Life*, 1991.

or by coastal vessels like the one that had brought us from Adelaide.' In this cosmopolitan and welcoming city Fanny transformed herself from Outlaw Fan into Francee Anderson, rising young actress, though she never lost the quality that earned her the pet name 'Frantic'.

The move to Sydney brought her for the first time into contact with families of wealth and comfort who were major contributors to the city's cultural life. The Hon. Henry Willis – the bereaved fiancé long ago of Mrs Anderson's sister and now the Speaker of the New South Wales Parliament – had facilitated their move. The Victorian ideal of the cultivated gentleman, he took them to lunch in the parliamentary dining room and entertained them at his great house, Innisfallen Castle, in Middle Harbour (now Castle Cove).

Full of fun and what people were starting to call 'personality,' Fanny quickly made friends. Campbell's studio was in the exotic Equitable Building, part of the fabled Palings precinct in George Street in the city centre, where musicians, actors and writers mingled and drank coffee at the Café Francais across the street. There she met his star pupil, Tien Hogue, the youngest of the eight children of the former Minister of Education, James Alexander Hogue. She was dazzled by this talented, lively family, whose members wrote, recited, sang, played instruments and prepared small concerts and plays – the home entertainment of Adelaide on a grander, more prosperous and ambitious scale.

Tien Hogue was already trying her hand at the new movies; and one of her brothers, John Roland Hogue, had graduated from J C Williamson's to become a rising musical comedy star on the American stage. 'Warm and loving and giving,' they had 'a wonderful family glow, that engulfed and welcomed me, made me belong and feel warm and happy,' Anderson remembered. In particular, Tien's older brother Oliver, a reporter on the *Sydney Morning Herald* – 'tall, craggy, adorable' in Fanny's eyes – was enchanted by his sister's engaging little friend, who remained for many years his 'Frantic.'[22]

The Hogues' friends, the Jewish lawyer-pianist Maurice Price and his younger brother Ellis, also 'held out their arms to me and brought me into their circle,' Anderson recalled. As Tien Hogue spent more time making movies, Fanny replaced her as Ellis Price's partner in his amateur performances and at his mother's At Homes. 'Theirs was a grander house than any I had yet known,' she wrote in her memoirs. 'I listened, watched, absorbed the nuances of manner and behavior.' Tutored by the Hogues and the Prices and the cultured families of other friends she made at Lawrence Campbell's, she developed the love of 'Beauty' that was her touchstone of artistic excellence for the rest of her life.

Fanny and her new friends went surfing at Manly, eating supper from hampers of home-cooked food, followed by the music of mandolins, guitars and songs under the moonlit southern sky. But these fun-loving young people were also ambitious, hard-working and civic-minded. Maurice and Ellis Price had been, like Fanny, child prodigies, Maurice on the piano and Ellis on the violin and as an elocutionist. They had studied from an early age with the best teachers, who were central figures in Sydney's thriving musical community. Like Fanny they were used, from childhood, to appearing before the public, often for charitable and cultural organisations, and had won prizes at local and national eisteddfods.

---

22 Tien was the nickname of Anne C. Hogue (1892-?). Soon after Fanny arrived in Sydney, Tien played in two movies written, directed and filmed by Franklyn Barrett, *A Blue Gum Romance* and *The Life of a Jackeroo*, and in *Pommy Arrives in Australia*, written and directed by Raymond Longford and filmed by Barrett, featuring Lottie Lyell. In 1914 she made *The Shepherd Of The Southern Cross* with Arthur Shirley, who left soon after for a successful career in Hollywood.

Surrounded by these loving, more worldly, friends, Fanny was free to experiment with different adult personas. This small plain provincial girl, with only the bloom of youth, energy and personality as assets, set her sights on becoming romantic, beautiful and strange – in other words, glamorous, a word that had not yet been invented, but which she would exemplify 20 years on. Trying out possible professional names, she moved from France to Francé to Francey and finally to Francee.

But her first priority as Francee Anderson was to master her craft. At Lawrence Campbell's studio – The Lawrence Campbell School of Public Speaking and Dramatic Art – she honed her deep, velvety voice and learned how to train her body to be strong and expressive. Campbell had the first recording device she had encountered, and he put it to good use, playing back her recitations, criticising an impure vowel here and a swallowed consonant there until her elocution was perfect.

She also learned to listen to the words, feeling the emotion through the writing, even if it was something she had never experienced herself. 'It's the words,' she told Campbell. 'If the author says it in the right words, the emotion's written for you. It's all there.' Years later, when she was acknowledged as one of the world's greatest emotional actresses, she still saw this as the foundation of her art.

Campbell also enforced a strict regime of exercise to strengthen breathing and make the body strong and agile. This was a pleasure to Anderson, who had, as a child, joined her brothers in their exercise on the parallel bars; and now, in Sydney, she took long walks with a stick threaded through her arms behind her back to make herself stand straight. Under Campbell's tuition, she developed the well-toned body she kept for the rest of her life. Proud of her strength, this tiny girl even managed to accidentally knock her beloved teacher unconscious when they were skylarking in his studio.

During her first year at the studio Francee saw her friend Tien Hogue starring in the public performances Campbell held regularly to showcase his best students. By early 1914, however, Tien, with her 'extraordinary magnetism and charm' and her 'golden voice with a fresh crisp quality,' was ready to move on.

Francee stepped easily into Tien's starring role in Campbell's entertainments, earning her first theatrical review in March 1914. The evening was 'most notable for the debut of Miss Anderson in the Potion Scene and two scenes from *Romeo and Juliet*,' the *Sydney Morning Herald* critic wrote. 'The youthful actress's voice was not fully formed for the fatigue of strenuous passages,' he continued, 'but her all-round talent for acting, her touches of character, and her facial expression were remarkable.' Three months later her 'genuine dramatic ability' was noted. By the time of Mr Campbell's Christmas Recital, where she was again singled her out as a 'clever player… who showed dramatic qualities,' she was ready, at age 18, to demonstrate those 'dramatic qualities' in her first professional role.[23]

As little 'Frantic' grew into the professional 'Francee' world events impinged on her happy group of friends. In August that year Australia had joined Britain and the other parts of the Empire in war against Germany. She and her playmate Oliver Hogue had made their last joy ride around nearby Darlinghurst, and Hogue had sailed as part of the 2nd Light Horse Brigade for faraway Egypt. 'I wish I had rigged you out

---

23 'The Lawrence Campbell Students,' *SMH* 12 Mar: 10; 24 Jun: 16; 16 Dec 1914: 14.

as a soldier & had you with me,' he wrote from the ship. 'You would have had plenty of adventures.' But he knew that his Frantic had other adventures ahead of her. 'Such a lot is going to happen next year,' he wrote. 'I hope to hear great things of you.'

Julius Knight as Napoleon

Talma

Chapter Four

Francee 1915

*Miss Francee Anderson took the fancy of
the audience as the flippant and flirtatious
Stephanie de Beauharnais*

Tamworth Daily Observer 1915

In April 1915 Australia's most beloved actor, Julius Knight, announced that he would make a farewell tour of the Australian provinces – the 'smalls,' as they were called. Eighteen-year-old Francee Anderson applied to Knight for a place in the company, hoping, unrealistically, to be cast as leading lady; but she was delighted when she was taken on to play the ingénue roles: Stephanie in *A Royal Divorce*, Jeffik in the one-act *Sacrament of Judas*, and supporting roles in *David Garrick* and *The Lady of Lyons*. The much more experienced Melbourne-born actress Nellie Bramley would play the leading roles of Josephine, Ada Ingot and Pauline.[24]

Francee was lucky – or shrewd – in her choice of Julius Knight's company and a strenuous provincial tour for her professional debut. Twenty years later, as she rose to the heights of Broadway stardom, she credited Julius Knight with teaching her everything she knew, not just about acting, but how to conduct herself as a professional woman; and she

---

24 *Theatre* 1 Apr: 23; 1 May 1915: 38; Clyde Packer, 'Dame Judith Anderson.' In *No Return Ticket: Clyde Packer Interviews Nine Famous Australian Expatriates*, 1984, 59.

always acknowledged that this early training in the rigours of touring prepared her for her first, difficult years in American stock and the many cross-country tours that made her a North American household name from the late 1920s to the 1980s.

When Julius Knight announced his farewell tour, he had been performing to rapturous Australasian audiences since 1897. Born in Scotland in 1863, he was rising through the British theatrical ranks when the keen-eyed George Musgrove picked him out for a leading part in the experimental stock company he and J C Williamson were putting together to tour Australia and New Zealand in 1897.

Knight had been in Australia before, as part of the less than successful Laura Villiers company in 1891. But under the Musgrove-Williamson management, he was taken to Australian hearts, and remained there well past his final departure in January 1917. During four long tours under J C Williamson management, he established himself in the Australasian mind as the perfect representation of Napoleon (in *The Royal Divorce*), the Roman prefect Marcus Superbus (in *The Sign of the Cross*), the famous actor David Garrick, the aspiring lover Claude Melnotte (in *The Lady of Lyons*), the unfrocked priest Jacques Bernez (in *The Sacrament of Judas*) and other romantic historical figures. Famous for his well-turned leg and gorgeous costumes, the 'only and adorable Julius' had a cross-gender appeal that made him a general favourite.[25]

---

25   *TT* 6 Jan 1910: 30; Veronica Kelly, *The Empire Actors: Stars of Australasian Costume Drama 1890s-1920s*, 2009; 'Julius Knight, Australian Matinee Idol: Costume Drama As Historical Re-Presentation,' *Australasian Victorian Studies Journal* 9, 2003: 128–44; 'A Complementary Economy? National Markets and International Product in Early Australian Theatre Managements,' *New Theatre Quarterly* 21.1, 2005: 77–95; Obituary, *Times* (London) 25 Feb 1941: 1; 'Mr Julius Knight,' *Theatre* 2 Dec 1912: 9; 'Exit Julius Knight,' *SMH* 1 Feb 1917; George Musgrove to J C Williamson, 20 Nov 1896, JCW.

Knight's leading ladies had usually been imported stars. When he came to Australia for his 1912–15 tour, he brought with him two actresses familiar to Australian audiences. Irene Browne, his leading lady, had become a favourite with Australian audiences when she toured as part of H B Irving's company the previous year; and Grace Noble was a seasoned actress who had been in Australia twice with Williamsons' main rival, the prestigious Brough and Boucicault company. In addition, he brought, as ingénue, Mary Goulding, a young woman who had recently been touring in Canada with the company of Miss Horniman, with whose London company Knight had been playing. From actresses already in Australia he recruited another former member of the Brough company, Mrs Brough's sister, Emma Temple, and Eily Malyon, a British-born actress in her thirties who had come to Australia the year before as understudy to Ethel Irving; she had married Plumpton Wilson from the same company and the pair had remained in Australia.[26]

This visit of Julius Knight's company to Australia coincided with strenuous attempts on the part of Australian actors to form a union. Prominent among the fledgling union's demands was the restriction of imported actors to two per company, with the rest made up from local talent. Although 'The Firm' – J C Williamson – strongly opposed the union and its demands, the sheer numbers of well-trained, talented Australian actors made it inevitable that the importation of young, relatively untried company members such as Mary Goulding was no longer necessary or viable.[27]

Indeed, Knight found plenty of female talent on the ground to back up, and finally replace, his leading lady and

---

26 *Australasian* 7 Oct 1911: 33; *EN* 2 Dec 1912: 5; *ST* 1 Dec 1912: 2. Malyon (1879–1961) and Wilson went to the US in 1907, where both made a career in the movies and she rivalled Anderson in severe-looking housekeeper roles.
27 *Register* 20 Nov 1911: 8; *SMH* 13 Jan 1912: 15.

other imported members of his company. He saw Lawrence Campbell student Dorothy Cumming in an amateur production soon after he arrived. A few weeks later she was playing a minor part in *Bella Donna*, the company's second production. A year later Cumming replaced Mary Goulding in *Man and Superman* after that actress had failed to satisfy the critics. Early in 1914 Knight recruited Lizette Parkes to replace the imported (and ageing) Grace Noble in the difficult part of Dora in *Diplomacy*. Parkes had been a child actor and a Williamson star ever since she replaced Tittell Brune as Peter Pan for their New Zealand tour in 1910. In her new role as ingénue, she quickly became a favourite of Australian and New Zealand audiences, attracting more attention than the British star, Irene Browne.[28]

By early 1915 a line seems to have been crossed. Sydney's *Referee* noted that the two forthcoming Williamson shows had young Australian actresses in the lead. Enid Bennett would support visiting American, Fred Niblo, in *The Travelling Salesman* and Lizette Parkes would play Mercia to Julius Knight's Marcus Superbus in *The Sign of the Cross*. In May that year *Lone Hand* featured 'Some Actresses Who Have Made Good' – a photomontage of Lizette Parkes, Enid Bennett and Sylvia Bremer, another young Williamson find. By the time the Knight-Browne company gave its farewell performance that same month, few playgoers mourned the return of Irene Browne to London.[29]

This was the context in which Julius Knight chose the company for his 'smalls' tour. Knight's choice of Nellie

---

28   *SMH* 17 Feb 1913: 3; *ST* 21 Dec 1913: 6; *Age* 30 Jan 1914: 6.; *The Newsletter* 14 Feb 1914: 3; *Referee* 20 Jan 1915: 15; *TWN* 30 Jan 1915: 5.
29   *Referee* 10 Feb 1915: 15; *LH* May 1915: 394.

Bramley as leading lady was a surprise; but she was a seasoned actress who had been attempting for some time to move beyond melodrama to more substantial roles. She proved a great success on the tour, and went on to a long career as the idol of the Gallery Girls – the vocal fan clubs who made their preferences known in the city theatres.[30]

Like Francee Anderson, however, most members of the touring company were unknowns. Ailsa Craig, who became one of her closest friends, had toured the previous year with the *Within the Law* company that had included Tien Hogue. Margaret Gordon had recently come to Australia as part of the Scottish company, *Bunty Pulls the Strings*. Lena McLachlan was a talented amateur singer who had a bit part in *The Chorus Lady* a few months before. Of the men in the cast, Kingston Hewitt had been in amateur performances with Francee; Ronald Byram was an up-and-coming actor who had played small parts with H B Irving and understudied Fred Niblo; and Harold Moran was an amateur actor, producer and drama teacher from the large provincial city of Ballarat.[31]

Actors based in Australia were no strangers to long tours. J C Williamson and The Firm's managing director, Hugh Ward, both American-born, had come to Australia on tour. Before they settled in Australia both had travelled with companies around the world. Australian actors were used to playing in Burma, China, the Straits Settlements and India as well as the UK, the US and Canada. Even the domestic Australian and New Zealand circuit established by Williamson and Musgrove in the late nineteenth century

---

30   *Critic* 15 Jun 1923: 3.
31   *Mail* 26 Dec 1914: 4; 20 Nov 1915: 4; *TT* 17 Dec 1914: 24; *Ballarat Courier* 4 Sep 1915: 7. Byram went to the US in 1916, where he appeared on Broadway and in movies until his death of pneumonia in 1917 while shooting Nell Shipman's *Back to God's Country* in Canada. Moran had a long career in professional and amateur theatre.

required considerable travel, mostly by train and coastal vessel, through the capital cities of Sydney and Melbourne in the southeast, westward to Adelaide and Perth, south to Hobart, north to Brisbane, and across the Tasman to a number of New Zealand's principal towns. Their companies also travelled regularly to South Africa.[32]

Despite the distances and difficulties involved, Australia's small towns were also well catered for. In 1915 eastern Australia had two major theatrical companies that played the 'smalls': Harry Clay's Vaudeville Company and Philip Lytton's Dramatic Company. They followed the Show Circuit, providing entertainment for the crowds who converged on the larger country towns for the annual agricultural show and for race week. Lytton travelled with his own capacious tent and presented 'the latest English and American dramas.' In 1915 he preceded Julius Knight on the northern 'smalls' circuit with the pantomime *Dick Whittington*, the specially written war play *For King and Country*, and the melodramas *It's Always the Woman* and *The Girl Without a Home*.

The most celebrated of the country tours of recent years was that of the great Australian soprano Nellie Melba. In 1909 she announced that she wanted all Australians to hear her sing, as Jenny Lind had done in Sweden a generation before. Her manager and flautist John Lemmone arranged a tour that took her to 70 towns as far west as Forbes, up the coast to Townsville, over 1000 miles north of Sydney, then south, ending her tour at Colac, a town of about 4000 people in the

---

32   Desley Deacon, 'Location! Location! Location: Mind Maps in Australian Transnational History,' *History Australia* 4.3, Dec 2008: 1–16; 'Cosmopolitans at Home: Judith Anderson and the American Aspirations of J C Williamson Stock Company Members, 1897–1918.' In Robert Dixon and Veronica Kelly, eds. *Impact of the Modern: Vernacular Modernities in Australia 1870s-1960s*, 2008, 202–22; 'Becoming Cosmopolitan: Judith Anderson in Sydney, 1913 to 1918.' In *Transnational Lives: Biographies of Global Modernity, 1700-present*. Ed. with Penny Russell and Angela Woollacott, 2009; Veronica Kelly, *The Empire Actors*; 'A Complementary Economy?'

Victorian Western District. Melba was feted at every town she visited, met at the railway station by the mayor and a large crowd of citizens, presented with bouquets, and entertained by prominent citizens.[33]

Julius Knight's farewell tour had something of the flavour of Melba's gift to the nation. 'They all want me,' he declared, and he was determined that as many people as possible would see him. His company of 50 began their tour in late May 1915, travelling by train through the larger western New South Wales towns from Tamworth to Tenterfield, and on to Warwick, Toowoomba and Ipswich in southern Queensland. They then took the coastal steamer *Bingera* 650 kilometres north to central Queensland's largest town, Rockhampton, where they played the seven nights of Show Week, when visitors from the cattle stations in the hinterland poured into town. From there they went by steamer 350 kilometres to Mackay for three nights, then another 350 to Townsville for six nights. From Townsville they headed west by rail to the old mining towns of Ravenswood and Charters Towers, where they stayed for the five days of Carnival Week. Returning to Townsville they took the steamer south to Bundaberg and Maryborough, then to Brisbane, where they boarded the train once more to go south to Murwillumbah, Casino, Lismore, Grafton, then west to Singleton, Armidale, Dubbo and Bathurst.

After a few days rest in Sydney in mid-August the weary company wended their way south and west to Goulburn, Wagga Wagga, Wangaratta, Seymour, and Shepparton to Echuca on the Victorian side of the Murray River. They then headed south, travelling large distances to St Arnaud in

---

33   *West Australian* 30 Jan 1909: 12; *SMH* 5 Jun 1909: 13; *Brisbane Courier* 9 Jun: 5; 13 Jul 1909: 5; *Colac Herald* 8 Oct 1909: 2.

the Wimmera, to Ballarat, the largest of the provincial cities, and on through Ararat to the coast at Warrnambool. There they turned east to Victoria's other large city, Geelong, west again to Colac and Camperdown, where they played in the Mechanics' Hall on the evening of the pig sale. From there they headed home, through Albury on the Victoria-New South Wales border, back to Wagga Wagga, north to Katoomba and Orange, arriving back in Sydney in early October, having been on the road for four exhausting months.

The towns Julius Knight's company played in ranged in size from Kyabram, in the rich Victorian irrigation district, with 1,600 inhabitants, to the gold mining city of Ballarat, with close to 40,000; but most had populations of about 5,000. In 1915 Australia's non-Aboriginal population was about 4.5 million (the censuses of the time did not include the indigenous population). With the economy based on mining and wool, 60 per cent of these lived outside the six capital cities, most in towns of less than 1,000 people. Only 16 Australian towns had more than 10,000 residents. The places the company visited were generally prosperous – although the mining towns were often declining in population. They had substantial civic buildings – courthouses, post offices, churches, colleges, convents, hotels and theatres – as well as the spacious houses of their leading citizens. Charters Towers in northern Queensland was typical: a gold-mining town established in the 1870s, it had a population of 30,000 at its height. Already half that size when Julius Knight visited in 1915, it had the wide street and mixture of veranda-ed shops, hotels and houses and neo-classical public buildings that characterised Australian rural centres.

The company had to be ready to play in a wide range of venues. Knight had the scenery built on a reduced scale so that it would fit anywhere; and where the railways would allow it, he carried his own lighting plant, 'so that nothing will, or could, occur to mar the completeness of this production,' he told one country newspaper. The larger towns, such as Ballarat, had theatres to rival those of the capital cities. Ballarat's Her Majesty's, which still survives, seated 1,700 patrons in its two dress circles and stalls, and provided comfortable dressing rooms backstage. More usual was the Mechanic's Institute or School of Arts, such as that at Ravenswood (also still surviving), an all-purpose timber building used as theatre, cinema, library and social hall.

In Victoria the venue was often the Town Hall, splendid buildings whose accommodations for theatricals were sometimes less than ideal. *The Daylesford Advocate, Yandoit, Glenlyon and Eganstown Chronicle*, for instance, deplored the lighting of the Daylesford Town Hall as 'a gloomy failure.' 'A great actor, such as Mr Julius Knight,' their reporter wrote, 'after his experience with the derelict footlights and antiquated headlights on the Town Hall stage, must not be condemned if he spreads abroad the evil tidings that for any first-class company to come to Daylesford is for them to court disaster.'[34]

Despite Daylesford's 'gloomy failure,' Julius Knight's country tour was a great success. The repertoire for the tour was carefully chosen to appeal to a wide variety of audiences. Most of all, people wanted to see him in his most famous role as Napoleon in the historical drama *A Royal Divorce*. First presented in London in 1891, the play depicts Napoleon's reluctant divorce from the Empress Josephine and his marriage, in the hope of an heir, to the Austrian archduchess Marie Louise, and follows his subsequent downfall. Knight's version of the play included four tableaux that further dramatised the great man's demise – The Retreat from Moscow, The Charge and The Rout at the Battle of Waterloo and, finally, Napoleon in exile on St Helena, gazing out over the sea as the sun sets. In the

---

34 The Daylesford Advocate, Yandoit, Glenlyon and Eganstown Chronicle 4 Sept 1915: 3.

year when Australian soldiers (including Oliver Hogue) were distinguishing themselves at Gallipoli, this play was especially appreciated for Napoleon's speech praising the victorious British at Waterloo – 'Those British Bulldogs' who 'know not when they are beaten, but fight on… fight on… !'

A Royal Divorce had three attractive roles for women – the beautiful and wronged Empress Josephine, the cold and haughty Marie Louise, and Josephine's gay and audacious niece, Stephanie de Beauharnais, who fearlessly protests her aunt's treatment by Napoleon. These royal characters provided plenty of opportunity for the gorgeous 'frocking' for which Knight plays were renowned.

From the beginning, audiences loved the young Francee Anderson as Josephine's spirited niece. The tour began on 26 May 1915 at Tamworth, 400 kilometres northwest of Sydney by rail. The *Tamworth Daily Observer* considered the production of *A Royal Divorce* 'perfect.' 'Country play-goers have of late been treated to some excellent theatrical performances,' the critic wrote, 'but nothing quite so finished, so thoroughly artistic in every detail has been put before Tamworth audiences… Miss Francee Anderson took the fancy of the audience as the flippant and flirtatious Stephanie de Beauharnais.' In Armidale the local newspaper considered her depiction of Stephanie as 'exceptionally good'. 'She squeezed every ounce out of the part which is one which comparatively few would make a success of,' they wrote. 'The scene in which she indignantly reproaches Napoleon for his treatment of Josephine, and also that in which she surprises her husband in the inn, showed her talent off to particular advantage, and she was deservedly applauded by the audience.' The Shepparton critic summed up the young actress's triumph in her first professional engagement: 'Miss Frances Anderson as Stephanie de Beauharnais was simply delightful.'[35]

---

35 Shepparton Advertiser 26 August 1915: 2.

Francee Anderson at 18
Table Talk 30 December 1915, State Library of New South Wales

Chapter Five

Marking Time 1915–17

Julius Knight has had not a few leading ladies, but he has seldom had the strong support on the woman side that he gets in The Three Musketeers. *Miss Olive Wilton's Miladi (a most difficult part) is played with unusual power, Miss Cumming's Queen of France with rare sympathy, and Miss Francee Anderson's Constance with a pertness that is adorable, and an admirable excuse for the hot-headed Gascon falling so suddenly and inextricably in love.*

Winner, 29 December 1915

When Julius Knight's tour of the smalls ended on 28 September 1915, he was ready to say goodbye to the Australian audiences who had taken him to their hearts for so many years. Indeed, he was, according to a newspaper report, looking up the sailing list for England when entrepreneur Hugh McIntosh, 'spying round for the biggest star procurable, determined to secure him at all costs' for his new Modern Amusements Limited.[36] Tempted by McIntosh's no doubt generous offer, Knight reorganised his company for two final seasons in McIntosh's vast New Tivoli Theatre in Adelaide and the refurbished Princess's in Melbourne.

---

36 Winner 22 December 1915: 12

The 'simply delightful' Francee Anderson was one of the members of his smalls company that he retained. The new company played a season of modern dramas in Adelaide – *The Silver King*, *Raffles*, *The Third Degree* and *Paid in Full* – that offered little opportunity to display her talents. But when they moved to the Princess's Theatre in Melbourne and a season of historical dramas, she was noticed for 'a pertness that is adorable' as Constance, the Queen's maid of honour in *The Three Musketeers*, providing, the critic noted, 'an admirable excuse for the hot-headed Gascon falling so suddenly and inextricably in love.'[37]

Still unable to tear himself away from his Australian audiences, Knight began what turned out to be his final season in June 1916, this time back in the Williamson fold. He chose as his leading lady the Australian Lizette Parkes, who had by this time become the Firm's most valuable dramatic actress. Francee Anderson once more played the minor roles – Susy the waitress in *The Silver King*, Jeanne the Belgian innkeeper's daughter in *Under Fire*, the Roman prostitute Ancaria in The *Sign of the Cross*, her former role as Stephanie de Beauharnais in *A Royal Divorce,* and Miss Nesbitt in the American courtroom drama *The Lion and the Mouse.*

Each of these parts, however, were noticed by critics for the skill with which Anderson gave them personality: Susy the waitress was 'very lackadaisical'; Miss Nesbitt was 'an exasperating little American hustler'; Stephanie de Beauharnais was 'coquettish, flirtation-loving, but loyal,' played with 'a delightful vivacity.' But it was in the role of Jeanne, the innkeeper's daughter whose father is shot before her eyes, and as the rejected prostitute Ancaria, that her unique talents began to be recognised by critics and audiences alike. 'The grief of Jeanne (Miss Francee Anderson) after the

---

37 *Winner* 29 Dec 1915: 8.

shooting of her father, Christophe, was a fine piece of acting, which deservedly earned the praise of the onlookers,' the *Sunday Times* noted when the war play *Under Fire* opened in Sydney in July 1916. Among the many who commented on her effective handling of this wrenching scene, *Table Talk*'s critic observed of her Melbourne performance that 'Francee Anderson's portrayal of Jeanne, the innkeeper's daughter, is an admirable piece of emotional acting, convincingly developed'; and the *Argus* reported that, although her opportunities were few, she made good use of them and they were 'full of red blood.' A writer for the *Australian Bystander* gave a similar prevision of Anderson's later career heights when he wrote:

> *A striking success was made by Francee Anderson as Ancaria in* The Sign of the Cross. *Ancaria is the lovely pagan whom Marcus deserts at his own party to enjoy the society of Mercia, the Christian outcast, in an anteroom. Ancaria follows, and summons the rest of the company to witness the reason of Marcus's defection. Former players have lightly mocked and taunted the Christian girl, but Francee Anderson really rose to great heights in this scene. She quivered with passion, and denounced the 'white sorceress' and her recreant knight like a flame.*[38]

But Francee Anderson was still only 19 and low on the totem pole of Australian actresses; and her patron and teacher Julius Knight did finally quit Australia in January 1917, at the end of the tour that had been so successful for the young actress. As the new year dawned, prospects did not look good for the

---

38   *SMH* 26 Jun 1916: 3; *Referee* 28 Jun 1916: 14; *ST* 9 Jul 1916: 2; *TT* 21 Sep 1916: 25; *Argus* 23 Oct 1916: 10; *Australian Bystander* 6 Jul 1916.

ambitious Francee. Despite a Melbourne critic's opinion that the actresses in *The Three Musketeers* provided an 'argument against the wholesale importation of English and American actresses,' the major firms were returning to old ways. J C Williamson had recently imported the American silent movie actress Florence Rockwell to star in the crime play *House of Glass*. They had also brought in five British actors with the comedy *Fair and Warmer*, including the leading lady Daisy Atherton and two other actresses.[39]

The track record of the new player on the block, J & N Tait, was not promising. Early in 1916 E J (Ted) Tait had left The Firm, where he had been general manager in charge of the Sydney office, and joined his brothers John and Nevin in their celebrity concert business. The livewire Ted immediately devoted his considerable energies to expanding J & N Tait to include theatrical productions in competition with his former employer. Their first venture was to bring the complete company of the worldwide hit *Peg o' My Heart* to Australia, led by its British star Sara Allgood. As *The World's News* pointed out sarcastically under the headline ADVANCE AUSTRALIA, 'There is at least one Australian in the *Peg o' my Heart* Company' – a Miss Yaldwyn, who had been in England for some time and 'has had a splendid all-round experience in stock in the provinces and in the suburbs of London.' 'She has not been heard much of in Australia,' the article added. Local actresses again had to make do with country tours and minor roles in these imported companies.[40]

Francee Anderson therefore found herself, in February 1917, taking on the tiniest of the four small roles available in the Taits' newest import, *Turn to the Right*. Ted Tait had

---

39   *EN* 1 Jan 1917: 2; *SMH* 27 Jan 1917: 6.
40   *Theatre* 1 Feb: 35; 1 Mar 1916: 5–6; *Brisbane Courier* 27 Jan 1917: 13; *TWN* 8 Apr 1916: 5.

organised this company during his trip to the US at the end of 1916. *Turn to the Right* was one of the most successful (and saccharine) of the recent spate of 'crook' plays on Broadway. Tait imported the four main (male) actors and the one actress required to play the important role of the mother in this comedy. Lizette Parkes, who had just been playing Empress Josephine opposite Julius Knight, was reduced to playing the sister of one of the 'crooks,' while Francee and Nancye Stewart, the daughter of the great Nellie Stewart, had minor 'girlfriend' roles. Gaston Mervale, that well-travelled and multi-talented former Australian resident, was brought back as producer.

Turn to the Right was an enormous success, although it was, as the *Australasian* put it, 'vacuous and soppy.' Opening in Melbourne on 24 February 1917, it toured the capital cities all year. Although she made a lasting friend of her fellow-sufferer Nancye Stewart, Francee had much to be depressed about during the long months of playing what the *Theatre* remarked truthfully was 'a part in name only.' She had hoped against hope that her long lost father would come to see her while she was playing in Perth the previous November. Whether she knew or not that her father was in a nearby hospital, probably suffering from alcoholism, is not clear. But the anticipation and the disappointment when he never appeared was enough to make her ill, and she had to miss several performances for probably the first time in her short career.[41]

Apart from the rock of her mother, her personal life was full of anxiety and uncertainty. Along with many others, she had a beloved brother, Jack, fighting in France. Her dear friend Oliver Hogue was battling his way through the Sinai and Palestine with the Australian Light Horse and the Camel

---

41   *Referee* 28 Feb 1917: 14; *LH* 2 Apr 1917: 229–32; *Australasian* 31 Mar 1917: 572; *Theatre* 1 May 1917: 23.

Corps, sending her letters of increasing longing for the little girl who had grown up in the three years he had been away.[42]

Like many 19-year-old girls, she had had a brief wartime romance. The most serious of her flirtations up to then, she met Adelaide-born Greg Bruer in Sydney during the happy winter of 1916, when he was waiting to go abroad again after a period of illness contracted at Gallipoli and she was getting notice in the Knight company. They saw each other rarely while she toured from September that year, and Mrs Anderson cautioned them against a hasty engagement as he embarked for England in February 1917. A year later he wrote from France, remembering 'a wee girl crying in a taxi' and 'a brave young lady standing on the platform waving goodbye.' A letter from Oliver Hogue gives an insight into her anxieties (and his own feelings). 'I was pleased to get your sad little letter of Jany 27,' he wrote. 'Sure it's a sad little lass you were then Honey.' 'Some of the brightest & best of the boys won't come back to Sunny Australia,' he conceded, [but] 'don't you worry about that bloke who says he's sure he won't get back.' 'I hope the bloke who is *more than a friend* will win thro!' he wrote generously. 'I'm awfully jealous of him.'[43]

With nothing in her life certain, Anderson brooded during 1917 on her career, which seemed to be going nowhere. Ted Tait had come back from the US with glowing accounts of Australians doing well there.[44] Certainly there had been a haemorrhage of talent to the US, especially to the increasingly attractive Hollywood. By 1917 two of the women featured in *Lone Hand*'s photomontage in 1915 – Enid Bennett and Sylvia Bremer – were in Hollywood, and the

---

42   Oliver Hogue, writing as 'Trooper Bluegum,' published many accounts of the fighting in the *SMH* during this time. His letters to Anderson are in UCSB.
43   Greg Bruer's letters to Anderson are in UCSB; Hogue to Anderson, 17 Mar 1917, UCSB.
44   *Theatre* 1 Feb 1917: 20.

third – Lizette Parkes – was making plans to follow them.

The most conspicuous success was the 24-year-old Enid Bennett. When Americans Fred Niblo and Josephine Cohen toured Australia from 1912 to 1915 Bennett had joined their company and eventually understudied and often replaced the fragile Cohen. She left Australia with the Niblos in June 1915 and began a successful movie career with the Triangle Film Corporation. In February 1917, as Francee and Lizette Parkes were playing insignificant roles in *Turn to the Right* back in Australia, Bennett was starring in *Princess of the Dark* with heartthrob Jack Gilbert. Sylvia Bremer joined her at Triangle in 1916. By December 1917 she had made five movies and Australian newspapers were advertising her alongside Enid Bennett as the second Australian star to make a decided impression in the American film world.[45]

Dorothy Cumming, who had played with Francee in Knight's company at the end of 1915, had also seen a brighter future in Hollywood. She had sailed in July 1916 and was immediately offered a contract with Famous Players. Preferring the legitimate stage (though she liked the money to be made in the movies), she was back in Australia the following June as leading lady to Cyril Maude, the British actor who had made a worldwide success with his current play, *Grumpy*. Her first movie, *Snow White*, starring Marguerite Clark, was playing at the Paramount in Melbourne when she arrived. *Lone Hand* described her in October 1917, 'chatter[ing] in her bright wholly Australian way despite the USA stamp on her beautiful clothes and much of her personality.' She returned to America with Maude's company for a tour of New Zealand, Hawaii and the American West and Southwest.

---

45 *Theatre* 1 Oct 1915: 36–38; 1 May: 14; 1 Jul: 6, 52; 1 Aug: 2, 24; 1 Sep 1916: 34; *LH* Jun 1916: 31–32, 50; 1 Mar 1917: 27–30, 48–5; *Grafton Argus and Clarence River General Advertiser* 7 Nov 1917: 2. Josephine Cohen died in Jul 1916 and Niblo and Bennett married two years later.

Her hometown newspaper, the *Goulburn Evening Penny Post*, considered that she 'had improved… wonderfully by her trip to America.'[46]

For an ambitious and talented young actress, the next step was clear. In July 1917 Oliver Hogue wrote to Anderson, in reply to a letter that was probably written early in June, 'So you are off to America. Well my little angel there will be many in Sunny New South Wales who will follow your career with interest.' 'I will think of you & pray for you & long for news of you & follow every step you take,' he continued. 'Perhaps you'll have left old Australia before this arrives.' A few weeks later he referred to her going to America with Nancye Stewart, suggesting that the two young actresses had shared their discontent. Nancye's plans, however, were disrupted when she had to come to her mother Nellie's aid, as she was often called upon to do. Nellie Stewart had embarked on a comeback after seven years away from the stage. Although she was greeted rapturously by audiences who remembered her as Australia's greatest actress – the theatre's equivalent of Melba – she was not in good health. When the *Turn to the Right* company completed their Sydney season in mid-June 1917, Nancye joined her mother's company, while Francee continued on to Brisbane, Hobart, Adelaide and then New Zealand, giving up, for the moment, their dreams of escape to America.[47]

In August *Lone Hand* announced that Lizette Parkes – a third dissatisfied member of the *Turn to the Right* company – was leaving for America. Lizette never did get there, and

---

46   *Queenslander* 23 Jun 1917: 29; *SMH* 6 Jun 1917: 1; *Argus* 9 Jun 1917: 26; *LH* Oct 1917: 531–32; *Goulburn Evening Penny Post* 9 Apr 1918: 2.
47   Hogue to Anderson, 25 Jul 1917, UCSB; *Theatre* 1 Jul 1917: 21.

Nancye Stewart did not for several years. Francee Anderson, however, persevered with her plan. She told Clyde Packer many years later that during the New Zealand tour she was urged by the American principals in the company to go to 'God's Country.' If she stayed in Australia, they warned her, she was destined to play second fiddle to overseas stars. This decided her, she recalled, and she cabled her mother to sell up and pack their bags.[48]

Her decision may not have been as decisive as she remembered 60 years later. Oliver Hogue wrote her in late January 1918, in reply to a letter written about this time, 'My dear Sweet Little Woman: There now… At last you've convinced me that you are a real big woman & not a little girl any longer… you were in quite a melancholy mood Honey when you churned out that recent letter. You were trying to solve the Riddle of the Universe & it was not very easy was it?' 'Don't you worry about the big problems of the world Honey,' he advised. 'Just you "carry on" & be a good little Angel, & the problems will solve themselves in due course.' 'I suppose you've seen Tien lately,' he concluded.' She is getting on fine. I'm awful proud of the pair of ye.'

But by this time her mind was made up. Frances Margaret Anderson's passport was issued on 2 January 1918. A week later she and her mother were on the *SS Sonoma*, heading for San Francisco and Los Angeles.

---

48   *LH* Aug 1917: 435–36; Hogue to Anderson, 23 Jan 1918, UCSB; Clyde Packer, 'Dame Judith Anderson.' In *No Return Ticket*, 1984, 59.

ACT II
Sensation

Broadway 1918

... a stepping stone to something bigger
Francee Anderson, Diary 1919

Scene Three
New York

Francee Anderson in America aged 21

Apeda NY/ UCSB

Chapter Six

Godzone Country 1918–22

When Francee Anderson and her mother arrived in San Francisco on the *S.S. Sonoma* on 28 January 1918, she could not contain her excitement. In a last burst of her old identity as 'Frantic,' she galloped the length of the dock, 'up and down, up and down, like someone possessed.'

'Miss Francee Anderson, who commenced her career with Mr. Julius Knight, and who appeared here in "Turn to the Right" and "The New Henrietta," left the Palace Theatre at the end of last week,' the *Sydney Morning Herald* reported. 'Miss Anderson expressed the hope that she would be able "to work her way to New York".'[1]

Her first stop was Los Angeles and Hollywood, where she had a letter of introduction to leading producer, Cecil B De Mille. She had the good fortune to meet at the dock Martha McKelvie, an enterprising motion picture journalist. Ten years older than Anderson, she was married to a future Governor of Nebraska. She was, Anderson wrote later, 'my first, permanent friend on American soil.' McKelvie admired the courage of the ambitious young Australian and her doughty mother and did everything she could to open doors for her in Hollywood.

Anderson's passport described her as having an oval face,

---
1   *SMH* 19 Jan 1918: 15.

with blue eyes, a small mouth, brown hair and a fair complexion. Her nose, it said, was 'Roman' and her height was over-stated at 5 ft 6 in. (She was barely 5ft 3 in.) She was, as *Lone Hand* put it, 'graceful, dainty, and pink with youth,' but that oval face and Roman nose, so attractive to caricaturists ten years later, was not what movie producers were looking for in 1918. As Martha McKelvie recalled many years later, 'I took her around Hollywood and introduced her to celebrities and other notables… We tried to get her into pictures but she didn't have Hollywood's formula of beauty and blonde hair.' Her screen tests revealed a nose that was not small enough and eyes that were too deep set. 'I went with my letter to Cecil B De Mille,' Anderson remembered. 'He took one look at this Australian waif – no looks, no clothes, no nothing. He wasn't interested.'[2]

'Have you starred in any pictures yet?' Greg Bruer wrote from France in June 1918. But his letter a month later revealed her disappointment at the four frustrating months she and her mother had spent in Los Angeles. 'Sorry you haven't gained what you came for,' he wrote.[3] From the perspective of a glittering career, she recalled in 1969 a story of pluck and optimism:

> *Momma had confidence in my ability and, despite my lack of beauty, we headed for New York. I went from casting office to casting office before I got a part as a heavy in a play with the 14th Street Stock Company. The next year I was playing the lead.*[4]

---

2 Gary Johansen, 'Judith Anderson: Grand Dame of the Theater,' *Sunday World-Herald Magazine of the Midlands* 1 Jun 1969: 14–15; Martha McKelvie to Anderson, Telephone Messages, Hollywood, 7 Feb to 25 Mar 1918, McKelvie Papers; Gloria [Martha McKelvie] to Anderson, 13 Apr 1918, postcard to Gordon Apartments, Los Angeles, UCSB.
3 Bruer to Anderson, 6 Jun & 3 Jul 1918, UCSB.
4 Johansen, 'Judith Anderson.'

The real story was, of course, much more rocky. A letter from Mrs McKelvie to Greg Bruer suggests a breakdown in Anderson's health under the strain of Hollywood's rejection. 'Buck up – there's a good time coming,' Oliver Hogue wrote from Palestine in response to an unhappy letter of mid-April. (Hogue and the Cameliers, meanwhile, were enduring the 'dust, fierce heat, flies, malaria, scorpions, spiders, snakes' of the Jordan Valley preparing for the final sweep that drove the Turks out of Palestine and Syria.) By June 1918 Anderson and her mother had crossed the continent by bus and were preparing to tackle New York, where their only contacts were Oliver's actor brother, Roland Hogue, and his wife Gwen.[5]

American theatre in 1918 was dominated by David Belasco, the 'Bishop of Broadway' as he was called because of his habit of wearing a clerical collar. Born in 1853, Belasco was famous for the infinite care he gave to his productions and his ability to make the most melodramatic story realistic. He prided himself on his ability to spot talent in the most unlikely places and his Svengali-like promotion of the female stars he discovered, over whom he demanded complete control. His current 'little girl' was Lenore Ulric, whom he had spotted when she replaced then-favourite Laurette Taylor as the Hawaiian girl, Luana, in *The Bird of Paradise* three years earlier. In the first of many exotic parts she played for Belasco, Ulric made a brilliant hit as 'Little Madam Butterfly of the Indian Reservation' in *The Heart of Wetonah* in 1916. In mid-1918, when Anderson arrived in New York, Ulric was coming to the end of a long run of *Tiger Rose*, in which she played a French-Canadian waif reared among rough men in a mining town.[6]

Anderson had dreams of being the next lucky young

---

5 Bruer to Anderson, 25 Feb 1918; Hogue to Anderson, 27 May 1918, UCSB; Major James Robertson, *With the Cameliers in Palestine*, 2006.
6 *NYT* 18 Apr 1915: X7; 14 Jan 1917: X6; *CSM* 28 Aug 1915: 6. For Ulrich, *WP* 21 Mar 1915: 66; *NYT* 1 Mar 1916: 9; *CDT* 14 Oct 1917: F1.

woman to be touched by Belasco's magic. She told an interviewer in 1948 how she and her mother took lodgings in a small hotel next to the Belasco Theatre on West 44th Street, confident that the great man would spot her and offer her a contract. This was not a total fantasy: in the international world of the theatre Belasco had many Australian connections. He had just given her former Williamson colleague Dorothy Cumming a small part in his new play *Tiger! Tiger!* which would feature his other 'little girl,' Frances Starr, along with former Adelaide actor O P Heggie; and he had under contract the young Australian actor Jerome Patrick, who had recently appeared with Frances Starr in *Little Lady in Blue*.[7]

The Master showed no interest, however, in seeing the latest Australian import, Francee Anderson. Crestfallen, she and her mother moved to a room in the house of a doctor's wife on West 56th Street. Her resourceful mother took in sewing while Francee did the rounds of the theatrical producers and agencies in the intense heat of the New York summer. These were, she told Hal Porter years later, 'months of poverty and despair.'[8]

The American stage, in 1918, was infatuated with the adolescent, a new category that was emerging in the larger community as a social type, a new mentality and a profitable market.[9] The 17-year-old Helen Hayes, who was to become the most beloved of the cohort of actresses that Francee joined, began her long career in 1917 touring in *Pollyanna*, the little girl in braids who was always glad. By the end of that year she was being hailed as the 'Youngest Leading Lady on the Stage.' Early the following year 22-year-old Ruth Gordon

---

7   Program for *Medea*, 1948, PAC; *Theatre* 1 Nov 1919: 5–9; *NYT* 22 Dec 1916: 9.
8   Hal Porter, *Stars of Australian Stage and Screen*, 1965.
9   See for example 'Fetching Indeed Are Fashion For The Flapper,' *CDT* 5 Dec 1915: C3; 'Sex Education: Anxiety About "Flappers",' *Manchester Guardian* 6 Jul 1916: 2; 'Ingenues Hold Sway. Their Dainty Graces Rule Along Broadway,' *LAT* 4 Sep 1916: Ii8.

and her partner Gregory Kelly entranced Broadway as the baby-talking Lola Pratt and her love-struck admirer in *Seventeen*, a play based on the popular Booth Tarkington novel that was widely seen as a faithful picture of the farcical and tragic aspects of first love. Over the next few years Hayes and Gordon perfected the role of the stage flapper – the 'Up-to-Date Miss' who 'Does Not Intend to Do Wrong [but] Means Only to "Have a Good Time",' who the *Washington Post* placed at about 16. Alfred Lunt rose to stardom in one leap in 1919 when he played with Hayes in another Tarkington creation, *Clarence*; and his future wife Lynn Fontanne made her name as the sparkling *Dulcy* with Gregory Kelly in 1921.[10]

Anderson, even at 21, was never the ideal ingénue; nor was she a comedian. However, armed with new portraits by the New York theatrical photographers Apeda that emphasised her sweetness, she diligently pursued all possibilities. Seeking a part as one of the aspiring maidens in Winthrop Ames' production of Maeterlinck's *The Betrothal*, she was passed over by the young Guthrie McClintic for the more beautiful Sylvia Field, Gladys George, Winifred Lenihan and June Walker. She was in good company however: also rejected were Margalo Gillmore and Tallulah Bankhead – the latter no doubt already too sophisticated at age 16 to play one of Maeterlinck's ethereal maidens.[11]

The Spanish flu was raging, and, weakened by fever, she fainted in the Paul Scott agency. But just as she had reached her lowest point, Scott had found something for her: second lead in Emma Bunting's 14th Street Stock Company. This was not quite what she had envisioned when she set off from Sydney ten months before, but she would be earning $40 a week. She and

---

10   *LAT* 9 Dec 1917: V12; *Theatre* Jul/Dec 1917: 361; 1918: 76, 150; *WP* 18 Sep 1914: 4; 8 Jul 1917: Fs8.
11   See Guthrie Mcclintic, *Me And Kit*, 1955, 169.

her mother moved to a rooming house on 14th Street.

The old Fourteenth Street Theatre, just off Sixth Avenue, was a relic of the Rialto, the theatre district that grew up between 14th and 23rd Streets after the Civil War. Once managed briefly by Laura Keene, its huge auditorium seated 1,600 people. Never a success, in recent years it had been neglected and dark, superseded by the elegant new theatres on Broadway.[12]

This was not a chance or negligible opportunity. Emma Bunting's touring stock company was one of the greatest in the US, with a large following throughout the South. She herself was, in the words of the *New York Times*, an undisputed star, as well known in the South as Ethel Barrymore in Times Square. 'A winning, red haired little thing with big, moving picture eyes… a manner ingenuously magnetic and a definite sense of the theatre,' Bunting had decided that she had 'served her time' and was trying out a metropolitan engagement.[13] Anderson's Australian experience of stock gave her an edge over local actresses, who were used to long runs in the one play.

Emma Bunting's name brought large audiences to the out-of-the-way theatre and Anderson's talent attracted notice. 'Frances Anderson is excellent, reading her lines intelligently and with feeling,' a *Variety* reviewer noted early in December. Five months later, as the season drew to a close, the reviewer remarked of her role in *Seven Keys to Baldpate*, that 'Frances Anderson as the heavy, the girl blackmailer, played it very well indeed.'[14]

By the end of the season, however, Anderson was glad to be done with the engagement. 'Finished 14th St Theatre

---

12   *Variety* 28 May 1920. Eva Le Gallienne turned it into the Civic Repertory Theater from 1926 to 1934.
13   *NYT* 4 Nov 1923: X1; *Variety* 15 Nov 1918.
14   *Variety* 6 Dec 1918; 2 May 1919.

for ever I hope,' she wrote in her appointment diary. These months had been tough for her. The 14th Street management had been difficult to deal with and she had had to lay down her terms firmly. The majority of the audience, as *Variety* put it, were 'exactly the picture type in the regular run of 10-cent houses.' She was unsettled, seeking out Mental Science lectures and lectures on Bolshevism and the League of Nations when she was not attending musical performances or assessing theatrical stars ('Walter Hampden – in *Hamlet* – an intelligent reading but by no means inspired'; 'Saw John Barrymore in *Redemption* – Thrilled A masterpiece of Art – such as I have never before witnessed').[15]

With the war over, Oliver Hogue and Greg Bruer were due to be demobbed. 'Walked in Washington Square this A.M. meditated on the future,' she noted in her diary on 5 April 1919. But two weeks later the blow fell: 'Ol is dead – March 3rd' she wrote starkly. Her 'baby love,' Oliver Hogue, had died of the flu in London after surviving Gallipoli and the Desert War. His brother Roland brought her the news at the theatre just as she was about to start the dress rehearsal of the week's play.[16]

Anderson wrote later that she had never been 'in love' with Oliver Hogue. She had been too young to respond to his devotion; but he was brilliant and fascinating and had been her ideal. A month later Anderson wrote wearily, 'Since April 20th the knowledge of Ol's death I find the exertion of living hurts more & more daily.' But life, and earning a living, went on. Three days after hearing of Oliver's death, she signed in a daze a contract for summer stock in Waterbury, Connecticut, 77 miles from New York City. 'It doesn't interest me in the

---

15 Diary 3 May 1919; *Variety* 17 Jan 1919.
16 'Trooper Bluegum. Oliver Hogue Dead. Victim of Influenza,' *SMH* 12 Mar 1919: 10; Diary 20 Apr 1919.

slightest,' she wrote in her diary. She arrived in Waterbury 'tired and depressed'; but they turned out to be a 'jolly decent company' and the production 'awfully good.' She decided that 'it's going to be alright' after all.[17]

By the end of summer 1919 she returned full of hope to 14th Street, where she accepted a contract as lead, with a salary of $100 a week. 'I feel it is a stepping stone to something bigger,' she wrote in her diary. She was no longer an outsider in New York. During her first season at 14th Street she had become firm friends with Olga Lee, a New Yorker who was also new to the company. Olga's parents, wealthy stockbroker Cosmond Hammerslough and his wife Hortense and daughter Julia were, in Anderson's words, 'warm, generous and fond,' and took her in as daughter and sister. With Olga, Anderson had 'earnest conversations about romance, marriage, sex.' 'I think our friendship will be true & lasting,' she wrote soon after they met – a prediction of their lifelong close relationship. From Australia, Nancye Stewart arrived in New York in April 1919 – 'Joy of Joys,' Anderson wrote; her sister Elizabeth ('Did') arrived in July; and in August she had a reunion with her old friend from Adelaide, Jean Robertson, who had been in the US since early 1917 and was about to appear on Broadway in *The Unknown Woman* with the tragic and talented Marjorie Rambeau.[18]

By this time, her Australian 'fiance' Greg Bruer seems to have disappeared from her life. With her new friends Anderson enjoyed everything New York offered. 'Greenwich Village lots of fun… a wild night,' she wrote in her diary in July. 'Palace… Dinner Theatre… Astor Roof with Lorna two Swedish chaps,' she noted a week later. In August: 'Yachting from Pt Washington to Bayside… dance at the Club in eve

---

17 Diary 23 Apr; 4, 5, 7 & 31 May 1919.
18 Diary 1 Feb; 19 Apr; 2 May; 2, 7 & 28 Jul; 10 Aug 1919.

Launch after dance'; 'Dinner with Ralph.' 'Open 14th St Theatre *Third Degree* Starred – Supper Little Club,' she wrote like a New York veteran on 25 August.

Her success at 14th Street the previous season brought her the stepping stone to something bigger that she hoped for. 'Met Wm Gillett – Charming man,' she had noted at the end of that season. William Gillette, then close to 70, was one of the great theatre and movie matinee idols of the time, famous throughout the world for his stage creation of Sherlock Holmes. A few months later Alf Hayman, general manager of Charles Frohman Inc, called on her and offered her the role of Joanna Trout in the Southern touring company of *Dear Brutus* with Gillette from October 1919 to April 1920. On 4 October she once more wrote, 'Leave 14th St for ever I hope.'

The enchanting Helen Hayes had made her first Broadway hit in J M Barrie's *Dear Brutus* in December 1918, just as Anderson started at 14th Street. A midsummer night's fantasy in which the characters have the magical opportunity to remake their lives, the play mixed dream and reality in a manner similar to Maeterlink's *The Betrothal*. It gave Helen Hayes the perfect role as Margaret, the dream daughter who never was.

When Anderson opened in *Dear Brutus* in Stamford, Connecticut on 13 October 1919 Madge Bellamy – later to become a major silent movie star – had replaced Helen Hayes, who went on to further acclaim as the incorrigible daughter in *Clarence*. In choosing the 22-year-old Francee Anderson for the role of Joanna Trout, an ebullient young woman too ready to fall in love, William Gillette shrewdly saw her ability to give personality and emotional definition to any character she played.

Anderson's experience of touring in Australia stood her in good stead as the *Dear Brutus* company began its run through New England, eastern Canada, Baltimore and the

South. Pittsburgh was a 'Dirty hole,' she recorded in her diary, and when she arrived in Chicago in mid-January 1920 she was 'miserably lonesome.' On her 23rd birthday, however, she decided that 'There are some very [?] & dear folk in this world. Afternoon & dinner with Miss Moore. Supper with Mrs Price lot of mail.' The final run through Detroit, Cleveland and Washington DC, to Newark had its bad moments: 'I long for my lost loved one. Miss & need him more daily,' she wrote in Dayton, Ohio, early in March on the anniversary of Oliver Hogue's death. But she formed an enduring friendship during the tour with fellow-actor Anne Morrison; and she liked earning enough money to buy her long-suffering mother a fur coat.[19]

The tour ended on 17 April 1920 just in time for Anderson to have a quick reunion with her brother Frank, who had been in New York since the end of December. By 19 April she was in Schenectady, New York, to take the lead with a local stock company, the Armory Players. Feeling depressed at the end of a long and difficult tour, she was unprepared for the *coup de foudre* that struck a month later when she met the company's manager. At Paul Scott's office she was introduced to a tall, rugged man a good many years older than her. That evening she rang Olga. 'I have just met the man I'm going to marry,' she told her. A few days later she wrote in her diary, 'I know now that this was a very crucial moment in my life leading to great & wonderful things.'[20]

This was indeed true; but it brought heartbreak too. 'Doug,' as she called him in her memoirs, was a Canadian with a law degree from Yale who had abandoned the law for the theatre. He was soon courting her with chocolates and roses, and

---

19   Diary 5 & 19 Jan; 10 & 23 Feb; 3 Mar 1920.
20   *Press and Sun-Bulletin* (Binghamton, NY] 1 Jun 1920: 12; *Variety* 25 Jun 1920; Diary 14, 16, 18 & 19 Apr; 14 Jun to 28 Jul 1920.

a month later kissed her for the first time. With both of them soon caught up in a passionate love affair, he confessed that he was married and that his wife and children were coming to join him from Canada. A few months later, when she discovered he had not told his wife of the affair, she picked up the phone and rang her. When she returned, exhausted, to New York from Boston, where she had been playing with the Arlington Players, in the middle of 1921, 'Doug' took a house for them and her mother in Babylon, Long Island, and they lived together as man and wife. 'No words were ever said in church, nor even in a civil ceremony. Yet it was the only real marriage I ever had,' Anderson wrote years later.[21]

This home on Long Island was the last oasis of peace she enjoyed before she settled in California in 1940. It had two streams and a lake, and a garden that reminded her of the small yard behind the shop in Adelaide. Doug gave her the 'noble and handsome' Great Dane – Rex – who was her constant companion for many years; and she and Doug rode horses on the beautiful grounds. During these years Olga Lee, now married, visited often, and she brought Rosalie Watson, a friend from Baltimore who lived in Greenwich Village with her new baby and her husband, the psychologist Dr John B Watson, inventor of behaviorism, both of whom became great friends.

This brief interlude of tranquillity and happiness came to an end when Anderson returned to the theatre in September 1922 to make her almost unremarked Broadway debut in the mystery, *On the Stairs*, starring the old favourite Arnold Daly. Doug's fortunes went up and down, and he was a drinker like her father, and Anderson found ambition beginning to assert itself again; but when *On the Stairs* ended, she got no more calls.

---

21   Diary 29 Jul 1920. For Arlington Players see *Boston Evening Globe* 18 Jan; 8 Feb 1921: 4; BG 23 Jan 1921: 38; BP 1 Feb; 22 Mar 1921.

IN "PETER WESTON"

MISS JUDITH ANDERSON and FRANK KEENAN.
[H. A. Atwell Photo.]

Forthright, old-fashioned acting holds the boards at the Harris these nights. Here is a pair of players who can tear an emotion to tatters, and do so nine times a week in the last act of "Peter Weston," a scene from which is pictured. Their rôles are those of father and daughter; their experiences, as may be observed, are stressful and stirring.

Chapter Seven

Judith 1923–4

acting of distinction… by a young woman, new to me, named Judith Anderson.
Sheppard Butler, Chicago Daily Tribune 1923

If no one was calling her, Anderson resolved to take matters into her own hands. Veteran actor Frank Keenan was looking for a new actress to play opposite him in *Peter Weston*, which he had been touring briefly on the West Coast. This company was to open in Toledo, Ohio, in mid-February 1923, moving on to Dayton, and then to Chicago on 25 February for the rest of the season.

Anderson knew she was the right person for the role – the anguished daughter of a dominating and unfeeling father – and that the scene between them as he crushes her spirit could make her name. She called him up, and the certainty in her voice persuaded him to see her. 'A voice called me on the phone at the hotel in New York,' Keenan recalled several years later. '"You have a part – the leading part – in *Peter Weston*. I would like you to see me and give me that part".' 'How do you know you could play it?' I said, liking the speaker's confidence and voice. '"Because I know what kind of a part it is, and what kind of an actress I am".' 'Where are you now?' '"Three blocks off".' 'Can you come right up?' '"I'm on my way – goodbye." And Miss Anderson came.' 'She had a long nose, and her eyes weren't big,' Keenan went on. 'She wouldn't last a day in motion pictures. I told her she was no ravishing beauty. She only smiled and went on talking. She talked for half an hour – long enough to talk herself out of a job. But she talked herself in.' Keenan had just one condition: she must change her 'sappy ingénue name.' They decided that 'Judith' sounded strong enough for a serious emotional actress; and Judith Anderson was born.[22]

Anderson's instinct was right about the part. She immediately caught the attention of *Chicago Daily Tribune* critic, Sheppard Butler, who noted 'acting of distinction… by a young woman, new to me, named Judith Anderson.' 'I suspect that whoever found her achieved a discovery of importance,' he wrote. 'Her deportment in her present surroundings stamps her unmistakably as an emotional actress of great promise.' In a long review he captured those aspects of her talent that captivated audiences for the rest of her career:

> *Traversing an extraordinarily difficult role, she emerges with flying colors. One scene in particular she enacts with remarkable vividness… Badly acted, the scene would be preposterous. In Miss Anderson's hands it becomes a haunting portrayal of collapse, bleak despair, and spiritual torture. I cannot, at the moment, think of anyone who would have done it better.*

In particular, Butler noticed Anderson's hands: 'Only her hands rebel,' he wrote. 'They twitch and move about endlessly, febrile tokens of the storm within. Eloquent hands, these. Somehow the actress contrives to make them actually seem thin and wasted.' Continuing Chicago's love affair with their new discovery, the *Tribune* published a beautiful sketch

---

22 'Personality, An Intangible Asset,' *ST* 13 Mar 1927: 3; 'Confident Adelaide Girl,' *Mail* (Adelaide) 19 Mar 1927: 16.

of Anderson looking frail and feminine in an organdie dress.[23]

This season in Chicago was a turning point in Anderson's career. Indeed, it was the beginning of her career as *Judith* Anderson, theatrical star. After Chicago, nothing would stop her rise to the top of her profession.

Peter Weston placed her in the line of emotional actresses who were replacing the chirpy adolescent as the favourites of theatre audiences. Chief among these was Pauline Lord, seven years older than Anderson and a veteran of 20 years in the theatre. Considered one of the most skilful actresses on the American stage, she had consolidated her place as its leading emotional actress in 1921 as the forlorn and bitter heroine redeemed by love in Eugene O'Neill's *Anna Christie*.[24]

More importantly, *Peter Weston* linked her fortunes to the young woman – Katharine 'Kit' Cornell – who had demonstrated her talent as an emotional actress as the anguished daughter in

JUDITH ANDERSON.
Of "Peter Weston."

"I'D much rather talk about dogs than clothes," exclaimed Miss Anderson, with a shrug of disdain. "I think people should wear what they're happy in—if they like bizarre things, let 'em wear 'em. For myself, I can't be bothered shopping and picking things out. Once in awhile I bring myself to time and try to look decent, but most times I just forget all about 'em. I'd like to wear trousers all the time."

And yet it would be hard to imagine a more feminine attire than the dainty white organdy frock of the sketch. It is suggestive of iced lemonade, leghorn picture hats, and green shade on a golden hot day. The bertha and the side panels are edged in deep Viennese point lace. There is embroidery on the tight, basquelike bodice and on the panels. The girdle is powder blue—the color named by Australia, from whence Miss Anderson came five years ago. The velvet ribbon is plaited, with a myriad tiny knotted streamers falling from one side, which is graced by a spray of pale peach taffeta roses and baby blue forget-me-nots. White satin brocade slippers fit the summery costume for any season.

Miss Anderson likes best to appear in black.

---

23 Sheppard Butler, *CDT* 26 Feb: 17; 4 Mar: D1; & 18 Mar 1923: B1.
24 Alexander Woollcott, 'Second Thoughts on First Nights,' *NYT* 13 Nov 1921: X1.

Clemence Dane's *Bill of Divorcement* that same year, and the aspiring director Cornell had just married – Guthrie McClintic.

Chicago also marked the end of her relationship with 'Doug.' In Dayton, Ohio, in the first week of the *Peter Weston* tour, she met Daniel Joseph Mahoney, the adventurous general manager and vice-president of the *Dayton Daily News*. Described as 'a roaring newspaperman in the rugged, old tradition,' Mahoney was the first of many semi-serious flirtations that helped her recover from the dream of romance she had shared with 'Doug.' Like many of her flirtations, he became a life-long friend as he climbed the ladder of success, becoming the influential editor of the *Miami Post* and president of the Cox newspaper dynasty.[25]

In Chicago Anderson continued to develop other important friendships. In the *Peter Weston* cast was a flamboyant Australian girl named Bernice Vert. She had travelled from Australia on the same steamer as the violin virtuoso Jascha Heifetz, who had just completed a tour of the East. Music was Anderson's great love, after the theatre, and some of her most treasured memories, in later life, were of after-theatre parties where Jascha played violin or piano. Through Bernice she also met Sam Behrman, then a struggling playwright, and the glamorous film star Dagmar Godowsky, who was soon to play a small but important part in Anderson's rise to fame.

Ted Tait, in the US to recruit talent for Australia, caught Anderson's performance in *Peter Weston* during its short season on Broadway in September and October 1923. 'One of the most notable recent successes,' he told the *Sydney Morning Herald* on his return, 'is that of a little girl who was with us in *Turn to the Right*, Miss Frances Anderson, now known in New York as

---

25   *CDT* 14 Feb 1923: 17; *NYT* 19 Feb 1923: 10; Obit, Daniel Joseph Mahoney, *Time*, 12 Apr 1963.

Judith Anderson. She is playing lead with Frank Keenan… She is on her way to making a world name for herself.'[26]

After her success in *Peter Weston* Anderson rarely had to look for work again. Her break-through moment on Broadway came early in 1924. A play had almost completed its out-of-town tryout when the management decided that it needed a complete change of cast. The play was *Cobra*, and Anderson was engaged to play a new sort of vamp, Elise Van Zile, and provide her own clothes.

With no time to look for a suitable outfit for a seduction scene by such a character, Anderson discovered hanging in her wardrobe a dress made for the much larger Dagmar Godowsky by the great New York designer Milgrim. As she tells it in her memoirs, she stood before the mirror and 'wound the yellow satin round and round, tighter and tighter around my waist, as tight as it could be pulled; and that… was the dress I wore at my opening performance that tense Wednesday afternoon.'

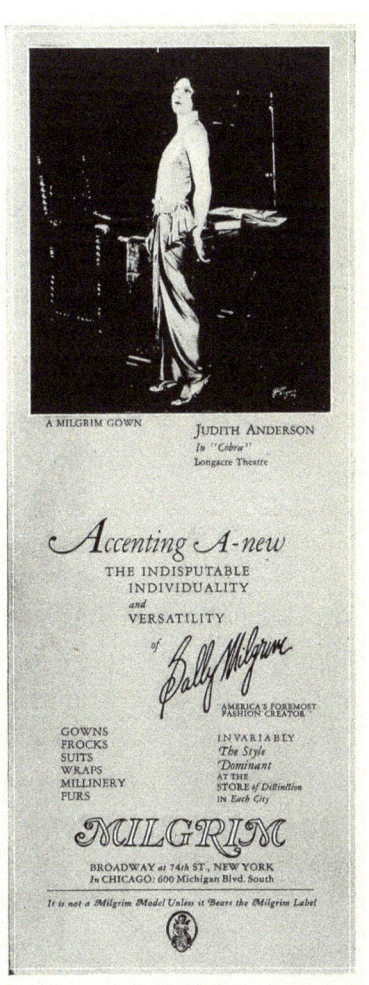

The dress was a smash hit. It

---

26   'Brilliant Australian Girl,' *SMH* 24 Nov 1923: 17.

was copied again and again and it featured in Milgrim advertisements. This was the beginning of Anderson's career as a fashion icon, representing a new sophisticated, sensual type who was as sexually active as the childlike flapper, but more urbane and stylish.[27]

It was not only the dress that caught New York's attention. 'It is a long time since Broadway has seen a better actress than Judith Anderson,' the critic in *Billboard* wrote soon after her opening on 24 April 1924. 'Sure in her technique, clear of diction, entirely without self-consciousness, her performance in *Cobra* is one of the best acting exhibitions of the season.' 'With the growth in her art which may be reasonably expected,' he concluded, 'Miss Anderson is surely designed for stardom.'[28]

The young Australian became one of the sensations of the season. She had 'personality' – that essential ingredient in a town where good looks and talent were two-a–penny. The *New York Herald Tribune* found her 'irresistible!' 'Miss Anderson isn't conventionally pretty,' their critic wrote, but she has that 'certain strangeness' which is 'something just as good.'[29]

That 'certain strangeness' attracted articles on the new type of predatory young woman she played (a 'New Type of Vampire,' a woman who is 'neither too good nor too bad'), her unusual looks ('mere prettiness fading before talent and personality'), and a certain exoticism from being Australian. Broadway had become truly international since the war, but Australians were still rare, and they represented to New Yorkers a modernity not conveyed so clearly by those from the old world of Europe.[30]

---

27   *Vogue* 15 Jun: 88; 15 Jul 1924: 41; *Variety* 30 Apr 1924: 7.
28   *Billboard* 10 May 1924: 23.
29   *NYHT* 11 May 1924, NYPL
30   *American*, 24 Apr 1924; *World*, 26 Apr 1924, NYPL; Elita Miller Lene, 'A Breakfast Interview With Judith Anderson and Her Dog, "Rex, the Great",' *Billboard* 24 May

Anderson's co-star Louis Calhern was one of her brief flirtations of this period.
Marcus, *New York Times* 4 May 1924.

In an era when *Vogue* was telling women how to 'Accentuate Your Youthful Lines,' and advising them that 'sports and semisports' were 'never so important,' much of this modernity stemmed from the sense of Australians being perfect physical specimens. The Australian swimmer Annette Kellerman had popularised the streamlined body beautiful in the teens; in 1924 she had just released her final movie, *Venus of the South Seas,* and *Vogue* was advertising her 'Two-in-One bathing suits with tights attached.' References to Australians in American newspapers emphasised their sporting prowess. As a headline in the *New York Times* put it in 1925, SPORTS IN AUSTRALIA ABSORB WHOLE NATION. Americans admired Australian sportsmen and women for their skill, and saw them as worthy opponents. The *Times* reported on a surprisingly large range of Australian sporting heroes – cyclists,

1924: 20–21; *Vogue* 1 May 1924: 78, 128.

boxers, golfers, swimmers and even cricketers. But most attention was focused on the Davis Cup – the annual international tennis championship. Australasia had dominated the series until 1920, when the US defeated them in a hard-fought match in Auckland. Since then, the US had managed to hold on to the Cup, but the Australasians always gave them a good, well-publicised fight.

1924 was the year of the Olympic Games in Paris, and the *New York Times* reported breathlessly on the battle between the American and Australian swimmers, with all eyes on the contest between Johnny Weismuller (of later Tarzan fame) and 'the Australian flash,' Boy Charlton. After the Olympics, the Australian swim team toured the US giving exhibitions. The American public was, therefore, ready to see the young Australian actress, Judith Anderson, as a beautiful physical specimen, healthy, lithe and fit, a perfect example of the new woman of the 1920s. This style was confirmed as *the* modern style by the Paris Exposition of 1925. Pretty was out, and moderne – smooth, streamlined, swift, or angular and geometric, like Anderson's profile – was in.[31]

Critics admired the way this young Australian used her body subtly to express emotion and character, and the manner in which she controlled her beautiful velvety voice. Anderson herself worked hard at keeping her body and her voice in shape, as she had as a girl in Sydney, and boasted throughout her life that she had never worn a corset or a bra.

Magazine and newspaper stories stressed her love of the outdoors, and photographed her riding her horse, boating and with her huge dog Rex. She loved throwing off 'the petty restraints of over-civilized city life,' she told an interviewer from *Theatre* magazine. 'Between seasons I get out into

---

31 'The Last Word in Paris Fashions: Modernistic Design In The Autumn Mode,' *CDT* 30 Aug 1925: B2.

the country with my Great Dane Rex and a horse and enjoy a perfect orgy of freedom,' she continued. 'No reason in the country why I shouldn't run and shout and sing and fling myself all over the place. These are the grand and glorious periods of relaxation for me.'[32]

Judith Anderson's success in *Cobra* turned her instantly into a person people wanted to know and to know about. As she put it, 'Suddenly... I had a small celebrity.' 'It was as though I had freshly arrived there, fully-fledged,' she remembered; 'as though the years in boarding houses and trains and road hotels had never been.' She took an apartment with her mother and Did on West 63rd Street and began to frequent nightclubs and attend balls and parties in the houses or apartments of the wealthy in gowns borrowed for the night from leading fashion houses.

She quickly got to know her rising contemporaries – some of whom would become close friends. Kit Cornell was stunning audiences as the crippled girl in *The Outsider* in a performance that was, according to one critic, 'like a peep through a hidden keyhole' at the heroine's heart and mind. Throughout the rest of the season she and Anderson went head to head in the grosses reported by *Variety* and the accolades heaped on their heads by the critics. Margalo Gillmore had just appeared as the 'beatific' wife in the hit, *Outward Bound*, with future film star Leslie Howard.[33]

Helen Menken was finishing up the two-year run of *Seventh Heaven*, the 'Golden ace' of the 1922–3 season, in which she was compared, in her 'haunting spiritual presence,'

---

32 Lene, 'A Breakfast Interview With Judith Anderson and Her Dog'; Anderson photo with Rex, *VF* Sep 1924, NYPL; Anderson, 'A Stage Vamp on Women,' *Theatre* Oct 1924: 22, 26, 63.
33 *Variety* 12 Mar: 17; 10 Jan 1924: 16.

to the great Duse. Helen Hayes, now 24 years old, was struggling unsuccessfully to shed her ingénue roles; but was demonstrating the quality that made her America's most loved actress for the rest of her life – her ability 'to hold most of her audience in her hand and to tie them into rosy and ingenious love knots whenever she liked.'[34]

From 1924 the theatre became Judith Anderson's life. There were to be no more Dougs. 'This was the time,' she recalled, 'of small flirtations, more numerous than significant, and temporary romances.' Her enduring love affair was with the stage, and she would remain faithful to it, with one brief interlude, for the rest of her life.

---

34 John Corbin, 'The Happy Pessimist,' *NYT* 5 Nov 1922: 97; Stark Young, 'The Play: How To Take The Cake,' 17 Dec 1924: 19.

Mr. Belasco's New Risen Star

Author's collection

Chapter Eight

Star 1925–6

Judith Anderson was little short of gorgeous, and this reviewer, for one, is hoarse from joining in the cheering.

Leo Marsh, New York Telegraph

When Francee Anderson arrived in New York in 1918 she wanted more than anything to be noticed by David Belasco. Six years later, as Judith Anderson, she had her wish. In June 1924, a month after she was described as 'surely designed for stardom' for her role as Elise in *Cobra*, Belasco sent for her, and offered her the part of Dolores Romero in *The Dove*, opposite the great actor Holbrook Blinn. When the play opened in Baltimore at the end of January 1925, the response to Anderson was so enthusiastic that Blinn insisted that her name be put up in lights alongside his. Suddenly, after six years of apprenticeship, she was officially a star.[35]

The Dove by Willard Mack was the sort of old-fashioned melodrama that Belasco made into an art form, presenting a heightened reality that 'bristles and tingles with life.' *Washington Post* critic John J Daly described the Belasco effect as 'putting a complete motion picture scenario on stage, with

---

35 'Judith Anderson: The *Cobra* Woman to Star in New Belasco Piece,' clipping [Jun?] 1924, NYPL; *Variety* 18 Jun 1924: 7; *Baltimore Sun* 26 Jan 1925, NYPL.

the blessing of human voices and the perfect shadings of silence.' Mack had written *Tiger Rose* for Belasco and Lenore Ulric in 1917. Tiger Rose had been Indian; Dolores Romero (The Dove) was Mexican, a good girl in a bad place, a cafe singer who catches the eye of the evil Don José Maria Lopez y Tostado and has to save her American sweetheart from his villainy. 'With Willard Mack in back of the manuscript,' Daly wrote, 'and David Belasco himself having his turn at casting, designing, directing – and all those things Belasco knows how to do well, when he feels the flare coming on – plus the magnificent histrionic ability of Miss Judith Anderson and Holbrook Blinn, aided and assisted by many others in a first-rate cast, the new play is a veritable knockout.'[36]

When *The Dove* opened at that loveliest of Broadway theatres, the Empire, on 11 February 1925, Anderson's name was up in lights, joining Leon Errol and O P Heggie as Australians thus honoured. 'The evening was all Mexican border, cabarets of gay sinners, patios with moonlight and soft music,' Stark Young wrote in the *New York Times*, 'a singing girl, a rich caballero and his passionate desire, an American boy and his devotion, with suspense, arrests, and a happy ending, and applause, curtain speeches and bravos for Judith Anderson and Holbrook Blinn and Mr Belasco.' 'Judith Anderson had to play a girl that exists only in opera and somewhere in the hum of guitars on a Summer night,' he went on. 'She created a figure that was full of variety, of a sense of wit, beauty and impulsive life. The cadence of the voice, the rhythm of speech and of body were always admirable.' 'The signs of talent were everywhere evident in her playing,' he concluded. Others praised her 'style, poise and unfailing distinction,' 'charm, ability and magnetism,' 'the come hitherest eyes below the Rio Grande' and 'voice of

---

36 *WP* 3 Feb 1925: 5.

contralto richness.' 'Judith Anderson was little short of gorgeous,' Leo Marsh wrote in the *Telegraph*, 'and this reviewer, for one, is hoarse from joining in the cheering.'[37]

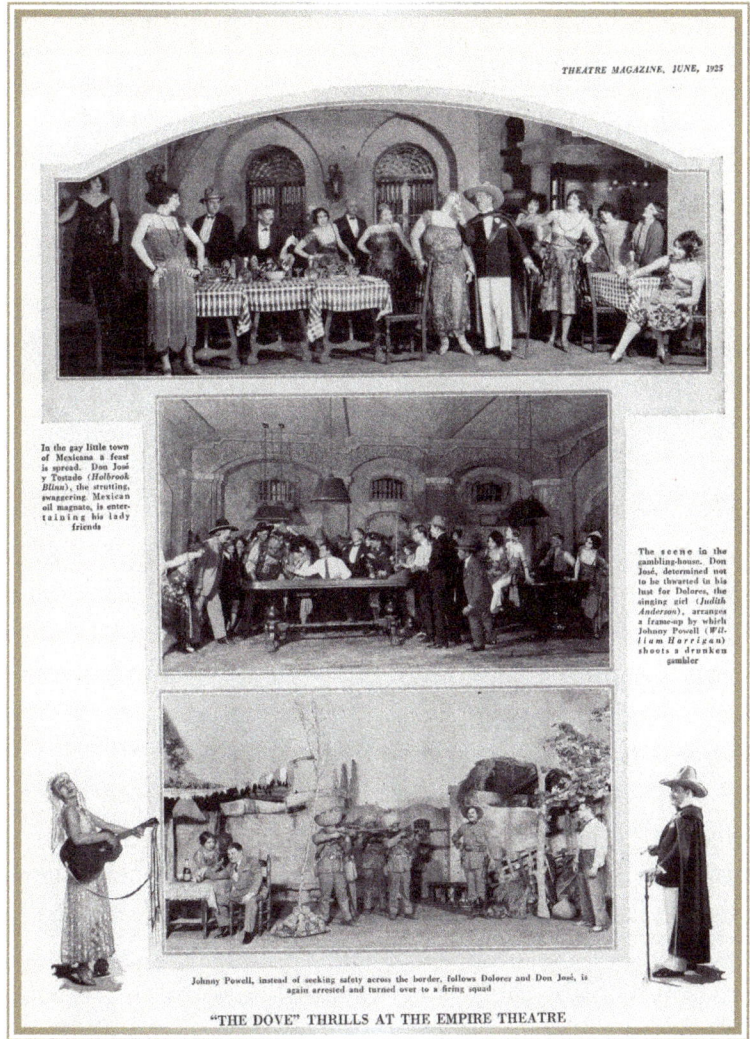

Author's collection

---

37   David Worral, 'Lights Of Broadway. The Australians In America,' *Mercury (Hobart)* 17 Oct 1925: 16; *NYEP* 12 Feb 1925, NYPL; *Variety* 11 Mar 1925: 20; *NYDM* 12 Feb 1925; *NYDN* 18 Feb 1925; *NYMT* 21 Feb 1925; 13 Feb 1925, NYPL.

Guthrie McClintic, from the heights of his position as one of America's leading producer-directors in 1955, described a star as 'an individual who is blessed with some indefinable chemical element that makes great masses of the public willing to pay money to see him or her irrespective of the play the star is appearing in.' Judith Anderson certainly proved herself deserving of this new honour. *The Dove* played to capacity houses until late June, earning grosses of $20,000 a week with only the screwball comedy *Is Zat So?* among the non-musicals making more.[38]

After a summer break, *The Dove* resumed in late August and played until early October. It then toured Philadelphia, Cleveland and Pittsburgh till it arrived in Chicago a few weeks later. There, it broke all records and was repeatedly extended until the company left for their final performances in Boston in April 1926. A *New York Times* story proclaimed that 'Leon Errol and the emu are no longer the only two thoroughly well-known importations from the Antipodes.'[39]

Images of Anderson, looking adorable in a Spanish mantilla, with a kiss curl on her forehead, were everywhere. Leading photographer Edward Steichen featured her in *Vogue*. She was on the cover of *Theatre Magazine* in June 1925, in an issue that included a spread of scenes from the play. Up-and-coming celebrity photographer Nickolas Muray, who photographed her for *Theatre*, fell in love with her – and later became one of her closest friends. Many years later he remembered her as she was then. 'She was playing in *The Dove*,' he recalled, 'a sentimental Mexican play with implications of tragedy, in which she played a young girl, innocent but with great charm and playfulness. This was the first and only play in which I ever saw her in a singing part.'

---

38   Guthrie McClintic, *Me and Kit*, 1955, 279; *Variety* 4 Mar 1925: 19.
39   'Anderson Sings In The Dove,' *BH* 21? Apr 1926, NYPL; *NYT* 15 Feb 1925: X2.

She had a most mobile and unusual face, and a very petite figure – perhaps five foot one inch – which grew on the stage to five foot ten. Her walk, her gestures, her voice could suggest authority, greatness, tragedy – or great callousness and tragic depth, as in MACBETH. *Her voice is penetrating – even when she whispers. She has the commanding ability of gaining everyone's close attention to what she is saying, whether on stage or off.*[40]

Anderson's status as a Belasco star, and her phenomenal success in *The Dove*, placed her among a select few of young American actresses. Robert Coleman, at the *New York Daily Mirror*, decided immediately that 'Judith Anderson's work as the singer stamps her as America's foremost young actress.' The *Metropolitan Guide* put it more colorfully: 'Miss Anderson,' their reporter wrote, 'is the most exciting trinket among the naughty and impassioned ladies it has thus far been our good fortune to see on the New York stage.' Among these 'naughty and impassioned ladies' were the two other Belasco stars, Beth Merrill, who was appearing in *Ladies of the Evening*, and Lenore Ulric in *The Harem*.[41]

More interesting, however, were the half dozen who would be her co-stars and rivals for the rest of her career. Helen Hayes and Ruth Gordon were attempting to work their way out of the flapper category in which they had earlier been so successful, Hayes in F Tennyson Jesse's *Quarantine*, and Gordon ('discovered' for the third time!) in *Mrs Partridge Presents*. Lynn Fontanne and Alfred Lunt had married and turned themselves into the country's most glamorous

---

40   *Vogue* 1 May, 1925: 83; Muray, notes for his book *The Revealing Eye* late 1960's, courtesy Mimi Muray Levitt; *Theatre* Jun: Cover, 38; Sep 1925: 25; Photos by White *TSM* May 1925: 290; Goldberg *NYT* 17 May 1925: RP6; Caricatures, *BT* 29 Apr 1926; *CN* 21 Nov [1925], NYPL.
41   *NYDM* 12 Feb; *Metropolitan Guide* 15 Mar 1925, NYPL.

and successful husband-and-wife comedy team under the auspices of the Theatre Guild. Margalo Gillmore and Helen Menken were carrying the adolescent vogue into its next incarnation – the ethereal young woman – in *Outward Bound* and *Seventh Heaven*. Pauline Lord, in *They Knew What They Wanted*, was Anderson's main rival as an emotional actress, having made an indelible impression in *Anna Christie* two years earlier.[42]

Most important of all was the exotic-looking Kit Cornell, who had made her name as the daughter in Clemence Dane's *A Bill of Divorcement* in 1921. Married to Guthrie McClintic, the young man who had rejected Anderson for *The Betrothal* in 1918 and now a rising producer-director, she was demonstrating her acting credentials in Shaw's *Candida*. Belasco had realised her potential and featured her in the unsuccessful *Tiger Cats* in late 1924; but she managed to evade the Great Man's further control. During 1925 she and McClintic would establish themselves as the New York stage's power couple in the sensational *The Green Hat*, in which she played the abandoned Iris March under McClintic's direction.[43]

As the sophisticated vamp of *Cobra* and the acclaimed Belasco star of *The Dove*, Judith Anderson found herself swept up as part of a wave of modernity that engulfed New York in the middle part of the 1920s. In February 1924 the 26-year-old George Gershwin had electrified the city with his 'Rhapsody in Blue,' presented by jazz bandleader Paul Whiteman in a concert at the Aeolian Hall designed to demonstrate 'that jazz was beginning a new movement in the world's art of music,'

---

42   *Vogue* 15 Feb 1925: 70, 114; 1 Jan 1922: 57; *NYT* 11 Jan 1925: X1; *Theatre* Mar; 20 Apr 1925.
43   *NYT* 20 Sep1925: X1; *Theatre* Jan 1926, Cover.

and that it 'had come to stay and deserved recognition.' Gershwin's composition, a concert work rather than a piece of dance music, was a rhapsody – 'a free-ranging mélange of diversified rhythms, loosely joined' – 'a musical kaleidoscope of America, of our vast melting pot, of our national pep, of our blues, our metropolitan madness,' as Gershwin himself described it.[44]

Several months later, in December 1924, George and Ira Gershwin, in their first collaboration as composer and lyricist, had a huge hit with *Lady, Be Good*, starring their old friends, Fred and Adele Astaire, whose beautiful loose-limbed dancing had thrilled London over the two previous years.

Anderson's friend Dagmar Godowsky, in her memoirs, recalls the mid-1920s as a time when 'everybody was so happy and so rich.' 'Everybody,' for Godowsky, included the friends she had introduced to Anderson in Chicago the previous year – the violinist Jascha Heifetz, his accompanist and emerging music critic Sam Chotzinoff, the composer Vincent Youmans and the would-be playwright Sam Behrman – who were in turn close friends of the young musical genius George Gershwin, his brother Ira, and their gregarious family. Indeed, this mixture of the greatest classical and popular musical talents of the period is a wonderful example of the 'Mongrel Manhattan' described so vividly by Ann Douglas.[45] Gershwin's friendship with Heifetz and his fellow Jewish musicians was immortalised in the song 'Mischa, Jascha, Toscha, Sascha' that he wrote in 1922; Heifetz and Chotzinoff were present at Gershwin's first presentation of 'Rhapsody in Blue'; and Chotzinoff wrote one of its most enthusiastic reviews. He married Heifetz's sister, Pauline,

---

44 Paul Whiteman and Mary Margaret McBride, *Jazz*, 1926, 93; Isaac Goldberg, *George Gershwin: A Study in American Music*, 1958, 139–40.
45 Dagmar Godowsky, *First Person Plural: The Lives of Dagmar Godowsky*, 1958; Ann Douglas, *Terrible Honesty: Mongrel Manhattan in the 1920s*, 1995.

in 1925; Behrman married his other sister, Elza in 1936; and Gershwin's sister, Frances, married Godowsky's brother, Leopold, in 1930.

Godowsky, Heifetz and the Gershwin crowd were the consummate party-givers in a time of spectacular parties. Anderson many years later recalled these carefree after-theatre parties. Sam Behrman described in 1929 parties dominated by Gershwin at the piano. 'The effect that he evokes is extraordinary,' he wrote. 'I have seen Kreisler, Zimbalist, Auer, and Heifetz caught up in the heady surf that inundates a room the moment he strikes a chord.'

> *Illuminated and vitalized by his own music, his own voice, his own eager sense of the rhythm of life, Gershwin instantly conveys that illumination and that vitality to others, and that is why he can at once pick up the confused and disparate elements of the average New York party and precipitate them—willy-nilly—into a medium warm and homogeneous and ecstatic.*[46]

At the Gershwins' parties Anderson met Fred and Adele Astaire. At Sam Behrman's she met Canadian-born comedienne Beatrice Lillie, and British stars Gertrude Lawrence and Jack Buchanan, who charmed New York in *Andre Charlot's Revues* of 1924 and 1926. In 1925 she began lifelong friendships with novelist (and later photographer) Carl Van Vechten, a longtime *aficionado* of modern music and friend of the Gershwins, his friend the wealthy playboy Eddie Wasserman, and Noël Coward, the 'young and omnipresent' British actor, composer and playwright who shocked and excited New York in the second half of 1925 with three plays, *The Vortex*, *Hay Fever* and *Easy Virtue*.

Coward sealed his friendship with Anderson when they

---

[46] S.N. Behrman, 'Profiles: Troubador,' *New Yorker* 25 May 1929: 27–29.

were both in Chicago in February 1926, Anderson touring in *The Dove* and Coward in *The Vortex*. Chicago audiences hated Coward's play, causing him to inscribe on his dressing room wall, 'Noël Coward died here.' To console himself, he enjoyed himself greatly with Anderson, along with Iris Tree and Diana Cooper (in Chicago in Max Reinhardt's *The Miracle*), on daily expeditions to the local riding club. In Chicago she also made friends with singer Grace Moore, an 'adorable, gay blonde from Tennessee' who was appearing in the *Music Box Revue*, and the fragile Jeanne Eagels, who was at the end of a long tour as the prostitute Sadie in her smash hit, *Rain*.[47]

This exciting period also brought Anderson into contact with the movie world, which at that time encompassed New York as well as Hollywood. *Cobra* had been purchased by J D Williams' Ritz Carlton Pictures for Rudolph Valentino, who was reported to have seen the play many times and wanted Anderson for the movie. But she was already performing in *The Dove* and under contract to Belasco by the time the studio was ready to film in spring 1925, and Elise van Zile was played by his longtime co-star, the sloe-eyed and darkly beautiful Nita Naldi. The screen rights for *The Dove* were bought in June 1926 by United Artists [First National], who released the movie, starring box office favourite Norma Talmadge in Anderson's role, in January 1927.[48]

More importantly, she met, through Holbrook Blinn, her co-star in *The Dove*, the cultured Walter Wanger, general manager of production for Famous-Players-Lasky's Hollywood and Astoria (Queens) studios. At a party for Michael Arlen, author of *The Green Hat*, she met one of

---

47 *CDT* 21 Feb 1926: F3; Sheridan Morley, *A Talent to Amuse: A Biography of Noël Coward*, 1985, 120–21; Photo: 'Actresses to Sell Programs at Riding Club Horse Show: Jeanne Eagels, Beth Beri, Jobyna Howland, Mrs Leander McCormick, Grace Moore, Vivienne Segal, Judith Anderson,' *CDT* 5 Dec 1925: 34.
48 *LAT* 29 Jun 1924: B21; *NYMT* 26 & 27 Jul 1924; Clippings, [27?] Jul? 1924, NYPL.

the studio's stars, Aileen Pringle, who had recently been proclaimed by popular romance writer Elinor Glyn as the most beautiful woman in the world. After an evening of 'an extraordinary amount of chatter,' Anderson and 'Pringie' became best friends. Wanger was to play an important part in Anderson's movie career many years later. Pringle was an intellectual, and through her Anderson met her lover H L Mencken and the publishers Alfred and Blanche Knopf.[49]

Anderson remembered the years 1924 to 1926 as a time of light-hearted flirtations when she wore an evening dress every night of the week. One of her admirers was Charlie Chaplin, who was in New York in August 1925 for the opening of his latest movie *The Gold Rush*. His rhapsodies after seeing her in *The Dove* were blown up by his publicity man into claims that he was going to build a theatre for her, which in turn evoked a tirade from Belasco, who had her under contract. Nevertheless, newspapers reported them together at society functions during his stay in New York.[50]

More seriously, Nickolas Muray, who had photographed her for *Theatre*, wanted to marry her. But she realised they were both ambitious, hard-working and strong-willed, and decided they would be better off as friends. 'I've had my dream of love,' she wrote him in her jagged style in July 1925, ' – it was very exquisite for a moment.'

> *I don't think it will come again – even if it did I don't think I'm quite prepared to meet it – my illusions are shattered – my ideals are in pretty bad shape – I've an awful lot of work to do before I can worthily give – in return – and so my very*

---

49 Matthew Bernstein, *Walter Wanger, Hollywood Independent*, 2000, 41–43, 53–57; *NYT* 8 Feb: RPA4; 18 Mar 1925: 21; 6 Jun 1926: X2.
50 *American* 27 & 31 Aug 1925; clipping [ca 29 Aug 1925], UCSB; *LAE* 31? Aug 1925; *NYDN* 3 Sep 1925; Photo: Wilda Bennett, Charlie Chaplin, Judith Anderson, Jeanne Eagels, *Mirror* 17 Sep 1925, NYPL; *NYT* 14 Sep; 16 Oct 1925: 18; *Mercury (Hobart)* 22 Jan 1926: 5.

dear – I shall speak no more of love – let's be friends Nick – that I can give you…

p.s. It just occurs to me that I've done a very sensible thing.[51]

Another would-be lover of this period, British actor Philip Merivale, spoke jealously of 'the hosts of young men and maidens whom you attract to you.'[52]

Avid for new experiences, Anderson sailed for Europe during her summer break in July 1925. Her destination was not England, but Paris, where the International Exposition of Modern Industrial and Decorative Arts was being held, showcasing what came to be called 'Art Deco' – the streamlined style that she herself epitomised. On the ship was fellow-actress Ilka Chase, the daughter of Edna Woolman Chase, the legendary editor-in-chief of *Vogue*. Anderson claimed years later that the elegant Chase taught her during that voyage about wines and liqueurs and how to dress with style. Anderson had already been noticed as someone who could wear clothes well (that yellow dress in *Cobra*), and under Chase's tutelage she became one of the fashion icons of the twenties and thirties.[53]

Anderson found, however – as Kit Cornell had done – that a contract with the great Belasco was a mixed blessing. The Bishop of Broadway was 72 years old in 1925, though, like his stars, he admitted to less; and he was in the last years of his extraordinary career, though he did not admit to that either. He had learned his craft in his native California before

---

51 Anderson to Muray, [early Jul 1925], 2nd letter, courtesy Mimi Muray Levitt.
52 Merivale to Anderson, 20 Nov 1926, UCSB.
53 *NYT* 3 Jul: 16; 12 Jul 12, 1925: RP2. See photo *NYT* 5 Jul 1925: RPA4 of her friends Grace Moore and Vincent Youmans at the Exposition; *Chicago Journal of Commerce* 23 Jun 1926, NYPL.

continuing that education in New York. He first made his name as a playwright; but from 1895, with his Civil War play *The Heart of Maryland*, he had established himself as a brilliant, perfectionist producer with an eye for talent and a reputation as a Svengali. In 1889 he had become involved with the ambitious and beautiful wife of a Chicago millionaire who styled herself 'Mrs Leslie Carter.' Under his tutelage she made a huge hit in *The Heart of Maryland*, the sensational *Zaza* in 1898 and *Du Barry* in 1901. In the first of many such breaks, Belasco cast her off when she remarried in 1906. His plays – and his leading ladies – followed this pattern for the rest of his career: stories of sexual temptation, abandonment or exploitation showcasing stars he moulded and controlled until they finally rebelled and disappeared into oblivion. Mrs Leslie Carter was followed by Frances Starr, a 'little girl' who excelled at playing fallen angels.[54]

When Francee Anderson arrived in New York in 1918, Belasco's latest 'little girl', Lenore Ulric, was playing a French-Canadian waif in *Tiger Rose*. Admired for her 'rich and sultry beauty' as well as her abilities as an emotional actress, Ulric had major, long-running hits in *The Son-Daughter* from 1919 to 1921 and as the 'naïve, ignorant, aspiring, ardent little Parisian chorus girl' *Kiki* from 1921 to 1923.

By 1924, however, Ulric had become restless under Belasco's benevolent yoke. She was a top draw for Belasco – 'an actress whose name in white lights blazing on a playhouse marquee was always more compelling of attention than the attraction in which she was appearing.' After three seasons in *Kiki*, she refused to continue in the role. Worse, she was threatening to marry her lover, the actor Sidney Blackmer. Belasco had been preparing *The Dove* for Ulric, who wanted the role,

---

54   *NYT* 10 May 1919: 19; 26 Jul 1922: 10; 12 Jun 1926: 15; 'Mrs. Carter Will Go on the Stage,' *CDT* 30 Jun 1889: 9; *CDT* 5 Dec 1911: 13; 19 Jan 1919: C3.

but, as Anderson put it in her memoir, 'little girls who are naughty deserve to be punished,' and Belasco's offer of the play to Anderson followed immediately on Ulric's departure for Europe on her first vacation in three years.[55]

By the time *The Dove* had completed its tour in April 1926 Anderson found herself further embroiled in Belasco's machinations. He had coaxed Lenore Ulric back to his fold by setting up a rivalry with Anderson and later with Helen Menken, but their relationship continued to be stormy and manipulative. The fiercely independent Anderson was unwilling to play Belasco's games. She quarrelled with him early in 1926, possibly over her reported engagement to Louis Calhern, her co-star from *Cobra*, and the *New York Times* reported that she was looking elsewhere for work.[56]

Belasco retaliated by leaving her out of his plans for the fall season. When she returned from her holiday in Europe at the end of August, they appeared to make up; but it wasn't until October that the *New York Times* reported that she would appear for Belasco in *Garden of Eden*. By then however, Anderson, fearing that she would be out of work, had accepted J C Williamsons' invitation to make a return tour to her homeland. 'Judith Anderson will leave New York today for tour of Australia in *Cobra*, *Green Hat* and *Easy Virtue*,' the *New York Times* reported on 19 November. 'She will return to Belasco in August 1927.'[57] She would never again appear in a David Belasco production, but it would take another two years before she shook herself free of Belasco's grip.

---

55 *NYT* 7 Jun 1924: 16; 29 Apr 1925: 24.
56 *NYT* 10 Jan: X2; 27 Jan 1926: 17.
57 *NYT* 11 Jul: X1; 31 Oct: X1; 19 Nov 1926: 23.

Interlude
Australia

The pylons of the Harbour Bridge had just been completed when Judith Anderson returned to Sydney in 1927.

NSW State Archives and Records

Chapter Nine

Failure 1927

Some people complain that the theatre is not true to life. And then, when a Judith Anderson comes along, in a play which, temperamentally and artistically, is so true to life that it bites like an acid, they howl that the theatre is giving us too much truth.

'Uncle James,' *Sunday Times* [Sydney]

Truth's *view of Judith Anderson's 'sex play,'* 16 January 1927

On 19 November 1926 Judith Anderson, Broadway star, and her mother left New York for a tour of the country they had left eight year before. As the *New York Times* announced, she would appear in three recent Broadway hits, her own *Cobra*, Katharine Cornell's *The Green Hat* and Noël Coward's *Easy Virtue*. Australian producers had been keen to lure Anderson back to Australia ever since she made her name in *Cobra*. But it wasn't until *The Dove* finished that she contemplated accepting J C Williamson's offer.[58]

J C Williamson Ltd – so familiar that it was just known as 'The Firm' – dominated the Australian theatrical scene. Its founder long dead, it had been led since 1920 by the four Tait brothers, John, Nevin, E.J. (Edward Joseph) and Frank, under the chairmanship of George Tallis, the only remaining original partner. The Firm scoured the world for what they considered the best operas, plays, musicals and concert performers, and the Taits were men of the world. Nevin and his artist wife Bess Norriss were based in London, while the other brothers spent much of each year travelling to Britain, Europe and North America attending shows, negotiating for rights and organising performers to appear in Australia. Among those they introduced to the Australian public during 1926 were 'The Greatest Dancer of all Time,' Pavlova; the 'Genius of the Piano,' Percy Grainger; and the great Russian bass singer, Chaliapin. In theatre, they imported major shows from London and Broadway, often presenting them within months of their success overseas and headed by leading British or American actors. During 1926 they had featured the Broadway hit *White Cargo*, with its author Leon Gordon in the lead role, and, from London, the long-time favourite, Dion Boucicault Jr

---

58   *NYT* 19 Nov 1926: 23; *Argus* 31 Jul 1924: 10; *SMH* 4 Oct 1924: 12; *Theatre, Society And Home* 1 Jan 1925: 32; *Advertiser* 11 Aug 1925: 19; *Variety* 5 May 1926: 44; JCW agreement *Cobra* 6 May 1926, JCW.

in a season of plays by J M Barrie.

E J 'Ted' Tait, based in Sydney, was The Firm's ambassador to the world of entertainment that flowed through that city's beautiful harbour. With his daughters Jessie (born 1907) and Dorothy (born 1909), he gave lavish parties at Firenze, their large mansion on Edgecliff Road, Woollahra, or at the Ambassadors, that 'Mecca of pleasure loving Sydney,' where he introduced his visiting artists to the city's social and artistic elite. The family were active in many of Sydney's charities, and the J C Williamson artists were often used as drawcards for balls, matinees, fetes, and other fund-raising events. These charitable activities gave the Taits and other theatrical personalities access to vice-regal circles, while the governor, his wife, and their circle frequently attended theatrical performances. Sydney's society was cosmopolitan and democratic, and its show-business families and their visiting artists played major parts in making it Australia's fun-loving capital.

These gaieties were generously chronicled in the newspapers of former theatrical entrepreneur Hugh McIntosh MLC – the sporting *Arrow* and *Referee*, the daily *Evening News* and most entertainingly in the *Sunday Times*, where 'Letters of a Social Gadabout' and 'Letters to Mariegold' were obviously the handiwork of intelligent and informed insiders.

The Australian newspapers, including the leading *Sydney Morning Herald* and the Melbourne *Argus*, greeted Anderson's return warmly. But Anderson herself was in low spirits when she embarked on this tour. She had quarrelled with Belasco earlier that year when newspapers published rumours of her engagement to her former co-star Louis Calhern, and Calhern had subsequently married her friend Ilka Chase – a hasty marriage that was over by the end of the year. As Belasco had done when Lenore Ulric had threatened to marry Sidney Blackmer, he punished Anderson by finding no play for her to follow her enormous success in *The Dove*. When he announced his attractions for the fall, he did not mention Anderson, and she saw him mounting two relative failures, *Fanny* with Fanny Brice in September, and *Lily Sue* with Beth Merrill in November; and newspapers announced, erroneously, that Katharine Cornell would appear in his other play, *The Desert*. There was newspaper talk of Anderson appearing in *The Garden of Eden*, for which Jeanne Eagels, finally released from the long-running *Rain*, had previously been named. Anderson rejected it, however – a sensible decision, given its later failure. Her mother was keen to see her sons; Olga Lee was willing to accompany them; so they took up the Williamson offer and set off for Australia.[59]

Things went well at first. When they arrived in Sydney on 16 December 1926, Anderson and her mother had a noisy, affectionate reunion with her brother Frank, now in his early 30s, and they met for the first time Jack's wife and his two daughters, Margaret and Jessie. They rented a pretty apartment in the fashionable Hampton Court in Bayswater Road, Kings Cross, close to their old home in Potts Point, and settled in to enjoy Sydney's summer weather and its pleasures.[60]

The local press found Anderson 'charming of manner, and quite unspoiled by her successes in New York.' She and Olga were quickly absorbed into Sydney's lively social life. She was interviewed on the radio, attended a dinner dance at the Wentworth Hotel with Olga in aid of the Cancer Stamp Fund and another at the City Café given by girl fans from the Sydney Permanent First Nights Club, where Anderson gave an impromptu speech. And she created a stir when she appeared on Bondi Beach in a pair of pale green

---

59   *CDT* 26 Apr 1925: D1; *NYT* 10 Jan: X2; 26 May: 25; 29 May: 11; 18 Jul: X1; 10 Oct: X1; 31 Oct 1926: X1; Charles Higham, 'Dame Judith: "Ugly! Dirty!"' *Bulletin* 12 Mar 1966: 38.

60   *Daily Telegraph* 17 Dec 1926; *Advertiser* 18 Dec 1926: 16; *Sunday Times* 2 Jan 1927: 3.

and pink pyjamas over her bathing suit.⁶¹

The Firm had imported three British actors to support Anderson and Olga Lee in *Cobra*. Henry Daniell, who would play the womanising Jack Race, had appeared on Broadway for three years and had played the role in the London production. Michael Hogan was to play his friend Tony Dorning. Doris Johnstone, who had appeared in previous Williamson productions, was announced to play Judith Drake, but she was replaced at the last minute by Sibyl Jane, another British actress who had been appearing in the American import *Is Zat So?* Veteran local actor Leslie Victor filled a minor role.⁶²

When it opened at the Criterion on 8 January 1927, critics found *Cobra* unoriginal and unconvincing, saved only by the restraint with which Anderson created the character of Elise and the admirable acting of her supporting cast.⁶³

The Cobra Woman
Daily Telegraph
17 February 1927

Despite her personal success in *Cobra*, Anderson recalls in her memoirs that the play was a failure. After only six weeks it was replaced by the more sedate old favourite, Roi Cooper Megrue's *Tea for Three*, in which she played with visiting Americans Leon Gordon and Wallis Clark from the middle of February until the end of March. Gordon and Clark were old friends of Anderson's who had just completed a year-long tour of Australia in Gordon's world-wide hit, *White Cargo*.

---

61 *SMH* 17 Dec 1926: 15; 3 Jan: 4; 5 Jan: 7; 1 Jan 1927: 6; *EN* 7 Jan 1927: 12; *Mail (Adelaide)* 12 Mar 1927: 19.
62 *Scotsman* 19 Aug 1925: 7; *MG* 14 Nov 1925: 7; *SMH* 23 Dec 1926: 6; 5 Jan 1927: 2; *EN* 6 Jan 1927: 12.
63 *SMH* 10 Jan 1927: 6; *Auckland Star* 22 Jan 1927.

Advertised as 'the most notable of J C Williamson productions because it has as co-stars two internationally famous artists associated for the first time in a play by the most successful of dramatic writers,' *Tea for Three* also proved a disappointment. 'The association of these stars caused a big first-night crowd to flock to the Criterion,' the *Sunday Times* wrote, 'but, try as they might, their valiant efforts failed to stir the house to any great depth of enthusiasm.' Critics agreed that the play was old-fashioned and long-winded, saved only by Anderson's 'inimitable artistry.'[64]

Moving on to Melbourne, Anderson and Gordon opened in *Tea for Three* early in April, following Australia's long-time sweetheart Nellie Stewart, in her beloved role as *Sweet Nell of Old Drury*. Anderson was welcomed with great enthusiasm. The audience 'saw the art of acting at its highest and understood why this young Australian had climbed to the top in other countries,' the *Age* reviewer wrote. Roy Bridges in the *Herald* wrote of 'Judith Anderson's Triumph.' '"I loved it," said one bright eyed girl, exchanging impressions with another after the performance; and "I simply loved her," said another,' reported the *Argus*. 'It was a joyous theatrical occasion.'[65]

McCrae in The World's News *caricatures Judith Anderson's sexual magnetism in* Cobra, *5 February 1927*

The special correspondent for the *Hobart Mercury* was more critical, voicing the complaint that followed Anderson

---

64   *SMH* 19 Feb: 12; 21 Feb: 6; 1 Apr 1927: 12; ST 20 Feb 1927: 2; EN 21 Feb 1927: 7.
65   *Age* 4 Apr 1927: 11; MH 4 Apr 1917: 23; *Argus* 4 Apr 1927: 22.

throughout her return to Australia and poisoned her triumph. 'Last night Miss Judith Anderson succeeded Miss Stewart on the boards of the Theatre Royal,' the critic wrote, 'and we might have expected a memorable evening... But, again,' he wrote, 'there was a fly in the ointment.':

> *We saw in Miss Anderson, a fine emotional actress, in her artistic springtime, a rare treat indeed, and with her Mr Leon Gordon and Mr Wallis Clark, two fine actors. But what a play. Another miserable triangle: Husband, wife and male friend.*

He ended 'Stars like Judith Anderson should be asked to play parts worthy of their best efforts, not wasted on questionable drawing room dramas'.[66]

By the end of April, The Firm was deeply anxious about the success of Anderson's tour. Leon Gordon, her co-star in *Tea for* Three and director of her next offering *The Green Hat*, worried that Australia had not yet seen her at her best, it was reported. He 'is straining every nerve to make *The Green Hat* a production worthy of the star,' he told the *Mercury*'s correspondent. But when the play opened on 30 April, it drew even greater vituperation. C J Dennis in the *Herald* called it 'a weak and sordid play.' The critic at the *Argus* admired Anderson's 'richly musical' voice and her 'wide range of expression,' but condemned the play as indecent, poorly constructed, and generally 'unworthy of her ability.' Another critic put the general reaction succinctly:

> *Certainly with her beautiful speaking voice and her very real histrionic ability, this young Belasco star (the significance of being a Belasco star is hardly appreciated here) does make something of the role of Iris March, but it is impossible, even*

---

66 *Mercury (Hobart)* 4 Apr 1927: 6.

for her, to do more than save it from being utterly pathetic. The trouble about The Green Hat is that it is not only too suggestive, but dull, and of that oppressive brand of dullness that depresses one almost beyond endurance.[67]

Despite the best efforts of the JCW management to lure the Melbourne audience with stories of her American successes, attendance dropped off so dramatically that they announced that Anderson would open in Adelaide at the end of the month in *Cobra*, and that she would appear in that play for the last week of her Melbourne season, only three weeks after *Green Hat* had opened. However, she continued in *Green Hat* until she left for Adelaide. The complete truth of her Melbourne season was revealed only by newspapers distant from the scene of her humiliation. The *Auckland Star* reported that people regarded *The Green Hat* as 'so bestial that the theatre is practically empty, and the failure cannot be concealed.' The *Queensland Figaro* was even more explicit: 'The play is considered quite too unpleasant for pleasant people, and it flopped so badly that it is alleged that at one matinee there were more ushers than audience in the dress circle.'[68]

Having decided to continue presenting *The Green Hat* for Anderson's Adelaide season, the JCW management tried to prepare her audience with warnings about its subject matter, reminders of her connections with Adelaide and her success with Belasco, and promises of beautiful frocks.

Interviewed by the *Adelaide News* on her arrival on the overnight express from Melbourne, Anderson told the reporter that she had come to Adelaide for her mother's sake; but she wanted to 'go out and walk about among the places I knew when I lived here.' She was 'slight in build, with dark,

---

67 *Mercury* 25 Apr 1927: 6; MH 2 May 1927: 8; *Argus* 2 May 1927: 6; clipping, UCSB.
68 *Argus* 17 May 1927: 13; *Advertiser* 14 May 1927: 16; *Referee* 18 May 1927; *Auckland Star* 28 May 1927; *Queensland Figaro* 4 Jun 1927: 7.

unshingled wavy hair and deeply set blue eyes,' the newspaper reported, and she 'gives the impression that there is much dynamic force behind her quiet, unassuming manner.' 'She has a rich, musical speaking voice, capable of expressing great depth of feeling, and a touch of sadness in it adds to its charm.'[69]

As in Melbourne, however, critics were repulsed by the subject matter of *The Green Hat*. 'With a theme which is unpleasant and verging at times on the sordid, *The Green Hat*, which was presented at the Theatre Royal tonight before a house crowded in every part, had little to recommend it as a story,' the Adelaide *Mail* wrote. 'Those who had read Michael Arlen's novel... were a little curious as to how he would deal with the unsavoury episodes.' 'He has shown a great deal of temerity in matters associated with sex relationship,' the account went on, 'and the result is a play of smart lines, dramatic climaxes, and decidedly unpleasant characters... The theme is a depressing one, and the well-known story deals with the sex problem with a stark realism and a frankness of expression that is often startling – and sometimes repulsive.'

Judith Anderson, the critic conceded, made the best of a thankless role:

> *It is difficult to make a pathetic heroine out of an immoral woman, who had not the slenderest excuse for immorality. On the rare occasions when she had a chance of exhibiting emotion she gave evidence that in a more realistic role she would prove to be an artist of rare histrionic genius. She did her utmost to make the part of Iris acceptable, and her superb work won the sympathy of the audience despite its better judgment. Though she is not the siren Arlen*

---

[69] *News* 28 May 1927: 1.

has pictured she is most alluring. Her voice is rich, full of emotional tones, and her work is amazingly natural.[70]

The Adelaide *Register* was more cynical. 'The huge popularity of Michael Arlen's play, *The Green Hat*, owes much to the author's fame as a delineator of the manners and morals – and particularly the latter – of London's smart set,' their critic wrote, 'and middle class audiences, enamoured of the sin and cynicism, reputed to be the stuff of which smart sets are made, have felt reassured at seeing the light-hearted sinners react with old fashioned British fervour to all the time honoured stage sentiments.' 'There is much sentiment in *The Green Hat*,' the writer continued, 'and "purity" and parenthood are exploited with all the thoroughness of old-time melodrama.'

This critic had nothing but praise for Anderson's performance. 'She revealed a rare capacity for expressing the greatest heights of emotionalism by quiet restrained acting and intelligent attention to detail,' he wrote. 'In all the scenes in which she appeared she commanded the undivided attention of all, and was splendidly aided in that respect by her attractive appearance and perfectly modulated speaking voice.'[71]

The *Advertiser* called the play 'a Turkish bath for the emotions' and mocked the fact that 'There are no inarticulate lovers in Michael Arlen's plays; they all talk too much and they all talk like Michael Arlen, with a conscious desire to be shocking.' But it did provide a personal triumph for Anderson:

She certainly gave the impression of a woman consumed by a devouring flame, and her hysterical sobbing in the first act and her shaking farewell to her lover in the third were the

---

70   *Mail* 28 May 1927: 10.
71   *Register* 30 May 1927: 10.

highlights of a remarkable performance. The jerky utterance, the quick defiant gestures were part of a fine character study, which was sustained from beginning to end.[72]

The *News* agreed that 'Judith Anderson is an actress whose technique is admirable.' 'She is far removed from the stereotyped stage star and has mastered the art of repose,' their critic wrote. 'She expresses a wealth of emotion by simply standing still.'

She is restrained and sincere. She has an unusual style of speech and gesture. When occasion arises she thrills by her dramatic force. Not once does she over-emphasise a situation, nor raise her voice unduly, but she compels attention because of her personality.[73]

Before the week was out, however, virulent attacks were made on the play. 'Idra,' in the women's pages of the *Advertiser*, launched a racist attack on Michael Arlen. 'Prior to the war,' she wrote, 'if anyone had been questioned concerning Armenians their knowledge would have extended far enough to permit of the statement that they were a remote, more or less primitive race, with the Continental aversion to baths.' 'After the war,' she went on, 'they came much into prominence, owing to Turkish atrocities, as having more starving children than any country in Europe.' 'Attention now,' she pointed out, 'is again drawn to Armenia, owing to an educated Armenian having written first a nasty book, and then dramatised it into a still more nasty play, having for its subject the decadence of the English people.' Pointing out the 'unnatural' character of most of the people in the play, she sneered that 'Of course, you could hardly expect an Armenian to understand things that are "not done".' 'The lady of the

---

72 *Advertiser* (Adelaide) 30 May 1927: 12.
73 *News* 30 May 1927: 2.

Green Hat is even worse than the black lady of *White Cargo*,' she adds in a parting shot.[74]

More hurtful for Anderson was the attack by 'Lady Kitty' in the *Register*. After condemning the play as not only sordid but stupid, she expresses her sympathy towards the young actress 'for having to make her debut in her native town in what one felt was a thoroughly unsympathetic part.' 'In private life,' she goes on, 'one finds Miss Judith Anderson full of charm, the chiefest attraction of which is a perfect naturalness. Her whole life is her work, and her mother, whom she loves dearly, and who always travels with her. Her mentality is deep and serious, and breadth of outlook wide as the seas. But the seriousness of mind shown in her grey eyes is often broken by a twinkle that emanates from a delicious sense of humour.'[75]

The final insult to Anderson from her home state came from 'Norma,' writing in 'Women's World' in the *Border Watch* in Mount Gambier, a small town close to the border with Victoria. 'To receive applause in the dignified way of the real artist has yet to be learnt by this clever Adelaide girl,' 'Norma' wrote. 'She follows the "curtain" too aggressively, and stands with some attitude of contempt for the opinion of any Adelaide audience. A dignified gracious bow would be more pleasing to the audience – but perhaps that will come later.'[76]

After only a week in Adelaide, in what seems to have been a last-minute decision, J C Williamson announced that Anderson would play a series of matinees of *The Green Hat* in Sydney before she left for New York. On the day of her last performance in Adelaide, a reporter from the *News* described Anderson and her mother in their hotel room surrounded

---

74   *Advertiser* 2 Jun 1927: 7.
75   *Register* 2 Jun 1927: 14.
76   *Border Watch* 9 Jun 1927: 6.

by flowers, chocolates and mail from admirers, with the telephone hardly ever ceasing from ringing. 'Adelaide feels proud of the clever actress,' she wrote, 'and its only regret is that no opportunity was afforded of seeing her in some other play of a more wholesome quality than *The Green Hat*. Her work in that is so fine that one longs to see her in something which would give more scope for her undoubted talent. But she had no say in the choice of play. The powers that be said it was to be *The Green Hat* and no argument on the subject was allowed.'[77]

'Woman's World' in the *Advertiser* the following week reported that 'Miss Judith Anderson was frankly angry at having to appear in *The Green Hat*. She declared on the Saturday before the play opened that she "expected to be asked to leave Adelaide on Monday morning." She detested the play, but curiously enough is an admirer of Michael Arlen himself.' 'She has not much more time for *Cobra*,' the report went on, 'and declared that next time she comes to Australia she will insist on having a voice in the choice of plays.'[78]

Meanwhile the play had to go on in Sydney. Some of the critics there were more sophisticated in their assessment of its subject matter and of Arlen's skill as a storyteller and a playwright. '*The Green Hat* is not a play for children,' the *Sydney Morning Herald* critic wrote. 'Had it been presented during the Victorian era, a proportion of the audience would undoubtedly have risen up and filed from the theatre in outraged propriety.' 'But,' he went on, 'provided one is prepared to hear certain matters referred to downrightly, with no attempt at delicate disguise, there is little that is positively repulsive in it. Instead of treating his theme in the cold, hard, semi-scientific way adopted by Brieux in *Damaged Goods*, the author has

---

77 *SMH* 2 Jun 1927: 2; *News* 3 Jun 1927: 6.
78 *Advertiser* 7 Jun 1927: 10.

developed it with dramatic vivacity, and a keen sense of the theatre.'[79]

The matinees of *The Green Hat* were so successful that, after two weeks, Williamsons decided, 'owing to public petition,' to begin a week of evening performances from 23 June. Coincidental with that change, they further announced that Anderson would appear in Somerset Maugham's *Rain* for a brief season from 2 July. A later report said that she had been booked to return to the US on the *Aorangi* on 30 June but had agreed to stay another three weeks.[80] As young women crowded in to see the scandalous *Green Hat*, a war of words swirled around the young actress. Replying to a critic who asserted that 'never in my life did I expect to hear, on our stage, such things as were spoken of, and before too, an audience comprised principally of young women,' 'Uncle James' in the *Sunday Times* rhapsodised:

> *Hurrah for Judith Anderson, her eyes of starry sheen —*
> *While woman is Philandersome, her hat will still be green!*
> *So many critics binge to us about this sparkling Show;*
> *They crawl around and cringe to us, and say we mustn't go!*
> *But Judith is a genius – a star of special size,*
> *Whom any dashed Arrhenius can see with naked eyes!*
> *No telescope is needed here, to see this lovely star —*
> *Our Judith has succeeded here, and likewise shines afar!*

After three more verses of such doggerel. He appeals:

> *If Iris comes or goes or not, need Judith disappear?*

Coming to her defence in prose, 'Uncle James' concludes:

> *Well and good. Some people complain that the theatre is not true to life. And then, when a Judith Anderson comes along,*

---

79 *SMH* 10 Jun 1927: 8
80 *SMH* 18 Jun: 10; 23 Jun 1927: 2; *Arrow* 24 Jun 1927: 16.

in a play which, temperamentally and artistically, is so true to life that it bites like an acid, they howl that the theatre is giving us too much truth. Poor things. They are a strange set of antibilious animals, some of these critics.[81]

But Uncle James's defence came too late. A few days later Anderson was too ill to go on; the opening night of *Rain* was postponed; and she was hospitalised with pneumonia and pleurisy. In later life Anderson collapsed from time to time from stress, and there is no doubt that her disappointment at her Australian reception contributed to her illness. There also seems to have been an unhappy love affair that exacerbated her condition. In her memoirs she says that she almost died. Among the complications of the pneumonia was an infection of the eyes, which temporarily blinded her. She attributes her recovery from her deep depression to her old friend Jascha Heifetz, who was touring Australia at that time. Heifetz brought her a stack of records, including Gertrude Lawrence singing in George Gershwin's latest hit 'Oh, Kay' and recordings of his own music, which, she says, restored her faith in the theatre and her will to live.[82]

Anderson spent six weeks in hospital before sailing for America on the *Sonoma* on 1 September 1927. Meanwhile her almost unknown understudy, Billie Lockwood, made headlines for the skill with which she took over Anderson's part in *The Green Hat*. Anderson's would-be saviour, 'Uncle James,' continued to boom her extravagantly as 'our Australian Mona Lisa of the stage.' She is 'a peerless flower of human genius,' he wrote, 'which – like some exotic-coloured Japanese chrysanthemums – has achieved its perfect blossoming under the

---

81 ST 26 Jun 1927: 4.
82 EN 29 Jun 1927: 13; *SMH* 29 Jun 1927: 13; Lyman Sevier to Anderson, Tue [after 10 Oct 1927], UCSB; 'Abe Greenberg's Voice of Hollywood,' *Hollywood Citizen-News* 28 Jan 1969, MHL.

dramatic guidance of David Belasco, in the hothouse theatrical atmosphere of New York.' 'She has re-visited her own country for a few brief months at the height of her dramatic powers,' he continued. 'It may be many years before she returns. Perhaps, when she comes back again, Australia may be sufficiently grown up to understand the dramatic tragedy and pathos of our own great Silent Wilderness. . . . Hearken, ye critics and criticasters. Judith of Adelaide passes by!' But only the *Auckland Star* noted on 3 September that 'Judith Anderson has stolen quietly away to America.'[83]

To the 30-year-old Judith Anderson, the failure of her 1927 homecoming was intensely personal. But larger forces were also at work. To be associated with American culture and American modernity in 1927 was to be open to derision and censure. In the Australia that Anderson knew before the Great War, Americans were agreeable and entertaining 'cousins,' exemplified in her world by popular comedian Fred Niblo. Since the end of the war, America and Americans were increasingly seen as illegitimate usurpers of the power and prestige previously enjoyed by Britain and its Empire. At the level of culture, they were seen as predators, colonising the world with their movies and plays, and spreading inferior tastes, morals and manners, as well as an offensive 'Yankee twang.'

This hostility to America's changing place in the world was exacerbated by attempts by the British government and British business to rebuild its local film industry, which had almost disappeared during the war. This was accompanied by calls for quotas to be applied to American films and for 'Imperial preference,' requiring former colonies (now

---

83   *Referee* 6 Jul 1927: 17; ST 17 Jul 1927: 6; *Auckland Star* 3 Sep 1927.

'Dominions') to show a certain percentage of British films.[84]

In Australia this agitation against the American domination of the film industry was also used to argue for protection of its own local industry. This came to a head with the appointment of a Royal Commission into the Moving Picture Industry in Australia in May 1927. In the discussion leading up to the appointment of the Royal Commission and as the Commission moved around the country hearing evidence, the power and influence of the American film industry was strongly criticised. The Americans had a 'stranglehold' on Australian cinemas; they supplied Australia with 97 per cent of its feature films; their grip on the market was strengthened by the block-booking system that controlled most picture theatres; many of these films were vulgar and harmful to the moral sense of young people; and they often acted as propaganda for their country of origin.[85]

The Royal Commission stirred up considerable fear and hostility about the 'Americanisation' of Britain, Europe and Australia. 'The cumulative social effect of this cosmopolitan advertisement of the ways of American life is tremendous,' an editorial in the *Sydney Morning Herald* commented in March 1927. 'Whether consciously or unconsciously, the makers of American films are Americanising the world.' 'The trouble is,' the writer went on, that 'a great many of the American films which Australia sees are tawdry and sordid to a degree; their moral standard is as low as their mechanical standard is high.' 'Desperate diseases require desperate remedies,' the editorial warned.[86]

Headlines referred to AN AMERICAN INVASION, THE FILM

---

84 *Canberra Times* 10 Feb 1927: 12.
85 See S. Gaunson, 'Australian (Inter)national Cinema: The Royal Commission on the Moving Picture Industry in Australia, 1926–1928, Australasian Films Ltd. and the American monopoly,' *Studies in Australasian Cinema* 6.3, 2012: 291–300.
86 *SMH* 5 Mar 1927: 14. See also 29 Apr: 10; 4 May 1927: 15.

OCTOPUS and the AMERICAN MOVIE MENACE. Concerns were expressed about 'demoralising American films,' slang and the divorce rate. This hostility inevitably spilled over into other forms of imported American culture, particularly the all-pervasive American plays. For some years American plays had been taking over the London theatrical scene. When British actor-producer Basil Dean returned from the US in December 1925 he stated flatly, 'The future of the English-speaking stage lies in America.' Dudley Glass, the Melbourne *Herald*'s music and drama correspondent in London, asked in August 1926: WHERE ARE THE ENGLISH PLAYS?[87]

The shift in outspokenness that was agitating theatrical censors, official and unofficial, in these years was what Grace Kingsley in the *Los Angeles Times* described as 'moving the bed downstage.' 'Instead of keeping it discreetly in the text of the play,' she wrote in May 1926, 'we are taking the bed seriously.' The great success of the 1924–5 Broadway season had been *They Knew What They Wanted*, a play about longing that has as its centre an illegitimate child. Acclaimed by all the critics as a gentle, moving story, brilliantly acted by Pauline Lord and Richard Bennett, the play remained on Broadway for 192 performances and won the Pulitzer Prize. It was equally successful in London in 1926 and opened in Sydney in a production by the Russian-born Jewish American Maurice Moscovitch in September the same year.[88]

Despite the acclaim it attracted, *They Knew What They Wanted* was one of the first targets of a newly-aroused demand for censorship of the theatre in America. In New York a Citizens Play Jury that reported to the District Attorney had been constituted of representatives of 30 religious, civic and

---

87   *Argus* 27 Jan 1927: 13; *Advertiser* 23 Aug 1926: 9; 10 Mar: 15; 29 Apr 1927: 10; *Recorder* (Port Pirie) 11 Mar 1927:1; *ST* 13 Mar 1927: 1; *News* 3 Feb 1927: 7; *SMH* 15 Mar 1927: 12; *Queensland Times* 31 Jan 1927: 9; *NYT* 27 Dec 1925: X2.
88   *LAT* 2 May 1926: C23; *NYT* 25 Nov 1924: 27.

reform organisations. The Citizen Jurors acquitted *They Knew What They Wanted*, but this was the beginning of urgent calls for censorship of Broadway plays that paralleled the demand for oversight of films.[89]

This movement came to a head in February 1927, just as the JCW management was announcing in Sydney that Judith Anderson would appear in *The Green Hat* following *Cobra*. On 10 February the New York police raided three shows, Mae West's *Sex*, the play about lesbian love, *The Captive* and *The Virgin Man*. Anderson's admirer Philip Merivale wrote her the next day with details of her friends Helen Menken and Basil Rathbone, who had been playing in *The Captive*.[90]

In Australia the theatre's 'sex mania' was also drawing criticism. When Leon Gordon's *White Cargo*, which portrayed a group of demoralised white men in West Africa and the marriage of one of them to a highly sexualised 'half-caste,' opened in Sydney in February 1926, the *Sydney Morning Herald* condemned some scenes as 'repellent,' and a lively debate ensued in the *Evening News*, with 'Christian' asserting that '*White Cargo* is rotten cargo that should be barged beyond the ten-mile limit to sufferance.' Members of Adelaide audiences also found it 'sordid and unsavoury,' stating that it 'left a nauseous taste in the mouth'; and the Melbourne *Argus* considered that 'it emphasises matters which are not fitted for stage treatment.' The Commissioner of Police obviously agreed and sent plainclothes policemen to take 'shorthand notes of certain expressions by the actors in the course of the play.' But audiences flocked to it, and it was even transferred to a larger theatre towards the end of its long run. When Judith Anderson arrived in Sydney in January 1927 this

---

89   *NYT* 14 Mar 1925: 15.
90   *NYT* 10 Feb 1927: 1; Philip Merivale to Anderson, 11 Feb 1927, UCSB.

controversial play was preparing for its third season there.[91]

Also attracting condemnation in Australia at the end of 1926 was *They Knew What They Wanted*. The *Sydney Morning Herald* attacked it as 'a coarse crude bit of so-called realism, containing a third act of such brutal directness that it ought never to have been staged.' In a speech after the final curtain that evening, Mrs Moscovitch pointed out that 'vulgarity and realism are two different things.' Unlike *White Cargo*, *They Knew What They Wanted* lasted only one month in Sydney. When it opened in Melbourne in late March 1927, it was reported that thousands of letters had poured in to the Moscovitches and the play was quickly taken off.[92]

A third target of the would-be censors was a farce called *The Cradle Snatchers*. A group of neglected middle-aged (40-year-old!) wives decide to give their straying husbands a lesson. They pay some young men to 'make love' to them, and in the ensuing confusion, they win back the attention of their husbands. A great success on Broadway during the fall 1925 season, it was banned in Great Britain in early 1926. Although it was described by the *Sunday Times* as 'the naughtiest' comedy 'ever seen in Australia' when it opened in Sydney in May 1927, the critic was ready to excuse its sexual innuendoes. 'Sydney likes to laugh,' he wrote, 'and at this show there is so much laughter that hostile criticism and perhaps conscience – for the time being – become numbed.' *Truth* considered it 'risque, but not at all vulgar.' The *Sydney Morning Herald* was more severe. 'Inasmuch as Saturday night's crowded auditorium roared in continuous laughter at *Cradle Snatchers*,' their critic wrote, 'there is evidently a market for decadent plays

---

91   *SMH* 22 Feb 1926: 6; Letters to Editor, *Evening News* 23 Feb to 16 Mar 1926; ST 7 Mar 1926: 22; *Advertiser* 17 Jun 1926: 15; *Mail* 3 Jul 1926: 19; *Argus* 28 Jun 1926: 14; 5 Jul 1926: 22; 23 Aug 1926: 14; *SMH* 8 Jan 1927: 12.
92   *SMH* 27 Sep: 7; 28 Sep 1926: 12; *Truth* 31 Oct 1926: 11; *Telegraph* (Brisbane) 16 Apr 1927: 7.

of this description – a fact presumably regarded by theatrical managers as complete justification for their production.' The Melbourne critics and audiences gave the *Cradle Snatchers* no quarter. 'It aims at being daring, but is merely gross,' the *Argus* critic wrote. 'Instead of providing skill and wit, it is crude and clumsy.' 'Some of the sayings that were meant to cause laughter produced only a silence which indicated that their significance was all too clear,' he continued. 'At the end of the piece many members of the audience applauded and many did not.' Again, the police were called on to report on the play, coming up with the verdict that it was not as bad as *White Cargo*.[93]

As the *Sunday Times* put it, comparing the different reception accorded *Cradle Snatchers* and *They Knew What They Wanted*, 'Apparently an Australian audience will stand any amount of "sex," provided it is treated as a joke… But once the dramatist treats sex as a serious matter, the box-office receipts grow very thin.'[94]

The Royal Commission hearings focused further attention on this 'invasion' of vulgar American sex plays. During the hearings *The Green Hat*, *White Cargo* and *The Cradle Snatchers* were often referred to as equally worthy of censorship as American movies. While hearing evidence in Melbourne early in May, when Anderson was playing there, the Chairman asked the witness, Senator Guthrie, 'Do you not think you might clean up your own stables in Victoria, and prohibit such plays as *The Green Hat* and *White Cargo*?' 'I would certainly like to see a censorship of plays, as well as of pictures,' he added.[95]

The question of 'sex plays' was a minor part of the furore

---

93 EN 27 Mar 1926: 6; ST 1 May 1927: 2; *Truth* 1 May 1927: 11; *SMH* 2 May 1927: 6; *Argus* 8 Aug 1927: 18; *Advertiser* 9 Aug 1927: 15; EN 9 Aug 1927: 7.
94 ST 8 May 1927: 35.
95 *SMH* 26 Aug 1927: 12; *Register* 26 Aug 1927: 9; *Brisbane Courier* 6 May 1927: 19.

over film censorship and Americanisation that pervaded Australian culture in 1927. But, caught in the slipstream of this nationalist and moral crusade, Judith Anderson returned to America, and Belasco, with a sense of failure that it took some years to overcome. At the same time, however, it strengthened her determination to return to Australia in a play that was worthy of her talents.

ACT III
Greatness

Scene Four
California Dreaming

Los Angeles, 1929, looking from La Brea towards Hollywood
Water and Power Associates, Los Angeles Public Library

Chapter 10
New Beginnings

Think 'Bernhardt, Bernhardt'...
George Kelly, playwright, 1927

Judith Anderson, by Nickolas Muray 1927
Eastman Museum / Mimi Muray Levitt

Judith Anderson returned from Australia in September 1927 feeling desolate in body and spirit. Hailed as a rising star only three years before, her career prospects now looked bleak. Although Belasco had written to her in Australia, assuring her that he was working day and night on a new play for her, she was bitterly disappointed on her return to find him still using her as a pawn in his power play with Lenore Ulric.[1]

The Old Master was getting on – 75 that year, even though he only admitted to 69 – and he had only four more years to live. Unable to move beyond the formula that had been successful for so many years, he had a series of failures in 1926 and 1927. During 1927 he was determined to lure his old love, Lenore Ulric, back to his fold; and she, in turn, was making the most of her bargaining position to wring concessions from him. In April he had announced that he would be presenting *The Red Mill* by the Hungarian playwright Ference Molnar, boasting that it would be the biggest production of his career. In her memoirs, Anderson says that he had promised the play to her, with Basil Rathbone as co-star; but by the time she returned, Belasco had decided to keep it for Ulric the following season, when it was renamed *Mima* and co-starred her fiancé, Sydney Blackmer. In its place he offered Anderson another play – probably *The Desert*, a translation from the Spanish that he had been promising the public for several seasons – which she rejected.[2] Although she remained under contract to Belasco for another two years, she never played in another of his productions.

Feeling betrayed, spiritually drained and convinced that she had no future, Anderson was saved from despair by

---

1 Lyman Sevier to Anderson, Tue [after 10 Oct 1927], UCSB.
2 *NYT* 26 Jul 1928: 28; 15 May 1931: 1; 6 Apr: 25; 8 May: X1; 22 May 1927: X1; *LAT* 22 May 1927: 17; *CDT* 24 Dec 1927: 9.

producer Rosalie Stewart, who invited her to take the lead in *Behold, the Bridegroom*, a new play by George Kelly. Best known these days as Grace Kelly's uncle, Kelly was a successful playwright whose previous play *Craig's Wife* had won the Pulitzer the year before. His muted and sensitive drama, with its selfish, worldly heroine, was completely up-to-date in its focus on character study, in contrast to Belasco's lavish, formulaic melodramas. Antoinette Lyle is a shallow, decadent flapper who pines away when she realises how little she deserves the morally upright man she falls in love with. Anderson told Australian journalist Judy Stone many years later that Lyle was the only character she had identified with, thinking 'Gosh this is me.'[3]

'I love my play if possible better than ever,' Anderson wrote her former lover, Nickolas Muray, as she braced herself to begin rehearsals. Here was a drama that engaged her intellect, allowed her to demonstrate her command of emotional acting, and required her to transform her body from health to physical decline to death. George Kelly, directing the play, urged her to think 'Bernhardt, Bernhardt'; and one critic heard a heavenly voice: 'As Miss Anderson passed away… in the flowing robes of an exotic invalid, her last words were almost as lute-like as those of CAMILLE when spoken by Bernhardt's *vox celeste*.'[4]

Heralded by photographs by Nickolas Muray of Anderson looking her most beautiful, *Behold, the Bridegroom* opened on 26 December 1927 at the lovely Cort Theatre. Critics loved the play – GEORGE KELLY AT HIS BEST according to Brooks Atkinson in the *New York Times*; and Burns Mantle included it among his *Best Plays of 1927–28*.

---

3   *NYT* 10 Oct 1927: 24; 28 Jan 1968: D27; *WP* 4 Mar 1928: F2.
4   Anderson to Muray, 19 Oct 1927, Muray Papers. See also for her despondent mood.

But most of all they accorded Judith Anderson a new respect as a serious dramatic actress.

That fierce critic Alex Woollcott noted 'Such force and art as I had not dreamed she possessed,' and gave her his highest accolade: 'such power, such subtlety and such distinction that I have been busy ever since revising my list of those who should be permitted to play *Hedda Gabler*.' Robert Littell in the *New York Post* identified clearly her distinctive use of her body to convey her psychological state: the restless, energetic young 'worldling' played with 'enamelled snap and brilliant speed,' who becomes by the end of the play the 'quavering,' 'feeble' invalid slumped back in her chair. Above all, as the critic in the *American* put it, 'She made it real.'[5]

Despite its brilliant reception by the critics, *Behold, the Bridegroom* was a failure. *Variety* had initially indicated that it 'stood out among welter of holiday premieres.' As a 'class draw,' the 'general critical praise and agency activity after opening indicated success.' Suddenly, however, in early February its sales dropped, and by mid-February Rosalie Stewart announced that it would close in two weeks and that her revival of Kelly's *The Torchbearers* was cancelled. The play was picked up by the Shuberts, who moved it to their large new Majestic Theatre, where John Gielgud's Broadway debut in *The Patriot* had just crashed spectacularly. It lasted there until mid-March, when it was tried out on tour in Boston for a 'doleful' two weeks before closing early in April. The only saving grace for Anderson from this unexpected failure was the lasting friendship she made with actress Mary Servoss.[6]

---

5   *NYT* 27 Nov: RP3, 4; 27 Dec 1927: 24; *Queen's Star* 10 Dec 1927; *NYP* 27 Dec 1927; *American* 27 Dec 1927; *World* 28 Dec 1927, NYPL; *Vogue* 1 Jan 1928.
6   *Variety* 4 Jan: 26; 11 Jan: 44; 8 Feb: 46; 15 Feb: 47; 29 Feb 1928: 50; *NYT* 26 Feb: 105; 1 Apr 1928: 120; *Variety* 4 Apr 1928: 50.

Although she starred in a number of failures from 1927 to 1934, Judith Anderson was a 'class draw' admired by critics and featured often in magazines

Author's collection

It is hard to tell why *Behold, the Bridegroom* failed. It certainly faced tremendous competition. The 1927–8 season had a record number of 264 new productions – a number never again reached; and during Christmas week, when *Behold* opened on Broadway, there were 19 premieres, eight of them on 26 December. The season was also a turning point in Broadway genre and style, bringing new producers and writers to the fore, and creating a new cadre of leading actresses. Among the week's notable openings was the innovative musical *Show Boat* – a harbinger of what was to come.[7] Also opening that week was *The Royal Family*, produced by the brilliant young producer Jed Harris. Harris had blazed onto the theatrical scene in 1926 with *Broadway*, an enormous hit that introduced what became the new Broadway style – 'clever, tense, urban, dynamic and, above all, contemporary.' Earlier in the season he had presented *Coquette*, in which former ingénue Helen Hayes became an adult star, and in 1929 he would do the same for Ruth Gordon with *Serena Blandish*.[8]

This auspicious season also saw the winning partnership of Guthrie McClintic and Katharine Cornell confirmed with Somerset Maugham's *The Letter*, in which Cornell was finally proclaimed a star. And Eugene O'Neill began his long partnership with the Theatre Guild, presenting two plays, *Marco Millions* and the Pulitzer prize-winning *Strange Interlude* in January 1928, starring Lynn Fontanne. As Brooks Atkinson put it three years later of these major changes to the New York theatrical world, 'You would have thought there had never been a Belasco.'

Anderson's final break with Belasco came when *Behold, the Bridegroom* closed at the end of March 1928. In place of the Molnar play he had promised her, he loaned her to an unknown producer for *The Young Truth* (later *Anna*), a play by Rudolph Lothar that she described in her memoirs as 'dreadful,' with a leading man – Lou Tellegen – who was 'catastrophic.' Although critics found her 'completely captivating' as 'a roguish little Trilby,' acting 'with her brains as well as her

---

7 *NYT* 5 Jun 1960: X1; 9 Dec: 29; 14 Dec 1927: 34; 1 Jan 1928: X1; *CDT* 1 Jan 1928: E1.
8 Jed Harris, *A Dance on the High Wire*, 1988, 81; Martin Gottfried, *Jed Harris, the Curse of Genius*, 1984, 82.

emotions,' they agreed it was a 'silly play.' 'Miss Anderson is an emotionalist of super-talent, but a poor soubrette of the Lenore Ulric type,' Burns Mantle concluded in the *Chicago Daily Tribune*, and Tellegen 'a player of limited charm in the spoken romance.'[9] To Anderson's relief *Anna* only lasted 31 performances.

The 'dreadful' *Anna* marked the end of Anderson's contract with Belasco. Her youthful dream of being a Belasco star had led her into a career cul-de-sac, while Katharine Cornell, Helen Hayes and Lynn Fontanne had caught up and passed her as audience favourites. After making her official debut as a star in September 1927 in *The Letter*, Cornell and McClintic presented a series of historical plays over the next few years that toured widely, building an avid audience for this charismatic actress. In 1931 Cornell set up her own production company to present her greatest hit, *The Barretts of Wimpole Street*, in which she played the romantic Elizabeth Barrett. With an efficient company at her back, and her husband as director, Cornell became what her publicity director, Ray Henderson, called 'America's First Lady of the Theatre.'

Cornell's main rival for the title of 'First Lady' in the early 1930s was the beloved former child actress Helen Hayes. Finally freeing herself from her ingénue roles, Hayes had been spotted by up-and-coming producer Jed Harris for the tragic heroine of his 1927 hit, *Coquette*. She broke further from her virginal persona the following year when she married divorced playwright Charles MacArthur.[10] When MacArthur began a successful career as a screenwriter, Hayes became a sought-after movie actress, enhancing her popularity in the

---

9 *Town Topics* 14 May 1928, NYPL; *LAT* 27 May 1928: C9; *WSJ* 19 May 1928: 3; *NYT* 17 May 1928: 23; *CDT* 27 May 1928: G1.
10 *NYT* 9 Nov 1927: 23; *CDT* 18 Aug 1928: 1.

theatre. In 1933 she made an enormous hit in *Mary of Scotland*, and two years later played her best-known stage role in *Victoria Regina*.

Ruth Gordon was also delivered from her 'beautiful but dumb' roles by Jed Harris when he starred her in S N Behrman's *Serena Blandish* in 1929 as a naïve young woman caught up in the marriage game in the 1850s. With her 'lovely, dainty, fragile acting, rare to see,' she placed herself once more among the contenders for theatrical honours.[11]

In a class by herself by 1928 was Lynn Fontanne, who, with Alfred Lunt, had become America's leading husband-and-wife team and the stars of Broadway's major new production company, the Theatre Guild. Seldom appearing apart from her husband, she was at her best as a high comedienne, especially in plays by S N Behrman and Noël Coward.

In January 1928 the Theatre Guild cast Fontanne in one of her most unusual roles – as Nina Leeds in Eugene O'Neill's *Strange Interlude*. O'Neill had become over the previous eight years America's leading playwright, winning the Pulitzer prize for *Beyond the Horizon* in 1920 and for *Anna Christie* in 1922. In 1928 he was taken up by the Theatre Guild, who produced two of his plays, *Marco Millions* and *Strange Interlude* in the same month. A highly experimental play that lasted five hours (with a break for dinner), *Strange Interlude* used asides for characters to reveal their true thoughts. Though approached warily by the critics, it proved an enormous success, attracting capacity audiences to the small John Golden Theatre and winning the Pulitzer once again for O'Neill.

When Fontanne was ready to abandon the exhausting role in June 1928, the Theatre Guild invited Judith Anderson, finally released from Belasco's control, to replace her. The

---
11   *NYT* 24 Jan 1929: 34.

Guild revealed that they had chosen among several leading actresses who wanted the part. (Silent-film actress Lillian Gish disclosed years later that she was one of them). Percy Hammond, in the *Los Angeles Times*, remarked that Fontanne would be a hard act to follow. 'Any artist who follows Miss Fontanne in *Strange Interlude* is putting her bobbed head into a lion's maw,' he wrote. 'Miss Fontanne… in the Theatre Guild's stupendous stunt is a religion,' he wrote. 'Few of the saints of show business have been adored as she is; or have deserved the worship more.'[12]

Anderson, however, was ideally suited to this psychological study of a modern woman's tangled relationships with the men in her life. *Strange Interlude* drew even bigger grosses with her in the role. As *Variety* put it in October 1928, the Theatre Guild 'has a little gold mine' in the play. Anderson claimed that she had driven a hard bargain with the Guild and was paid more than Fontanne. Nevertheless, her marathon two years in the nine-act play – 18 months on Broadway and six months on tour – exacted a physical toll. In December 1928 the Guild formed a second company led by Pauline Lord to tour to the West Coast. As Anderson's Broadway company continued to play to full houses during spring 1929, she had several absences due to illness.

In April 1929, she finally took a short vacation.

Then she took over from Lord in Los Angeles.[13] She had made her name, with *Strange Interlude*, as a serious emotional actress of modern roles.

In California she began to imagine herself achieving greatness.

---

12   *NYT* 31 May: 28; 3 Jun 1928: X1, 2; *Brooklyn Citizen* 24 Jun 1928; Stuart Oderman, 'Lillian Gish: A Friend Remembered,' *Journal of Popular Film and Television* 22:2, 1994: 52–57; *LAT* 24 Jun 1928: C11.
13   *Variety* 31 Oct 1928: 52; *NYT* 13 Dec 1928: 34; 6 Apr 1929: 20.

Robinson Jeffers 1930s

Author's collection

Chapter Eleven

Love and Ambition 1929

It was an instant love affair. He was beautiful to look at: strong and quiet, with his faithful dog beside him.

Judith Anderson on meeting Californian poet
Robinson Jeffers in 1929

In 1928, in the wake of her disastrous Australian tour, Judith Anderson had expressed the wish 'to do something really worth-while.' 'After I have made much money,' she vowed, 'I might give the public just one fine play.'[14] Now, a year later, she met the men who would help her keep that dream alive – and ultimately to achieve it in her masterpiece *Medea*, almost 20 years later. That fateful year she met the producer Jed Harris and her future husband, the Berkeley academic Ben (Peter) Lehman, who introduced her to the Californian poet Robinson Jeffers.

The first of these momentous meetings was with the 'Wonder Kid' Jed Harris. It is not clear when or where they met. In her memoirs, written in the 1960s, she places the meeting in California, possibly to heighten the drama of this conjunction of fate. Harris's biographer places it in Florida immediately after Harris's triumphant opening of *The Front Page* in August 1928. But it seems most likely that the two met

---

14 *BG* 25 Mar 1928, NYPL.

in February 1929 when Harris was vacationing in Florida after the opening of *Serena Blandish*, and Anderson was recovering from an illness that kept her out of *Strange Interlude* for several weeks. Whatever the date and place, Anderson immediately recognised a kindred spirit – someone who 'would bring a powerful influence of color, stimulus and a vaulting imagination into my life.'[15]

When Harris appeared on the cover of *Time* in September 1928, he was at the peak of his fame and notoriety. In a bare two years the 27-year-old had revolutionised the Broadway stage, bringing fast-paced, topical, vernacular drama in an

Jed Harris on the cover of Time *3 September 1928*
Wikipedia Commons

---

15   Martin Gottfried, *Jed Harris, the Curse of Genius*, 1984, 92–4; *NYT* 1 Jan: 61; 18 Feb: 33; 24 Feb: 113; 6 Mar: 32; 9 Mar 1929: 24; *Variety* 6, 13 & 20 Feb; 6 Mar 1929; *CDT* 21 Feb 1929: 29.

unprecedented run of success with *Broadway* (1926), *Spread Eagle* (1927), *Coquette* (1927), *The Royal Family* (1927), and *The Front Page*. The caption to *Time*'s cover photo also signaled the young man's abrasive personality: 'Jed Harris. He knows it teases,' referring, the accompanying article explained, to his overweening self-confidence and his 'strange irritable fervor.'

But Jed Harris was also captivating, especially to anyone who loved the theatre and had ambitions to reach its heights. Moss Hart, a young theatrical aspirant at that time, recalled Harris's 'dazzling cascade of eagle-winged and mercurial words.' Lillian Gish had 'never heard anyone talk about the theater with the intelligence and the excitement and the interest that that man had.' As Hart put it, every aspiring playwright's prayer in those days was, 'Please, god, let Jed Harris do my play!' And Gish probably spoke for many actors when she exclaimed: 'I'd work for that man for nothing.'[16]

Not only was Harris a brilliant persuasive speaker, he was, producer George Abbott remembered, 'a hypnotic listener' whose whispered replies created a seductive sense of intimacy. With what his biographer described as his 'pale, bony, ivory face; dark and piercing eyes; glossy black hair brushed flat like shelf paper,' Harris was highly attractive to men and women alike.[17]

Whether they met in late 1928 or early 1929, Anderson's ambition to do something 'worth-while' coincided with that of Harris, and made a combustible combination. Having conquered Broadway in just two years, Harris had visions of a company of his own that staged the best of classic and modern theatre. Early in 1928 he had announced a repertory venture in association with veteran actor Holbrook Blinn (Anderson's old mentor). Newspaper baron William

---

16 Gottfried, *Jed Harris*, 117, 120.
17 Gottfried, *Jed Harris*, 42, 2.

Randolph Hearst had agreed to acquire land on Central Park South to build a theatre for the company. Just as Harris was about to sail for England to recruit actors, however, Blinn died suddenly in a fall from a horse. In what Harris described as the unhappiest period of his life, the young producer saw his ambitious plans come to nothing.[18]

Harris did not give up, however. He decided instead to present the classics – Pinero, Feydeau, Ibsen, Chekhov, Strindberg – as commercial ventures, beginning in fall 1929, alongside other, modern, productions. As the *New York Times* reported somewhat snidely, Harris's grandiose plans for the troupe included half the town's well-known players. During 1928 these included one of his current lovers, Ruth Gordon, and the talented comedian, Ina Claire.[19]

Judith Anderson was the sort of smart, talented actress Harris was attracted to. He, in turn, embodied the sort of 'worth-while' theatre that she longed for. Anderson thought she had found the perfect producer-manager-lover, while Harris thought he had found another star for his dream repertory company. They became lovers and began to plan the brilliant role Harris envisioned for Anderson – Medea.

Anderson carried this vision of a splendid future to the West Coast when she toured there in *Strange Interlude* a few months later. In San Francisco she met the 'charming, witty, erudite' novelist and professor of English, Benjamin Lehman (whom she always called 'Peter'). There was an instant attraction between them, which was intensified by Anderson's delight in the benevolent ambience created by Lehman's wealthy friend Noël Sullivan.

In a magic weekend visiting Sullivan at his retreat

---

18   *NYT* 4 Mar: 115; 6 Jun 1928: 23; *CDT* 25 Jun 1928: 1; Jed Harris, *A Dance on the High Wire*, 1979, 142–5.
19   Gottfried, *Genius*, 94–5; *NYT* 24 Jun 1928.

in Carmel, Anderson met Robinson Jeffers, the stern Californian poet whose *Poems* Lehman had introduced for the Book Club of California. 'It was an instant love affair,' she told an interviewer many years later of her first meeting with Jeffers. 'He was beautiful to look at: strong and quiet, with his faithful dog beside him.' Although she told Lehman later that she would love to be 'a Robinson Jeffers wife,' their love affair was always at the level of intellect and imagination.[20]

Robinson Jeffers was 42 years old in 1929. Lean and athletic, he lived an austere life in Carmel with his devoted wife, Una, and their twin sons, Garth and Donnan. His epic verse, which valued the wild natural world over that of civilization, was enjoying the strong critical acclaim that had begun in 1925 with *Roan Stallion, Tamar, and Other Poems* and was reinforced in 1927 with *The Women at Point Sur* and in 1928 with *Cawdor and Other Poems*.

Ben Lehman was one of Jeffers' earliest admirers. As well as introducing Anderson to Jeffers, he urged her to read the poet's work. Writing from the Union Pacific that was taking her back to New York in June 1929, she was reading Jeffers' poems, *Roan Stallion* and *Tamar*. 'I was too sunk in the stark tragedy of the tales to listen fully to the torrent of beauteous language that is Jeffers,' she wrote Lehman; '– what luxury to have it to read.'[21]

With her head full of Jeffers' poetry and Lehman's charm, Anderson reluctantly left California to meet up with Jed Harris in Paris. 'I have left so much behind – to go to – a mirage?' she wrote Lehman in her jagged mis-spelled style as she embarked on the *Berengaria*. 'I don't know – time will tell

---

20   *LAT* 5 Nov 1989: I53; Anderson, in hand on Lehman to Anderson, 26 Aug [1929], UCSB.
21   Anderson to Lehman, posted 22 Jun 1929 St Louis, to c/o Noël Sullivan, 2323 Hyde Street, San Francisco, UCSB.

clearly. I have hopes & desires what will emenate [sic] from them I don't know –'[22]

Anderson had good reason to be apprehensive. Harris was a notorious philanderer with a wife he was about to abandon and numerous lovers. What she did not know, however, was that one of his current lovers, Ruth Gordon, was pregnant, and was ensconced in an apartment in the Paris suburbs awaiting the birth. Gordon had been starring in Harris's latest hit, *Serena Blandish*. When he returned from the trip to Florida where he had met Anderson, she had told him of her pregnancy and her intention of keeping the child. He closed the play soon after, announced that he was quitting Broadway for London, and the two sailed for Paris in separate ships.[23]

Anderson's first few days in Paris were wonderful. 'I am a balloon – bouncing bubbling along the streets,' she wrote Lehman. 'Today "We" went for a long walk in the Bois – then drove to Versailles – back – stopped at St Cloud – walked miles down on the bank of the Seine – Had dinner at the Maisonette Russe – fun with the orchestra had them play sweet old tunes walked home.' Harris was insisting that she must do *Medea*, she recalled in her memoirs.

Then suddenly, mid-letter, Anderson wrote two days later in a daze, 'A situation so unbelievably fantastic has arisen that it has left me without mind or reason – So you will for the time being have to accept the disjointed muddle of my thoughts and be patient with me till I can give you some sort of explanation.'[24]

Stunned by the revelation of Gordon's pregnancy,

---

[22] Anderson to Lehman, c/o Sullivan, posted Staten Island 28 Jun 1929. See also Tue [2 Jul 1929], posted 3 Jul 1929, c/o Sullivan, from Cherbourg, UCSB.
[23] Gottfried, *Genius*, 101–03; Ruth Gordon, *My Side: The Autobiography of Ruth Gordon*, 1976, 233–4; *NYT* 11 Apr; 19 & 29 Jun 1929; *LAT* 28 Apr 1929: C14; *CDT* 27 Jun: 31; 20 Aug 1929: 37; *Variety* 28 Aug 1929.
[24] Anderson to Lehman, posted 10 Jul 1929 from Hotel Chambord, Paris, UCSB.

Anderson fled to Antibes with her friend, the opera star Grace Moore. She returned to New York in mid-August, just as Harris was sailing for London after a whirlwind visit home to wind up his affairs. On her return she had to face a further eight-month tour of *Strange Interlude* starting in Boston in early September.²⁵

On 1 December 1929, the *New York Times* asked, 'Whatever became of Jed Harris?' They got their answer a few days later when he returned to New York, following the (undisclosed) birth of his son in October. He had not forgotten his plans for a repertory company. While in London he had scouted for talent. Maurice Evans – later one of America's best-known actors – was 28 years old when Harris spotted him in *Journey's End*. As Evans reported in his memoirs, 'a very persuasive American producer named Jed Harris nearly succeeded in getting his claws into me, but when I heard his grandiose plans for establishing a repertory company on the Great White Way, I decided to steer clear of his cultural ambitions.'²⁶

Back in New York, Harris 'awed' New York audiences with his April 1930 production – directed for the first time by himself – of Chekhov's *Uncle Vanya*, starring former silent star Lillian Gish. Announcing plans to stage *Othello* with Gish as Desdemona and Osgood Perkins as Iago, Harris set off for London to try to engage Paul Robeson for the lead role.²⁷

'I go to New York on Saturday heaven be praised & live for a while in my apartment,' Anderson wrote Ben Lehman in May 1930, as the *Strange Interlude* tour finally wound to

---

25 Gottfried, *Genius*, 111–15; Anderson to Lehman, postcard [early Aug] 1929 from Cannes; postcard posted 10 Aug 1929 from Paris, UCSB; *Vogue* 28 Sep 1929: 68–70, 124–8; *CDT* 20 Aug 1929: 37; *NYT* 23 & 25 Aug 1929; *Variety* 2 & 9 Oct 1929.
26 *NYT* 10 Dec 1929; *Variety* 11 Dec 1929; *LAT* 27 Dec 1929: 7; Maurice Evans, *All This… and Evans Too!* 1986, 52.
27 Harris, *Dance on a High Wire*, 125; Gottfried, *Genius*, 118–22; *NYT* 2, 10 & 12 Mar; 16, 19 & 20 Apr; 6 & 22 May; 8 Jun 1930; *LAT* 4 May; 31 Aug 1930; Stuart Oderman, *Lillian Gish*, 2000, 259–60.

an end. 'We play Newark for 2 weeks after that I will put my delightful self on a boat or a train & go someplace.' 'The great magnates know my future movements,' she wrote, teasing him, '& when they impart their knowledge to me – I'll keep it to myself – so that one of these days I'll be an uncomfortable surprise to you.'[28]

One of the 'great magnates' deciding Anderson's future was Jed Harris, who had lured her back to his fold with talk of *Medea*. From Paris, he wrote:

> *My dear Judy: It's almost two weeks since I last heard from you. I suppose you have really gone off and married somebody. My one consolation is that I am in Paris where a favorable rate of exchange makes it possible to buy wedding presents at a reasonable price. I have sent you three wires and three letters and feel very proud of myself. Not only will your jilting me give me a legitimate excuse to feel sorry for myself but this lack of balance in our correspondence will serve as fuel for moral indignation. I find it very pleasant to be thus deceived and injured. For once I cannot be called: cad.*[29]

The summer was hellishly hot, but Anderson was resting her 'old nina-bound bones' and reading *Lysistrata* (which the Theatre Guild was planning to put on that fall) and *Medea* when she wrote Lehman in mid-June. A manager, she told him, was talking about *Medea*.[30]

But the dream of starring in a brilliant production of *Medea* with Harris proved elusive. As he announced plans for Gogol's *The Inspector General* starring Dorothy Gish, and

---

28   Anderson to Lehman, Sunday Eve In bed, posted May 8 [1930] from Hotel Belvedere, Baltimore to 2323 Hyde Street, San Francisco, UCSB.
29   Harris to Anderson, May 1930, UCSB.
30   Anderson to Lehman, 8? Jun 1930, c/o Noël Sullivan, 2323 Hyde Street, San Francisco, forwarded to Apt 205, 932 Tiverton Ave, West Los Angeles, UCSB.

a new play, *Mr Gilhooley* with Helen Hayes, Anderson began to realise that Harris was at the beginning of a sharp decline almost as swift as his ascent. *Mr Gilhooley* was a flop and *The Inspector General* lasted only seven performances. Harold Johnsrud, fiancé of the future novelist Mary McCarthy, had a bit part in the production. As McCarthy recalled many years later, 'John [Johnsrud] was in a disastrous production Jed put on of *The Inspector General*... That was a harrowing time... one of the principal actors, a very fat person, killed himself by jumping out of a window, driven to it, people said, by Jed's tormenting sarcasm.'[31]

Meanwhile, producer Lee Shubert returned from Europe with the rights to Pirandello's *As You Desire Me*, and on 25 June the *Chicago Daily Tribune* announced that Judith Anderson would play the mysterious Unknown One in this tantalising drama of fluid identity.[32]

---

31   *NYT* 8, 11 & 17 Jun; 4 Jul 1930; *CDT* 27 Jul 1930; Mary McCarthy to Carol Brightman, 4 March 1988, McCarthy Papers; *NYT* 24 & 28 Dec 1930.
32   *NYT* 16 Jun 1930: 28; *CDT* 25 Jun 1930: 15.

... *moulded in the most exquisite gown of the theater season*... Judith Anderson in As You Desire Me, Vogue *1931*

Author's collection

Chapter Twelve

Sophisticated Lady 1930–33

> ... *too scattered, too many loose ends, too far too many rough corners... I'm old raggedy Peggety...*
> Judith Anderson to Benjamin Lehman, 1934

As *You Desire Me* opened at the Maxine Elliott's Theatre to a celebrity-studded audience on 28 January 1931 after an initial tour of Washington DC, Philadelphia and Chicago, and ran for 142 performances on Broadway. Although Anderson was longing for *Medea*, the role of Cia, the dissolute cabaret singer who is mistaken for the long-lost wife of a wealthy Italian, displayed her talents to perfection. 'Moulded in the most exquisite gown of the theater season,' Anderson was 'the most decorative' as well as 'one of our finest young actresses,' her long-time admirer Claudia Cassidy wrote in the *Chicago Journal*. 'Her voice is a vibrant thing, alive with response to any demand she puts upon it, and her body has fluid grace that knows no static moment.'[33]

Although Brooks Atkinson hated the play and Anderson's performance and John Mason Brown was lukewarm, the other New York critics (and the audiences) agreed with Cassidy. Anderson's performance is 'electric, compelling, enthralling,' Robert Coleman wrote in the *New York Mirror*, such as 'one is seldom privileged to see in these days of so-called realistic

---
33 *Chicago Journal*, 30 Dec 1930, NYPL.

acting. Here is a performance that is at once true and grand theater.' John Anderson in the *New York Journal* found the play 'fascinating but tenuous.' But, he pointed out, 'there was always Judith Anderson to look at in a long, ornamental and frequently affecting performance.' She 'gives it much tension and glamour,' he continued, 'and the nervous vitality which tells so vividly in her best work.' 'As The Unknown One, Miss Judith Anderson gives what is perhaps the outstanding performance of her honorable career,' Robert Garland wrote in the *New York Telegram*. 'When I say that her Antoinette Lyle in *Behold the Bridegroom* is improved upon, I can think of no higher praise.' Even that former arbiter of stardom, Alexander Woollcott, who seldom went to the theatre by the 1930s, wrote to the Shuberts to praise Anderson's fascinating performance. An advertisement for Lux Toilet Soap featuring Anderson spoke of her 'electric beauty.' And Hirschfeld published the first of several caricatures he made of her famous profile.[34]

All of this seemed to have little effect on Anderson's spirits. 'Im just going rather mad places people anything anywhere to get away as far away as possible from myself,' she wrote Lehman early in March 1931 in her inimitable style. 'Im quite allright physically & mentally only impatient for the dream that won't live for me – heart whats left of it whole & fancy liberal.' It seemed for a moment that Anderson might be called to Hollywood to star in the movie of *As You Desire Me*; but MGM announced that they had bought it for their star Norma Shearer. When it was finally produced in 1932, Greta Garbo played Anderson's role in an exquisite performance that mirrored Anderson's in many ways.[35]

---

34   *NYT* 29 Jan; 5 Apr 1931:104; *NYP* 29 Jan 1931; *NYM* 20 [29?] Jan 1931; *NYJ* 29 Jan 1931; *New York Telegram* 29 Jan 1931; *Standard Union* 17 Feb 1931; advertisement, NYPL.
35   Anderson to Lehman, posted 7 Mar 1931 from Hotel Seymour, 50 W45, New York, to 29 Mosewood Road, Berkeley, UCSB; *LAT* 7 Apr: A9; 9 May 1931: A7;

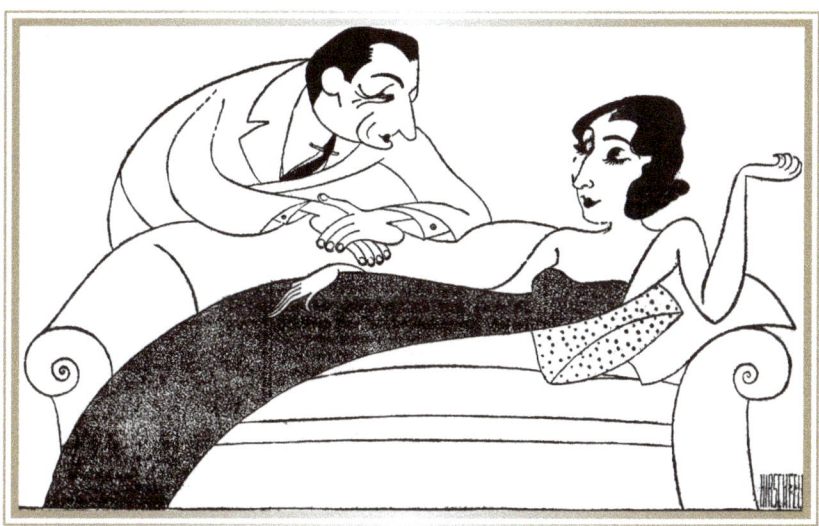

Judith Anderson and José Rubin in As You Desire Me, *by Hirschfeld*
New York Times 5 April 1931. © The Al Hirschfeld Foundation

The Unknown One was the first of a number of sophisticated roles Judith Anderson played from 1931 to 1934. The epitome of glamour, she was acclaimed more for her dress sense than her choice of plays – though critics never failed to comment on the brilliance of her acting. Throughout these years, Anderson continued to long for a 'worth-while' play.

When *As You Desire Me* closed for the summer in late May 1931, Anderson was still hoping to do something with Jed Harris. As she wrote to Lehman early that month, 'Peter my sweet – I don't know yet what I am going to do during the summer: motor tour through Adirondacks to Montreal and through Maine to Cape Cod with Jean Dixon; or a picture on the coast or *As You Desire Me* also coast or take three plays to London *Dove – Bridegroom* & *As you* etc – Or – play "Medea" – here after I close which will be early in June.'[36]

Her dream of playing *Medea* dragged on through 1931.

Anderson to Lehman, 10 May & 23 Jun [1931], UCSB.
36 Anderson to Lehman, 10 May 1931, UCSB.

She was under contract to the Shuberts for a tour of *As You Desire Me* in the fall, and as usual she was restless under this restriction. 'Next season will start with a sticky law wrangle I think,' she wrote, ' – they plan to bring me to NY January in a new one all of which I find myself unable to digest.' 'Why,' she asked, '– because I have a swell commercial play with one "Harris" – which I think would make a much richer & therefore happier woman out of me – and the Guild have landed me with the new ONeil Trilog.'[37]

The 'new ONeil Trilog' was *Mourning Becomes Electra*, Eugene O'Neill's reworking of Aeschylus's *Oresteia* in post-civil war New England. Because of her contract with the Shuberts, she was unable to take up immediately the Guild's offer of the part of Lavinia Mannon in this three-part tragedy. It opened triumphantly on 26 October 1931 with Alice Brady in Anderson's role and Nazimova as her mother, Christine Mannon. After Anderson toured in *As You Desire me* to Rochester, Toronto, Montreal and Boston in September and October 1931, she managed to get out of the Shubert contract and set off in the Guild's second company of *Mourning* on a tour of Chicago, the mid-West and the West Coast, beginning in January 1932, with Florence Reed and Walter Abel.

'Peter darling,' Anderson wrote hurriedly on a postcard at Christmas 1931, 'No time now O'Neill has got me again Electra – so when Im normal again – if ever – I'll tell you all – how are you my sweet.' 'We don't open – Baltimore till the 4th 32,' she continued. 'Then we wound slowly to the Coast. Arms around & deep love to you my one sweet. Judy.'

Anderson hated *Mourning Becomes Electra*, though she enjoyed playing with the veteran actress Florence Reed. *Washington Post* critic Nelson B Bell called O'Neill 'the high priest of morbidity' and found the play 'somber,

---

37 Anderson to Lehman, 10 May & 23 Jun [1931], UCSB; NYWT 10 Mar 1931, NYPL.

psychologically and physiologically repulsive.' A trilogy of plays that lasted five hours, with an hour's break for dinner after the first, it had, according to Bell, 'a driving, cumulative, irresistible power that compels unwavering attention.' As the central character linking the three plays, Anderson's 'ominous and forbidding monosyllabic automaton,' Vinnie, was 'vividly set forth without mercy or compassion.'[38]

The negativity of *Mourning Becomes Electra* exacerbated a sense of anxiety and depression during this tour. By now she realised that she could not rely on the mercurial Harris, who continued his downhill slide. And family problems began to bulk large. Before she left on tour her mother had received a letter from her husband's sister in Scotland saying that he was very ill and asking her to write and make peace with him. She did so reluctantly, and Anderson also wrote him a long letter. She finally received an answer when she arrived in Chicago in mid-February that plunged her into despair: he did not want to hear from his wife, he wrote frostily. Anderson does not record whether her father had any warm words for her, but this seems to have been the last time she heard from him. (He died, seemingly alone, in 1939 at the age of 81.) 'Peter, my sweet, sweet Peter,' she wrote from Detroit in March, 'Why arent you here *now*. I need to talk with you badly... Life is the same with few good moods bad moods – a little calmer I'm afraid – its all quite an effort & shadows of resignation I fear me are deepening. I wish it were despair – there's be hope then.'[39]

Much to Anderson's disappointment, the company did

---

38   Anderson to Lehman, posted 18 Mar 1932 from Detroit, UCSB; *WP* 12 Jan: 10; 13 Jan 1932: 10.
39   Anderson to Lehman, posted 18 Mar 1932, UCSB.

not go on to the West Coast as she had hoped. Instead, they returned to New York for a final two weeks at the Alvin Theatre. Despite her bleak mood, her performance was as dazzling as ever. Brooks Atkinson welcomed Anderson's new Lavinia, 'sharp and malignant and tightly knotted' and growing in stature as the play moves towards its conclusion. 'She charges her part with originality,' he wrote; 'her scenes are electric.'[40]

After *Mourning Becomes Electra*, Anderson recalled in her memoirs, she had two years of continual work that got her nowhere. Her mood of resignation deepened as she moved, apparently rudderless, from one play and producer to another. During the summer of 1932 newspapers reported that she and Helen Menken were to appear in *The Establishment of Madame Antonia*, a play based on a set of stories about women in a Paris brothel, to be produced by Peggy Fears. But while she was in Europe Gilbert Miller, the American producer who regularly brought hits from the London stage to Broadway, arranged for her to play in *Firebird*, an adaptation from the Hungarian in which Gladys George was having a success. The part of Carola provided Anderson with one of the finest scenes she had ever played, according to *Herald Tribune* critic Percy Hammond. 'By her quiet and forceful if often obvious magic she dominates every play in which she appears,' he wrote, while Robert Garland, in the New York *World Telegram* considered that 'Miss Anderson more than maintains the gifts and the glamour which have placed her securely among the first ladies of the American theatre.' But the play was weak and only lasted 42 performances when it opened at the end of November 1932. Its most important legacy was the pair of dachshunds, Gooney and Micklosh, she had acquired for the play – the replacements for Rex, who had died in 1928,

---

40   *NYT* 10 May 1932: 25.

and the forerunners of the many dachshunds that were her companions till the end of her life.[41]

Her next play, *Conquest,* was an even greater disaster. Arthur Hopkins, one of Broadway's most innovative producers, had recently expressed his despair at the dearth of good plays. Lovers of the theatre were therefore keen to see this new work, which he himself had written. When it opened in the middle of February 1933 with Anderson in the lead as an 'asp-like lady,' Brooks Atkinson wrote in the *New York Times* that it was 'full of high motives and fine perceptions but bloodless.' Percy Hammond pronounced it 'daffy.' It lasted 10 days.[42]

The Theatre Guild then put her into *The Mask and the Face,* an adaptation by Somerset Maugham of Luigi Chiarelli's 1913 comedy of marital deceit. The play was in the Guild's long tradition of reviving important foreign plays; but what was confronting in 1913 seemed to Anderson in 1933 a 'mossy milestone.' Audiences agreed, and the play ran for only 40 performances when it opened on 8 May 1933, despite excellent performances by Anderson as the elegant Countess Savina Grazia, Humphrey Bogart, still relatively unknown despite his long stage career, as her would-be lover, and Shirley Booth as a faithless wife.

This part gave Anderson a wonderful opportunity to wear spectacular clothes and the publicity surrounding the play provided some of the most beautiful images of her career. *The Stage,* in an extended feature on Anderson, proclaimed that 'The clothes of the month are definitely those of Judith Anderson in *The Mask and the Face,* a meaty collection of

---

41 *NYT,* 4 Jul: F6; 9 Jul: 7; 13 Oct 1932: 22; *CDT* 17 Jul 1932: F7; *Variety* 12 Jul 12; 2, 12 & 30 Aug; 6 Sep; 6 & 13 Dec 1932; 3 Jan 1933; OT 11 Aug 1932; *Reno Evening Gazette* 27 Aug 1932; *WP* 28 Aug 1932: A3; *NYHT* 22 Nov 1932; *NYWT* [22 Nov 1932], NYPL; *Vogue* 15 Jan 1933: 38–9, 73, 80.
42 *NYT* 20 Feb: 11; 25 Feb 1933: 20; *LAT* 26 Feb 1933: A2; *Variety* 21 & 28 Feb 1933.

imports culled by the deft hand of Margaret Pemberton.' The article describes 'the wickedest gown' – a mauve teagown with a very narrow skirt, a sleek high waistline, a slit at the side, a clinging train, and a straight lace coat. 'Very nnn-yuh,' was the writer's summing-up. But the outstanding gown, by the French designer Vionnet and illustrating the article, was ingeniously cut, 'twisted and wrapped, with an almost bandaged look.'[43]

Critics as usual loved Anderson as well as her clothes. Stephen Woolseley, in *The Stage*, found her Countess Savina enticing. 'She has a way with her,' he wrote, 'particularly since she is Judith Anderson.' 'We approve of giving Judith

Judith Anderson in The Mask and the Face *as Countess Savina Grazia, with Humphrey Bogart as her would-be lover*

Author's collection

---

43   *The Stage*, Jun 1933: 36–8.

Anderson titles,' he went on, '(this is the second time she has been knighted this season, *Firebird* was the other occasion), because as an actress she is to the manor and the title born. Her figure, her voice, and her bearing, without any sentimental beauty of face, spell "lady" with character.'[44]

---

44 *The Stage*, Jun 1933: 32–3.

Judith Anderson and George Bancroft in Blood Money *1933*

Author's collection

Chapter Thirteen
Hollywood Calling 1933

The unknown Miss Judith Anderson is capable of stealing a film from anyone... You don't know her, that is Hollywood's fault
The London Times, 1934

Anderson's reputation as a brilliant and glamorous actress with a thrilling voice brought her her first opportunity in the movies – *Blood Money* – in 1933. Since the advent of sound in 1929 the movies had been poaching the legitimate theatre for talent. The elegant and beautifully-spoken Kay Francis, the current queen of Warner Bros, had made the move immediately (in the Marx Brothers debut *Cocoanuts*) and had enchanted audiences in the delightfully amoral *Trouble in Paradise*, directed by Ernst Lubitch, in 1932. The aristocratic Ruth Chatterton (who had played Judy in the original *Daddy Long Legs* in 1914) depicted career women who took what they wanted sexually. Bette Davis moved to Hollywood in 1930 and began to make her name in stories of sexual adventure and misadventure such as *Three on a Match* in 1932; and Barbara Stanwyck portrayed illicit inter-racial sexual attraction in *The Bitter Tea of General Yen* in 1933. Of Judith Anderson's cohort, only the delicate Helen Hayes, married to scriptwriter Charles Macarthur, had made the leap to Hollywood, appearing as the unhappy prostitute in *The Sin of Madelon Claudet* (MGM 1931) and the nurse involved in a doomed love affair in *A Farewell to Arms* (Paramount 1932).

In the brief period between 1929 and 1934, when the Motion Picture Production Code was enforced, Hollywood – and especially Warner Bros – revelled in stories of strong, sexually-active women, gangsters, prostitutes, drugs, and sex. The best of them followed Lubitch's formula: 'At once elegant and ribald, sophisticated and earthy, urbane and bemused, frivolous yet profound… amused by sex rather than frightened of it.'[45] Judith Anderson, with her aura of sophistication, her gorgeous dress sense and her skill in conveying emotion, fitted well with the sort of women being portrayed in what came to be known as pre-Code movies.

Anderson was tested early on for the talkies when she made the short, *Woman of the Jury*, for the Warners subsidiary Vitaphone, in their Brooklyn studios in 1930, soon after she completed her tour with *Strange Interlude*. Over the next few years her plays were considered eminently filmable: *Strange Interlude* was sold to MGM, who put their leading star, Norma Shearer, into the role of Nina, with the up-and-coming Clark Gable as her lover. Warner Bros bought *Firebird* as a vehicle for Ruth Chatterton. MGM also snapped up *As You Desire Me*, and for a brief moment it seemed that they might use Anderson in the part: at the end of May 1931, as the play was closing, she wrote Ben Lehman that she was 'trying to get a picture contract settled'; but a month later she wrote, 'Peter darling – I am not going to the coast worse luck – The deal has all fallen through, so —.' A few months later the newspapers revealed that the part had been reserved for Garbo.[46]

In 1933 however, Joseph Schenck, the former president

---

45   Michael Wilmington, quoted in https://en.wikipedia.org/wiki/Ernst_Lubitsch
46   Roy Liebman, *Vitaphone Films: A Catalog of the Features and Shorts*, 2003; OT 22 Nov 1930: 4; *LAT* 24 Nov 1930: A7; *Variety* 3 Dec 1930: 15; 22 Sep 1933; *NYT* 10 May 1931: X5; Anderson to Lehman, 10 & 30 May 1931; 23 Jun [1931], UCSB; *Sheboygan Press* (Wisc) 11 Aug 1931: 33; *LAT* 3 Feb 1932: 6.

of UA, and Darryl F Zanuck, former head of production at Warner Bros, started up their new studio, 20th Century Pictures. Determined to out-Warner Warner Bros, over the next couple of years, until they merged with the Fox studio in 1935, they made some of the greatest pre-Code movies.

Blood Money was one of the studio's first productions. Written and directed by the talented but difficult Rowland Brown, the movie depicts a wide-open Los Angeles under-

Blood Money *featured cross-dressing women and elegant clothes, as well as the usual gangster violence and vice*

Author's collection

world, with Judith Anderson as a stylish nightclub owner, Ruby Darling, and musical comedy star Blossom Seeley singing a Rodgers and Hart ballad which was later rewritten as *Blue Moon*. (A 22-year-old Lucille Ball played a girl at the racetrack in her third – fleeting – movie appearance). Now considered one of the greatest of the pre-Code movies, it featured cross-dressing women, rough sex and elegant clothes, as well as the usual gangster violence and vice.[47]

Judith Anderson later dismissed her role in *Blood Money* as a failure. It was certainly received coolly, for the most part, at the time. Critics who were used to seeing her on the stage in more upscale roles were disconcerted to see her playing against type. On its release in November 1933 Mordaunt Hall in the *New York Times* felt that the part did not give her an opportunity to display her real ability. Norbert Lusk in the *Los Angeles Times* agreed. Anderson was impressive, he wrote, but with her elegance of bearing, her flawless stage English and her superb taste in costuming, she was out of her element as an underworld character. The *Christian Science Monitor*, in a review condemning the movie as 'rather silly,' lamented the fact that 'Miss Anderson has had the misfortune to be miscast in her first screen part.'[48]

Not everyone was disappointed, however. William Boehnel in the *New York World Telegram* considered that 'The quiet and forceful power of Judith Anderson's performance in *Blood Money*, at the Rivoli, saves that foolish artless melodrama from being altogether a bore.' *Variety* was sure that 'femme lead' Judith Anderson 'will find plenty of followers after this screening.' At a time when the studios were competing for fashion honours, the writer gave Anderson top marks. 'Always a dresser of charm Miss Anderson has a well chosen wardrobe,' she wrote. 'Black is the shade of all gowns but one. An evening frock has a unique treatment in a shoulder drape. Another gown with a pointed décolletage has diamond

---

47 'Cinema Club 9 Program Notes,' WTOP-TV 9, Washington DC, ca 1970s, MHL; 'The Hollywood Gangster, 1927–1933', in Danny Peary, *Cult movies* 2, 1983; *LAT* 17 May 17: E.1; 22 May 2003; Andrew Sarris, 'Big Funerals,' *Film Comment*, May/Jun 1977: 6–9, 64; Guy Madden, 'Blood Money,' May 2007: 8; Elliott Stein, 'Fox Before the Code,' *Village Voice* 29 Nov 2006.
48 *NYT* 16 Nov 1933: 30; *LAT* 26 Nov 1933: A2; *CSM* 27 Nov 1933: 4.

ornaments on the shoulders. Two black satin tailored suits are shown with the new pointed shoulders.'[49]

The London *Times* appreciated Anderson's performance for more than her dress sense. 'The unknown Miss Judith Anderson is capable of stealing a film from anyone,' their critic wrote. 'Her portrait of Ruby, conceived in cool, clear tones of tolerant sophistication, is quite brilliant and is in perfect harmony with the spirit of the whole film.' Nominating her for the week's best performance in March 1934, he commended her 'cool, level-headed figure, with a touch of fire about her,' and sent a rebuke across the Atlantic: 'You don't know her, that is Hollywood's fault.'[50]

As in her experience in Australia in 1927, Anderson felt her failure to 'take' in Hollywood in 1933 as a personal failure. When Darryl Zanuck signed her for *Blood Money* in July he announced that he had acquired her services for an extended period and that he was sure that she had the personality and ability to become one of the screen's most striking box office magnets. By September, however, when filming was over, Anderson was 'seething with impotent rage' as Zanuck procrastinated over the promised longer-term contract. When he finally decided not to take up her option, Anderson wrote to Lehman with 'the silent coursing of bitter tears & life passing me by.'[51]

But Anderson's timing, as in the Australian fiasco, was fateful. *Blood Money* and Zanuck's other boisterous productions of 1933 were the final hurrah of the pre-Code movie. The new code, which had been introduced in 1930 to self-police the industry, had not worked, and church groups and moral crusaders were threatening outside censorship if the industry did not toughen its stance.

---

49 NYWT Nov 1933, NYPL; *Variety* 21 Nov 1933.
50 *Times* 26 Mar 1934: 10; 'The Week's Best Performance,' Mar 1934.
51 *WP* 8 Aug 1933: 14; Anderson to Lehman, posted 19 & 24 Sep 1933 from Chateau des Fleurs, Hollywood to 97 Tamalpais Road, Berkeley, UCSB.

As Andrew Sarris put it in his commentary in 1977, 'with Judith Anderson's compliant, low-cut-gowned night club hostess and Frances Dee's wild-eyed nymphomaniac,' *Blood Money* gave Hollywood 'one last fling with grown-up sensuality before the age of Shirley Temple officially began.' After the movie was banned in Ohio and Maryland, Joseph Schenck wrote to Will Hays, the notorious president of the Motion Picture Producers and Distributors of America and enforcer of the Code, that they were 'through with any gangster elements.' A few months later the studios granted MPPDA authority to enforce the Production Code, creating a strict regime of self-censorship that endured for decades.[52]

'I embrace you with all my memories,' Judith Anderson wrote to Ben Lehman from Montreal in October 1931. 'I wish I had a magic carpet – now I wouldn't think twice about my wish – We would all be there at Noëls [Sullivan] – same thoughts same emotions – nothing changed – 19—? Lordy me how time flies.' Throughout the years 1931 to 1933, as she pursued what she considered a 'secondrate' career, Lehman retreated into a memory of a fleeting moment of happiness. Again and again she hoped her tours or a movie would take her to the West Coast, but they never did until July 1933, when she arrived in Los Angeles to make *Blood Money*.[53]

Their reunion was bitter sweet. Again Anderson was involved in another romantic entanglement – this time with the handsome and unstable actor Ian Keith, who had appeared with her in the short-lived *Firebird* at the end of 1932. Keith had spent the previous year in an on-again

---

52 Andrew Sarris, 'Big Funerals'; Schenck to Will H. Hays, 7 Feb 1934, MHL.
53 Anderson to Lehman, posted 1 Oct 1931 in Quebec, written from Ritz Carlton Hotel, Montreal; Xmas [1931], card; posted 18 Mar1932 from Book-Cadillac Hotel, Detroit, UCSB.

off-again divorce from his second wife (his first wife was
the actress Blanche Yurka) and had recently married a third
wife, probably illegally. 'Film Couple Re-Divorced,' the *New
York Times* had announced in July 1932. In July 1933, following *Firebird* and *The Mask and the Face*, Anderson and Keith
appeared together in *Reunion in Vienna* at the Castle Theatre at
Long Beach, Long Island, and they were announced for a tour
in *Design for Living* that September (which never eventuated).
When Anderson went to Los Angeles to make *Blood Money*,
Keith was there filming *Queen Christina*, with Garbo and
Laurence Olivier (who was subsequently fired from the role)
and appearing in *Othello* at a local theatre. The two appeared
together in November in Anderson's next, short-lived
play, *The Drums Begin*. In early December the newspapers
announced that he and his (third) wife had parted.[54]

This is the background against which the somewhat
anguished meeting between Anderson and Lehman took
place. They had of course not seen each other since they first
met in 1929, and that had been a brief *coup de foudre* when
she was already entangled with Jed Harris. When they met
again in August or September 1933 the strong attraction was
still there; but Anderson was involved with Keith, and geog-
raphy (he in San Francisco, she in Los Angeles) and propriety
seemed to limit the time they spent together.

When she wrote him from New York in December confessing that she had been 'flirting again' (the entanglement with
Keith), it is clear why both had collapsed into illness during
her last weeks in Los Angeles and had not seen each other
again. 'Peter this mustn't hurt you,' she wrote, 'it won't will
it darling.' 'There was a strange subcontious desire,' she
explained with her usual shaky spelling, 'that had been

---

54 *NYT* 20 Jul 1932: 20; 21 Jun: 20; 3 Jul: 14; 10 Dec 1933: N7; *Variety* 25 Jul 1933; *LAT* 24 Jul: A9; 31 Jul: 7; 26 Sep: A7; 30 Nov: 11; 13 Nov 1933: 7.

slumbering for a year, I was not aware of it truly, and then suddenly alive and awake, do you know about it?' 'There is a nasty tangle involved,' she went on, 'and I don't know what the outcome will be, but I know I can't fight against it anymore than I will fight for it, if it is to be it will take hold and possess me and you will be the first to know about it my sweet.'[55]

The 'nasty tangle' continued through the early months of 1934, as *The Drums Begin* quickly failed. 'My regrets are laid as sincere homage before the proud figure of Miss Anderson,' the reviewer in the *New York American* wrote, 'too singular an artist to be allowed to lay waste her powers in poor plays.'[56]

In February 1934, following headlines of 'Former Baroness Accuses Mate of Desertion' and 'Film Actress Seeks Divorce,' a strange announcement was made by the *Chicago Daily Tribune*. 'Won't Confirm or Deny Marriage: She Won't Talk,' the headline ran. Accompanied by photos of Anderson and Keith, the story reported that Judith Anderson, stage and film star, 'simply won't discuss' the report that she is secretly married to Ian Keith, English matinee idol. '"I won't confirm it; I don't deny it," the dynamic "Electra" declared".'

And like that same O'Neill heroine in a soul rending 'aside' she added, when asked if possibly she and Keith had any marriage plans, 'I won't say either "yes" or "no."'[57]

A *Los Angeles Times* report a month later had Keith and his wife together again; and a further report of 17 April had them remarried. In May 1935 their divorce was announced.[58]

At the beginning of 1934, as her youth faded, Judith Anderson appeared to have found nothing worthwhile, either personally or professionally. All that talent, all that hard work,

---

55 Anderson to Lehman, [ca 10 Dec 1933], UCSB.
56 *New York American* 25 Nov 1933, NYPL; *NYT* 25 Nov 1933: 10; *Variety* 5 Dec 1933.
57 *LAT* 21 Dec: A3; 22 Dec 1933: A1; *WP* 21 Dec 1933: 4; *CDT* 14 Feb 1934: 5.
58 *LAT* 18 Mar: A2; 17 Apr 1934: 13; 19 May 1935: 1.

all that charm seemed to have come to naught. She was, she had written to Lehman in December, 'too scattered, too many loose ends, too far too many rough corners... I'm old raggedy Peggety.'[59]

---

[59] Anderson to Lehman, [ca 10 Dec 1933], UCSB.

Scene Five
London Calling

The Old Vic where Judith Anderson performed Macbeth *with Laurence Olivier in 1937*
New York Public Library

Chapter Fourteen
The Quality of Greatness 1934

Her figure is beautiful, she moves like a poem and, from the moment she speaks her first line, one is translated immediately to another, and infinitely thrilling world. Heaven, one feels, is just around the corner... Magnificence had returned to the Theatre.

English playwright Keith Winter

Judith Anderson dressed by Valentina in Come of Age 1934
Author's collection

December 1933 was not the first time Judith Anderson had despaired of herself or her career; and it would not be the last. But she had put all that behind her by March 1934, when she finally broke her silence to Peter Lehman. 'Peter darling Can't write,' she wrote, '– have been trying to ever since the big California Mistral – it was all very shocking & embarrassing to me – but I suppose if children will play with fire they are bound to get dirty fingers & ashes in their eyes – anyway – finis.'[60]

Just when Anderson had been at her lowest ebb personally and professionally, her fortunes had begun to change. At a lunch party during December, she had met producer Delos Chappell, who was looking for an actress for an experimental play, *Come of Age*, by the British playwright Clemence Dane. Anderson loved everything about the play – its unusual colloquial free verse; its delightful author, whose work she had admired ever since she saw Katharine Cornell in *Bill of Divorcement*; the music composed and played by the tall fair young Englishman, Richard Addinsell; her youthful co-star Stephen Haggard; and the design by James Reynolds. Above all, she regarded her role, as the sophisticated older women who rejects and then mourns for her young lover, as the perfect part for her. And she was able to marry the perfect part to the perfect dress, as she made theatrical history by commissioning the Russian-born Valentina to design her gowns.[61]

Come of Age opened at the Maxine Elliott on 12 January 1934, accompanied by glamorous photos of Anderson in Valentina's classically-inspired draped and twisted ensembles. Although critics were strongly divided – Brooks Atkinson

---

60   Anderson to Lehmann, [Mar 1934] from New York, UCSB.
61   *NYT* 18 Dec: 24; 29 Dec 29: 27; 18 Dec 1933: 24; 15 Sep 1989; Kohle Yohannan, *Valentina: American Couture and the Cult of Celebrity*, 2009, 121; photos 120, 122.

considered it a failed work of high endeavour and others criticised its 'trite phrases and orchestral syncopation' – its devotees greeted it with rapturous praise.[62] 'Last night I had a great experience,' wrote the English playwright Keith Winter. 'I saw a truly great actress in a truly great play. This was theatre as one dreams of it. Here, at last, was something to tell the grandchildren about.'

"There are,' Winter continued, 'in the English speaking world, three actors who have genius of a quite staggering order – Charles Laughton, Edith Evans, and Judith Anderson. Perhaps, Laurence Olivier.'

'La Anderson… looked not a minute over thirty,' he wrote:

Her figure is beautiful, she moves like a poem and, from the moment she speaks her first line, one is translated immediately to another, and infinitely thrilling world. Heaven, one feels, is just around the corner… I do not as a rule think, still less write in superlatives but I cannot compromise about the events of last night.

The audience greeted the final curtain with prolonged and heartfelt cheers. Magnificence had returned to the Theatre.[63]

Robert Garland, in the *World-Telegram*, considered the play 'A rare adventure in the theatre' in which 'Miss Anderson's performance has the quality of greatness.' Arthur Pollock, in the *Brooklyn Daily Eagle*, agreed: 'The stage's most lovely treasure of the season came to view at the Maxine Elliott Theatre last night,' he wrote, 'a play unfolded in music and words… There has been nothing in a long while to offer so rich an emotional experience. It made a rare evening.' Leo Fontaine,

---

62 *Variety* 16 Jan 1934: 29.
63 [Jan 1934], UCSB.

in the *Morning Telegraph*, was moved to 'ineffable transports.'⁶⁴

Despite this enthusiasm and the support of such cultural leaders as Fannie Hurst and Jascha Heifetz, *Come of Age* closed in mid-February after what *Variety* reported as 'a month in the red.' At its final performance its admirers gave it 17 curtain calls. *Come of Age* remained Anderson's favourite play, and she fought for many years to have it performed in London and on the West Coast.⁶⁵ It was finally revived in 1952, directed by Guthrie McClintic, to whom Clemence Dane introduced her in 1934 and changed the direction of her life and work.

There were persistent rumours during the summer of 1934 that Anderson would take *Come of Age* and *Mourning Become Electra* to the Coast. When she wrote to Lehman in late March she reported that 'negotiations are on to do *Mourning Becomes Electra* on the Coast in April.' 'If they materialize I'll be leaving in a few days – now how do you like that – or will it raise hell with the curriculum – or do I flatter myself,' she wrote, fantasising that they could then 'take a slow moving boat' to England 'to regain my slightly befogged vision in Devonshire with Clemence Dane – she has a little farm house there & wants me to visit –'⁶⁶

None of these plans and fantasies eventuated, however. Instead Lehman came to New York with his son during the summer and did not contact Anderson; and in a letter during the fall he intimated that he was contemplating marriage. 'I

---

64   NYWT [13 Jan 1934]; BDE [13 Jan 1934]; MT [13 Jan 1934], NYPL.
65   *NYT* 10 Feb 1934: 20; 14 Apr 1935: X1; *Variety* 20 Feb 1934: 44; Anderson to Lehmann, [late Mar 1934], UCSB; Anderson to Maurice Browne, 29 May 1934, Browne Papers; NYWT 7 Apr 1934, NYPL.
66   *NYT* 8 Apr: X1; 20 May 1934: X1; *Variety* 6 Apr: 1; 29 May 1934: 47; Anderson to Lehmann, [late Mar 1934], UCSB.

shall never forgive you though for being in New York and not letting me know, I can't understand that Peter,' Anderson wrote in November, ' – you didn't want to see me for reasons of your own – what were they Mr Lehman, you surely don't think Im married no sir never have been and as the years go on it seems to me that if it isn't you it won't be anyone else.' 'And while we are on the marriage subject let me say this,' she continued, 'that I didn't know how much I'd revolt at the very idea of your marrying anyone else until I got this letter not hearing from you for such a long time, the things that have come to both of us shadows between, then another letter from you and I had a horrible feeling when I opened it, then "two special things to speak of" well I tell you right there and then I hated the woman with a stupendous magnificent hate so don't do it Peter please. Period.'[67]

But by the time she wrote this letter, Anderson's life had changed in a remarkable way, and issues of romance and marriage had been put aside – at least for the immediate future.

---

67 Anderson to Lehman, 14 Nov 1934, from c/o Mrs Daniel J. Mahoney, Miami Beach, Florida, UCSB; Lehman to Sullivan, 12 Jul 1934, postcard from New York; 24 Jul 1934 from Maine, Sullivan Papers.

Judith Anderson and Helen Menken in The Old Maid *1935*

Author's collection

Chapter Fifteen

Directed by Guthrie McClintic
1934–5

> *I am just walking around my house acting like*
> *a fool mad drunk with the riches you have given*
> *me and drenched in beauty. Thank you so much.*
> *Do you mind if I love you both very much*
>
> Judith Anderson to Guthrie McClintic and
> Katharine Cornell, 1934

Apart from attracting the usual praise for her acting, *Come of Age* was responsible for a decisive turn in Judith Anderson's career. Clemence Dane was a close friend of Katharine Cornell and Guthrie McClintic – the young man who had rejected her as not pretty enough in 1918, now a brilliant director. The four became friends; and Anderson's ascent to recognition as one of America's greatest actresses began later that year, when Guthrie McClintic invited her to take the lead in *Divided by Three*.

Anderson had long admired and envied McClintic and Cornell. Together McClintic the producer-director and Cornell the actress had built a brilliant organisation that cast Cornell as 'The First Lady of the American Stage.' As a young talent-spotter for Winthrop Ames McClintic had noted early in 1921 that the 28-year-old Cornell was someone to watch. They were married in September that year, a month before Cornell made her name in Clemence Dane's *A Bill of Divorcement* and three months before McClintic made his successful directorial debut with A A Milne's *The Dover Road*.

Cornell had what critic Burns Mantle described in 1924 as 'a certain subtle something… a Duse quality.'[68] She was snapped up that year by Belasco; but she managed to elude his control to appear in the sensational *The Green Hat*, staged by her husband, in 1925. McClintic became known as a producer with an eye for talent and a director who could bring out the best in his actors. Since 1925 Cornell had appeared only under her husband's direction, and from the early 1930s the couple had their own production company, Katharine Cornell Productions, with a highly efficient management team led by Alan Attwater (later by Stanley Gilkey) and Gertrude Macy, with publicity handled by Ray Henderson.

In August 1934, after *Come of Age* had closed, McClintic signed Anderson for a new play, *Divided by Three* by Margaret Leech and Beatrice Kaufman. A photo in the *New York Post* of Anderson with McClintic and other members of the cast in the McClintics' garden overlooking the East River underlined her new status as one of the chosen. In the ebullient, garrulous McClintic Anderson found a temperament that matched her own hectic personality. Her telegram to McClintic on opening night reveals her gratitude and the playful, affectionate relationship that had quickly developed between them: 'Puss,' she wrote, 'thank you on bended knee and kissing your royal ahem of course.'[69]

The magic of McClintic's touch did not work immediately. *Divided by Three* is now chiefly remembered as the play that launched the career of Jimmy Stewart. It is also memorable as

---

68   *CDT* 3 Feb 1924: F1.
69   *NYP* 17 Sep [1934]; *Midweek Pictorial* 22 Sep 1934, NYPL; Anderson to McClintic, tel, 2 Oct 1934, Cornell Papers.

Judith Anderson and Guthrie McClintic in his garden discussing Divided by Three *September 1934*
Museum of the City of New York / New York Public Library

the last Broadway performance of Hedda Hopper before she became the famed Hollywood gossip columnist. Brooks Atkinson praised it as a 'tenderly moving drama' in which Anderson 'played with deep compassion,' spreading an 'incandescent glow of emotion that illuminates the whole drama'; but Arthur Pollack in the *Brooklyn Eagle* put the majority opinion bluntly: 'No Marrow in its Bones.' While fashion editors enthused as usual over Anderson's wardrobe, Robert Garland, in the *New York World Tribune*, noting that 'Judith Anderson moves with a vast serenity of talent' in the midst of the play's 'chitting' and 'chatting,' makes the usual wish that 'she'd get a play worthy of her endeavors.'[70]

Divided by Three ran for only 31 performances. But for Anderson it was 'one of the grandest and most exciting experiences in my theatre life.' McClintic is 'a thrilling director and a grand person,' she wrote Lehman from Miami, where she was vacationing. Lehman appears to have sent Anderson a copy of Robinson Jeffers' poem 'Solstice,' an adaptation of the Medea myth that would be published in *Solstice and Other Poems* in 1935; and she was already imagining McClintic as the director of a version of *Medea* written by Jeffers. 'Darling,

---

70 *WP* 11 Sep 1938: TT3; *NYT* 3 Oct 1934: 24; *NYWT* Sep 1934; BDE 3 Oct 1934, NYPL.

the Jeffers situation is all wrong,' she wrote Lehman. 'I wanted him to simplify Medea, the Baker, I think it is, translation is of course magnificent, but at the time we were dreaming of doing it, we wanted a simpler form.' 'But your idea is entrancing,' she went on, 'no I haven't read it but will do so as soon as I return to New York… I shall present the idea to [McClintic] after I have reread the poem and then tell you what happens.' [71]

McClintic was equally pleased with Anderson. But he had his own, more businesslike, plans for her. In a stroke of genius, he paired her with Helen Menken in *The Old Maid*, Zoe Akins' adaptation of the 1924 Edith Wharton novella.[72]

Anderson had known and admired Menken since she appeared in her first major hit, *Seventh Heaven* in 1924, when Anderson was making a splash in *Cobra*. She had been a child actor, the daughter of deaf parents, rising through burlesque and stock to stardom in *Seventh Heaven*. Described as 'an emotional actress with the lovely face of a heroine of romance' and a 'darkly emotional, clear-edged' voice, she had briefly been married to Humphrey Bogart when he was a struggling young theatrical actor. Menken's 'haunting eyes and wistful smile' made her a perfect fit for the tragic role of Charlotte Lovell, whose illegitimate daughter is brought up thinking her aunt Delia – played by Anderson – is her mother. [73]

Two weeks into rehearsals, Anderson telegraphed McClintic rapturously. 'I am just walking around my house acting like a fool mad drunk with the riches you have given me and drenched in beauty,' she wrote; 'thank you so much.

---

71   Anderson to Lehman, 14 Nov 1934, from c/o Mahoney, Miami Beach, Florida, UCSB.
72   *NYT* 26 Nov 1934: 13.
73   Obituary, *NYT* 28 Mar 1966: 33; *WP* 5 May 1918: SM5; *CSM* 30 Sep 1924: 6; A.M. Sperber and Eric Lax, *Bogart*, 1997, 33–7.

Do you mind if I love you both very much. Judy.'[74]

When *The Old Maid* opened at the Empire Theatre on 7 January 1935, Anderson's 'glowing performance' drew the admiration of the critics. 'Miss Anderson... settles with magnificent and impressive dignity to an effectively repressed style of acting that becomes her greatly,' Burns Mantle wrote in the *Chicago Daily Tribune*. 'Although her Delia has a calm, sure, deliberate manner, her blood is hot and her determination terrible,' Brooks Atkinson wrote in the *New York Times*. 'Without a single nervous gesture, Miss Anderson drives through the play with remorseless vitality.' But the reviews were mixed: some critics did not like Menken's characterisation of the tortured Charlotte, and the play was damned with faint praise as having 'a strong feminine appeal.'[75]

After a faltering start, however, *The Old Maid* became a firm favourite with audiences. Its appeal was helped by the stunning drawings and photos of the striking pair of cousins, one fair and beguiling and the other dark and stern. Anderson's enthusiasm had worn off by April. 'What news,' she demanded of Lehman in a letter of 3 April 1935. 'I have absolutely none, except for the fact that I am working, which is a constant source of surprise to me, A that I am working, B that "The Old Maid" has this much of a kick in her.' 'Business is very good,' she continued, 'and we are likely to run on for quite some time. I am personally contracted until the 1st of June, and I would like very much to kiss the old girl goodbye then, its no fun a pretty silly nice play, no fire of emotion literature, acting anything.'[76]

---

74 Anderson to McClintic, tel 21 Dec 1934, Cornell Papers.
75 *NYT* 8 Jan 1935: 26; *CDT* 20 Jan 1935: D3; *WSJ* 11 Jan 1935: 13; *Variety* 14 Jan 1935: 1; *CSM* 12 Jan 1935: 8.
76 *WP* 15 Mar 1936: SS1; 17 Mar 1935: A1; *NYT* 31 Mar 1935: X1; drawing Menken by MARCUS, *NYT* 30 Dec 1934: X1; full page photo Anderson and Mencken by Vandamm, 17 Feb 1935: X2; Anderson in wedding gown, *The Stage*, Feb 1935, cover;

Anderson hoped to go to London to play in *Come of Age* in the fall. To her surprise, however, *The Old Maid* was controversially awarded that year's Pulitzer prize; and it immediately leapt to first place at the box office. 'Silly Old Maid got the Pulitzer,' she wrote morosely to Lehman. 'That wretched medal threw my fine plans from high to low gear… felt that I should stay with this really dull and depressing opus and make a little money for a change.'[77]

She needed the money. During the summer of 1935 her sister, Did, began to exhibit signs of the mental disturbance that would hospitalise her for many years. Their mother was in England visiting Frank, who had settled there, and Anderson had to manage this tragic emergency as well as earn enough money to support her mother and Did. As she trudged through a summer of *Old Maid* performances, she also had to deal with the sudden death of her dear friend, Rosalie Watson – dead at 36, leaving two small boys. 'Peter darling,' she wrote at the end of August. 'So much to say and no heart to say it with! My Rosalie Watson died a few weeks ago and shattered my world around me – my sister is desperately ill – and "The Old Maid" goes on forever!'[78]

After a two-week vacation, she set off with a heavy heart on tour at the end of September accompanied by a maid and her two dogs. As John Scott noted in the *Los Angeles Times*, 'Practically dead and buried these many years, except for sporadic exceptions, the "road" is now coming very much alive.' Ethel Barrymore was to tour in *The Constant Wife*,

---

New Yorker, 2 Mar 1935; photo Anderson and Menken in *Old Maid* by Alfred Cheney Johnston; Anderson to Lehman, 3 Apr 1935, UCSB.
77   Anderson to Lehman, 3 Apr 1935, UCSB; *NYT* 14 Apr 1935: X1; Anderson to Maurice Browne, 29 May 1934, Browne Papers; *Variety* May 7, 1935: 1; *NYT* 7 May: 1, 2; 7 May: 21; 8 May: 21; 12 May: X1; 19 May: X2; 24 Oct 1935: 23; *CSM* 7 May 1935: 18; *Variety* 8 May: 68; 15 May 1935: 53, 55; *WSJ* 10 May 1935: 13; *WP* 12 May: M1; 12 May: B2; 12 Jul 1935: 9.
78   Anderson to Lehman, 30 Aug 1935, UCSB; *NYT* 19 Jun 1935: 19.

Katharine Cornell in repertory including *Romeo and Juliet*, Grace George in *Kind Lady*, and Eva Le Gallienne with her repertory company, bringing classics like *The Master Builder*, *John Gabriel Bjorkman* and *Camille* to the provinces. [79]

The "road" as Scott described it, 'refers to the many hamlets, towns and cities visited by touring theatrical companies.' The road for Anderson would involve eight months of travel, 12,940 miles through 79 cities and 31 states before she was free of the 'old girl.' As she wrote Lehman in her erratic spelling, 'Going to carrear, yes I can see that wrong dear, all over the country.'[80]

In money terms the tour was a brilliant success. *Variety* reported that the 10 days of one-night stands between Boston and Pittsburgh had played mostly to standing room. In Detroit the public 'flocked in droves.' In Cincinnati they were accorded a 'powerful' reception. Chicago as usual welcomed Anderson with enthusiasm. *The Old Maid* was 'an affair of great distinction,' Charles Collins wrote in the *Chicago Daily Tribune*. Both actresses, with their 'vivid personalities and impressive careers,' gave 'notable performances in contrasting veins – Miss Anderson as the calculating woman of the world, Miss Menken as the tremulous, romantic heroine who unluckily bore an illegitimate child to her cousin's ex-lover.'[81]

When *The Old Maid* opened in Los Angeles on 25 February 1936, *Variety* reported that 'Hollywood's first nighters, decked out in gala finery, filed out of the Biltmore half hour before midnight wondering where among film-dom's first line of actresses could be found two players who could match the performances they had just seen.' 'To match their interpretations,' the reporter went on, 'is to achieve near perfection in dramatic art.'[82]

---

79 *NYT* Sep 3, 1935: 24; *LAT* 7 Sep 1935: 5.
80 Anderson to Lehman, 30 Aug 1935, UCSB.
81 *Variety* 13 Nov: 53; 27 Nov: 55; 4 Dec 1935: 47; *CDT* 24 Dec 1935: 13.
82 *Variety* 26 Feb 1936: 3. See also *LAT* 26 Feb 1936: A16.

Anderson had continued to dash off her ungrammatical letters to Peter Lehman. 'A word or two about punctuation grammer etc.,' she wrote breathlessly in April 1935, 'what does it matter you know that I love you deeply and that I'm only a one syllable girl and not a correspondent and what does it really matter if there are two r's and one L or vice versa I always was willing to grant you all the brains of the family and I didn't stop to figure where we were going to get the looks from.'

Lehman had written her that he had not married after all. 'I'm glad you didn't marry her though darling,' she replied. 'I think its nicer the way it is don't you, well you know very well what I mean.' 'Darling do write me all your news,' she continued, 'how are you feeling what are you doing whom are you seeing fun you are having it if you are in love or out again… goodnight my dear love, be well be happy and think tenderly of me often. Always & through all time Your Peg.'[83]

As the *Old Maid* tour came closer to San Francisco, Anderson wrote happily, 'turn down the bed, and get my slippers out, put out the Cat and pour out the Gin.' But Lehman, wary of being stung again as he had been two years before, was full of anxiety. 'I wrote you a long letter, self-analytical that I didn't send,' he wrote to Noël Sullivan at the end of January 1936. He had been for two days 'unequal in body to anything,' but now he was 'inwardly sure and at ease.' He would not risk opening night of the *Old Maid* when he had to work next day, he told Sullivan. 'If Friday would do as well for you, I'll chance it, & prepare for it, thus.' He seems to have got cold feet, however, and left town, pleading illness. After she had left Los Angeles, Anderson wrote in anguish, 'Dear

---

83   Anderson to Lehman, 5? Apr 1935 from New York, UCSB.

Peter, my dear lost Peter, what has happened to our sweet love, has it gone, was my intuition right at our first reunion, have you built a wall that has no open gateway for me, and if I am right why?' 'Today a letter from Peg brought everything else in the way of pain and pang,' Lehman wrote Sullivan when he received this letter.[84]

Lehman must have replied confessing his fears and his wish to marry her. 'Peter Peter: I am more ridiculously happy than I have been in ages,' she wrote him in early April. 'I had been for the first time lonely for you, it never occurred to me that you could shut me out, you were always supposed to be there, silences did not matter, the love was enduring but richer with time.' 'I went to you flying, more free than ever before,' she continued, 'but the tables were turned, you had withdrawn health excusing but not fooling me all the while.' 'Don't you know that if it had been financially possible I would have gone to you years ago,' she concluded. 'And what can I do now. I thought I would have the summer to laze and holiday as I pleased, but I have family affairs to arrange that will be more difficult and painful but that must be done if I am to have any peace at all, how long it will take I don't know, but I must finish it finally and as comfortably as possible for all concerned…'[85]

The two seem to have come to some understanding over the next few weeks. In early May, when she got back to New York, where her mother had joined her, she wrote Lehman about her family problems and told him she had 'talked to Ma pretty seriously about you read her one of your letters she said he seems to love you can he support you?' But ambition stood in the way of love once more. 'I am having dinner with

---

84   Anderson to Lehman, 5 Dec 1935 from Cincinnati; posted 29 Mar 1936 from Dallas, Tx; posted 14 Apr [1936] from Nashville, UCSB; Lehman to Sullivan, 28 Jan [1936]; Sunday [23? Feb 1936]; 31 Mar [1936], Sullivan Papers.
85   Anderson to Lehman, from Kansas City, Mo, UCSB.

Kit Cornell tonight which is setting me in a dither,' she wrote Lehman. 'Guthrie cabled her about something and I am in a fine state of palpitation to know.' McClintic's exciting plan, telegraphed from London, was to cast her as Queen Gertrude in *Hamlet*, with the brilliant young British actor John Gielgud as co-star.[86]

---

86 Anderson to Lehman, from The Navarro, New York, 6 May 1936, UCSB; *NYT* 8 Jun 1936: 22.

Judith Anderson and John Gielgud in Hamlet *1936*

Author's collection

Chapter Sixteen

Co-starring John Gielgud 1936–7

… the best Queen in Hamlet anyone in this generation ever has seen –
Brooklyn Daily Eagle

With the prospect of appearing in a great play with one of the greatest young actors, Anderson's plans to travel with Lehman during the summer were quickly shelved. McClintic wanted her to go to England with him to talk with Gielgud and the designer Jo Mielziner. 'I wanted so much to be with you,' she wrote Lehman on 13 June, 'but the fine finger of fate seemed to direct me in the opposite direction – away from you.' 'Guthrie wanted me very much to go to England… and Clemence Dane was eager for me to come over and see about a possible production of Come of Age next Spring.' 'I love you & miss you,' she added, '& wait for Xmas.' 'My plans are changed, in large (I think) and in particular (certainly),' a disappointed Lehman wrote Noël Sullivan.[87]

Guthrie McClintic had seen and noted the 28-year-old Gielgud in his London production of *Richard of Bordeaux* in spring 1933, when he had made a three-month sweep through Europe studying the latest drama. When Gielgud triumphed

---

87 *NYT* 19 Jul 1936: X1, 2; Anderson to Lehman from The Navarro, New York, 13 Jun 1936, UCSB; Lehman to Sullivan, 22 May [1936], Sullivan Papers.

in fall 1934 in his own, fresh, production of *Hamlet*, McClintic quickly began negotiating to bring the young star to Broadway. Meanwhile, Gielgud had 'captured' London with his production of *Romeo and Juliet*, in which he alternated as the hero with his rival, the 25-year-old Laurence Olivier, with Peggy Ashcroft as Juliet.[88]

John Gielgud was born to the stage. His great aunt was Ellen Terry, the famous Victorian actress, and his mother was, according to him, 'a great actress who had retired very early.' In 1929 he was part of the innovative young company put together by Harcourt Williams at the Old Vic, the 'people's theatre' where his 1931 *Hamlet*, with its pace and psychological interpretation, was hailed by leading critic, James Agate, as 'the high-water mark of English Shakespearean acting in our time.' Like Anderson, he had a voice, in Laurence Olivier's words, 'that wooed the world.'[89]

In London, making her headquarters at the Ritz, Anderson joined Gielgud, Mielziner and McClintic in their noisy late-night discussions and researched in the National Portrait Gallery for Restoration clothes and hairstyles for the production. She spent a 'heavenly' weekend in Kent with Clemence Dane, where Dane fashioned a bust of Anderson. Best of all, she was able to visit her brother, Frank, and they drove together to Scotland – 'my native hearth,' as she wrote Lehman in late July.[90]

Thoughts of her deserted lover haunted her throughout the summer. 'Peter Darling – Against this magnificent silence that you have imposed upon me I shall try to write to you,' she wrote him when she returned from Scotland. 'Oh Peter

---

88   *NYT* 18 Jun 1933: X1; 15 Nov 1934: 25; 7 Apr: X1; 12 Apr: 27; 18 Oct 1935: 27; *WP* 5 Jul 1935: 18.
89   Margaret Webster, *The Same Only Different*, 1969, 45–50.
90   Johnathan Croall, *Gielgud: A Theatrical Life, 1904–2000*, 2000, 220–21; Anderson to Lehman, 28 Jul 1936, postcard from Edinburgh, UCSB.

how I wished for you in Scotland… we went up to visit my Aunt Father's sister in Arbroath & saw the home of my fathers birth & graveyards & relatives it was all very sentimental and beautiful – as we drove in to Arbroath a band of kilties came to greet us The sky was shining & the air crisp & caressing & I was deliriously happy & sad & lonely.'[91]

A few days later she was more cheerful. 'I am going to be gay tonight & go to the theatre – Diana Winyard [Wynyard] in a new play directed by Guthrie McClintic… if plans go through I shall come back here & play during Coronation [probably referring to *Come of Age*]… I hope you will take your holiday here… '[92]

Anderson arrived back in New York on 27 August, followed a few days later by Gielgud. She sent Lehman a hurried note as she prepared for their first rehearsal: 'I am full of fittings, photographers, and rehearsals to begin tomorrow morning.' 'I have crowned Gertie [Queen Gertrude] with a titian halo!' she added. 'I look pretty odd in the daylight, but then I am a night girl… ' The next night, after the rehearsal, she scribbled at the bottom of the letter, 'if you don't come on to see me – you must to see hear & wonder at Gielgud – he is magnificent.'[93]

As they prepared for their out of town opening in Toronto on 30 September, Anderson wrote Lehman in high excitement of Gielgud's 'genius.' Years later she recalled her feeling that she was in the presence of a master and hated each rehearsal day to end. 'Danish government has invited Gielgud to come over with the company,' she wrote Lehman, '– then we might play Norway and Sweden & to London.'[94]

Gielgud was also happy, despite what he described as

---

91   Anderson to Lehman, 14 Aug 1936 from London, UCSB.
92   Anderson to Lehman, posted London 14 Aug 1936, UCSB; *NYT* 15 Aug 1936: 6.
93   Anderson to Lehman, 2 Sep 1936 from The Dorset, New York, UCSB.
94   Anderson to Lehman, 21 Sep 1936 from The Dorset, New York. UCSB.

'appallingly and damply hot' weather. He got on well with McClintic, he wrote Peggy Ashcroft, and he liked the production very much. The women [Anderson and Lillian Gish, who played Ophelia] were both excellent, as well as being dears; the American accents were not bad; and the preliminary photos were very good indeed. 'Anderson has five beautiful dresses,' he wrote his mother a few days later. They had two dress rehearsals at 2 and 10 the day before they opened, and completely rearranged the last scene hours before the curtain went up. The Toronto critics hailed the production as a triumph.⁹⁵

After four days in Toronto (which Gielgud dismissed as a 'one horse town') and two in Rochester, *Hamlet* opened at the Empire in New York on 8 October 1936. Gielgud is 'young, slender and handsome,' Brooks Atkinson wrote in the *New York Times* the next day, 'and he plays his part with extraordinary grace and winged intelligence.' 'This is no roaring, robustious Hamlet,' he continued, 'but an appealing young man brimming over with grief.'

> *His suffering is that of a cultivated youth whose affections are warm and whose honor is bright. Far from being a traditional Hamlet, beating the bass notes of some mighty lines, Mr Gielgud speaks the lines with the quick spontaneity of a modern man. His emotions are keen. He looks on tragedy with the clarity of the mind's eye.*

'This is an admirable *Hamlet* that requires comparison with the best,' Atkinson concluded. 'For intellectual beauty, in fact, it ranks with the best.' But, he added, it lacked 'a coarser ferocity to Shakespeare's tragedy that is sound theatre.'⁹⁶

---

95 Gielgud to Ashcroft, 21 Sep 1936; to mother, 26 Sep & 2 Oct 1936, in *Gielgud's Letters*, 2004; *NYT* 1 Oct 1936: 28.
96 *NYT* 9 Oct 1936: 30.

Although it was clearly Gielgud's play, critics also heaped praise on Anderson's lushly sexual interpretation of Gertrude. Atkinson admired the way she 'abandoned the matronly stuffiness that usually plagues that part and has given us a woman of strong and bewildered feeling.' The *Brooklyn Daily Eagle* flatly proclaimed Anderson 'the best Queen in *Hamlet* anyone in this generation ever has seen.'[97]

The public loved the new *Hamlet*. Allene Talmey, in *Vogue*, had portrayed the audience who usually attended McClintic's first nights as 'the intellectuals, a bit dowdy, somber.' But *Variety* described the *Hamlet* first-nighters as 'the ritziest first-night audience in years,' and they proved anything but sombre. 'The first night was extraordinary,' Gielgud wrote to his mother. He had received huge applause on his entrance, and, after 15 curtain calls, people, headed by Noël Coward, rushed backstage in great emotion.[98]

E C Sherburne, in the *Christian Science Monitor*, described a stage 'always dazzling with color… for the play has been costumed in a sort of Van Dyke cavalier style – silks, jewels, laces – rather than in the soberer manner associated with the usual Elizabethan costumes or those of the legendary Denmark of this tragedy.' He particularly admired the scene between Hamlet and the Queen in her chamber for its 'richness of characterization, tragic force, heartbreak and variety of emotion as acted by Mr Gielgud and Judith Anderson, for both make their roles powerful antagonists in the duel of reproaches between mother and son.'[99]

Illustrated by Steichen's arresting photograph of Gielgud and Anderson 'twisted like ribbons,' *Vogue* welcomed 'the season's first Shakespearian venture into adultery, incest, and

---

97 *BDE* 18 Oct 1936, NYPL.
98 *Vogue* 1 Sep 1936: 85, 154; Gielgud to mother, 12 Oct 1936, in *Gielgud's Letters*.
99 *CSM* 13 Oct 1936: 7.

murder.' 'If you buy *Stage* & *Vanity Fair* for October – you can see some pretty nice pictures of your girlfriend,' Anderson wrote Lehman in mid-October. 'The opening night was all that I dreamed people were entranced & moved either to a voluble torrent of ecstasy or a glistening silence.'[100]

Lehman appears to have forgiven Anderson for scrapping their summer reunion and was now planning to join her for Christmas in New York. 'I expect a daily letter, and don't you expect any answers,' she had warned him as she began rehearsals, 'but if you are a very good boy and very entertaining I might surprise you.' 'Keep well, darling, and buy your ticket for Christmas time,' she wrote. 'I am longing to see you.' Swept up once more in her aura, he wrote Sullivan of the 'rainbow of feeling' her letter radiated – 'The most wonderful letter I think ever my eyes moved over – emotion & wit, excitement and laughter, and something so loving deep that if its not real she is the world's miracle.' 'Another letter like this,' he concluded, '& I'll have to go to New York Christmas or wherever they have *Hamlet* by that time – if I fly or walk.'[101]

But he continued to be wary of the spell she cast over him. 'I do not see how I can get into the clear of it, without going to New York,' he wrote Sullivan in November. Meanwhile, Anderson urged him to be bold. 'Peter Sweet,' she wrote. 'What to say to your letter – reams words words words that won't prove a thing. The seeing – being with – enjoying things learning each other with delight or disappointment that will do it.' 'It's a gambol [gamble] Peter for me as for you,' she urged him, '– is it worth it – to know the strength of the enchantment that has bound us so strongly though the years & distance & our separate flights – mine that have grounded

---

100 *Vogue* 15 Oct 1936: 76–77; Anderson to Lehman, 20 Oct 1936, UCSB.
101 Anderson to Lehman, 2 Sep 1936, UCSB; Lehman to Sullivan, 26 Sep [1936], Sullivan Papers.

me always in the same heart.' With increasing cold feet Lehman wrote to Sullivan that he feared he had 'over-said [himself] in letters to JA.' 'Though I dread the Eastern winter I shall have to go to get free,' he continued. 'For your most private ear, I report that deep inward I shall always have to be free.' 'Can any enchantment change that?' he asked.[102]

When Lehman did arrive just before Christmas 1936, he found that enchantment irresistible.

Attending Anderson's matinee, he told Sullivan, he 'endured an excitement almost ravaging' and at moments her performance shook him 'in the remembered way of Duse.' In person she was even more extraordinary – 'talk & sight & touch & laughter & passion – unbelievable mélange, each moment hardly credible.' He hardly noticed New York's near-freezing weather and the rain that lashed the city as he was plunged into Anderson's chaotic hours – 'Sunday morning 4; Monday 5.15; this morning 8.10… I wish I was five years younger but will live in the present gratefully… She stirs me, enchants me, fills my nerves with dreams. Her raillery, her fantasy… her beautiful freedom, her communication with the dogs – sensitive to them over & through everything – everything. Three weeks or three years, it is unmatched being. And whatever lies ahead, I have done right to *come*.'[103]

Anderson's mother had returned to England to live with Frank, and she herself had moved to an apartment hotel at 1 Fifth Avenue, where Gielgud took the apartment below. 'Right down in Greenwich Village, on the 24th floor with three windows in each room, marvellous view, huge sitting room – and service,' he told his mother. Lehman's visit was filled with the gay social life of a Broadway star: lunch with

---

102   Lehman to Sullivan, 16 Nov [1936]; 29 Nov 1936, Sullivan Papers; Anderson to Lehman, Fri [20 Nov], posted 24 Nov 1936, UCSB.
103   Lehman to Sullivan, Tuesday nite [22 Dec 1936] from Hotel Brevoort, Sullivan Papers.

the Van Vechtens, Fanny Hurst and Bennett Cerf; a visit to Helen Hayes' country house with Gielgud, Lillian Gish, Noël Coward and Beatrice Lillie; drinks with Gielgud, who he found 'unintelligible in speech – though every word fell clear in the theatre – and beautiful and feminine in person.' 'When a young man of 23 or 24 came in before we left,' he told Sullivan, 'he took on an obvious glitter, & mentioned casually next day that he was an hour late for Alex Woollcott's dinner, though Peg and I left betimes and he was dressed when we came in.'[104]

As his visit drew to an end, Lehman wrote to Sullivan of his intoxication: 'Forty thousand tongues could not describe the increase of appetite raised by the setting devised by that personality. The potency of youth springs from it, and the heart and ringing ears can wait on their future – if any.' But they seem to have parted with a mutual agreement that their lives were too different for marriage to be possible. 'I'm glad you are getting on with the book,' Anderson wrote Lehman a few weeks later, '– that is your happiness Peter – & that's what it must be – misgivings no more – I had them yes – but its clear now – you for your work & your people – I for my channel where the current takes me. I haven't enough to give you nor you me, but what I have will last always.'[105]

Hamlet closed on Broadway on 30 January 1937 to huge houses, with over 500 standing to see the final matinee and evening performances of what had been a record run. The company then moved on to triumphant short runs in Washington DC (where Anderson lunched with First Lady, Eleanor Roosevelt), Boston and Philadelphia.[106]

---

104   Gielgud to mother, 1 Nov 1936; 4 Jan 1937, in *Gielgud's Letters*; Lehman to Sullivan, Tue nite, Sullivan Papers.
105   Lehman to Sullivan, Christmas [25 Dec 1936], Sullivan Papers; Anderson to Lehman, posted 6 Feb 1937, USCB.
106   *NYT* 31 Jan 1937: 48; *WP* 8 Feb 1937: 9; Gielgud to mother, 1 & 17 Feb 1937.

As Gielgud sailed back to England, Anderson planned to follow him soon after to visit her mother and Frank and to pursue her dream of presenting *Come of Age* in London. But an offer from Lux Theatre to broadcast *Mary of Scotland* from Los Angeles brought her to California in late March. 'If I go I shall stay with Mary [Servoss] at Villa Carlotta, and with Pringie [Aileen Pringle] too I guess so if you are interested you will know where to find me,' she wrote Lehman. 'I shall stay only a few weeks and then go back and to England… if you are in a good mood I might let you show me your desert.' 'I am longing to see the Lobos haunt again – & you too – & I promise not to slay you, if you assure me of like consideration,' she wrote him as they made plans to meet.[107]

'Judith is in Hollywood,' Lehman wrote Sullivan, '– wants to see you, to see me, wants to go to the desert to which I have truly said I cannot escort her. Nor can I go down, these weeks at all events: so I ask her when can she come up, that I will show her the Cats, Tor House, Ennisfree, the Farm, with your due cooperation.' 'Good Easter,' he concluded: 'at the moment I have less faith than usual in resurrections, – anyway the woe of Friday suits me better.' As he waited, with apprehension, Anderson's visit, he mapped out with Sullivan a plan for 'the re-orientation and reconstruction which I can no longer put off… that I dream of making into a working program for a final phase… this coming summer and winter.'[108]

---

107 Anderson to Lehman, posted 17 Mar; 21 Apr [Mar?] 1937, UCSB.
108 Lehman to Sullivan, Thur [25 Mar 1937]; Sun [28 Mar 1937], Sullivan Papers.

Judith Anderson and Laurence Olivier in Macbeth *at the Old Vic 1937*
Lebrecht Music & Arts / Alamy Stock Photo

Chapter Seventeen

Marriage and Olivier 1937–8

Darling I consider it my finest performance
Judith Anderson to Noël Sullivan, 1937, on her marriage

When Anderson and Lehman did meet in mid-April, however, the old magic returned. 'Darling I hated furiously everything at the last moment,' Anderson wrote Lehman after her visit to Berkeley, '& most of all you moving swiftly into the dark night. It was so stupid that we weren't with you – but frustration seems to be our middle name – but I will work something out before I leave – I will see my agent tomorrow & know more about time then… I loved every minute of our hours together & even when I was at the other end of the street.' Another visit early in May left Anderson with 'a sheer shining mist of delight & beauty of the past days & the promise of life ahead… At this moment I want more than anything to come back. Then drive with you across the continent – but we will both think more about that – in that case I wouldn't come back till you were ready to leave. It might be a good idea to weather a trip like that together… I live in the beauty of our gentle days – be happy & well my darling… '[109]

Two weeks later they were married by a justice of the peace in Kingman, Arizona. 'The marriage would have tickled

---
109 Anderson to Lehman, 14 Apr; 3 May 1937 from Los Angeles, UCSB.

you to death,' Lehman wrote to Sullivan a few days later, '& Peg got the giggles and we hung on the wire between tears and roaring laughter.' 'Darling I consider it my finest performance,' Anderson scrawled on a joint postcard.[110]

From Kingman they set off across the continent, visiting friends along the way. 'You will gather I am in heaven,' Lehman wrote Sullivan. 'Last night her beauty at dinner… took my breath and wet my eyes, as it dazzled all others. Very pride-making, all of it, – and best of all the sense of daring is supplanted by confidence.' After a week in New York, crowned by a farewell party at McClintic's till dawn with 'Fania [Marinoff], Carlo [Van Vechten], Florence Reed, Helen Menken & Henry, Morris Ernst, Margalo Gilmore & her husband, Lil Gish, etc, etc, with Kit Cornell calling from Boston at midnight,' the honeymooners sailed for England on the *Roosevelt* on 6 June 1937.[111]

In London Anderson was immediately caught up in lengthy negotiations over *Come of Age*, introducing her new husband to her mother and brother and her numerous theatrical friends. They visited Clemence Dane at Hollywych Farm in Kent and John Gielgud and his partner John Perry at Foulslough Farm in Essex. From Foulslough Farm Lehman wrote Sullivan, a homosexual who was intensely interested in human relationships, 'The Johns are a ménage you would delight to observe, and would approve as the best that that relation can achieve – or any other.'[112]

---

110 Lehman to Sullivan, 21 May 1937, on El Tovar, Grand Canyon notepaper, Sullivan Papers. See SFE 19 May 1937, NYPL; *LAT* 20 May 1937: 16.
111 Lehman to Sullivan, 21 May 1937; 15 Jun [1937], Sullivan Papers.
112 Peggy Ashcroft to Lillian Gish, 23 Jul 1937; see also Gielgud to Gish, 14 Aug 1937, Gish Papers; Lehman to Sullivan, 8 Jul [1937] from Foulslough Farm, Sullivan Papers.

In mid-July, when *Come of Age* seemed reasonably certain, Anderson and Lehman set off for a two-month trip through the Continent. By the time they got back to Paris in early September, the plans for *Come of Age* had fallen through, and the London Old Vic management had invited Anderson to play Lady Macbeth opposite the 30-year-old Laurence Olivier in a production by the French director Michel Saint-Denis. By the end of the month she had made up her mind to accept the role, and departed for London, leaving Lehman in Paris, where he hoped to get some writing done.[113]

Cracks (or reality) had already begun to appear in their perfect bliss in New York; and London, with its inevitable family and career stresses, had given Lehman 'strange unseizable threats' to their 'undreamed of delights, unimagined adventures.' Anderson, in turn, had noticed his tightness with money and his tendency to procrastinate. During their European trip they had several 'rows' that Lehman shrank from detailing to Sullivan, and back in Paris, he was hoping for 'progress in conjugality as distinguished from amatory success.'[114]

Before Anderson left for London, however, they had a major confrontation, with each hurling insults that were impossible to forget. 'I *could* not write,' Lehman wrote Sullivan after Anderson left. 'I have lived an alternative of ecstasies and *de profundis* miseries incredible now to even me.' 'I have the *greatest* dreads for this girl,' he concluded. 'What we shall salvage from it, I do not even guess.'[115]

---

113 Lehman to Sullivan, 25 Jul [1937] from Paris; 5 Aug 1937, postcard from Cortina D'Ampezzo; 26 Aug 1937, postcard from Zurich; 5 Sep [1937] from Paris, Sullivan Papers; Gielgud to Gish, 14 Aug 1937, Gish Papers; Gielgud to Anderson, 9 Sep [1937], UCSB; Anderson to McClintic, 11 Sep [1937] from Paris, Cornell Papers; *NYT* 1 Aug 1937: 138; *MG* Sep 1937: 12.
114 Lehman to Sullivan, 8 Jul; 9 Jun; 5 Sep [1937]. See also 13 Jul [1937], Sullivan Papers.
115 Lehman to Sullivan, 30 Sep [1937] from Saint-Malo, Sullivan Papers.

In a letter to Lehman a week later, Anderson tried to get to the root of their 'infantile misunderstandings.' 'I wonder if you envy despise or hate me most sometimes,' she wrote, '– I cannot forget the words said I cannot forget that you the man I married – have insulted me more than any human being I have ever known.

> *Your love wanted to stand between me & adversity enhance good minimize ill – it is not irony that the reverse happened – it is an illness have you medicine to cure Peter – can you be positive that you would not loose your temper & give voice to it again. I don't think I would be responsible for my actions if ever I heard such words again.*

'I have compared the days of our marriage with my life before it,' she went on, '– I know what I have given up & what I have adjusted to – I knew that I have & done the wifely duties the laundry & the packing – but then you were doing no more than you always had done & I was doing much more than I ever had done before.'[116]

'You should remember Peter that the last rows were all of your making,' she wrote 10 days later, '– Vienna Tre Croce St Malo & two when we returned to Paris.'

> *I have detailed their beginnings & you know them as well as I – & when you called me a fishwife & I retailed in kind… I know that the trouble with you is that when you are wrong you won't admit it – with your fine command of words you use them trust them & convince yourself that you & your meaning is right as with Fishwife… You say that you would not abdicate your way of life – do you mean that I should mine completely isn't marriage a 50–50 business.*

'I have never found your mind dull,' she continued, '– nor

---

116 Anderson to Lehman, 8 Oct 1937 to Paris, written Thu [7 Oct 1937], UCSB.

have I been uneasy at the prospect of your conversation – or anybody elses for that matter.

> *It was unfortunate for me that in my youth I didnt have a good education – it is shameful to me now that I haven't used the years in more study – I have no terror at the prospect of life in Berkeley I have qualms & regret that I would not be able to appreciate & enjoy & control the talk at my table… Because I commented on the faculty life as against my own you let your imagination pick it up & make a monstrous ogre. Im not as stupid as all that Peter – who wouldn't be nervous about leaving all ones friends & way of living to take up an entirely different life among different people.*
>
> *I married you because I loved you – not physically enough perhaps – & the new knowledge of your life with women has shocked and amazed me – & has made the sexual adjustment more difficult – I thought we had more than enough in common to give one another – to found an unshakable life of goodness & glory & I respected you.*
>
> *But we have lived together & I know you now – & you me – & you have let me see the innermost of your being – such that I know you would never have let your friends see & I find you confused complicated inhibited & evasive. Of course you are saying – 'but you are all of those things' – yes but Im not evasive. Im not afraid Peter & if Im wrong I'll admit it.*[117]

Macbeth – undertaken in the face of this major emotional crisis – was a troubled production. Laurence Olivier had made his

---

117   Anderson to Lehman, posted 20 Oct 1937, written Sun? 17 Oct 1937 to Paris, UCSB.

name as a Shakespearean actor two years before when he alternated the roles of Romeo and Mercutio with John Gielgud. Already a movie star and well-regarded actor in modern plays, he was determined to consolidate his reputation as a classical actor when the Old Vic featured him as their star during 1937 and 1938. By October 1937 he had played in *Hamlet*, *Twelfth Night* and *Henry V*, all produced by Tyrone Guthrie to mixed reviews.[118] For his first professional attempt at *Macbeth*, he had invited the experimental teacher-director Michel Saint-Denis to mount the production – the Frenchman's first experience of directing a Shakespearean play.

Michel Saint-Denis, the nephew and follower of the French theatrical legend Jacques Copeau, had established his innovative drama school, the London Theatre Studio, two years previously. Although he was enthusiastically supported by emerging actors such as Gielgud and Olivier, the public and most critics were less welcoming of his 'foreign' ideas. His concept of *Macbeth* was highly unusual, with lighting, stage setting and costumes designed to reflect Macbeth's delusional state of mind, his signature use of fantastic masks for the witches and Banquo, and mask-like makeup for Olivier and Anderson. Saint-Denis 'let his imagination run amok,' Olivier recollected. 'We arty lot were at this time going through a phase of avid preoccupation with size. Everything had to suggest godlike proportions, and the results could be pretty extraordinary.' 'The audience was given some sort of warning by one's appearance with deliberately mask-like make-up,' he continued, 'but appearances, sets, costumes and props were none of them whole-heartedly abstract: it was "stylized".' 'Noël [Coward] nearly died laughing when he came to see it,' he added.[119]

---

118 *Observer* 3 Nov 1935: 19; *NYT* 6 Jan 1937: 19; MG 8 Apr 1937: 12.
119 Jane Baldwin, 'The Rediscovery of Michal Saint-Denis.' Introduction to Baldwin,

The choice of Anderson to play the important role of Lady Macbeth also added to the 'foreignness' of the production. She was unknown to the British public, although she had many admirers among its leading actors and playwrights. She and Olivier knew each other, probably from the time in 1929 when they crossed the Atlantic together in the *Aquitania* – he an unknown and she a respected star in *Strange Interlude*. They would certainly have become acquainted through longtime admirer Noël Coward when he appeared with Coward in *Private Lives* in 1931 and she was starring in *As You Desire Me*. Olivier had also appeared in several plays by Keith Winter, the playwright who lauded Anderson in *Come of Age*, placing her with Charles Laughton and Edith Evans (and 'perhaps' Laurence Olivier) as one of the three actors of the English speaking world who have 'genius of a quite staggering order.'[120]

In addition to these artistic problems, both Anderson and Olivier were going through major personal crises. Olivier had fallen in love with actress Vivien Leigh the previous year, and after the pair had appeared together in *Hamlet* at Elsinore, Denmark, in June 1937, they moved in together, each abandoning their spouse and child. As Olivier recollected in his *Confessions*, he 'had to steel myself for it [*Macbeth*], set my shoulders, brace my tights, put on my chain-mail jock-strap and hope for the best.' To add to the general disarray, Lilian Baylis, the legendary manager of the Old Vic, died suddenly two days before opening night. 'They had an appalling time before they opened,' John Gielgud wrote to Lillian Gish in early December, '– illness, postponement and finally the death

---

ed., *Michel Saint-Denis, Theatre: The Rediscovery of Style and Other Writings*, 2009; Laurence Olivier, *The Autobiography: Confessions of an Actor*, 1994, 111–12.
120 *NYT* 13 Jan 1931: 34; *CDT* 20 Jun 1936: 15; Winter, '*Come of Age*,' [Jan 1934], UCSB.

of Lilian Baylis the very night before.'[121]

The play opened on 27 November 1937 to mixed reviews. Olivier himself admitted that he had not been 'an unparalleled success.' The *Manchester Guardian* critic, A D, always ambivalent about the young Olivier, described him as an actor who went from strength to strength, but still put too much strain on his voice. Charles Morgan in the *New York Times* also criticised Olivier's speech, which he considered was 'violent at expense of beauty'; but, he conceded, his Macbeth was still interesting, 'doomed by own character.'[122]

Critics were less conflicted about Anderson's performance. A D was full of praise. 'Miss Anderson's performance suggests that she has been born with a rich technique in Shakespeare,' he wrote. 'She has nothing like the physical stature desirable in the present part, but she has almost everything else that it demands. Evil grandeur, iron, blood-rusted implacability, remorse, white lassitude, and the evocation of our pity – all these images and qualities are brought out by this fiend-like little Queen.' 'She takes the stage with authority,' wrote H H in the *Observer*, noting that she 'has come from America to show that experience in modern tragedy can be an asset to Lady Macbeth.' She did not escape criticism, however. Charles Morgan, in the *New York Times*, considered her Lady Macbeth a failure, despite the considerable reputation she brought from the United States. He found her interpretation confused – perhaps, he speculated, the result of differences between her and the director.[123]

Whatever the critics thought, the audiences came. 'In spite of a dreadful press,' John Gielgud wrote after attending an early performance, 'the theatre was packed yesterday

---

[121] *MG* 2 Jun 1937: 11; Olivier, *Autobiography*, 111–12; Gielgud to Gish, 4 Dec 1937, Gish Papers; *NYT* 26 Nov 1937: 2.
[122] Olivier, *Autobiography*, 111–12; *MG* 27 Nov 1937: 18; *NYT* 19 Dec 1937: 3.
[123] *MG* 27 Nov 1937: 18; *Observer* 28 Nov 1937: 13; *NYT* 19 Dec 1937: 3.

afternoon, when I went, and they are moving to the West End for four weeks at Christmas.' Although, in his opinion, the production was uneven, he considered it the best he'd seen. 'Judith is very good,' he told Lillian Gish, 'especially in her scenes with Larry, and the whole of her performance is finely conceived in a continuous line.' In particular, he wrote, 'She managed the sleep-walking scene, I thought, astonishingly well – never put down her lamp, as they always do, but used one hand for all the business, which I thought very clever and effective.' 'I am sure Judith must feel that it is a distinguished thing to have done,' he concluded, 'and worth all the agony she must have suffered, and though people are divided about her performance, it is a very distinguished debut for her in this country.'[124]

---

124 Gielgud to Gish, 4 Dec 1937, Gish Papers.

Interlude
Marriage and Career

Berkeley from the hills 1940, by Don Kingman

Chapter Eighteen

Faculty Wife 1938

*... now wouldn't it be perfect if I sign it
Your loving Wife Peg*
        Judith Anderson to Benjamin Lehman, January 1938

Judith Anderson and Ben 'Peter' Lehman September 1937, by Carl Van Vechten
                    Beinecke Library, Yale University

'I can't face another upset & will not be disturbed while I am contracted to give my dearest best,' Judith Anderson had written her new husband on 20 October 1937, as she prepared for the first rehearsal of *Macbeth*. 'Unless you can put suspicion out of your being & face facts honestly & hide nothing there is no foundation for our house – I know wherein I am wrong & I know where you are.'[125]

Sometime during the next few weeks, Lehman joined her in London. By the time he left for New York and California on 27 December, they had resolved their differences. 'We will have glorious new year my darling. Peg,' she telegraphed Lehman on New Year's Eve.

On paper she wrote:

This is the last day of the year darling & I shall make all kinds of resolutions for next… I hope we have a beautiful year Peter my darling. These past few weeks have been clarifying & have filled me with hope & courage – we should make it – we must make it – not go but glow in glory & dignity of it being – our line must be like that… I shall think of & be close to you at midnight tonight & at this moment as you are reading in our house do you feel funny – I love you darling – surer than ever before – please be well – be my own for I am thine – now wouldn't it be perfect if I sign it Your loving Wife Peg.[126]

Anderson had been sounded out to play in the London production of *Mourning Becomes Electra*, which was to replace *Macbeth* at the New Theatre in mid-January; but she had committed herself to becoming a 'wife' and was anxious to join Lehman in Berkeley. As *Macbeth* wound up and she prepared to say goodbye to her mother and brother and her

---

125 Anderson to Lehman, 20 Oct 1937, UCSB.
126 Anderson to Lehman, 31 Dec 1937, UCSB.

London friends, she telegraphed, 'My lips are on yours now darling. All love, Peg.' 'Ive got a devilish full week of luncheons & teas & I shant start packing till Sunday I think,' she wrote on 10 January. 'I thought of you all day yesterday wondering what time you got in & who met you 0 & how happy you must have been to get back, unpack & sit in the Brown chair & in the same bed…'[127]

'It was really frightful leaving Mother,' she wrote from the ship a week later, ' – poor old Frank looked so sad.' Her *Come of Age* co-star Stephen Haggard was on board and wanted her to play in *Whiteoaks*, which he was to direct on Broadway, but she said no. From the Algonquin when she arrived in New York, she wired an ecstatic, 'Luv luv luv, Peg.' She was welcomed by old friends. She had married Lehman from California, so she had lots of loose ends to tie up in New York. Her sister Did was in the Battleboro Retreat, a psychiatric hospital in Vermont, and Anderson had to visit – 'a pretty shattering business… It will be sad but must be done & the sooner the better. Mary [Servoss] will go with me.'[128]

An important piece of business was gynecological – perhaps related to her September comment about their sex life. 'I lunched with John [Watson] today,' she wrote Lehman, 'hes fine & talked over every thing & he thinks I should have an examination so I shall go to Dr Elias Rosalies Dr on Monday then I shall know when I can leave. Im sure Im allright so don't worry – also I might see Dr Hannah Stone John advises also.' 'It was a clubby little lunch we had,' she commented dryly. 'Also advise at once,' she added, 'Carlo [Van Vechten] wants to take some nude pictures. You said at Xmas time that you were agreeable – how do you feel now – no one would

---

[127] *NYT* 9 Jan 1938: X2; Anderson to Lehman, 7, 9 & 10 Jan 1938, UCSB.
[128] Anderson to Lehman, Sat [22 Jan], posted 27 Jan 1938 New York; 6 Jan; posted 23 Jan 1938 New York, written Wed [19 Jan 1938] from RMS *Aquitania*, UCSB; *Variety* 31 Jan 1938: 2.

ever know – or see a picture that we didn't possess – but do you want me to do it or not. That would be Wednesday night if we took them Mary [Servoss] & Fania [Marinoff] would be there.'[129]

On Monday 7 February she was on her way. 'I am excited & happy & longing to see you 8.20 AM Thursday. Love – & – Peg,' she wrote.[130] She arrived in Berkeley on 10 February, her 41st birthday, and settled into Lehman's house at 97 Tamalpais Road, in the Berkeley hills a little more than a mile from the university.

Lehman's California friends were apprehensive about the marriage. 'Ben Lehman has just been a week-end at Noëls [Sullivan],' Una Jeffers wrote to Mabel Dodge Luhan. 'His new wife Judith Anderson he left playing Lady Macbeth in London—He has had enough experiences now with the stage to write several full-length novels! Seems as enamored of his wife as ever & somewhat more optimistic than he was at their beginning, of making their marriage last. His pride in her acting helps.' Soon after Anderson's arrival Una reported to Luhan that 'Ben Lehman & his wife Judith Anderson are to [spend] this weekend at Noëls… They are madly in love & both very temperamental. Hard to [shake down].'[131]

But shake down they seemed to manage in their first months of domesticity. After the weekend at Carmel, Lehman wrote to Sullivan, 'Everything my life has dreamed of came together in the party and the evening – love, loyalty, friends through all the rich, the enriching gamut… And moving through it like the life giving blood it is that girl's beauty, and

---

129   Anderson to Lehman, posted 28 Jan 1938; see also posted 4 Feb 1938, UCSB. These photos were taken and are in the Van Vechten Papers, Yale.
130   Anderson to Lehman, posted 7 Feb 1938, UCSB.
131   Una Jeffers to Mabel Dodge Luhan, 25 Jan 1938, in RJN autumn 1993; 18 Feb 1938, in James Karman, ed., *The Collected Letters of Robinson Jeffers With Selected Letters of Una Jeffers Volume Two, 1931–1939*, 2011.

charm, and graciousness. Very pride-making, every way, and fostering humility, too.' Anderson seemed equally happy. 'How proud – how happy – and at peace Mother would have been to have seen me so protectingly wrapped round in your love,' she wrote Sullivan. 'I embrace you with all my love – that doesn't belong to Peter.'[132]

During the spring Anderson seemed satisfied with occasional radio work in Los Angeles. From Hollywood in April, after giving Lehman her news, she signed off, 'I remain & probably will for a long time to come – Your faithful Wife.' On their anniversary in May, Lehman wrote to Sullivan from the Yosemite Lodge, 'Here we are – the circular year closed among the crags and falling water of Nevada & Vernal falls!' As summer went on, Anderson echoed Lehman's satisfaction. 'We – all seven of the Lehmans have been in the garden all day, a lovely hot sun,' she wrote Sullivan, 'it was glorious.' (The dachshunds had just had pups.) She was even persuaded to 'pour' at the summer session tea. 'When I'm not pouring at faculty teas I do a Ferdinand,' she wrote McClintic, 'just sit and smell and think.'[133]

By September, however, seven months after she had settled down to the life of a faculty wife, Anderson reported 'that sickening grease paint feeling boiling up in inside me.' 'Had some thrilling holidays in Yosemite, Crater Lake – the redwoods, the summer has been lovely and the pups are

---

132   Lehman to Sullivan, 23 Feb [1938]; Anderson to Sullivan, 28 Feb 1938, Sullivan Papers.
133   *Variety* 11 Mar: 24; 14 Apr 1938: 4; *LAT* 17 Mar 1938: 9; *CDT* 24 Apr 1938: W4; Anderson to Lehman, Sat night [23], posted 25 Apr 1938, UCSB; Lehman to Sullivan, Wed [18 May 1938]; 24 Jun [1938]; Anderson to Sullivan, Wed 8 [Jun] 1938, Sullivan Papers; Anderson to McClintic, 20 Sep 1938, Cornell Papers. See Mother [Jessie Anderson] to Lehman, 3 Aug [1938], UCSB.

adorable,' she wrote to McClintic. 'I've been back to nature and now I want a whif of a good old dirty dressing room.'

A major cause of Anderson's restlessness was the announcement, in the middle of August, that the Theatre Guild was considering a production of Robinson Jeffers' *Tower Beyond Tragedy*, adapted by their resident play reader John Gassner. The Guild had sounded her out about this magnificent play, she told McClintic, but she didn't know if it would materialise. 'Much love to Kit and you lamby, and Stan [Gilkey] and Gert [Macy],' she signed off nostalgically.[134]

'Judith goes to New York the week of the tenth,' Lehman wrote to Sullivan early in October; 'she is greatly drawn to Broadway.' 'This a secret,' he added.[135] She did not leave, however, until the end of the month, staying to celebrate Lehman's birthday, where she consulted with Una and Robin Jeffers about the rights to *Tower Beyond Tragedy*.

Finally on her way to New York, she wrote Lehman from the Santa Fe Chief, 'Oh Lord – people talking – family – troubles – friends telephones – business – arguments – shopping – clothes – rehearsals – actors probably my taste for liquor & cigarettes will come back & there I'll be – same old thing over again – Well well –.' When she got there, however, her delight was palpable:

> *It was very exciting – Mary [Servoss] met me & we got to the hotel about 3.30. Talked with Lewis & Terry Helburn [Theatre Guild] over phone. Then over to Marys for dinner – liver – & then Lawrence [Langner] called & asked me to come down – so I had my liver & Tony Minor [Worthington Miner] – director called for me & off to the Langners. We had a very interesting talk – upstairs for an hour or so. I still can't quite make it all out. I shall have to see [Philip] Moeller*

---

134 Anderson to McClintic, 20 Sep 1938, Cornell Papers.
135 Lehman to Sullivan, 2 Oct [1938], Sullivan Papers.

& Terry [Helburn] first – but L is madly enthusiastic about it – he was very glad that I came on – I go to the Guild in the morning for an hour or so to hear some readings & meet Margaret Webster – a possible Cassandra. Will probably lunch with K Hepburn Monday – she is either frightened to play it – or wants to do a comedy – but I'll find out about that later. Uta Hagen is tied up with the Lunts Sea Gull – Erin [O'Brien-Moore] is going to read it. They are really trying & I think we will get it settled. Had my hair curled & nails painted a pretty pink this morning then off to 21 to lunch with Al Lewis – he is very nice & astute. Noël Coward just arrived & was very amusing & full of messages & Larry [Olivier] is here – Helen [Menken] picked me up after lunch & we went to Bloomingdales to get some vacuum Cleaners & then to see her house Oh but it is enchanting. She moves in on Saturday – Nick Murray [Muray] & Steichen called for half an hour & Steichen says although he first photographed me 14 years ago – I only look 21 or maybe 22. Dinner with Carl [Van Vechten] & Fania & Sat night I go to see & hear Toscanini!! with them. Lewis & Mrs Roberts at 4 tomorrow & Len [Hanna] for dinner & theatre – Max Gordon telephoned to urge me to do Linus's[?] play – said that both he & Sam Harris will do all they can for the play don't know if they are financially interested but I guess so. Can do any play I like in Maplewood NJ stock for a week my salary any week I want to – was out when Radio man called so don't know what prospects are there & now I think that isn't bad for 24 hrs in NY so I put my virtuous little head on the pillow now... I miss you & wish you were here. .[136]

A week later she was still exhilarated:

---

[136] Anderson to Lehman, posted 30 Oct 1938, from New York, written on the Santa Fe Chief; Thu 11.30 pm [3 Nov 1938], posted 11 Nov 1938, from Hotel Algonquin, UCSB.

This morning Nick [Muray] drove me to the country – we lunched with Mary [Servoss?] & Fred & drove back – I to dine with Dick [Hunt] Georgina & Peter – but traffic ???? I saw Georgina at theatre night before & they had just come back from Europe. I had not called Dick I have had little time to call any friends – thought I would arrive for dinner – but didn't get back till 8 pm. Erin [O'Brien-Moore] came over for an hour & we went over a little of Electra – she has a reading tomorrow – yesterday I looked at apts all afternoon & think I have found a charming one – but will decide tomorrow – cocktails with Dorothy Parker who is here for a few days – dressed for theatre – little visit with Louis Beamfield[?] who left tonight for Ohio – Len [Hanna] called for me – dinner at 21 – to Oscar Wilde – I started crying 2 minutes after the curtain was up & my throat was thick & hot the rest of the evening a heartbreakingly magnificent performance & a sensitive & moving play – on to 21 – saw Larry [Olivier] – Viv [Leigh] is not with him – he flew to the coast tonight – Friday an hour at the Guild seeing impossible Cassandras met Gassner a pompous little man but knowledged – lunch with Helen [Menken] – from 4 to 6 Lewis Miss Roberts & Sanford [Meisner?] – before they left Elizabeth [Young] arrived then Cheryl Crawford. They are going to do [John] Coltons play [Two Queens]. Charlotte Greenwood erstwhile musical comedy comedienne to do Elizabeth – would I play Mary – No. This morning another play came from them – about Mary Mother of God – They assure me modestly that Mary is the greatest role in the world – They left at 7.10 pm, dinner 21 – with a new dish – salmon fume & caviar – oil & parsley – very delicious – to Abraham Lincoln one of the finest staged produced & acted throughout plays I have ever seen – simple true & [Raymond] Masseys is a great performance – he is Lincoln – saw [Robert] Sherwood there & met Carl Sandburg, had supper that night with Len [Hanna], Baron au Ginsberg – the Duke de Verdura & a young Englishman who knows John [Gielgud]. The Irish Girl – Molly's play is a great success. Tomorrow I go to the Guild to hear readings of possible Electra's & Cassandras – & Orestes. In [Robert] Morleys – Oscar Wilde – dressing room met an English producer who wants me to play Isadora Duncan – Alfred Lunt told him I was the only actress to play it & now I go to bed to read a new 3rd act of the 'Tower.'[137]

Amongst all this activity, Anderson's main concern was to pin down the Theatre Guild on *Tower Beyond Tragedy*. As she wrote to Lehman, Lawrence Langner, founder and director of the Guild along with his wife, Armina Marshall, were 'madly enthusiastic' about the play, and over the next few weeks she worked with the adapter John Gassner, the play's director, Worthington Miner, and various board members to find a suitable cast.[138]

When the board finally decided to go ahead with *Tower*, Anderson telegraphed Lehman, who was spending the weekend at Carmel with Noël Sullivan:

Tower *settled, Rehearsals probably Monday week opening around Christmas. Cast not completed but presents no problems. Terribly happy though bedded by cold. Loving congratulations Una Robin [Jeffers]. Love babies [dogs], Noël, Lee, you. Peg.*

The following day the *New York Times* announced, 'Judith Anderson to Emerge From Retirement.' 'Judith Anderson,' the article ran, 'who last was seen hereabouts in *The Old Maid*

---

137   Anderson to Lehman, posted 30 Oct 1938, from New York, written on the Santa Fe Chief; Thur 11.30 pm [3 Nov], posted 11 Nov 1938, from Hotel Algonquin, UCSB.
138   Anderson to Lehman, Thur 11.30 pm [3 Nov], posted 11 November 1938; Sun Eve [13 Nov], posted 14 Nov 1938; Wed [16], posted 17 Nov 1938, UCSB.

in 1935, will be returning to the Broadway stage under the Guild's banner in the John W Gassner dramatization in blank verse of *The Tower Beyond Tragedy*, the poem by Robinson Jeffers.' A week later, however, she arrived back from a weekend away to find the Guild 'still fiddling' about a production date. 'So after talk with Morris Agency – I sent the play to Guthrie [McClintic],' she wrote Lehman. 'Guild still say 'calling California tonight' to know about cast for another play & if that doesn't [?] will do Tower first – to hell with them – if Guthrie doesn't buy it I shall. I have been phoning madly & am quite upset about it – when I left Wed afternoon it was definite – but now the same old muddling.'[139]

A few days later she received a 'body blow': 'Telephone all day finally at 5 PM Langner called me to tell me that they had finally decided not to do the play,' she wrote Lehman. 'Guthrie doesn't want to do the play his plans are all set – & he has just had a bad failure,' she ended dejectedly.

But this was show business, and she 'picked up the bits & pieces & telephoned to make other connections.'

> *Dinner & theatre with Len [Hanna] who left for Cleveland – & today – Radio men here at 11 a.m. for an hour. Herman Shumlin at 12 for an hour about a play that he wants me to do [Little Foxes] – haven't finished it yet much telephoning – Radio rehearsal at 4 to 8 – here for talk with Cheryl Crawford about the Jesus play that she wants me to do. José Rubin for an hour wanting me to arrange interview with Noël Coward for his]? ?] with beautiful voice – Mary for dinner Telephone ringing all through, & here it is 10.30 & I have 2 plays to read before I sleep – Also a silly play from Lillian May [Ehrman] that I read last night before I slept.*[140]

---

139 *NYT* 19 Nov 1938: 8; Anderson to Lehman, Fri 2 P.M. [25? Nov 1938], UCSB.
140 Anderson to Lehman, Tue [29] 10.30 pm, posted 30 Nov 1938, from 433 East 51st Street, New York, UCSB.

Judith Anderson as Mary, mother of Jesus, in Family Portrait *1939*

Author's collection

Chapter Nineteen

Family Portrait 1939

You say you love me – love is being not demanding & so with my love for you I gave & gave up so much – & you demand more – I still love you but I cannot give you the freedom of my spirit & being

Judith Anderson to Ben Lehman, 1939

Out of this confusion one play emerged. The producer Cheryl Crawford had recently gone out on her own after being associated for many years with the Theatre Guild and the new, revolutionary Group Theatre. Soon after Anderson's arrival Crawford had brought her a new play, to be directed by British director, Margaret Webster, 'about Mary Mother of God,' she wrote Lehman. 'They assure me modestly that Mary is the greatest role in the world,' she added drily. A few days later she was not so sceptical. 'Read most of the "Mary" play which might even be great,' she told Lehman. The next day she reported 'Dinner with Elizabeth [Young] & Margaret Webster to talk about the Mary play – Webster a very charming & intelligent girl.' Checking out the production of *Hamlet* starring Maurice Evans that Webster was currently staging, Anderson found it a 'thrilling evening' with 'magnificent direction.'[141]

---

141 Cheryl Crawford, *One Naked Individual: My Fifty Years in the Theatre*, 1977;

By early December she had decided to do *Family Portrait* – the 'Mary' play. It is 'a fine play,' she wrote Noël Sullivan. New York, although 'shattering,' was once more exciting. She was 'being very gay and enjoying the loved faces and endearing friendships that I have missed in the past months'; 'the little theatre I have seen is excellent and exciting'; and the Philharmonic and Toscanini 'glorious.'[142]

Family Portrait, which opened at the Morosco Theatre on 8 March 1939, was a second turning point in her career, and in her life. Based on a story by Anatole France about the family of Jesus, it portrayed Mary as an ordinary loving mother, puzzled by, but proud of, her unusual son. Everyone agreed with Brooks Atkinson that Anderson's portrayal of Mary was 'inspired.' 'Her simple-hearted mother of men, full of wonder, pride and misgiving, is played with deep compassion and adds considerable stature to Miss Anderson's reputation as an actress,' he wrote in the *New York Times*. Arthur Pollock in the *Christian Science Monitor* vividly described the effect of Anderson's acting. Some of the play's scenes are beautiful, he wrote. 'Judith Anderson, who plays Mary, the mother of Jesus, helping magically to make them so.'

> *When she and her sons follow Jesus to Capernaum because the boys want her to bring him back to Nazareth and his carpentering, the play is at its best. It glows then, she bringing the glow to its words and its action, for as she sits in the little inn of the fishing village and hears the talk, she learns of Jesus' greatness, of the eagerness of the people to listen to him, of the effect his words have upon them, and she is moved and quietly proud. Those are moments of great beauty. Miss Anderson, a seasoned actress, mistress of the*

Anderson to Lehman, Wed [16], posted 17 Nov 1938; Sun Eve [13], posted 14 Nov 1938, UCSB.
142   Anderson to Sullivan, 8 Dec 1938, Sullivan Papers.

theater's tricks, seems to forget them all and to play from the heart alone.'[143]

WTC in the *Wall Street Journal* pronounced that 'Judith Anderson, as Mary, attained heights of theatrical force not seen in any feminine part on Broadway this year.' 'The fullness of tragedy, whether one regards it as all the world or as greater than the world, is in this part,' he went on. 'Obviously, this requires the talents of an actress who is one of the great performers of her generation. That is precisely what Miss Anderson is.'

Whether it be in the quiet, gradually growing tenseness which leads up to the fulfilled climax of the first act; whether it be in the full expression of a great dramatic actress' powers, as ends the second act; whether it be in the restrained and sensitive ending, Miss Anderson is everything a dramatic artist can be.[144]

Tom Ewell, who as a 30-year-old actor played in *Family Portrait* with Anderson, remembered years later, no doubt with a little exaggeration, the excitement generated by her performance. 'I was once lucky enough to have been in a play where the great conductor, Arturo Toscanini, almost fell out of a box because he was so moved by the performance of the lady I was working with – Judith Anderson,' he recalled, 'and where the famous German writer Thomas Mann, who was sitting in the front row, crawled over the footlights to kiss the hem of her gown at the end of the performance. That sort of thing doesn't often happen.'[145]

---

143 *NYT* 9 Mar 1939: 18; *CSM* 10 Mar 1939: 14.
144 *WSJ* 10 Mar 1939: 11.
145 Ainslie Baker, 'Judith Anderson comes home for season of Greek tragedy,' clipping, PAC.

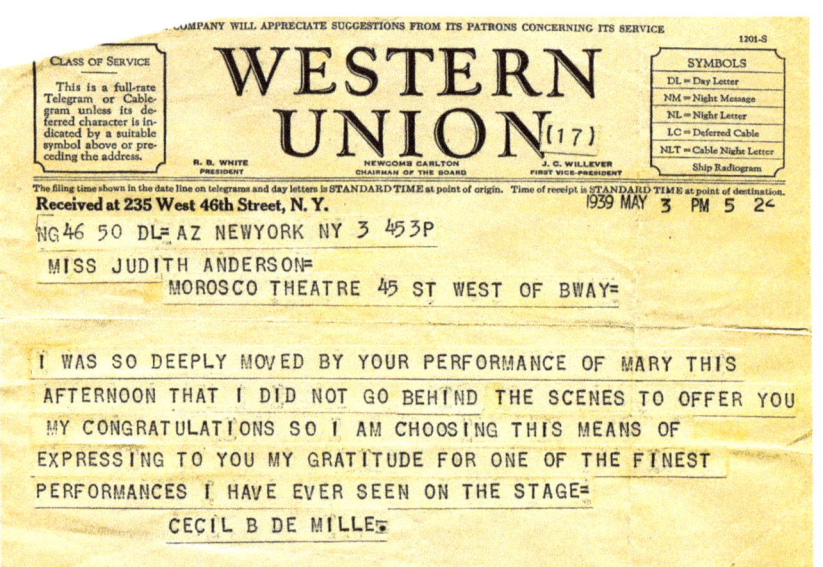

Telegram to Judith Anderson from Cecil B De Mille, 3 May 1939. UCSB. He later bought the film rights to Family Portrait

It is hard to tell from the available correspondence what Lehman's attitude was towards his wife's return to New York and her phenomenal success in *Family Portrait*. Initially he seems to have seen it as a temporary separation while she did a 'great play' – his friend Robinson Jeffers' *Tower Beyond Tragedy*. But her obvious exhilaration at being back in the thick of her old life filled him with apprehension, and probably anger. Ten days after her arrival she wrote, 'Your two cold letters here – & since you give me little further than a recital of the days activities – I give you mine.' After doing so, she ended with a heartfelt plea:

> I got little comfort from your letters & I think I warrant help – I did what I thought was right & had to be done & it was not easy – You say you love me – love is being not demanding & so with my love for you I gave & gave up so much – &

you demand more – I still love you but I cannot give you the freedom of my spirit & being.
No more. Im tired & sad & lonely. Goodnight – Peg[146]

A few days later, 'feeling cold heavy & NY weariness,' she had an invitation to fly back to California to do excerpts from *Come of Age* on the Rudy Vallee Show. 'Had I had any word from you of warmth & regret of this last fantastic demand of yours – I would have said yes immediately & by this time have been nearly there,' she wrote Lehman, 'but it was not possible – so I had to forego the $1100 for 10 minutes.'[147]

After consulting with Noël Sullivan, Lehman decided that he must support her if he was to save the marriage. 'Intended to write daily,' he wrote Sullivan in late November, 'but – work, NY letters to read, get calm over, & answer, the dogs... It was the deepest satisfaction to have talked with you... Some clarity I gradually come at. I have written Peg to say I will come if she says to do so: play sustainer as I can.' 'Of course you must come on for Xmas for all & obvious reasons,' she wrote a few days later. 'What happens after is up to us.'[148]

This New York visit, however, was disastrous. Again, we do not know exactly what happened. Anderson had by then decided that she was going to do *Family Portrait*, and it was probably obvious that her days of playing faculty wife were over. A letter from Lehman to Sullivan in late January 1939, written from the home of his California doctor, suggests a physical collapse from the stress of the visit: 'Thursday caught me at the worst: INFECTION PLUS SERUM THAT PARALYZED MY LEG – escaped a long illness; Reynolds [the doctor's family]

---

146   Josephine Miles to Lehman, 1 Nov [1938]; Anderson to Lehman, Sun Eve [13], posted 14 Nov 1938, UCSB.
147   Anderson to Lehman, Tue [29] 10.30 pm, posted 30 Nov 1938, UCSB.
148   Lehman to Sullivan, Sat [26 Nov 1938], Sullivan Papers; Anderson to Lehman, posted 30 Nov 1938, UCSB.

have been wonderful. Judith is in bed in Ardmore (a friend) with a cold on the chest – disturbing as always for her.'[149]

Anderson wrote with concern about his health a few days later:

> *Peter dear – I was relieved to get your letter this morning but at the same time shocked and sickened by its contents You know that I fully expected you to have an operation for [?] removal on Saturday at the latest… I wrote to Ric [his doctor] asking him to let me have some facts… I am much better up & dressed today for the first time – I came home too soon apparently… Agnes [Yarnell]'s Dr was afraid of pneumonia.*

'I'm sorry that I couldn't have been of more help and comfort to you while you were here,' she ended.[150]

Anderson wrote to Lehman once more in early February – then, with the opening of *Family Portrait* on 8 March, silence. 'Of Judith's opening, I hear indirectly more & more approval,' Lehman wrote Sullivan, 'but no word from her.'[151]

With the enormous success of *Family Portrait*, Lehman no doubt realised that his hopes of having a 'wifely' wife were gone. Anderson, for her part, knew that she could not live without the theatre, and that Lehman was not capable of giving her the freedom to pursue her career. There is no record of their final words. In April Lehman wrote to Sullivan, 'The days with you lifted me out of my heavy sorrow, or lifted it from me, somewhat.' 'Was it ten years ago on Good Friday we were together at Montalvo?' he asked rhetorically, remembering when they had all met that fateful weekend in 1929.[152]

---

149 Lehman to Sullivan, Sat [21 Jan 1938], Sullivan Papers.
150 Anderson to Lehman, Wed [25], 26 Jan 1939, UCSB.
151 Anderson to Lehman, c/o Dr E. Reynolds, 2 Feb 1939, UCSB.
152 Lehman to Sullivan, [after 9 Apr 1939], Sullivan Papers.

Scene Six
Hollywood

I love the earth. I love the space. I love the sunshine. I love the trees... Now I have a house. Eucalyptus. Mimosa, pepper trees. Daphne, vegetables. Marvellous!

Judith Anderson, California, 1940

Pacific Coast Highway looking north to Santa Monica, Pacific Palisades and Malibu 1940
Water and Power Associates

Chapter Twenty

Directed by Alfred Hitchcock
1939–40

You have long been interested in this magnificent actress. She would be marvellous.

Kay Brown to David O Selznick March 1939

Judith Anderson menacing Joan Fontaine in *Rebecca* 1940

Author's collection

Family Portrait put an end, for Judith Anderson, to 10 years of flirtation with the hope of marriage and children. But it also opened up a new career path and a completely new way of life that gave her a home and a garden of her own, and the money that allowed her to give the public 'one good play.'

Producer David O Selznick was looking for an actress to play the housekeeper, Mrs Danvers, in *Rebecca*, the movie that was to follow his much-publicised *Gone with the Wind*. In March 1939 his New York agent, Kay Brown, sent him the glowing reviews of Anderson in *Family Portrait*. 'You have long been interested in this magnificent actress,' she wrote. 'She would be marvelous.'[153]

This was another career-changing opportunity. David O Selznick had founded Selznick International Pictures in 1936, determined to establish 'a Tradition of Quality.' Based at the RKO-Pathé Studio in Culver City built by Thomas Ince in 1919, he was, in March 1939, just completing post-production for his most ambitious opus, *Gone with the Wind*, which opened the following September.

Selznick had purchased the rights to Daphne du Maurier's best-selling *Rebecca* in September 1938, a month after its publication. Brought to his attention by Kay Brown, this romantic thriller, which was likened to the best of the Brontes, was seen as the perfect successor to *Gone with the Wind*. It was also the ideal vehicle for the British director, Alfred Hitchcock, whom Selznick and Brown had been courting for some time. Selznick quickly signed him up, and they began the long process of casting the movie.[154]

As with *Gone with the Wind*, the search for the perfect lead actress was played out in public. Selznick originally wanted Carole Lombard to play the shy young Mrs de Winter, and later considered Olivia de Havilland, Margaret Sullavan, Loretta Young, Vivien Leigh, Anita Louise, Jean Muir and

---

153 Katherine Brown to David O. Selznick, 9 Mar 1939, HRC.
154 *Variety* 2 Sep 1938: 3; *Observer* 7 Aug 1938: 4; *NYT* 16 Sep 1938: 17; 19 Apr 1939: 20; *WP* 1 May 1939: 14.

Anne Baxter. He finally took a gamble on de Havilland's younger sister, the 21-year-old Joan Fontaine, who proved to be ideal in the role.[155]

The search for the actor to play Maxim de Winter was no less arduous. Selznick's original choice had been the heart-throb Ronald Colman, but Colman did not want to play in what he considered a woman's starring vehicle. His second choice was William Powell; but Laurence Olivier, who was currently playing Heathcliff in *Wuthering Heights*, was cheaper and finally, in late June 1939, was given the part.[156]

Selznick and Hitchcock recognised the importance of the role of Mrs Danvers, the housekeeper whose loyalty and devotion to the first Mrs de Winter creates much of the mood of the story. They immediately agreed to try to get British actress Flora Robson for the part. Robson arrived in Hollywood soon after to play the housekeeper in *Wuthering Heights*; but she left early in March 1939 to do a play in London, and her availability was uncertain.[157]

This was when Kay Brown introduced the possibility of Judith Anderson as Mrs Danvers. Anderson wrote in her memoirs, 'I made the screen test. I got the job.' But it was much more complicated than that. There were other major contenders, such as Nazimova, the eminent Russian-born actress, who was 'crazy to play Mrs Danvers,' and Eily Malyon, who had spent much of her career in Australia and was now a well-established character actress in Hollywood; and Selznick and Hitchcock still preferred Robson. But when

---

155   *LAT* 7 Jun 1939: 8.
156   *NYT* 14 Dec 1938: 32; 22 Jun 1939: 26; *WP* 24 Mar 1939: 12; *LAT* 3 Apr: 18; 8 May 1939: A15; David O'Shea to Kay Brown, [20?] Jun 1939, HRC.
157   Hitchcock to Selznick, cable to London, 13 & 14 Oct; Selznick to O'Shea, 14 Oct 1938; O'Shea to Selznick, 13 Mar; Selznick to O'Shea, cc Mrs Rabwin, 4 Apr; Marcella Rabwin to O'Shea, [early May 1939], HRC; *LAT* 24 Dec: A9; 7 Nov 1938: 13; *WP* 7 Mar 1939: 8; *Daily Mirror* 2 Jun [1939], NYPL; *NYT* 7 Jun 1939: 30.

Robson decided to play in *Family Portrait* in London, Kay Brown urged them to move quickly to secure Anderson. *Family Portrait* was closing in New York, she wrote Hitchcock early in June, and they needed to get her before she left on tour.[158]

Anderson arrived in Hollywood at the end of June 1939 to take a screen test for *Rebecca*. *Variety* was sure almost immediately that 'Judith Anderson, Main Stem celeb, has inked deal with David O. Selznick, is beginning to look like a safe bet.' But Edwin Schallert in the *Los Angeles Times* and Bosley Crowther in the *New York Times* were still reporting that Robson was the main contender; and the popular British actress Constance Collier was writing to Hitchcock asking him to think of her for the part. Trying to keep Anderson on a string, Selznick wanted to test Robson and Nazimova before they made a decision. 'Under no circumstances lose Anderson,' Selznick wrote to his contracts negotiator David O'Shea. Robson declined to take a test and after seeing Nazimova's test, Selznick told Brown, on 14 July, that they were going ahead with Anderson.[159]

David O'Shea informed Anderson's agents Leland Heyward and John McCormick on 18 July that she had the role. Shooting was expected to commence at the end of August at a salary of $1,750 a week. A press release from Selznick International Pictures two days later announced: 'Judith Anderson Wins Role of Mrs Danvers in *Rebecca*.' Anderson was one of leading actresses on the American stage, the press release emphasised, and she had recently been

---

158 Brown to Selznick, 9, 23 & 25 Mar 1939; Selznick to Hitchcock, 20 Apr 1939, cc Mr Schuessler; Fred Schuessler to Selznick, 2 May 1939; Brown to Hitchcock & Selznick to Hitchcock, 6 Jun 1939: cc O'Shea, HRC; *NYT* 17 Jun 1939: 17.
159 *LAT* 30 Jun: A2; 5 Jul 1939: A11; *Variety* 3 Jul 1939: 3; *NYT* 9 Jul 1939: 113; Collier to Hitchcock, 8 Jul; Selznick to O'Shea, 10 Jul, cc Hitchcock; to Kay Brown, 11 Jul, dictated 10 Jul; to David O'Shea, 14 Jul; to Kay Brown, [14 Jul 1939], HRC.

selected as the Best Actress of the Year by New York Drama Critics.[160]

Judith Anderson's definitive entry into movies was not the only change in her life marked by *Family Portrait*. From the time the play was announced in early February she appears to have regarded her marriage as over. Sometime before she left for Hollywood at the end of June, Anderson must have written Lehman asking for a divorce. On 30 June he wrote to Sullivan that he had just received 'a longer letter of the most chilling demands & implications.' 'There will be more sparring!' he added. She visited Berkeley to pack up her belongings, without seeing Lehman, before she returned to New York. On 13 July Lehman rewrote his will. Two weeks later the newspapers announced that Anderson was in Nevada seeking a divorce. A month later, on 24 August, the *New York Times* reported 'Judith Anderson Freed. Actress Divorces B H Lehman, Professor and Writer.' Louella Parsons noted Anderson two days later 'fresh from her divorce from her professor husband, at the Café Lamaze with a party of friends.'[161]

As Anderson drew a firm line under her second dream of love, she experienced two other important personal transitions. At the Kalgoorlie Government Hospital on 14 February 1939 her father James Anderson Anderson had died, aged 80,

---

160 O'Shea to Hayward, Beverly Hills, 18 Jul 1939, HRC; press release, 20 Jul 1939, NYPL.
161 Lehman to Sullivan, Thu [29 Jun], cont. Fri [30]; Sun [2 Jul]; [13 Jul 1939]; Sullivan Papers; *CDT* 30 Jul 1939: 10; *NYT* 24 Aug 1939: 23; *WP* 26 Aug 1939: 4. In 1957 Lehman married Henriette de Saussure Blanding, who had been married in turn to two of his colleagues, Chauncey Goodrich and Willard Durham. He lived at the historic Hayfield House in Saratoga until his death in 1977. See Benjamin Lehman, Recollections and Reminiscences of Life in the Bay Area from 1920 Onward. Regional Oral History Office, UC Berkeley, 1969.

of chronic myocarditis. With the undertaker the only informant, his death certificate gave 'children: unknown.' At the other end of the earth, her brother Frank, aged 44, married Laura Bowman on 29 December 1939, beginning the family that became so important to Anderson 10 years later.[162]

As soon as Anderson's casting as Mrs Danvers was decided, David Selznick peppered his staff with instructions about her makeup, hairdo and costumes. 'Get hold of Anderson immediately about letting eyebrows grow,' he ordered his makeup chief Monte Westmore. When it was finally announced, in early September, that Joan Fontaine would have the coveted

Judith Anderson and Joan Fontaine in Rebecca *1940*

Author's collection

---

162 Mother [Jessie Anderson] to Lehman, 13 Feb 1940, from Bristol.

role of the second Mrs de Winter, shooting started on 8 September.[163]

The story of *Rebecca* is well known. The young insecure second wife, who is never named, is subtly terrorised by the housekeeper, Mrs Danvers, who is obsessed by the memory of her former mistress, Rebecca. There are strong sexual overtones to this obsession (the caressing of Rebecca's fur, the stroking of her undergarments kept lovingly in their original drawers) which Anderson manages to convey convincingly despite the censor's admonition to Selznick that there must be no suggestion that the first Mrs de Winter was 'a sex pervert.'[164]

'Judith Anderson, in the plum role of Mrs Danvers, is quite unforgettable:... significantly modified from du Maurier to make her younger and more clearly a coded lesbian.'
Tim Robey 2009

Author's collection

---

163   Selznick to Westmore, cc Sch, 16 Aug 1939, HRC; *WP* 5 Sep 1939: 14; *HR* 9 Sep 1939, NYPL.
164   Joseph I Breen to Selznick, cc Mr Val Lewton, 5 Sep 1939, MHL; *NYT* 1 Oct 1939: 139. Production 8 Sep-20 Nov 1939; retakes began Dec 1939; release 12 Apr 1940;

Rebecca has become one of the favourite movies of all time, with Anderson's performance as the chilly Mrs Danvers considered one of the most memorable. Anderson remembered the movie and the role with affection. 'I felt secure in that character,' she told a reporter early in 1940. 'Sometimes there are little hurdles in character... and you have to get over those lines as best you can. But Danvers never deviated – just one clear drive from the beginning.' 'Mr Hitchcock is a very tolerant director and a very kindly man,' she went on. 'In the scene where Danvers suggests the girl jump out the window, he said to me, "Go to the window, open it, look at her, look away and say, quite matter-of-factly, "You need a little air, madam." Very quiet, very gentle, very terrifying.' She also remembered, with some amusement, how Selznick drove everyone mad with memos: 'I was going through a divorce at the time and he sent me a note saying: "Do not pluck your eyebrows." That was the least of my worries at that moment!'[165]

Tim Robey, film critic on the *London Telegraph*, noted in 2009 that Hitchcock, late in his career, in an interview with Francois Truffaut in 1962, had all but disowned *Rebecca* because it lacked humour. But, Robey argued, 'the supporting cast supply great wit and shading.' 'Judith Anderson,' he went on, 'in the plum role of Mrs Danvers, is quite unforgettable: the credit for this character – significantly modified from du Maurier to make her younger and more clearly a coded lesbian – is all hers and Hitchcock's.'[166]

Critics and audiences at the time agreed. *Hollywood Magazine* noted how Anderson's principal gifts as a stage actress – her 'smooth voice and fluid body' – 'give the part of

---

premiere New York 28 Mar 1940.
165   *NYWT* 20 Mar 1940, NYPL; *Times* [London] 10 Nov 2005: 18.
166   *DT* [London] 17 Oct 2009: 9.

'Mr Hitchcock is a very tolerant director and a very kindly man.' Judith Anderson 1940
Author's collection

Danny [Mrs Danvers] the quality of living danger and waiting disaster so essential if the story is to be believed at all.' As Ed Sullivan put it, 'It was the first time a performer has achieved a quality of menace by simply folding her hands. That's what Miss Anderson accomplished, but if those folded hands had concealed a hooded cobra the alarm could not have been more intense or the fear more emphatic.'[167]

Variety devoted a two-page spread to the New York opening at the Radio City Music Hall on 28 March 1940, showing crowds jamming the street, hoping to get a ticket. 'In the first five days,' their headline noted, 'Radio City Music Hall played to more than 150,000 admissions and turned away close to 75,000 additional ticket-buyers.' When it finished its six-week run at 'The Showplace of the Nation,' it had been seen by an estimated 900,000 people. Named on *Film Daily*'s

---

167   *Hollywood Magazine* Jun 1940: 16; *CDT* 21 Apr 1940: E4.

and the National Board of Review of Motion Pictures' 'ten best list' for 1940, along with *The Grapes of Wrath* (first), *The Great Dictator*, *Our Town*, *Fantasia*, *The Long Voyage Home*, *Foreign Correspondent*, *The Biscuit Eater* and *Gone with the Wind*, it grossed six million dollars that year, ranking fourth behind the Disney animations and MGM's *Boom Town*.[168]

The quality of living danger and waiting disaster

Author's collection

In February 1941 *Rebecca* was nominated for 11 Academy Awards: Best Picture, Best Actor, Best Actress, Best Supporting Actress, Best Director, Best Cinematography, Best Screenplay, Best Black and White Art Direction, Best Film Editing, Best Musical Score and Best Special Effects. Edward Schallert, in the *Los Angeles Times*, predicted a 'hot' race for Best Supporting Actress among Judith Anderson in *Rebecca*, Jane

---

168   *Variety* 3 Apr 1940: 28; *NYT* 5 May: 158; 23 Dec 1940: 25.

Darwell in *Grapes of Wrath* and Ida Lupino in *They Drive by Night*. On the awards night 27 February at the Biltmore Bowl, *Rebecca* was voted the best picture of the year – a triumph for Selznick; and cameraman George Barnes won for Best Cinematography; but Hitchcock, Fontaine, Olivier, and Anderson were disappointed when John Ford was named Best

David O Selznick, Joan Fontaine, Alfred Hitchcock and Judith Anderson, Academy Awards Dinner February 1941

Author's collection

Director for *Grapes of Wrath*, Ginger Rogers Best Actress for *Kitty Foyle*, James Stewart Best Actor for *Philadelphia Story* and Jane Darwell Best Supporting Actress for *Grapes of Wrath*.[169]

Henry Fonda as Tom Joad in *Grapes of Wrath* and Judith Anderson as Mrs Danvers have remained among the greatest heroes and villains respectively in movie history. Initial publicity for *Rebecca* featured the romantic couple, Laurence Olivier and Joan Fontaine. But gradually scenes of Judith

---

169   10 Feb 1941: 21; *LAT* 10 Feb 1941: A1; *CDT* 28 Feb 1941: 1.

Anderson menacing the timorous young Fontaine took their place. The *Chicago Sunday Tribune*, always a fan of Anderson, featured on the front of their Movie section what has become a classic image of Anderson standing behind Fontaine urging her to 'Jump, jump.' 'Ominous and ever present stands the still, bitter housekeeper Mrs Danvers, at the elbow of the gentle, timorous second Mrs de Winter,' the caption read. 'Joan Fontaine and Judith Anderson portray the role of wife and housekeeper in the screen version of Daphne Du Maurier's novel.'[170] This image has gradually overtaken the romantic one, and invariably accompanies discussion of the movie in recent years.

Los Angeles Times film critic Edwin Schallert wrote in March 1940, as *Rebecca* was about to open in that city, that it was going to prove more important to the future of film-making than *Gone with the Wind* because of the brilliant risk-taking of its casting. 'It was a pretty striking thing to choose Judith Anderson, whose screen possibilities have always been debatable, for the role of Mrs Danvers,' he wrote; yet 'the performance she gave will make it difficult for anyone to top her for next year's academy supporting award honors despite several fine portrayals already bidding for that prize.' 'Miss Anderson's success demonstrates anew,' he concluded, 'that there is no stage personage who cannot find her rightful place on the screen providing the casting is as astute as in Rebecca.'

Schallert continued to be hopeful that a splendid film career was going to open up for Anderson. When she completed *Rebecca* early in November 1939, her prospects seemed good. She tested for Warner Bros movies, *Dr Ehrlich's*

---

170   https://en.wikipedia.org/wiki/AFI%27s_100_Years...100_Heroes_%26_Villains; *CDT* 7 Apr 1940: 11.

Magic Bullet, Till We Meet Again, Madame Ravioli (originally *Two Sons*; produced as *East of the River*) and *All This and Heaven Too*. In early December, when Paramount bought the movie rights to *Family Portrait* for Cecil B De Mille, she discussed the screen treatment with him, reminding him of his dismissal of her 20 years before. In December she began work on the MGM production *Forty Little Mothers* – a run-of-the mill Eddie Cantor comedy. Anderson was then persuaded by her friend, MGM executive Benny Thaw, to sign a term contract that guaranteed her $1,500 a week for 40 weeks and forbade her from making stage appearances. She was reluctant to do so, but the money was an inducement – and she wanted to be in the Margaret Sullavan-Jimmy Stewart film, *The Mortal Storm*. 'Miss Anderson seems destined finally to create that cinema future for herself,' Edwin Schallert wrote in the *Los Angeles Times*.[171]

But MGM did little for her. She began work on *The Mortal Storm* in February 1940, but director Sydney Franklin did not want her, and she was replaced almost immediately by Irene Rich. There was talk of her being in *Escape*, but the part went to Nazimova, one of her rivals for the Mrs Danvers role. The truth was MGM did not know what to do with her. Her fans were perturbed as she wasted her talents as the stern headmistress in *Forty Little Mothers* and the plain Lady Joan Culver in *Free and Easy*. As *Variety* put it in March 1941, just as the Academy Awards were about to be announced, 'Judith Anderson, of all the members of the cast [of *Free and Easy*], should have the greatest grievance against Metro. She's cast

---

171   *LAT* 28 Apr 1940; C3; 3 Oct 1939: 12; 11 Jan 1940: 8; 28 Nov 1939: A15; 1 Jan 1940: 6; *NYT* 3 Oct: 27; 9 Nov 1939: 26; 29 Jan 1940: 18; *HT* 8 Nov [1939], NYPL; *WP* 22 Jul 1940: 9; 12 Dec 1939: 16; *Variety* 2 Dec 1939: 4; *Peninsula Herald*, 15 Oct 1945. The film, to be called *Queen of Queens*, was never made, reportedly stymied by the Production Code. De Mille was working on it when he died in 1959. See Phil A. Koury, *Yes, Mr. DeMille*, 1959 ; *NYT* 16 Aug 1959: BR7; *Variety* 29 Dec 1939: 2; *MPH* 9 Mar 40: 63.

as the rich but ugly duckling, and in a role that was meant for someone about 15 years younger than she. It's a mortifying and trying part for the accomplished actress.'[172]

Despite the fact that her movie career was going nowhere, Anderson found that she enjoyed life in Los Angeles. Leopold Stokowski, conductor of the Philadelphia Symphony Orchestra ('Stokie' to columnist Hedda Hopper), was often on the Coast in 1939, where he was recording *Fantasia* with Walt Disney and romancing Greta Garbo. Anderson was among the city's cultural elite in late October when she attended the concert at the Philharmonic Auditorium in aid of Polish Relief where Stokowski conducted the Los Angeles Philharmonic Orchestra; and was at the party cultural leaders Edward G Robinson and his wife Gladys gave for him later. In November she was entertained by Carl Van Vechten's friend, Anna May Wong, at a tea in honour of Chinese author Lin Yutang, along with Una Merkel, Hedda Hopper, Mercedes D'Acosta and Ramon Novarro. In December she and Anna May Wong lunched with her New York friends, Paramount Chairman Stanton Griffis and his wife, who were welcoming the Milanese financier Count Gian Luca Cicogna and his American wife. In January 1940 Ed Sullivan had her dating Garson Kanin, who was to marry Ruth Gordon a year later. She was befriended by director George Cukor and the Australian designer Orry Kelly.[173]

In March 1940 she threw in her fate with California and bought a modern house with a beautiful garden on a

---

172 *NYT* 29 Jan; 18 & 22 Feb: 32; 31 Jan: 23; 10 Apr: 35; 16 Apr 1940: 30; HR 3 Feb 1940; *LAT* 30 Jan: 1; 28 Apr; C3; 2 Jun 1940: C3; *WP* May 11, 1940: 16; *Variety* 19 Mar 1941: 16.
173 *LAT* 26 Oct: 12; 20 Oct: 13; 24 Oct 24: 17; 26 Nov 1939: D8; *Variety* 1 Dec 1939: 3; *CDT* 22 Jan 1940: 15; *WP* Jan 15: 18; 31 Jan 1941: 20.

three-acre block looking out over the ocean at 601 Amalfi Drive, on the Riviera section of Pacific Palisades, where her neighbours were Aldous Huxley, Anna May Wong – just back from Australia – and Warners producers David Lewis and James Whale. 'I have been a sardine in a can all my life,' she told a reporter during a brief trip to New York for the premiere of *Rebecca*, 'on the road, on a train, in a hotel room or a little apartment… I want a home, I want to live in it and be a part of it.' 'I love the space. I love the sunshine. I love the trees,' she enthused to another journalist, talking like 'a press agent for Southern California's All-Year Club.' She could no longer afford the theatre, she maintained. Instead 'she would stay in Hollywood forever… playing the hard, unsympathetic but meaty roles Hollywood gives her.'[174]

California remained home for Anderson for the rest of her long life; and better – and sometimes sympathetic – roles gradually came her way. Sometime early in 1941 she got out of her contract with MGM and announced that she would accept one character role a year. She was immediately snapped up for *Lady Scarface* with RKO ($2,500 weekly for 3 weeks), and *King's Row* (produced by David Lewis; costumes by Orry Kelly) and *All Through the Night* ($1,750 weekly for 4 weeks), both with Warner Bros, with Hal B Wallis as executive producer.[175]

Freed from her contract she was available once more for theatrical roles. Her first thought was to do Jeffers' *Tower Beyond Tragedy*. Invited to play *Family Portrait* for the Del Monte summer theatre, she agreed on the condition that the producer Charles O'Neal (the brand-new father of

---

174   *Variety* 9 Mar 1940: 2; *LAT* 10 Mar 1940: E2; Wong to Van Vechten, 20 Feb 1940; clipping [20 Mar 1940]; *NYWT* 20 Mar 1940; clipping 30 Mar [1940], NYPL; *CSM* 20 Mar 1940: 8. See also *WP* 31 Mar 1940: S6.
175   *Dallas Morning News* 3 May 1941; *LAT* 15 Apr 1941: A10. See Warner Bros Archives, USC for *All Through the Night* and *King's Row*.

Ryan O'Neal) would put on *Tower* in the outdoor theatre at nearby Carmel. With her old friend Hilda Vaughn a brilliant Cassandra and local actor Henry Brandon as Orestes, and directed at the last minute by experienced actor-director Moroni Olsen, this production of *The Tower Beyond Tragedy* was so nerve-wracking that she momentarily forgot her lines on the first night. But it was generally deemed a success. Jeffers, who had cautioned her that he probably would not attend, did come – and he stayed; and most important for Anderson was that her mother told her for the first time that she was great.[176]

New York drama critics Frank Farrell and William Hawkins were determined to see the production. 'Carmel is two hours and 10 minutes north of Los Angeles according to plane schedule,' they wrote; but it took them considerably longer and they missed the first two acts. The story was carved to the bone, they reported, and it was played in the open air on bare steps that led to a temple backed by mist-softened Carmel pines. 'Moroni Olson directed the poetic pageantry with a sure sense of movement against the static classicism of the

---

176   *LAT* 1 Jun 1941: C4; *Variety* 18 Jun1941. See Una Jeffers to Phoebe Barkan, 27 Jun 1941; to Anderson, [2 Jul 1941], Tor House; Anderson to Una Jeffers, 17 Jul 1941, HRC; *SFC* 7 Jul: 7; 13 Jul 1941: 8.

setting,' they concluded; and 'Miss Anderson consistently enhances the pictorial quality of the play with her expert ability to create tableaux.' But, they noted, 'The Forest Theater can pass the chill point when evening fogs roll up the hill.'[177]

At the same time as she was struggling to bring her vision of 'a great play' to life, an exciting new opportunity opened up. The rumour had gone around that John Barrymore – in his last year and a serious drunk – had suggested they do *Macbeth*. But she had a more substantial offer when Maurice Evans invited her to play Lady Macbeth in his forthcoming production, directed by Peggy Webster, to open on Broadway in November.[178]

---

177 NYWT 12 Jul 1941, NYPL.
178 *Evening Independent* (Massillo, Ohio) 12 May 1941: 4; Michael A. Morrison, *John Barrymore, Shakespearean Actor*, 1999; Evans to Anderson, 5, 11, 12 & 26 Jun 1941; Anderson to Evans, 18 Jun; [14 Jul 1941], Evans Papers; *NYT* 14 Jun 1941: 20.

Maurice Evans and Judith Anderson in Macbeth *1941*

Author's collection

Chapter Twenty-one

Macbeth 1941–2

In truth, Her Lady Macbeth, following in the theater her Mother of Christ in Family Portrait, demonstrates what her admirers have long been insisting: that Miss Anderson is one of the truly great actresses of the modern stage.

Richard Watts Jr, Washington Post

'With a prayerful heart I now sign our contract, therefore divorcing myself from my heaven on earth for 33 weeks,' Judith Anderson wrote to Maurice Evans from her Californian home in mid-July 1941, agreeing to play Lady Macbeth opposite his Macbeth.[179] After completing the filming of *All Through the Night* at the end of September, she flew to New York for rehearsals.

Maurice Evans was, in 1941, at the beginning of a career as America's most successful actor-manager. Born in London in 1901, he had joined the Old Vic in 1934 when John Gielgud was attracting new audiences to Shakespeare's plays. Guthrie McClintic had brought him to New York in 1935 after seeing him in *Hamlet*, to join Katharine Cornell on tour in *Romeo and Juliet*. He again toured with Cornell as the Dauphin in *Saint Joan* during the spring of 1936.[180]

---

179 Anderson to Evans, 19 Jul 1941, Evans Papers.
180 Maurice Evans, *All This… and Evans Too!* 1986; WP 5 Jul 1935: 18; Nov 14, 1937:

Evans had an entrepreneurial spirit that flourished in the New York environment. With funds raised by his old mentor, Dame May Whitty, from what she called the 'Incorporated Incompatibles,' Evans staged the rarely seen *Richard II* in January 1937 with Dame May's brilliant daughter, Margaret 'Peggy' Webster, as director. Brooks Atkinson praised it as 'one of the most thorough, illuminating and vivid productions of Shakespeare we have had in recent memory,' pronouncing Evans 'one of the finest actors of our time' and Webster a director of 'brilliance and versatility.' 'The public raves which have greeted Maurice Evans have even beaten those accorded John Gielgud when he turned loose his *Hamlet* last fall,' Alice Hughes wrote in the *Washington Post*. 'New York likes Mr Evans very much,' John K Hutchens wrote in the *New York Times* at the beginning of the fall 1938 season, 'and it seems safe to add simply – vice versa.'[181]

'Very business-like, friendly, self-assured – an actor-manager, 37 years old, who knows what he wants, and why,' Evans had by 1941 produced and acted in an uncut four-hour version of *Hamlet*, *Henry IV Part I* as well as *Richard II*, all directed by Peggy Webster. Expecting to be called up at any moment, in 1940–41 he played a 'superb' Malvolio in *Twelfth Night* for the Theatre Guild with Helen Hayes and Ruth Gordon, again directed by Webster. Early in 1941, however, he and Peggy Webster were able to plan for a production of *Macbeth*, as Evans began the process of becoming an American citizen.[182]

T2; *NYT* 13 Nov 1938: 179; *CDT* 29 Sep 1935: D4; 29 Dec 1935: D3; McClintic to Evans, 14 Jun 1935, Cornell Papers.

181 *NYT* 2 Dec 1936: 34; John Gielgud to mother, 14 Dec 1936, from New York, in Gielgud, *Letters*. See Margaret Webster, *The Same Only Different: Five Generations of a Great Theatre Family*, 1969, 59, 65; *NYT* 6 Feb 1937: 14; 11 Sep 1938: 185–86; *WP* 25 Feb 1937: 15.

182 Hutchens, 'Mr. Evans, Actor-Manager'; *NYT* 23 Mar: X1; 1 Jun 1941: X; Webster, *The Same Only Different*, 127–28.

Judith Anderson had met Peggy Webster when she auditioned her as a possible Cassandra for the Guild's *Tower Beyond Tragedy* in November 1938; and she quickly began to admire her as a possible director as they negotiated to put on 'the Mary play' *Family Portrait*. When she and Mary Servoss went to see Maurice Evans in *Hamlet*, it was Webster's 'magnificent direction' that made it a 'thrilling evening' for them. Evans did not have the magic of Gielgud: he 'mouthed all the time,' she wrote Ben Lehman, 'no heart no feeling sound & articulation signifying – Elocution.'[183] This was a brilliant opportunity, however, and Hollywood was bringing her money and a home but little professional satisfaction.

When *Macbeth* opened in New York on 11 November 1941, it was an overwhelming personal triumph for Anderson. Brooks Atkinson proclaimed it Miss Anderson's 'most distinguished work in our theatre':

> *It has a sculptured beauty in the early scenes, and a resolution that seems to be fiercer than the body that contains it. It is strong without being inhuman. And she has translated the sleep-walking scene into something memorable; the nervous washing of the hands is almost too frightful to be watched.*[184]

George Freedley in the *Morning Telegraph* declared that 'What makes their production majestic is not its Macbeth, but the tortured magnificence of Miss Judith Anderson.' In her performance, he wrote, 'I heard the lines as if for the first time.'[185] Richard Watts Jr in the *Washington Post*, agreed.

---

183 Anderson to Lehman, Nov 1938, UCSB; Diary 17 Nov 1938.
184 *NYT* 12 Nov 1941: 30.
185 *MT* 13 Nov 1941, NYPL.

This was the ablest presentation of *Macbeth* in the modern American theatre, he asserted:

> *It is vigorous and alive. It is fresh and dynamic in its approach. It captures the excitement of the story and the terror of its black and vengeful mood without losing the singing eloquence of the text. And, above all else, it has Miss Judith Anderson as Lady Macbeth.*

'There is little doubt about the magnificence of Miss Anderson's performance,' he continued:

> *It is a portrayal both carefully thought out and deeply felt. It has force and imagination and passion. It is completely human and completely understandable, and it reveals in its brightest aspect a superb knowledge of tragic acting combined with an instinct for the dramatic that must certainly have been born rather than made.*

'In truth,' he concluded, 'Her Lady Macbeth, following in the theater her Mother of Christ in *Family Portrait*, demonstrates what her admirers have long been insisting: that Miss Anderson is one of the truly great actresses of the modern stage.'[186]

When *Macbeth* closed on Broadway on 28 February 1942 after a record 131 performances for the play in the US, the production toured 17 cities until the end of May.

This was not the end of their plans for *Macbeth*, however. Evans and Anderson, as British citizens, had been working for war relief ever since World War II had broken out in August 1939; they had used cotton instead of wool for their costumes in *Macbeth*; and they had pledged the earnings from their

---

186   *WP* 23 Nov 1941: L3.

highly successful five-disc recording of the play to the British cause.[187] Since the United States had joined the Allies in December 1941, they had eagerly devised plans to bring first-class entertainment to the troops. When they offered, after their tour ended, to present *Macbeth* at Fort Meade, the large training centre in Maryland, the military authorities were sceptical. But Evans and Anderson were convinced that the men would appreciate serious drama – especially something as action-packed as *Macbeth*.

They were right. Even though *Macbeth* was competing with three camp movies, 1000 soldiers enjoyed the play so much that they gave it what *Time* magazine described as 'ten excited, claqueless curtain calls.' 'When question cards were passed out,' *Time* reported, '900 of the spectators replied emphatically that they wanted shows like *Macbeth*.'[188]

Delighted with the success of their experiment in bringing Shakespeare to the troops, Evans, now an American citizen, set out to convince the military to allow them to tour Army camps in a condensed version of *Macbeth*. 'Youre a filthy beast darling to ask me now,' Anderson responded from California a month later when he wrote asking her to join him, pretending reluctance to leave the 'heaven' she had just returned to.[189] Within the month, however, Evans was drafted into the Army Specialist Corps. His task was to promote amateur theatricals for posts where it was impractical to sponsor professional theatrical equipment.[190] For the moment, their plans had to be put on hold.

---

187 *Variety* 6 Aug 1940: 7; *LAT* 9 Aug 1940: 25; *NYT* 11 Aug 1940: 101; 17 Nov 1941: 13; *WP* 27 Oct 1940: 38; Evans to Anderson, 25 Jul 1941, Evans Papers.
188 *Time* 15 Jun 1942. See also *WP* 9 Jun 1942: 8; *NYT* 21 Jun 1942: SM25.
189 Mim [Anderson] to Evans, 14 Jul 1942 tel to 2 East 56th, Evans Papers.
190 *Variety* 13 Aug 1942: 1; *NYT* 18 Aug 1942.

Katharine Cornell, Judith Anderson and Ruth Gordon, Time, December 1942
Author's collection

Chapter Twenty-two

Three Sisters 1942–3

> *Generous, lavish array of star-gleaming players as will stir theater-goers at the mere sight of their name*
> Washington Post, 22 November 1942

Anderson and Evans were not the only theatre and movie professionals to want to contribute their talents to the war effort. Women in the theatre led by playwright Rachel Crothers had organised the Stage Women's War Relief Society during World War I. In 1940 they reorganised as the American Theatre Wing, a branch of British War Relief, raising close to $82 million in various forms of civilian aid to Britain before the US entered the conflict. During 1942 and 1943 they established Stage Door Canteens in New York, Washington, San Francisco and Hollywood as social centres for service men and women. They organised speakers' bureaus to help sell Treasury bonds, set up knitting and sewing workshops, and donated blood. Anderson's friend Helen Menken was in charge of preparing radio programs, and she herself joined the Theatre Wing's first-aid classes, knitted – as she had done with Julius Knight in 1915 – and made speeches and broadcasts.[191]

---

191 *Vogue* 15 May 1942: 44, 45; WP 26 Jul: L5; Feb 25, 1942: 8; *NYT* 15 Feb: X1; 3 Mar: 26; 17 Jan: 12; 22 Jan: 15; 26 Jan: 32; 14 Feb 1942: 11; *Variety* 4 Feb 1942: 2; *LAT* 30 Aug

In Hollywood the industry quickly set up the Hollywood Victory Committee to coordinate the contributions to the war effort of those theatre and movie workers who could not join the forces. Their Hollywood Talent Committee chaired by leading agent Charles K Feldman, and the Actors Committee chaired by Clark Gable, supplied stars to support Red Cross fund-raising and Treasury Bond sales. In spring 1942 Bob Hope led the Hollywood Victory Caravan, a two-week tour of 12 American cities by 50 leading Hollywood stars, raising a billion dollars for war relief. The Victory Committee also coordinated with the United Services Organization, the civilian body that arranged entertainment for the troops, to send 'Camp Shows' to army camps and naval stations.[192]

One of the most active members of the Hollywood community was Bette Davis, the reigning star and briefly, during 1941, president of the Academy of Motion Picture Arts and Sciences. She was the force behind the Hollywood Canteen, which opened in October 1942.[193]

In late spring 1942 Katharine Cornell, Raymond Massey and Burgess Meredith had, under the auspices of the Theatre Wing, raised over $80,000 for war relief with performances of George Bernard Shaw's *Candida*. When Anderson's plans to tour army camps with *Macbeth* fell through, she interested Bette Davis in a fund-raising tour of *Tower Beyond Tragedy*, with Davis playing Electra. *Los Angeles Times* movie critic Edwin Schallert announced 'Bette Davis' Return to Footlights Likely,' in late September. Anderson's friend, Monty Woolley, who had worked with Davis in *The Man Who Came to Dinner* the previous year, would direct and play Agamemnon, and

---

1942: H1.
192   *Variety* 13 Jan: 1, 3; 18 Feb 1942: 23; *NYT* 11 Mar: 40; 5 Apr: X10; 23 Jan: 16; 1 Mar 1942: X1; *WP* 25 Apr 1942: 3.
193   Davis resigned after two months. *Variety* 5 Aug: 2; 14 Aug: 4; 2 Sep: 61; 21 Sep: 3, 10; 24 Sep 1942: 8; *CDT* 15 Sep 1942: 16.

there was a chance, Schallert thought, that the Shuberts might take it to New York. *Variety* stated further that Anderson would proceed with the play as soon as she completed work on her current movie, *Edge of Darkness*; and Elsa Maxwell added the enticing gossip that Tyrone Power would play Orestes. A few days later Anderson wrote to Jeffers, 'I had a telegram from Bette Davis from hospital tonight, telling me that as soon as she is well, we will get together and talk about the Tower – keep your fingers crossed.'[194]

But this exciting possibility was not to be. Before Bette Davis recovered from the cold that had hospitalised her, Anderson had received an offer she could not refuse – to play the oldest sister, Olga, in Katharine Cornell's production of Chekhov's *The Three Sisters*, in an all-star cast with Cornell as the second sister Masha, and Ruth Gordon as their sister-in-law Natasha. Guthrie McClintic would direct.

McClintic and Cornell had been preparing for this production of Chekhov's *Three Sisters* since April. Their first priority was to find a male star to play Vershinin opposite Cornell's Masha, because the men were quickly disappearing into the services or the movies. Orson Welles, basking in the glory of *The Ambersons*, had film commitments; Brian Aherne expected to go into the forces; Maurice Evans was already called up; Basil Rathbone, Reginald Owen, Charles Boyer, Melvyn Douglas and Ronald Colman were not available. Finally, Dennis King replied emphatically with a one-word telegram: YES.[195]

---

194   *NYT* 11 Jun 1942: 26; *LAT* 24 Sep 1942: 14; *Variety* 24 Sep 1942: 8; *Pittsburgh Post-Gazette* 12 Oct 1942: 25; see also *NYT* 27 Sep 1942: X1, 2; Anderson to Jeffers, [28 Sep 1942], HRC.
195   Tad Mosel with Gertrude Macy, *Leading Lady: The World and Theatre of Katharine Cornell*, 1978, 447–53; *LAT* 26 Sep 1942: A7; corres 15 Apr to 24 Sep 1942, Cornell Papers.

With no prospect of touring immediately with Evans, Anderson was replenishing her coffers with another Warners movie, *Edge of Darkness*, starring her fellow Australian Errol Flynn. Playing a Norwegian hotelkeeper who outwits the Nazis, she was glad to be portraying a sympathetic character at last on film. Also in the cast was Ruth Gordon, who had been engaged by Cornell to play Natasha in *The Three Sisters*. 'What about Judith as Olga?' she wrote Gertrude Macy, Cornell's manager, in August 1942, when she learned that Evans was going into the army, leaving Anderson free. A month later, Anderson had agreed to join the production.[196]

McClintic and Cornell had hoped to begin rehearsals in early October. But the filming of *Edge of Darkness* dragged on, with frantic telegrams flying back and forth across the continent. 'We wanted gold and now gold is ruining everything,' Ruth Gordon telegraphed dramatically in mid-October. Rehearsals began in early November, with Gordon and Anderson arriving a few days late. Anderson recalled years later 'that day when I came from Hollywood, and saw the second act of *Three Sisters*.' 'Oh, the magic of it,' she remembered, 'the wonder of great theatre, well you gave me that and I will be everlastingly grateful to you both.'[197]

This all-star cast assembled by 'the first lady of the theater' created great excitement among theatre critics. MISS CORNELL BRINGS BRILLIANT CAST TO NATIONAL the *Washington Post* headline proclaimed as the play was about to make its out-of-town opening there on 30 November. 'Generous, lavish array of star-gleaming players as will stir theater-goers at the mere

---

196   *LAT* 4 Aug 1942: 15; *AWW* 10 Oct 1942: 20; Gordon to Macy, 23 Aug [1942]; Macy to Anderson, nd; Anderson to Macy, tel 30 Sep & 3 Oct 1942; McClintic to Anderson, tel 8 Oct 1942; Anderson to McClintic, tel 9 Oct 1942, Cornell Papers; *NYT* 13 Oct 1942: 18.
197   Gordon to Macy, tel 17 October 1942; Anderson to McClintic, nd [Apr 1951?], Cornell Papers; *WP* 3 Nov 1942: B8.

sight of their names.' Veteran columnist and former actress, Florence Fisher Parry, anticipating the impact of the ensemble, analysed the qualities of the three stars. 'Judith Anderson is an actress of strange magnetism,' she wrote. 'She casts a mesmeric spell upon the eye of the audience, compelling it to rivet upon her and her only... I have never been able to take my eyes off her so long as she is on the stage.' Ruth Gordon is similar, though not in same way, she noted. Like Pauline Lord, they both 'generate a subtle aura about their every word and move so rare and so intangible and quiet that it baffles analysis.' Cornell's impact, on the other hand, was more physical: she was 'an eye-filler' and it was hard to look elsewhere when she enters the scene. Imagine the sense of awe, therefore, of the young Kirk Douglas – about to play his first Broadway role as an orderly in *The Three Sisters* – when he joined these goddesses at thanksgiving dinner at McClintic and Cornell's house.[198]

When *The Three Sisters* opened in Washington a few days later the audience, which included first lady Eleanor Roosevelt and Ivy Litvinoff, the British-born wife of the Soviet Ambassador, responded warmly to the 'genuine distinction' of the play. 'Surrounding herself with a cast of magnificent capabilities and bestowing thoughtful intelligence upon the material investiture of three acts that plumb deeply into the fundamentals of human aspiration, bewilderment and frustration, the American theater's sole actress-manager illuminated the Chekhov work with the brilliance of many talents,' Nelson B Bell wrote admiringly in the *Washington Post*.[199]

After performances in Baltimore, Fort Meade and Philadelphia, *The Three Sisters* opened on Broadway on 21

---

198   *WP* 2 Nov 1942: L3; *Pittsburgh Press* 25 Oct 1942: 24; Kirk Douglas, *The Ragman's Son*, 1989, 82.
199   *WP* 1 Dec 1942: B8. See also Ivy Litvinoff: B8.

December 1942, to the accompaniment of a *Time* magazine cover featuring Cornell, Anderson and Gordon. Some critics found *The Three Sisters* 'old, mouldy' – 'a bore' – but most were fascinated by the spectacle of three of their greatest actresses appearing together. (The exception was Alvah Bessie in *The New Masses*.) *Billboard* praised its 'beautiful ensemble playing.' *Vogue* found it exciting 'because Katharine Cornell and Judith Anderson, both great stars, play non-star parts; because Ruth Gordon plays her fat part with spiteful expertise; because of Guthrie McClintic's compelling adaptation of the play.' Newspapers and magazines followed *Time* in printing striking pictures of the three stars in costume, sometimes accompanied by Gertrude Musgrove, the British actress (wife of Vincent Korda) who played the youngest sister, Irina.[200]

The critics were unanimous in praising what the *Wall Street Journal* called 'Anderson's severe, tortured portrait' of the frustrated schoolteacher, Olga. The *Los Angeles Times* considered that Olga was 'brilliantly performed by Judith Anderson in those shadowy, musical tones she has.' *Billboard* admired her 'quiet dignity and restraint.' Cecil Smith in the *Chicago Daily Tribune*, pronounced simply that Anderson 'takes the palm.'[201]

After a long season on Broadway – the longest of any Chekov play to that date – *The Three Sisters* began a road tour in Boston on 5 April 1943, playing in Cleveland, Fort Meade, Detroit and Chicago, where they ended in early June a season that the *Washington Post* declared 'confounded sceptics.'[202]

---

200   *Time* 21 Dec 1942; see also inside story; *Billboard* 2 Jan 1943: 53; *CDT* 3 Jan 1943: E4; *New Masses* 5 Jan 1943: 30–31; Vogue 15 Jan 1943: 44. For photos see *NYT* 20 Dec 1942: X1; 7 Mar 1943: X1; *CSM* 22 Dec 1942: 8; Cover, *Cue*, 26 Dec 1942; *Life* 4 Jan 1943: 33; *Vogue* 15 Jan 1943. For drawings, *CSM* 6 Apr 1943: 4; *CDT* 6 Jun 1943: F6.
201   *WSJ* 23 Dec 1942: 4; *LAT* 28 Dec 1942: 13; *Billboard* 2 Jan 1943: 53; *CDT* 17 Mar 1943: 24.
202   *WP* 8 Jun 1943: 10.

As *The Three Sisters* ended its record run on Broadway, *Variety* had announced that Judith Anderson and Ruth Gordon were being sought by Warners for lead roles in a movie adaptation of Ibsen's *Pillars of Society*. And as the play was about to open in Chicago in mid-May, the *New York Times* revealed that Jed Harris had sent the script of Robinson Jeffers' *Dear Judas* to Anderson. Hollywood columnists were still touting the possibility of Anderson and Bette Davis doing *Tower Beyond Tragedy*. But Anderson had read in the *Times* that Maurice Evans was in Hawaii, staging plays with a soldier cast. She immediately wrote to him, offering to do *Macbeth* with him and his soldier actors. By the end of July, Anderson was on her way to Hawaii in a shared cabin with two Red Cross workers.[203]

---

203   *Variety* 8 Apr 1943: 4; *NYT* 16 May: X1; 11 Apr: X1, 2; 9 Jun 1943: 16; *LAT* 15 Mar 1943: A8; *WP* 22 Jul 1943: 14.

Judith Anderson in New Guinea 1944

Australian War Memorial

Chapter Twenty-three

In the Pacific 1943–4

... just sweet Judy...
former Private George Schaefer 1996

'For fighting men, this grimmest of wars is in one small way also the gayest,' *Time* magazine wrote in September 1943 in an issue featuring Bob Hope and a chorus girl's leg on the cover. 'Never before have the folks who entertain the boys been so numerous or so notable; never have they worked so hard, traveled so far, risked so much. In the Middle East last week were Jack Benny, Larry Adler with his harmonica, Al Jolson with a harmonium; Ray Bolger was in the South Pacific, Judith Anderson in Hawaii.'[204]

In 1943 Captain Maurice Evans, Shakespearean actor, was in charge of the Entertainment Section, Special Services, for the Central Pacific Theatre, based in Hawaii.[205] The US victory at the battle of Midway the previous year had turned Hawaii into a training ground for the Pacific offensive. Troops poured into the islands, and, housed in barracks and makeshift camps, they needed entertainment.

Evans had assembled a talented group, which eventually grew to 60. His director was Private George Schaefer, a

---

204 *Time* 20 Sep 1943.
205 *NYT* 18 Aug 1942: 2; Jack Shulimson, 'Maurice Evans, Shakespeare and the U.S. Army,' *Journal of Popular Culture*, Fall 1976: 255; *WP* 30 Apr 1944: B6; Diary Aug 1943.

graduate of Yale Drama School. Private Harry F 'Freddy' Stover, formerly of Paramount's art department, designed the scenery. Painter and sculptor Corporal Paolo d'Ana was in charge of costumes. Sergeant Howard Morris was a former actor. Private Roger Morris had been a music librarian at Warners. Hal David, later an Academy award-winning lyricist, wrote the songs.[206]

Arthur E Wyman, head of theatre at the University of Hawaii, had put the university's well-equipped theatre, Farrington Hall, at Evans's disposal, as well as the travelling theatre he had built to take shows to the scattered camps. In addition, the Entertainment Section had a circuit of 'half-way decent' wooden stages; but they were prepared to play anywhere on any kind of platform. They carried their set and lighting and wardrobe with them.[207]

Suffering from fever from her tetanus shot, Judith Anderson arrived in Honolulu on 29 July 1943 to play *Macbeth* with Evans and his GI actors. The normally relaxed holiday resort was in full alert mode, with barbed wire guarding the beaches, military police everywhere, and a full blackout enforced in the tropical heat. She went immediately into rehearsals, and they opened on Sunday 8 August in a camp in the mountains that held about 900 men. Evans was a great believer in the entertainment value of Shakespeare's plays. 'These plays are made of great stuff,' he told a reporter. 'They are never boring. These plays strike fire, they make you listen.' He was right. The production played to 60,000 servicemen during the three months they toured the Hawaiian bases, and was considered a great success, especially because of Anderson's name and charm.[208]

---

206 *Variety* 26 May 1943: 25; *LAT* 31 Dec 1970: C15.
207 George Schaefer, *From Live Tape to Film: 60 Years of Inconspicuous Directing*, 1996, 14.
208 Diary 29 Jul to 8 Aug 1944; Evans, *All This... And Evans Too!* 1987, 159–66; *CDT*

Anderson's capacity for enjoying herself made her ideal for the multitude of tasks involved in 'entertaining the troops.' As Maurice Evans put it in his memoirs, 'In her breezy Australian way Judith was a good sport.' At one end of the social spectrum, she dined with Lt General Richardson, the Commanding General of the Hawaiian Department,

---

26 Sep 1943: E2; *Variety* 6 Oct 1943: 1; 17 May 17, 1944: 2; *LAT* 29 Apr 1944: A4.

and Admiral Nimitz, the Commander in Chief of the US Pacific Fleet, and made a good friend of Admiral Bill Halsey, commander of the United Nations' forces in the South Pacific. At the other, she chatted to the men, mixing with them in their recreation centres. 'I ate with them, danced with them and talked with them,' she told a reporter later. Her appointment diary is littered with references to special friends that she made – 'Benny's party,' 'Kevin Wallace lunch,' 'Supper Howard Bill' 'Reggie Benny' – and adventures – 'Moonlight swim,' 'Sea shore,' 'Hawaiian music Dancing,' 'Moonlight party,' 'Flying,' 'Cattle round-up,' 'Goodbye to boys.' One day she lunched with Garth Jeffers, one of Una and Robin Jeffers' twin sons, who was stationed on Hawaii, and on another she dined with First Lady Eleanor Roosevelt, who was on her way home from a tour of the Pacific for the Red Cross. To the 'roly-poly Sergeant,' George Schaefer, who directed her in *Macbeth* and who was to become an important person in her later career, she was 'just sweet Judy.'[209]

Judith Anderson in Hawaii with future television producer and director George Schaefer 1943
Author's collection

But above all she went to the hospitals. 'It was not easy,' she told a reporter. 'I saw the cost of war, not in guns or ships

---

209   Evans, *All This… And Evans Too!* 166; Schaefer, *From Live Tape to Film*, 17. See also for photos of production.

or money, but in men, in boys, in glorious youth sacrificed for our freedom, our comfort, our liberty.'[210]

When Anderson got back to Los Angeles at the end of October 1943, she quickly reported on Garth Jefffers' welfare to his parents. 'Judith Anderson long-distanced from Hollywood the other night. – my boys' birthday,' Una Jeffers wrote a friend. 'She said Garth looks well and very handsome! etc., etc. Would I could see for myself.' She wrote to a number of the 'boys' she had met in Hawaii; and she participated in various fund-raising shows.[211]

Anderson wanted to return to the New York stage; but she hadn't worked for 10 months and needed money. She immediately tested for the role of Elizabeth Taylor's mother in MGM's *National Velvet*; but she lost out to Anne Revere, who won an Academy Award for her performance. She did, however, win a plum role as Ann Treadwell in Twentieth Century-Fox's *Laura*. A reporter interviewing her during the filming of *Laura* found her 'well-groomed and very friendly.' At the studio a Marine arrived from overseas. Picking her up and kissing her, he exclaimed, 'Isn't she lovely!'[212]

Indeed she was lovely in *Laura*. As a chic Park Avenue socialite with a weakness for tall younger men, she and her gigolo played by Vincent Price, stole the show, along with columnist, Clifton Webb, from the beautiful Gene Tierney in this very successful psychological thriller. At the age of 47, elegantly dressed by Bonnie Cashin, she was the epitome of sophisticated glamour, while Miss Tierney, according to one

---

210   *CSM* 4 Jan 1944: 8.
211   Una Jeffers to Barth Carpenter Marshall, 13 Nov 1943, RJSF; *Variety* 10 Nov: 47; 17: 1; 22: 9; 23: 14; 26: 11; Dec 1: 27; 13, 1943: 9; 23 Feb 1944: 19; *NYT* 25 Nov 1943: 51; Diary 25 Nov 1943; *Billboard* 27 Nov 1943: 4; *LAT* 4 Feb 1944: A1; *Auckland Star* 12 Feb 1944: 4.
212   Diary 8 Nov 1943; *WP* 24 Nov 1943: B6; *MGM News* Feb 1944, MHL; *NYT* 31 Mar 1944: 27; *Cleveland Plain Dealer Pictorial* [after 25 Apr 1944], NYPL.

An elegant Judith Anderson with Vincent Price in Laura *1944*

Author's collection

critic, 'plays at being a brilliant and sophisticated advertising executive with the wild-eyed innocence of a college junior.'[213]

Directed by Otto Preminger, *Laura* is now considered a

---

213 *NYHT* 12 Oct 1944, MHL; *Variety* nd, UCSB.

major film noir classic, selected for preservation in the US Film Registry by the Library of Congress as being 'culturally, historically or aesthetically significant.' The movie follows the investigation by detective Mark McPherson, played by Dana Andrews, of the apparent murder of advertising executive Laura Hunt (Gene Tierney). Clifton Webb plays Laura's effete mentor, Waldo Lydecker; Vincent Price is her playboy fiancé, Shelby Carpenter; and Judith Anderson her wealthy socialite aunt, who is also Shelby's lover and patron. The movie critic Roger Ebert in 2002 described *Laura* as 'contrived, artificial, mannered, and yet achieving a kind of perfection in its balance between low motives and high style.' 'What makes the movie great, perhaps,' he added, 'is the casting.' Indeed, the role of Ann Treadwell allows Anderson to look stylish in what Howard Barnes in the New York *Herald-Tribune* called 'a brilliantly modulated performance of the gigolo's "protectress".' Edwin Schallert in the *Los Angeles Times*, always a promoter of Anderson's screen potential, admired the way she 'provides a sultry, sinister character that dynamically emerges from the background' – a brilliant illustration of the important new role of character actors that he championed.[214]

In August 1944 Anderson had not appeared on Broadway since April the previous year. Veteran critic George Jean Nathan predicted that 'If Judith Anderson re-appears on the stage, she will achieve a personal success no matter what the play or the role in which she offers herself.'[215]

Patriotism, however, kept her from the Broadway stage for another year. When the United Services Organization began

---

214 *Chicago Sun Times* 20 Jan 2002, UCSB; *NYHT* 12 Oct 1944, MHL; *LAT* 17 Nov 1944; 10.
215 *American Mercury* Aug 1944: 226–29.

their overseas Camp Shows in July 1944, Anderson was one of the first to volunteer. The USO was a civilian organisation, strongly backed by Hollywood and Broadway, that provided recreation services to US military personnel. USO centres and clubs around the world acted as Homes Away from Home for GIs.

'Imagine my joy upon opening my sealed orders on the plane to find I was coming home to Australia,' she told the Australian press. On 10 July 1944 Anderson landed in Brisbane as part of USO Overseas Unit #297 with pianist-composer Albert Hay Malotte (who wrote the music for *The Lord's Prayer*), accordionist Anne Triola, violinist Shirley Cornell and singer Helen McClure. In a travelling suit of tailored khaki, with long pants and form-fitting tunic with a scarlet spread eagle on the shoulders and brass US insignia on the coat lapels, she won over the *Courier Mail* reporter with her 'charming smile' and 'sparkling eyes, denoting a sense of humour.' 'My movements are controlled by the US Army,' she told the reporter. 'I know not where I go.'[216]

A week later she was in Sydney, where her troupe presented an hour's program in US military camps and hospitals. She just had time for a reunion with her brother Jack, her three nieces, and her old friend Eileen Robinson Brooks, a visit to the Borovansky Ballet at the Theatre Royal, a Guest of Honour broadcast on the ABC and a photo session with the *Australian Women's Weekly* before the unit set off for New Guinea. Three weeks later, the Adelaide *Advertiser* reported from 'Somewhere In New Guinea' that, in spite of adverse weather, the American concert party featuring Judith Anderson had given concerts at Dobodura, Lae, Nadzab, and Finschhafen and that 'Large audiences have shown their

---

216   *AWW* 29 Jul 1944: 12; *SMH* 11 Jul: 4; *Courier-Mail* 11 Jul 1944: 3; *Variety* 19 Jul 1944.

appreciation of the more classical type of entertainment provided by the party.'[217]

Australia and its Territory of New Guinea had been under attack since January 1942, when Japanese troops captured Rabaul and soon after bombed the northern Australian port of Darwin. In response, the United States had committed itself to the defense of Australia, establishing General Douglas MacArthur as Supreme Commander, South West Pacific Area with headquarters in Brisbane, and American troops began arriving, turning Queensland into the 'one huge training camp and staging area' that Anderson found when she arrived in 1944. General Sir Thomas Blamey, Commander-in-Chief of the Australian Military Forces, was appointed Land Forces Commander under MacArthur. From July 1942 Australia and American troops fought the Japanese in New Guinea, finally making progress against them early in 1943.[218]

Dobodura, Lae, Nadzab, and Finschhafen were airbases that had been captured late in 1943. Since then the allied troops had been sweeping up the northern coast of New Guinea to Hollandia, the enemy base in Dutch New Guinea, which was secured by the end of June 1944 and established as General MacArthur's main base for his planned invasion of the Philippines. When Judith Anderson and her unit moved on to Aitape and Hollandia in late August, the allies were still clearing remnants of the enemy troops, especially on Biak Island, which had been captured, with great loss of life, only a few weeks before.

This assignment was something quite different from anything Anderson – a great dramatic actress – had done before. As she put it in her memoirs, 'in the jungle

---

217   *SMH* 18 Jul: 3, 6; 19 Jul: 7; 24 Jul 1944: 5; *Townsville Daily Bulletin* 4 Aug 1944: 4; *AWW* 29 Jul 1944: 12; *Advertiser* 21 Aug 1944: 6.
218   http://www.battleforaustralia.org/battaust/JapaninvadesNewGuinea.html

amphitheatres of New Guinea which were customarily devoted to movies, home-grown GI entertainments, and boxing and wrestling matches, the crudely lettered billboards announced:

> SATURDAY NIGHT! NO FIGHTS!
> JUDITH ANDERSON SHOW!
> 4 GIRLS!

'We had no sets, no costumes, no large company, no play,' she remembered, 'a "quality" variety show, I like to think, with more than a passing resemblance to an old fashioned concert party.'

Anderson was the mistress of ceremonies for this 'quality' show, and was listed to present two monologues. In Lae, however, their troupe was joined by a young naval officer, Robert Wallsten, who had been with Anderson in *The Old Maid*. Together they sliced a one-act play from *Macbeth*, and once again she introduced 'boys newly trained to kill' to 'the bloody story of an old Scotch killing.' 'Never have I known such close contact with an audience,' she later wrote, 'or felt one that hung, as this one did, with such alertness on every nuance of a text that for many of them was brand new.'

'The carriage trade arrived in jeeps, command cars, trucks and even bulldozers,' she recalled in her memoirs. 'while others trudged on foot, wearing ponchos against the inevitable rain, carrying stools or crates to sit on, beginning to fill the sky-roofed auditoriums as early as three in the afternoon for a seven-thirty show.'

Anderson was always apprehensive as to how 'the boys' would receive her 'classy' show. Lieutenant General Robert Eichelberger, who had led the troops in their capture of Hollandia, gave a firsthand account of her reception in a letter to his wife. 'Last night I heard by chance that Judith Anderson, the great actress, and a troupe would give a performance in a nearby camp,' he wrote. 'We went over... and it turned out to be by far the best thing that has been given. In fact, there has been nothing that would even run second to it.'

> *The male pianist played everything from Tschaikowski to swing; a girl violinist was pretty and very accomplished; a singer who sang; and an Italian girl who was also easy to look at furnished the naughty songs. Judith Anderson herself and a Naval officer who formerly worked with her on Broadway gave parts of Macbeth and she also gave some other recitations. The soldiers reacted ten times better than they did to the Bob Hope show.*[219]

Judith Anderson and Shirley Cornell entertained by RAAF officers after a wartime show at Aitape, Northeast New Guinea, 1944

Australian War Memorial

---

219   Robert Eichelberger to Em, 27 Aug 1944, in *Dear Miss Em: General Eichelberger's War in the Pacific 1942–1945*, 1972, 153–54.

As Maurice Evans had said of Anderson in Hawaii, she was always 'a good sport.' Her Daily Reminder for 21 August reveals a typical day: 'Biak, Owi, 1 Show Seabees, 2 Hospitals, Sleep in tent, fox-hole. She 'bounced in jeeps… over roads, carved into mountainsides by the Engineers or Sea bees and frequently pitted with water-filled shell holes or bomb craters, past blasted hillsides and palm trees decapitated by bombardment.' She slept in nurses' quarters in Quonsets, in pup tents, and on cots on the boat deck of a decommissioned ship in Hollandia harbour, while just over the hill dog-fighting planes spat fire. In Biak, still the scene of a mopping-up operation, she was driven past cliffs where enemy corpses 'lay in the grotesque attitudes of some wild frozen dance.'

Part of the task Anderson had set herself, as in Hawaii, was to pay a daily visit to the hospitals, especially the psychopathetic wards. She had discovered in Hawaii that 'an unfamiliar face, a civilian, a woman' helped these patients, and she was always thrilled when, after the war, these young men, recovered, sought her out.

A woman of strong feeling, helping to boost the morale of the troops seemed to bring out the best in her.[220] Her heart 'broke a hundred times a day' she wrote later, remembering her experiences in New Guinea, 'and was lifted as often, to see the simple, even merry taking-for-granted of the most appalling conditions – danger, pain, or more unrelieved day-after-day tedium in mud or dust.'

> *No more than any of us were these youths saints; but New Guinea was our crucible, our test, and I would hope that in my smaller orbit I emerged as they did, at the peak of my form. In the end the memory holds the knowledge of having witnessed a tragedy more overwhelming than any*

---

220 Robert Wallsten, in Anderson, 470–80.

ever set down on paper: a whole generation of high-hearted young men threatened and decimated by death, mutilation, madness. I shall never forget those wonderful, gallant, smiling faces, or the hurt ones, or the dead ones. At this distance the experience still seems the finest, most ennobling of my life. It was a privilege to have been there – and to known them.

Was she, one wonders, when she saw the realities of war at first hand, thinking of her young love, Oliver Hogue, toiling through Gallipoli and the Desert War, only to die of influenza so many years ago?

Judith Anderson, Teresa Wright and Robert Mitchum with the prone figure of John Rodney in Pursued *1947*

TCD/ Prod.DB/ Alamy Stock Photo

Chapter Twenty-four

Character Actress 1944–7

... in a role of fatefulness and power the 50-year-old Judith Anderson is all but elevated to movie stardom in her role as Jeb's adopted mother, Medora Callum

Edwin Shallert, Los Angeles Times

While she was entertaining the troops in the Caribbean at the end of 1944, Anderson got a cable from Jed Harris, suggesting they revive their plan to produce *Medea* in a translation by Jeffers. She returned to New York almost as fast as her cable of acceptance. Early in the new year Harris contacted Jeffers asking him if he was willing to take on the project. The usually obdurate Jeffers turned to the translation (or, rather, loose adaptation) immediately, much to his wife Una's surprise. In April 1945 Anderson and Harris drove to Carmel for a 'sparkling' talk with Jeffers and Una, in which Harris came up with many ideas that were incorporated in the script and the production. As Una wrote to Melba Berry Bennett, 'Harris is the most stimulating person – the first person in a very long time who interested Robin or me by his talk (of art!)… Harris kept us up very late completely absorbed.'[221]

---

221 Una Jeffers to Melba Berry Bennett, Apr 1945, quoted in Bennett, *The Stone Mason of Tor House: The Life and Work of Robinson Jeffers*, 1966, 194; 'Introduction:

But Harris was, as usual, mercurial and difficult to deal with. Two months later he pulled out, unwilling to accept the contract Jeffers offered. Absorbed in his task, however, Jeffers completed the play and it was published in March 1946. The Theatre Guild acquired the play in September 1945, but they let their option lapse. In April 1946 John Chapman in the *Chicago Daily Tribune* lamented that 'What might have been a real first actress performance was postponed to next season – the appearance of Judith Anderson as Medea.' 'I have read Robinson Jeffers' new treatment of *Medea* and find it magnificent,' he wrote; 'and Miss Anderson is just the one to project it with all its racking pity and all its shattering horror.'[222]

Meanwhile, Anderson's life changed in an unexpected direction. In fall 1945 she had met aspiring theatre producer and director Luther Greene. Born in 1910, 13 years after Anderson, he had just separated from his wife, Ellie, with whom he had two children, Lenka, aged about four and Luther Jr, 18 months. He had had a small success before the war, but after a short time in the services he had taken up ranching outside Santa Barbara. After the breakdown of his marriage he was trying to get back into the theatre.[223]

Greene's enthusiasm for a magnificent production of *Medea* was no doubt a powerful aphrodisiac for Anderson. It was probably his interference that led to the Guild dropping the project. He immediately took up the option himself and they began planning such a production. As Una Jeffers wrote

---

1845–1950,' in James Karman, ed., *The Collected Letters of Robinson Jeffers With Selected Letters of Una Jeffers, Volume One, 1890–1930*, 2009. See Una Jeffers to Bennett, 5 Mar 1945, RJHRC; to Hans and Phoebe Barkan, 6 Apr 1945, RJSF; to Frederick and Maud Clapp, 21 Apr 1945, RJYale; to Anderson, 23 Apr 1945, RJTH, in Karman, *Collected Letters*.

222   Harris to Anderson, tel 24 & 30 Apr; 15 Jun 1945, UCSB; Una Jeffers to William Fitelson, [May 1945], RJHRC; to Bennett Cerf, 29 May 1945, RJBerk; to Anderson, 18 Jul 1948 [1945], RJTH, in Karman, *Collected Letters*; *LAT* 13 Jun 1945: A2.

223   Toby Rowland to Angna Enters, 6 Nov 1945, Enters Papers.

to Anderson in March 1946, 'We are thrilled just to let our minds dwell on the set-up you had planned.' 'Patience, my heart,' she counselled, 'I believe that some wonderful arrangement will yet be arrived at.'[224]

Anderson's first move was to approach Igor Stravinsky to write the music. The Russian-born Stravinsky, one of the most important composers of the twentieth century, had settled in 1940 in Los Angeles, where he enjoyed the company of writers and poets. He had explored classical Greek themes in his ballets *Apollon* (1928) and *Persephone* (1933), and in 1947 would compose *Orpheus* in collaboration with choreographer George Balanchine. He welcomed the opportunity to work with Anderson and Jeffers, and began work on the music, to be ready by mid-July. Sadly, it was never finished, as Anderson and Greene could not meet his terms.[225]

In June 1946, as Anderson sold her Los Angeles home, the *New York Times* reported, 'Greene Has Plans for Trio of Shows.' Two involved Anderson: a revival of *Come of Age*; and *Medea*. A month later, a few days after his divorce decree was finalised, Greene and Anderson were married.[226]

Anderson maintained many years later that she had still wanted children and that she had hoped Greene would make a good manager, in the mould of Guthrie McClintic. At 49

---

224 Una Jeffers to Bennett Cerf, 29 Apr 1946, RJBerk; to Greene, 8 Jun 1946; to William Morris Agency, 15 Jun [1946], RJHRC; to Anderson, 16 Mar 1946, RJTH; to Blanche Matthias, 24 May 1946, RJYale; to Melba Berry Bennett, 31 Oct 1946, RJHRC, in Karman, *Collected Letters*.
225 Una Jeffers to Saxe Commins, 2 Apr 1946, RJBerk, in Karman, *Collected Letters*; Stephen Walsh, *Stravinsky: The Second Exile: France and America, 1934–1971*, 2006, 41–51. There is no record of what those terms were.
226 *LAT* 12 Jun: A3; 12 Jul 1946: 7; *SMH* 13 Jul 1946: 1; *Argus* 13 Jul 1946: 7; *NYT* 14 Jun 1946: 17; *Time* 22 Jul 1946; *News*? 30 Nov 1946, NYPL; Luther Greene to Una Jeffers, Thu [18/25 Jul 1946], from 213 S. Reeves, Beverly Hills, RJHRC; Una Jeffers to Melba Berry Bennett, 31 Oct 1946, RJHRC, in Karman, *Collected Letters*.

years old, it is doubtful if she had realistic hopes for children of her own (although Louella Parsons reported in November that Anderson was pregnant).[227] She did, however, establish loving relations with Lenka and Luther Jr (and, indeed, several years later, with their mother). But the desire for a manager was genuine, and Greene had obviously talked a good talk, promising her the much-loved *Come of Age* and the dreamed-of *Medea*.

From the time she had finished *The Three Sisters* in mid-1943 Anderson had made no money in the theatre. To enable her to offer her services to the troops, to maintain her home and support her mother and sister – and now an unemployed husband – she had turned to the movies, 'the actors' refuge' as she called them.[228] She was in her late forties, an elegant woman with a striking face who was capable of playing any character, from a suave sophisticate to a capable frontierswoman. During this period, as plans for *Medea* gradually came to fruition, Anderson made seven movies: *And Then There Were None*, *Diary of a Chambermaid*, *The Strange Love of Martha Ivers*, *Specter of the Rose*, *The Red House*, *Pursued*, and *Tycoon*.

Each of these movies is interesting in its own way. *Ten Little Indians* (released as *And Then There Were None*) was made when Anderson returned from Australia and New Guinea and the Caribbean late in 1944, directed by the exiled French filmmaker Rene Clair. *The Diary of a Chambermaid*, a project of her old friend Burgess Meredith and his wife Paulette Goddard, was directed by one of the greatest directors of all

---

227 *SFE* 11 Nov 1946; Una Jeffers to William Turner Levy, 13 Nov 1946, NYPL, in Karman, *Collected Letters*.
228 *NYHT* 15 Jun? 1941, NYPL.

time and another French exile, Jean Renoir.[229]

The most unusual, *Specter of the Rose*, was an experiment by Hollywood's highest-paid screenwriter Ben Hecht, in making a prestige art film for the budget production house Republic Studios. With stunning photography by Lee Garmes and score by George Antheil, *Specter of the Rose* has been called the first ballet-noir. Anderson's miniscule role in *The Strange Love of Martha Ivers* (original title *Love Lies Bleeding*) is interesting only as the first instance of Barbara Stanwyck's aggression against Anderson in a movie. (The second, more spectacular, is when Stanwyck takes Anderson's eye out with a pair of well-aimed scissors in their 1950 film *The Furies*).[230]

During 1944 and 1945 Judith Anderson had made four movies, more than she would ever make in a two-year period again. George Jean Nathan continued to lament her absence from the theatre; but she would make three more movies before she returned to her true *metier*. In May 1946 she played Edward G Robinson's sister in the noirish mystery, *The Red House* (original title *No Trespassing*). Early in 1947 she made *Tycoon* for RKO with John Wayne and Laraine Day, playing the young heroine's eagle-eyed governess – a part that allowed her to look austerely elegant, but was, like the film, eminently forgettable.[231]

Among all the movies Anderson made in this period, only one took the risk of casting her in a totally different role. This was *Pursued*, an innovative psychological western produced

---

229   *LAT* 13 Jun 1945: A2; *CDT* 1 Mar 1946: 27; UCLA Festival of Preservation 14 Aug 2004, MHL.
230   *Variety* 1 Nov 1945: 10; *WP* 8 Nov 1945: 7; http://www.albany.edu/writers-inst/fns03n12.html *Film Notes* Specter Of The Rose; Budget Bureau, 24 Sep 1945, *Love Lies Bleeding* [*The Strange Love of Martha Ivers*], UCSB; *WP* 27 Nov 27, 1945: 8. Stanwyck pushes her aunt, played by Anderson, down the stairs to her death in *The Strange Love*.
231   Nathan, *American Mercury* Aug 1945: 175; *LAT* 16 May 1946: A3; 25 Dec 1947: A12.

by Milton Sperling at Warners Bros and directed by Raoul Walsh, filmed on location outside Gallup in New Mexico just after Anderson and Greene married in 1946. Hailed as one of the first and finest examples of a new hybrid genre, the cowboy noir, its New Mexico mesas are dark and claustrophobic, with high cliffs, low clouds and ruined houses casting shadows over its protagonists and their secrets. What one critic has called 'that icon of noirish ambiguity,' Robert Mitchum – not yet a major star – strolls through his role as Jeb Rand, besieged on all sides by forces he cannot understand. And 'in a role of fatefulness and power' – to quote Edwin Shallert – the 49-year-old Judith Anderson is 'all but elevated to movie stardom' in her role as Jeb's adopted mother Medora Callum.[232]

The moody lighting of Pursued *casting shadows over its protagonists and their secrets.*
Author's collection

---

232   *LAT* 25 Jul; 7 Sep 1946: A5; 15 Mar 1947; A5. Anderson was paid $25,000 for the movie: see *NYT* 9 Mar 1947: X5; Douglas Doepke, customer review of *Blood on the Moon*, Amazon.com.

The story unfolds through a series of flashbacks in which Jeb Rand struggles to remember an incident of his early childhood – the memory of which might give him the key to a series of tragedies that befall him for no apparent reason. The film begins with a young boy (Jeb) being rescued by Ma Callum – the Judith Anderson character – from his hiding place in a house where something catastrophic has taken place. All he recalls is the flash of light off a pair of spurs – an image that returns to him again and again throughout the movie. He remembers calling for his Daddy and then being saved by a strange woman he has never seen before: Ma Callum.

Ma Callum takes Jeb into her family, bringing him up with her son Adam and daughter Thor. As they grow up, Thor and Jeb fall in love, and Adam comes to hate Jeb, who he considers an interloper. All the while, many unexplained attempts are made on Jeb's life, and he is shadowed by a brooding character also named Callum. After many twists and turns in the plot, Jeb and Thor end up back in the ruins of the old house, where he begins to remember the source of the 'black dog' that has been ruining his life.

Throughout the film, Ma Callum has kept the secret of her deadly love affair with his father from Jeb, trying to make a family where the secret continually causes hate instead of love. There is a beautiful scene that evokes the loving family Ma tries to make, but which Adam is unable to share, when Jeb, returning from the Mexican war, sings the *Londonderry Air*.

Stumbling across his old homestead while out riding one day, Jeb brings his anguish to Ma Callum, but she refuses to help him remember. In the final climactic scene, Ma Callum's secret is revealed, and she faces up to what she has to do to release Jeb from his childhood trauma and allow the two young lovers to move on to the future together.

There is much that could be said about *Pursued*. The

Jeb (Robert Mitchum) sings the Londonderry Air *while Adam (John Rodney) can't bring himself to join in*

Author's collection

filmmakers themselves billed it as 'the first psychological western'; and commentators have called it 'one of the top five westerns.' Certainly, as one critic put it, the movie 'smoothly integrate[s] the bedrock Western with the inky film noir,' especially in James Wong Howe's moody cinematography. Contemporary critic Leo Mishkin called it a 'Combination of Horse Opera and Psychoanalysis.' Putting it in blunt Hollywoodese, the *Hollywood Reporter* announced: 'Sperling Blazes New Oater Trail.' Western screenwriter Jack Moffitt put it more elegantly in *Esquire* when he wrote that *Pursued* 'overhauls and modernizes the entire tradition of western movies.' It is 'not so much a western as a strong human interest story located in the West. It has its hard riding and its fast shooting, but Sperling is less interested in perforating his characters than in showing what makes them tick. He gets inside the personalities of ranch women and

Judith Anderson as Ma Callum saves Robert Mitchum from a lynching
Author's collection

frontier gun fighters and treats them as human beings.'[233]

Viewers now – and viewers then – would immediately recognise the story as one of trauma and its healing. Those who suffered trauma – whether it be a childhood tragedy like Jeb's or a trauma resulting from war experiences (remember, this is 1947) would continue to repeat that experience in their nightmares until its original cause was confronted.

The American public had become familiar with trauma and its treatment as soldiers returned from the war with what was often called 'shell-shock.' Yet many people denied the existence of the syndrome or argued that it was 'better to forget.' Running concurrently with *Pursued* was *The Best Years of Our Lives* – the feel-good movie about three returning servicemen, one with physical wounds and all of them with

---

233   Don Chriscoe and Richard T. Jameson [*Film Comment* critic], customer reviews, Amazon.com; *NYMT?* 8 Mar 1947, USC; *HR* 12 Mar 1947; *Esquire* Apr 1947: 65, 209–14.

psychological ones. The movie, which won eight Academy Awards and was the biggest box office success since *Gone with the Wind*, dealt sensitively with the problems of the men's return home, but takes an optimistic stance to America's future, symbolised by the concluding wedding scene which forms, as one recent commentator put it, 'a closing of the ranks of the tribe… a getting beyond the pain and tumult of the past and a jittery present in commitment to the vision of a happier future.'[234] Although *Pursued* also ends with a couple going off together, it conveys a very different picture of America – a much more anxious and precarious one. This marriage between the feuding Callums and Rands has only been achieved by bloodshed and mayhem and we wonder how long its happiness will last.

Pursued was an interesting example of the important role of psychoanalysis in the films of the 1940s, and the way the theme of trauma and the use of noir characters and photographic effects conveyed a sense of foreboding as America emerged from World War II into the shadow of the Cold War.

Rebecca – and Anderson's performance as Mrs Danvers – had established the increasing importance of the character actor in movies during the forties, making it possible for a 50-year-old non-movie star like Anderson to be given such a central part as Medora Callum. Edwin Schallert, the *Los Angeles Times* movie critic, musing on *Rebecca*'s impact on the movie world in a series of articles in 1940, had predicted that its impact would be greater than that of *Gone with the Wind*. '*Rebecca* is the most striking picture ever made in terms of women character players,' he wrote. Judith Anderson 'is responsible for increased respect by the producers in casting of character players… ' '[Her] performance will, I believe,

---

234   Philip D. Beidler, 'Remembering the Best Years of Our Lives,' *Virginia Quarterly Review* Autumn 1996: 591–604.

prove the most far-reaching in giving a new complexion to the studio's appreciation of the exceptional talent of these people.' 'The cycle for the character actress has dawned,' he wrote in June 1940; 'here is a discovery for the studios of the first water... what [these notable stage actresses] can say with eyes and thought registered in facial expression is naught short of momentous.' [235]

Alton Cook in the *New York World Telegraph* considered that 'probably no other Western ever has been played with such delicacy and subtlety... Judith Anderson brings the wisdom of a great actress to her role of a seething woman of the frontier.' In *Esquire* Jack Moffitt admired Anderson's 'brilliant delineation of a pioneer mother who found the wilderness a hell.' Nelson B Bell in the *Washington Post* admired the movie's underplaying, noting that 'Judith Anderson's interpretation of the tortured Mrs Callum is only another demonstration of the finish and finesse of an accomplished actress.' Howard Barnes in the *New York Herald Tribune* stated flatly that Miss Anderson 'knows more about acting than most Hollywood actresses will ever learn.' And John T McManus in *PM* commented that Teresa Wright and Judith Anderson – draped mostly in the drabs of early ranch life – 'have to do it all with acting, at which they are of the very best.'[236]

Researcher Doris G Bazzini and her associates, writing in the journal *Sex Roles* in 1997 on 'The aging woman in popular film: Underrepresented, unattractive, unfriendly, and unintelligent,' have demonstrated that the large disparity in numbers of men and women over 35 (the aging woman!) in character roles diminished in the 1940s to a percentage which was only again reached in the 1970s.[237] In other words, these were good

---

235   *LAT* 24 Mar: C3; 28 Apr: C3; 2 Jun 1940: C3
236   *NYWT* 8 Mar 1947; *WP* 1 Apr: 5; 3 Apr 1947: 2; *NYHT* 8 Mar 1947.
237   Doris G. Bazzini *et al*, 'The aging woman in popular film: Underrepresented, unattractive, unfriendly, and unintelligent,' *Sex Roles* 36:7–8, Apr 1997.

years for older female character actors, as Edwin Shallert had predicted. The casting of Anderson – a middle-aged stage actress – albeit a star in her own firmament – in the role of Medora Callum, allowing her to play the role as the unglamorous, drably dressed frontier woman she is meant to be, and the adulation that she received for her acting, at least from critics, is, therefore, an interesting case study in the elevation of the female character actor in the 1940s.

This new interest in the female character actor can be seen as another symptom of the decline of the studio system during that decade.[238] Independents were ready to try new talent, they were ready to try out the best that Broadway offered, and they were more willing than the established studios to give theatrical stars the freedom they wanted to move easily between Hollywood and New York. Audiences were changing, becoming more educated and 'culture-wise,' and appreciating, like the reviewers quoted earlier, the 'delicate and subtle' acting of the best of Broadway. The award of the Academy Award in 1948 to Laurence Olivier's *Hamlet* is an interesting sign of this thirst for culture.

---

238 The studio system, or Golden Age of Hollywood, usually regarded as the period 1927 to 1949, was dominated by 8 major studios who produced movies on their own lots and maintained tight control over their personnel, distribution and theatres. See Thomas Schatz, *The Genius of the System: Hollywood Filmmaking in the Studio Era.* Faber and Faber, 1988

ACT IV
Climax

Scene Seven
Medea

Although Miss Anderson has left some memorable marks on great women in the theatre, Medea *has summoned all her powers as an actress. Now everyone realizes that she has been destined for* Medea *from the start.*

Brooks Atkinson, New York Times

Judith Anderson as Medea 1947. Photographer unknown

Museum of the City of New York

Chapter Twenty-five

Judith the Great 1947–8

Anderson 'plots the doom of her enemies with the intelligence of a priestess of black magic.' Brooks Atkinson, 1947

Author's collection

Between 1944 and 1947 Judith Anderson had made a lot of money in the movies: *Pursued* alone had earned her $25,000. 'After I have made much money,' she had vowed in 1928, 'I might give the public just one fine play.'[1]

---

1 *BG* 25 Mar 1928, NYPL; *NYT* 9 Mar 1947: X5.

Since 1929 she had been determined that that fine play would come from the pen of Robinson Jeffers; and he had written that play, *Medea*, for her in 1945. A postwar audience was hungry for such a play. After many disappointments, that long-held dream looked like coming true when she married producer Luther Greene in July 1946.

Luther, however, turned out to be another impediment to her dream. This marriage quickly seemed as if it was going to be even more short-lived than her previous one. As they set off in September for their delayed honeymoon in Europe, she wrote in her memoirs 20 years later, she knew almost immediately that it had been an error. In Luther Greene Anderson seemed to have found a temperament as stormy as her own. In Bristol, where they were staying with her brother Frank and his family in what were no doubt cramped and uncomfortable postwar quarters, he unleashed the temper that was the other side of his expansive optimism. And he demonstrated an enthusiasm for spending her money. When they returned to New York early in November, they separated immediately. 'I have just finished 3 days of complete misery & nastiness & I am sick to death of Luther & Judith & separations & trunks & whose whos!' Luther's former roommate Toby Rowland wrote his friend Angna Enters in late November. 'What horrible things they have both said & done – at least I give her credit for something, she's told me the bad things she's done; that's more than he has done —— – oh Angna what a mess.' 'It Lasted Four Months,' the *New York News* reported on 30 November, displaying a photo of the pair at the time of their wedding. 'You have heard, no doubt, that I called off the Judith mistake,' Greene wrote to Enters. 'It takes more than a fine actress to make a wife, I guess.'[2]

---

2 Toby Rowland to Enters, Fri [late Nov 1946]; Greene to Enters, 11 Dec [1946], Enters Papers; *News*? 30 Nov 1946, NYPL.

This unhappy adventure behind her, Anderson welcomed John Gielgud to New York, where he was about to appear in *The Importance of Being Earnest*, while her estranged husband dined with Buddy and Mary (Pickford) Rogers in Hollywood. Meanwhile the new firm of Robert Whitehead and Oliver Rea had been writing seductively to Jeffers. In January 1947 they had taken over the production of *Medea*, which they promised for the spring.[3]

The handsome Robert Whitehead was 31 years old – 'an aging juvenile' as he later put it – and Oliver Rea 23 in 1947. The two had met on a beachhead at Anzio and had shared their plans for the theatre after the war. In December 1946 they had opened for business. *Medea* would be their first – and daring – production.[4]

Among the other woes of her short-lived marriage, Anderson had broken her thumb while in Europe, and Hedda Hopper reported at the end of January 1947 that 'Judith Anderson, with a broken heart and thumb,' was in Hollywood to film *Tycoon*. While she was there, she and the two young producers went to Carmel to consult with Jeffers. Early in February a lavishly illustrated cover story in the *Los Angeles Times* Home Magazine profiled the poet – 'the man who lives with the isolate splendor of the hawk, sternly removing himself from the easy pleasures and pursuits of mankind.' 'The crashing of the sea, the wild, sweet smell of wind-brushed mint, heather and sweet alyssum that grow at will around the house, and the golden pheasants in the trees, made me feel as if I were in an enchanted forest,' the

---

3   Gielgud to mother, 20 Jan 1947, in *Gielgud's Letters*, 2004; *LAT* 21 Jan 1947; Whitehead to Mrs Jeffers, [Sep]; 24 Oct 1946, RJHRC; Una Jeffers to Robert Hass, 24 Jan 1947, RJBerk, in James Karman, ed., *The Collected Letters of Robinson Jeffers With Selected Letters of Una Jeffers Volume Three, 1940–1962*, 2015; *NYT* 22 Jan 1947: 31; *Variety* 22 Jan 1947.
4   *NYT* 4 Dec 1946: 44; 7 Dec 1947: 177

Judith Anderson with Robin and Una Jeffers outside Tor House. Donnan Jeffers and his wife Lee are on the left, 1947

Bancroft Library, University of California, Berkeley

journalist wrote. Describing in detail the stone house Jeffers and Una had created, she concluded, 'This is the house of California's celebrated poet, whose play, *Medea*, starring Judith Anderson, is now under contract.'[5]

Over the next few months Whitehead and Rea searched for a director. During February the *New York Times* reported that they hoped to open in March. Anderson's fellow Australian, Robert Helpmann, was interested in taking the production to London and Paris during the summer, the article added. A few days later the plan was to open on the West Coast in April and to bring it to New York in the fall.[6]

More definite plans began in late April, however, when

---

5   *LAT* 24 Jan: A7; 2 Feb 1947: F4–6; Una Jeffers to Frederick and Maud Clapp, 28 Mar 1947, RJYale, in Karman, *Collected Letters*.
6   *NYT* 9 Feb: X1; 11 Feb 1947: 36.

Anderson persuaded John Gielgud to direct *Medea* in a fall production. 'I think it is a fine thing and am very anxious to have a stab at it,' Gielgud wrote his mother.⁷

Over the next few months Anderson rented a little house at Malibu, where she prepared for this strenuous role by swimming, running, stretching, and limbering. Twice a day she shouted in full voice at the waves to strengthen her breath and lungs.⁸

Her cross-country negotiations with Gielgud, however, soon ran into difficulties. This had been her dream project for many years, and she had strong ideas on how it should be staged. They quarrelled over her costume and the casting of Jason. Early in July he wrote, exasperated, to say that he wished to abandon the project. A few days later he explained his decision to his mother:

*Judith Anderson, who has been in a very odd state since a bad marital fiasco in the spring, saw fit to ring me up from California where she has been lurking all this while, find fault and disagree with everything I and the management had been planning for the Medea, and the net result is that I have resigned from the production. It is typical Mrs Pat, Edith Evans behaviour – injured vanity at not being consulted on every detail, yet a canny instinct not to really be responsible herself. We are all very disappointed, and I resent the effort and waste of time.*⁹

They patched up their differences, however, and in late

---

7   *NYT* 26 Apr: 10; 6 May 1947: 34; *AWW* 22 Mar1947: 40; Gielgud to mother, 29 Apr 1947, in *Letters*.
8   *Variety* 13 May 1947: 2; NYT 30 May: 24; 9 Jun: 26; 11 Jun 1947: 32; Una Jeffers to Anderson, 12 May 1947, RJH; to Bennett Cerf, 26 May 1947, RJBerk, in Karman, *Collected Letters*.
9   John [Gielgud] to Anderson, tel 3 Jul 1947, to 19232 Roosevelt Highway, Pacific Palisades, UCSB; to mother, 6 Jul 1947, in *Letters*; see also 21 Jul 1947.

July a weary Whitehead and Rea reported that they had secured Albert Hecht for Creon, Aline McMahon for the Nurse, and Grace Mills, Kathryn Grill and Leone Wilson for the chorus. They were still looking for a 'manly looking fellow' of about 45 for Jason. Gielgud, meanwhile, was writing to Jeffers about changes he and Anderson wanted to make.[10]

A telegram from Gielgud to Anderson early in August suggested that she was also having problems with Whitehead. 'I don't want endless bickering,' he wrote, conceding that he would accept her candidate for Jason, John Barrymore look-alike John Emery, who had played Laertes in *Hamlet* with her in 1936 and was a McClintic-Cornell favourite. But by this time Emery was otherwise engaged and George Coulouris had been offered and refused the role.[11]

When rehearsals began early in September and there was still no Jason, Anderson begged Gielgud to take on the role. Not really suited to this 'manly' part, which would display his spindly legs, he agreed reluctantly to play it for six weeks if Whitehead and Rea would produce his *Crime and Punishment* immediately after. 'Judith is all graciousness and charm,' he wrote his mother, 'and is now trying to persuade me to

Anderson's vision of Medea, captured by Freuh
National Portrait Gallery

---

10   *NYT* 20 Jul 1947: X1; Gielgud to Jeffers, 26 Jul & 19 Aug 1947, tel from London; Jeffers to Gielgud [Aug 1947], RJHRC; to Anderson, 26 Aug 1947, RJH; Una Jeffers to Melba Berry Bennett, 5 Aug 1947, RJHRC; to Frederick and Maud Clapp, 21 Aug 1947, RJYale, in Karman, *Collected Letters*; Anderson to Robin and Una Jeffers, 27 Aug 1947, RJHRC.
11   *LAT* 17 Feb 17, 1947: A2; John [Gielgud] to Anderson, 7 Aug 1939 [1947?], from New York to 1123 Corey Drive, UCSB; *Variety* 17 Jun 1947: 4.

play Jason for the first four weeks.' 'It is not a good part, not very much up my street,' he continued, 'but I am tempted to agree, as I think it would be quite a popular gesture from me to her and also I cannot get a really suitable actor.'[12]

Despite Anderson's initial 'graciousness and charm,' rehearsals had many stormy passages. Marian Seldes, at the beginning of her career as one of Medea's attendants, felt Anderson's certainty as an actor: 'There was no question, there was no other way to do it than the way she did it.' Gielgud was, on the other hand, 'indecisive, dilatory, often mistaken in judgment,' in Anderson's opinion – a verdict shared by even his greatest admirers. He himself admitted many years later that he had made a hash of it. The friction between them was so bad that he threatened once more to leave the production 10 days into rehearsals. Their major confrontation continued to be over her costume. She had seen a boy in Menotti's *The Medium* and had her hair cut in a similar ragged, stringy style, coloured various shades of red. She wanted her costume to be similarly barbarous, leaving her feeling free and unencumbered, as if she were naked. Ten days before the Princeton opening she protested against the costumes Gielgud had commissioned from his good friend, David Ffolkes – which were, he admitted later, 'picture book-y and operatic,' and asked the designer Castillo to create something for her out of grey wool.[13]

The play had its out-of-town opening in Princeton on 3 October 1947 and then had a two-week tryout at the Locust Street Theatre in Philadelphia. Gielgud reported 'tremendous ovations at all three performances at Princeton'; but, *Variety* warned, it 'will have box office appeal largely confined to the literati classes.'[14]

---

12   *NYT* 9 Sep: 28; 10 1947: 30; Gielgud to mother, 4 Sep1947, in *Letters*.
13   Gielgud to George Pitcher and E. Cone, 3 Jun 1987; to Lawrence Langer, 19 Sep 1947; to mother, 19 Sep; 6 Oct 1947, from Philadelphia, in *Letters*.
14   Gielgud to mother, 6 Oct 1947; *Variety* 7 Oct 1947: 8.

Writing to his mother from Philadelphia, Gielgud reported on the 'endless conferences, heartbreaks and difficulties of all kinds' he had to deal with after their opening. The scenery was magnificent, he told her, but they had a ghastly post-mortem on lighting and costume. 'We are scrapping all the clothes,' he wrote. 'Judith fortunately rebelled ten days ago and hers are brilliant, designed by a French-Italian who works for Elizabeth Arden, so we have now asked him to do all the others.' They also replaced Aline McMahon, the actress playing the Nurse, with Anderson's old friend, Florence Reed, with whom she had played in *Mourning Becomes Electra* and whom she had envisaged in the part from the beginning.

'My own appearance is not at all good yet,' Gielgud told his mother, 'the wig too fair and the dress too pretty and fairy tale... Judith's alone has style and barbaric authenticity. I *must* look vulgar, overbearing and violently masculine on my first appearance. We now talk of black armour, leather and scarlet cloak and short, brown hair.'

At the final dress rehearsal in the new costumes in mid-October, Gielgud was in beige with a grey-brown breastplate and boots and dark green cloak, a huge helmet in his hand, with curly brown hair and a full curly beard. 'The new costumes are quite lovely,' he wrote his mother, 'against the grey scenery, grey porticoes and walls, pearly grey sea and mountains in the background, and costumes in every shade of pale beige, lavender, pink (Creon) leading up to Augeus who wears two shades of red': Judith is in grey with first a black, then a wine-red drapery, the Nurse in purple and grey... The three women of the chorus in shades of purple, brown and grey, most beautifully draped and the colours blended very cleverly so that they look a unity, yet each has its individual character. I wish you could see it yourself.[15]

Strikingly costumed just as Anderson had envisaged, *Medea* opened at the National Theatre on 20 October 1947. It was a triumph. At intermission the audience were already standing in the aisles and shouting. As Anderson gave the final speech:

> *Now of all men*
> > *You are utterly the most miserable. As I of women. But I, a woman, a foreigner, alone*
> > *Against you and the might of Corinth – have met you throat for throat, evil for evil. Now I go forth*
> > *Under the cold eyes of the weakness-despising stars: not me they scorn*

she was met with cheers and 13 curtain calls. Una and Robinson Jeffers had decided at the last minute to fly to New York to be present – Una in a borrowed Valentina gown and green velvet cloak by Worth – after 'violently excitedly enthusiastic' reviews from Princeton and Philadelphia and constant wires and telephone calls from the exultant Anderson; and this most reclusive of writers responded with a bemused bow to the insistent cries of 'Author, author.'[16]

Brooks Atkinson in the *New York Times* proclaimed Anderson's Medea 'a landmark in the theatre.' 'It would be useless now for anyone else to attempt the part,' he wrote. His admiration for Jeffers' words was just as great. 'Mr Jeffers' "free adaptation," as it is called, spares the supernatural bogeymen of the classical Greek drama and gets on briskly with the terrifying story of a woman obsessed with revenge,'

---

15 Gielgud to mother, 6 Oct 1947. Antonio Canovas del Castillo was Spanish. See Lindy Woodhead, *War Paint: Madame Helena Rubinstein and Miss Elizabeth Arden*, 2010.
16 Una Jeffers to Melba Berry Bennett; to Frederick and Maud Clapp, 14 Oct [1947]; to Blanche Matthais, 5 Nov 1947, RJYale, in Karman, *Collected Letters*; *CDT* 21 Oct 1947: 25.

he wrote. 'His verse is modern; his words are sharp and vivid, and his text does not worship gods that are dead':

> *Since Miss Anderson is a modern, the Jeffers text suits her perfectly and releases a torrent of acting incomparable for passion and scope. Miss Anderson's Medea is mad with the fury of a woman of rare stature. She is barbaric by inheritance, but she has heroic strength and vibrant perceptions. Animal-like in her physical reactions, she plots the doom of her enemies with the intelligence of a priestess of black magic – at once obscene and inspired. Between these two poles she fills the evening with fire, horror, rage and character. Although Miss Anderson has left some memorable marks on great women in the theatre, Medea has summoned all her powers as an actress. Now everyone realizes that she has been destined for Medea from the start.*

Atkinson liked almost everything about the production, praising Florence Reed's performance as the Nurse, and even finding Gielgud's Jason 'well expressed,' though others found him 'like a rather nice fellow who is caught in bad company' or even 'Ivor Novello in whiskers' or 'a tenor Siegfried cast as a bass Hagen.' He did, however, find Ben Edwards' setting, which Gielgud was so pleased with, pedestrian; and he felt that some of the conventional theatrical effects – the lightning and surf especially – should be 'locked up in the lumber room' out of respect for Anderson's acting. 'For she has freed Medea from all the old traditions as if the character had just been created.' 'Perhaps that is exactly what has happened,' he concluded. 'Perhaps Medea was never fully created until Miss Anderson breathed immortal fire into it last evening.'[17]

Radie Harris in *Variety* simply headlined her article

---

17 CDT 21 Oct 1947: 25; George Jean Nathan, *The Theatre Book of the Year, 1947–1948*, 1975 [1947], 106; *NYT* 21 Oct 1947: 27.

JUDITH THE GREAT. 'Judith Anderson,' she wrote, 'whose brilliant talent has been dissipated in Hollywood these past few years, playing "Danverish" housekeepers and pioneer women, is back on Broadway – and all is right in this best of theatrical worlds.' 'It isn't often when the perfect star meets the perfect part,' she continued, 'but when she or he do as Laurette Taylor in *The Glass Menagerie* – Larry Olivier in *Oedipus Rex* – Lunt and Fontanne in *The Guardsman* – Gertrude Lawrence and Noël Coward in *Tonight at 8.30* – Helen Hayes in *Queen Victoria* – Katharine Cornell in *The Barretts of Wimpole Street* and Raymond Massey in *Abraham Lincoln* to recall a few – the memory of it remains forever indelible':

> *Such a perfect combination is Judith Anderson in Robinson Jeffers' free adaptation of Medea. In a season still young, I'd like to go on record now in predicting that no other actress will come along to top her for every award as the finest performance of the year.*
>
> *Perhaps the greatest accolade paid Judith on opening night at the National was not the cheers and bravos of an audience that wouldn't leave their seats until the house lights were up – an audience that practically turned up en masse in her dressing room afterwards. No, the acclaim of Noël Coward, Gertrude Lawrence, Margaret Case, Dorothy Fields, Max Gordon, Louis Calhern, Louise Atherton, Richard Aldrich, Jack Kapp, Lawrence Langner, Armina Marshall, Howard Rheinhimer and other enthusiasts was overshadowed by the presence of a man who seldom visits backstage. But it takes one great artist to appreciate another one, and that's why Arthur Toscanini struggled through the mob to offer his personal compliments.*[18]

With *Medea*, Judith Anderson reached that acme of

---

18   *Variety* 24 Oct 1947: 8.

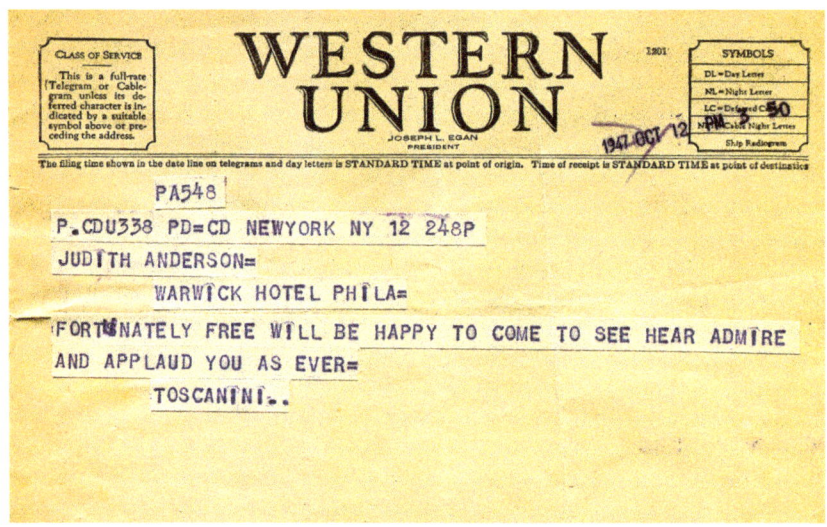

Toscanini's telegram to Judith Anderson before opening night of Medea *1947*

UCSB

stardom where, to quote *Vogue*, 'audiences go not to see the play, but to see Judith Anderson.' Providing a vivid evocation of her performance, the *Vogue* critic acclaimed 'Judith Anderson, Our Greatest Actress':

> *Judith Anderson's Medea begins with her lioness' roar of rage and anguish off stage, ends with her spent walk into exile carrying the dead warm bodies of her children, whom she has just killed. In between there is a nerve-wrought performance. As Medea, who killed her own father and brother for love of Jason, who later left her for a golden-haired young girl, Miss Anderson is barbaric, suffering, plays with her whole body, the terror of her jealousy rippling through her flesh. She throws the whole book of classic acting at Medea, throws it intelligently, in a wildly cadenced voice.*[19]

Louis Kronenberger writing in *PM*, again proclaiming

---

19   *Vogue* 1 Dec 1947: 168–69. See also *NYT* 14 Dec 1947: X4; *Billboard* 1 Nov 1947: 48.

Anderson 'our most distinguished dramatic actress,' gave her the greatest accolade, comparing her to Bernhardt in the role. And back in Australia Brisbane's *Courier Mail* boasted that 'She is considered one of the finest emotional actresses on the American stage; some think her the greatest.' 'Crowds are flocking to see her performance,' the *Courier*'s special correspondent wrote, 'waiting outside the theatre after the show just to catch a glimpse of her, trying to get her autograph. She gets as many as eight or 10 curtain calls at the end of the play.'[20]

---

20   *PM* 22 Oct 1947, NYPL; *Courier-Mail* 3 Jan 1948: 2.

Judith Anderson as Medea, by Richard Avedon
New York Public Library Digital Collection

Chapter Twenty-six
Medea and Friends 1948–9

Though Guthrie retained the general physical pattern of the production, he recreated our interpretations, improving them greatly... For me, it was like having a bright light shone on the character. We would sit on the floor in the middle of the rehearsal hall talking about the part — 'Like two children on the seashore,' Marian [Seldes] noted in her diary

Judith Anderson, unpublished memoirs 1962

Variety and *Billboard* had predicted that *Medea* would appeal only to the intelligentsia; but like *Strange Interlude* 20 years before, it proved to be box-office magic. Before it even reached Broadway it was a smash hit. In its first week at the 1164-seat National it grossed around $29,000, bettered only by another classic – Maurice Evans in Shaw's *Man and Superman* – which drew $31,000 at the slightly larger Alvin Theatre. By its fifth week it was bringing in $30,000. As *Vogue* wrote in January 1948, *Medea* was 'a must-see.'[21]

In the midst of all this success, however, a sense of grievance began to fester. *Medea* was Anderson's dream project,

---

21   *Variety* 24 Oct: 8; 22 Oct: 59; 29 Oct: 59; 26 Nov 1947: 57; *Billboard* 1 Nov 1947: 48; *Vogue* 1 Jan 1948: 121–25.

which she had willed into existence over a period of years. She had been critical from the start of what she considered the unnecessary costs the inexperienced young producers incurred. The imbroglio over the costumes was the prime example; but there were others that invoked her wrath. This came to a head in early December, when Whitehead and Rea announced they were moving *Medea* to the smaller Royale Theatre to make way for the production of *Crime and Punishment* they had promised Gielgud.

This move seriously affected Anderson's earning capacity, because she had agreed to a weekly salary of $1,000 until the play earned back its costs of $75,000. In the smaller theatre this would take longer; and what is more, the moving and rebuilding of sets would add to its costs. She had already made Jeffers a rich man – as author, he received ten per cent of the gross – and she did not begrudge this to the beloved collaborator she considered a genius.[22] But Gielgud, in his dual role as director and actor, had earned $2,000 a week. It appeared to Anderson that everyone but her – the originator and star of this phenomenal success – was being enriched by it.

As Anderson conceded, she did not have a serene temperament, and the production, after Gielgud was replaced by Dennis King in early December and they moved to the Royale, was rent by conflict. Her bitterness toward Whitehead and Rea was only increased when *Crime and Punishment* – which had replaced them at the National – turned out to be a failure.

As her sense of grievance grew, Anderson collapsed at the end of January 1948, complaining of exhaustion and anaemia. Over the next few weeks she had several blood transfusions

---

22   Una Jeffers to Anderson, 4 Nov 1947, RJTH; to Bennett Cerf, Jan 1948, RJBerk, in James Karman, ed., *The Collected Letters of Robinson Jeffers With Selected Letters of Una Jeffers Volume Three, 1940–1962*, 2015.

and took a week off at the end of February to rest. Una Jeffers wrote sympathetically from Carmel, 'Judy darling: How *are* you – I just saw the note in Time that you were out of the play for the week… No one can understand your endurance for so long.' Her fellow actor Helen Hayes sent her a note: 'God knows what's going to happen to the rest of us actresses now that you have some blood in you.'[23]

Rejuvenated, Anderson set about single-mindedly to release herself from her contract with Whitehead and Rea. In late March they had reached an impasse over her claim of 15 per cent of the gross when the costs had been recovered. She announced that she would quit at the end of May, and would not appear in the projected summer performance in Central City, Colorado or tour with them in the fall. Nor would she take it with them to England. Whitehead immediately set off for London, where he arranged for Eileen Herlie, who had played Gertrude in Laurence Olivier's movie of *Hamlet,* to appear in the part in Britain, directed by Gielgud. Infuriated, Anderson announced that *Medea* would close even earlier, on 15 May.[24] The conflict caused a serious rift between Gielgud and Anderson, and one with Whitehead that was only healed 30 years later when he produced, with her blessing, a revival of *Medea* starring his wife, Zoe Caldwell, with Anderson as the Nurse.

The audience's appetite for Medea had not been satisfied when it closed in May 1948. Claudia Cassidy in the *Chicago*

---

23 Diary 8 Jan to 8 Mar 1948, UCSB; *NYT* 29 Jan: 29; 30 Jan: 20; 31 Jan: 14; 4 Feb: 27; 20 Feb: 20; 6 Mar: 9; 8 Mar 1948; *LAT* 23 Apr 1948; 21; clipping, 11 Sep [1948], UCSB; Una Jeffers to Anderson, 5 Feb 1948, RJTH, in Karman, *Collected Letters*; *Advertiser* 17 Feb 1948: 3.
24 *NYT* 26 Mar: 26; 4 May: 29; 30 Apr 1948: 27; *Variety* 11 May 1948: 6; Una Jeffers to Anderson, 29 Mar & 7 May 1948; to Hans Barkan, 30 Apr 1948, RJSF, in Karman, *Collected Letters*; Gielgud to Mrs Robinson Jeffers, 12 Sep 1948, in *Gielgud's Letters*, 2004.

Daily Tribune described the scene on the play's last night. 'Medea – Closed to a clawing mob that wouldn't take sold out for an answer, even in terms of standing room,' she wrote:

> *A magnificent actress of tragic stature almost unknown in a generation of theatrical understatement, Judith Anderson has a superb role in Robinson Jeffers' otherwise less than fully satisfying adaptation of Euripides' play. As the tortured barbarian whose vengeance is beyond the comprehension of the Greeks who unleashed it, she is like a black panther writhing under vitriol but clawing its torturers with fearful accuracy even in its death throes. She dwarfs even the great columned façade of the Corinthian palace Ben Edwards flung up as background, and makes stooges of a hapless cast – except Florence Reed, who doesn't stooge.*[25]

Tributes continued to pour in as, in a period of confusion and vituperation, Anderson fought for the right to tour in *Medea* in the fall with a producer and director of her choice. On 28 March she had been awarded the Tony Award, along with Katharine Cornell and Jessica Tandy, for the Best Actress in a Play. At the end of May she was named the best actress of the season by *Variety*'s poll of 12 Broadway critics, 10 of whom gave her their vote. She was also awarded one of 15 grants for artists, writers and composers by the American Academy and National Institute of Arts and Letters, and was honoured by the Drama League of New York for the most distinguished performance of the season. In July she won *Billboard*'s Donaldson Award for best actress.[26]

Una and Robin Jeffers supported Anderson in her battle to ensure the producers did not hire any other actress to play her part in America. 'Impossible ever to separate Judith & Medea

---

25   *CDT* 23 May 1948: D8.
26   *NYT* Mar 29: 23; 22 May: 16; 12 May: 34; 18 Jul 1948: 46; *Variety* 26 May 1948: 1.

in our minds – ever,' Una assured her. Anderson negotiated with producers Lewis and Young to take over the American tour, then found that Guthrie McClintic was available as both producer and director. Whitehead and Rea opposed this change, as they stood to lose money by it; but they eventually gave in, after much to-ing and fro-ing, at the beginning of July.[27]

Writing to Noël Sullivan in June, Una Jeffers exploded with frustration after several days in New York as she and Robin left for a visit to Ireland, 'I cannot begin to speak of the dozens of interviews we had about Medea, & the confusion and hatred.' 'Judith must have been infuriating,' she went on, '& she frustrated them so much that they are unable now to keep from being revengeful though they won't admit it.'[28]

Robert Whitehead, many years later, when the two were friends again, was remorseful about his part in this contretemps and was hazy about the cause of their falling-out. 'Our difficulties had a lot to do with casting,' he told a reporter in 1982. 'Judith and I had a stormy relationship and the end of it was explosive. We didn't speak until a couple of years ago. I was young and she thought me an upstart.'[29]

At the height of her success, Anderson felt abandoned. After the theatre she went home alone, she wrote in her memoirs. She had moved to a light-filled apartment in the Artists'

---

27 Una Jeffers to Anderson, 7 May 1948, RJH; Jeffers to Whitehead and Rea, 12 May 1948, RJTH; to The Dramatists' Guild, 1 Jun 1948, RJHRC; to Anderson, tel 25 Jun 1948; Robin and Una Jeffers to Charlotte, Garth and Maeve Jeffers, from Donegal, RJLB; Una Jeffers to Anderson, 30 Jun from Donegal; 1 Jul from Ballymore, Eire; 3 Jul; [19] Jul; 5 Aug 1948, RJTH; to Noël Sullivan, 4 May [4 Aug] 1948, RJBerk, in Karman, *Collected Letters*.
28 Una Jeffers to Sullivan, 12 Jun 1948, RJBerk, in Karman, *Collected Letters*. See also Una and Robin Jeffers to Anderson, 11 Jun 1948; Una Jeffers to Anderson, 26 Jun 1948, from Ballymore, Eire, RJTH.
29 Rebecca Morehouse, 'A Theatregoer's Notebook,' *Playbill* May 1982.

Studio Building on West 57th Street, complete with a grand piano, oriental rugs, Russian icons and a Limoges dinner set.[30] But, still married to Luther, she had no idea where he was; her mother was in England with Frank and his growing family; Did was in her retreat in Vermont; and no one had invited her for Christmas until her old friend Helen Menken swept her up for a warm family dinner.

In the midst of this fracas Luther appeared once more in Anderson's life. Millie Rowland, whose stage name was Martha Downes, had a tiny role in *Medea* and was acting as Anderson's secretary. Her husband, Toby Rowland, who had been Luther's flatmate in New York, brought the two together again in early May. A month later they were holidaying together in Florida and the Bahamas. In mid-June the newspapers reported that the couple had dropped their divorce suit. As they drove across the continent to Los Angeles Anderson uttered 'a prayer for our life.' They settled in Malibu, where they relaxed with Luther's children Lenka and Spike, who were now six and four.[31]

In August, when the children returned to their mother, Anderson and Greene moved to his house, the mock-Venetian Villa Vallambrosa at 2074 Watsonia Terrace in Whitley Heights above Hollywood. McClintic had just announced that Anderson's tour of *Medea* would begin in San Francisco on 6 September, and she hoped this time to secure John Emery as Jason and her old friend Hilda Vaughn as the Nurse. But Emery was again unavailable. In his place was local favourite Henry Brandon, who had played with Anderson in *The Tower Beyond Tragedy* in 1941. Brandon's tall frame and craggy good looks made him a perfect Jason. According to a Los Angeles

---

30   Financial Records 1948–49, UCSB.
31   Rowland to Enters, postcard 17 Apr 1948; Greene to Enters, [Jul 1948], Enters Papers; Diary 4–11 May 1948; Bahamas 2 Jun to 2 Jul 1948, Financial Records, UCSB; *LAT* 16 Jun 1948; *Variety* 18 Jun 1948: 8.

columnist, 'No one could stride on wearing the shin plates, breastplate, and regalia of an ancient warrior and take stage like Henry.'[32]

Playbill for Medea II

Author's collection

For this long tour Anderson surrounded herself with friends: Marian Seldes and Millie Rowland (Martha Downes) were promoted to the three-woman chorus and Mary Servoss played the First Lady of Corinth. Hilda Vaughn – a brilliant actress – played the Nurse. Don McHenry continued as the Tutor. Anderson remembered the tour as 'wonderful,' 'exhilarating' and 'very sociable.' She found Luther, who accompanied her, companionable, though they still quarrelled over money. Marian Seldes recalled them hooking a rug – a common pastime on tour – and antiquing together.[33]

Advertised by a striking poster by the young Richard Avedon featuring an anguished Medea, the McClintic version

---

32 Greene to Enters, [Dec 1947], Enters Papers; *NYT* 28 Jul 1948: 27; *LAT* 18 Mar 1990: E5.
33 Interview with Marian Seldes, New York, 2004.

of the play opened at the Lobero Theatre in Santa Barbara on 3 September 1948, with Ben Edwards' setting and the Castillo costumes. *The New York Times* reported that 'In the crowd that cheered Robinson Jeffers' adaptation of the tragedy were Ethel Barrymore and Lotte Lehmann.' The great soprano Lehmann, who later became one of Anderson's closest friends, was reported to have walked away weeping, exclaiming that 'All that I am I left in there.'[34]

On 6 September the company opened for three weeks at the Geary in San Francisco. *Variety* spoke of 'rave notices.' Journalist Fred Johnson found a calm and gracious Judith Anderson fortified by her enthusiastic reception for the long exhausting tour ahead; and by the news that Lieutenant General Eichelberger, who she had last seen in the jungles of New Guinea, would be in the audience that evening.[35]

Anderson's next opening, in her hometown at the Los Angeles Biltmore on 27 September, elicited 'tremendous' applause. Edwin Shallert, her longtime fan, wrote in the *Los Angeles Times*, 'Long an actress of great capability, Judith Anderson becomes a veritable superwoman of the stage in *Medea*':

> *While the legend of her triumph in this play has been bruited here for more than a year, to see her in her actual performance in Robinson Jeffers' adaptation of a Euripides tragedy about a demon woman is an unparalleled experience.*
>
> *Hers is undoubtedly the most sensational interpretation of this generation.*

'Miss Anderson's calm exact approach to the emotions of the role,' he concluded, 'and her attainment of its final

---

34 NYT 4 Sep 1948: 9; CDT 21 Sep 1948: A1.
35 Variety 8: 51; 15 Sep 1948: 57; Billboard 11 Sep 1948: 46; Fred Johnson, 'Interlude With The Calmer Judith Anderson,' clipping, 11 Sep [1948], UCSB.

frenzies, do not permit a vestige of what might be termed "going overboard." She brings the portrayal an individual and regal magnificence.'[36]

ANDERSON'S MEDEA SETS LANDMARK FOR LEGIT *Variety* headlined in its own colloquial style. 'Judith Anderson brought Theatre to Los Angeles Monday night,' their reporter wrote. With its 'crisp, biting script,' the play 'comes to fiery flesh-and-blood life.' It is 'a flaming thing of stunning impact.'[37]

'Judith Anderson is holding nightly classes on the Biltmore stage,' *Variety* reported the following day, 'showing Hollywood gals a good many things they never suspected about the art.'[38] The *Los Angeles Times* noted that 'Miss Anderson has drawn more of the film colony to the Biltmore during the past week than any star to appear on a Los Angeles stage for some time… It is doubtful if anyone before the public today is more highly regarded within the profession itself than Judith Anderson.' Gossip columnist Brandy Brent observed that 'Everybody in town evidently turned out.' She spotted pianist Lester Donahue, actress Constance Collier, Anderson's friend, the Russian ballerina Tamara Geva, with her husband John Emery, movie director Rupert Hughes and the actress Ann Miller, along with the city's socialites.[39]

After three successful weeks in Los Angeles the *Medea* company set off through the smaller Californian towns to Seattle, and on to Salt Lake City, Des Moines and Columbia. Audiences initially were disappointing. When they arrived in Chicago, however, at the end of November, that city's audiences welcomed Anderson with their usual fervour. Claudia Cassidy in the *Daily Tribune* found her 'magnificent.' Her

---

36 *LAT* 28 Sep 1948: A6.
37 *Variety* 29 Sep 1948: 4.
38 *Variety* 30 Sep1948: 2.
39 *LAT* 3 Oct: D2; 29 Sep 1948: B1.

description of Anderson's performance is one of the most detailed and insightful:

> *The curtain rises on Medea's anguish, the twin edged dagger of love betrayed. She is an animal in torture. Asiatic, with slanting eyes sunk deep in their sockets, hair slipping from high coils to little tongues of snakes, a mouth as gashed in dryness as it has been voluptuously curved, a panther body with hands that curl to claws – this is the woman who bargains with her tormenters to coax them into the net of her black arts. Her voice is honey, or forked lightning, or an animal sound welled up from inner torment. Only when the blood in her heart is red on her hands is that pain assuaged.*

Cassidy found McClintic's production better than the one she had seen in New York the previous spring. She admired Hilda Vaughn's ability, as the Nurse, to tell a tale of horror; and in particular, she appreciated the 'stalwart' Henry Brandon who 'looks as Jason might, a golden weakling whose way with his sons has just the right note to whet Medea's bloody purpose.'[40]

Such was Chicago's enthusiasm for the play that it was extended from four to six weeks. When the company finally left Chicago in mid-January 1949, they criss-crossed the Midwest in bleak winter weather. In Minneapolis, according to *Variety*, the company moved across from St Paul on the coldest night of the year 'but still managed to grab a neat $17,000 in five performances.' In March and April they moved up and down the East Coast. In Boston at the end of April Katharine Cornell attended every performance.[41]

---

40 *Variety* 10 Nov1948; *NYT* 15 Nov1948: 21; Una Jeffers to Greene, 30 Oct 1948; to Anderson, 17 Nov 1948, tels to Seattle; Jeffers to Anderson, tel 23 Nov 1948, RGTH; to Albert Taylor ,tel 27 Nov [1948]; Anderson to Robin and Una Jeffers, tel 28 Nov 1948, RJHRC, in Karman, *Collected Letters*; *CDT* 24 Nov 1948: a1.

41 *CDT* 27 Nov 1948: 12; *Variety* 8 Dec 1948: 48; 26 Jan 1949: 59; *BP* 29 Apr 1949,

The company finally arrived in New York at the beginning of May 1949. It opened for two weeks at the City Center on 55th Street, where audiences could enjoy top quality theatre at bargain prices. At this huge auditorium, which seated over 3,000 people, Anderson broke all existing records for a legitimate play, grossing nearly $41,000 in a single week. 'L F' [Lewis Funke] in the *New York Times* found that under McClintic's direction her acting had 'a greater variety, a widened approach and a sharper comprehension of gradation and understanding.' 'Gifted with a voice that has the range to cover many moods,' the critic wrote, 'she is haughty, disdainful, tender, cunning.'

> *Daughter of a king, yet barbarian, she gives us a Medea that is demented with rage and jealousy over her lost husband, yet understandably pathetic, too. It is indeed a memorable characterization that is a splendid technical achievement.*

'L F' also preferred Henry Brandon's Jason to that of Gielgud. In his opinion Brandon gave 'a completely virile and masculine performance… credibly disdainful of his erstwhile love, a little ashamed of his once consuming passion.'[42]

Anderson brought the 37-week tour to a dramatic climax at the end of May when she performed *Medea* in the outdoor Sylvan Theater at the base of the Washington Monument in Washington DC. With an overflow crowd of 10,000, a poor amplification system meant that half the audience was enthralled and the other half dissatisfied, Richard L Coe wrote in the *Washington Post*. Then she had one more chore to do – two weeks of *Medea* in Honolulu at the end of June.[43]

As she and Luther prepared to take the Chief across the

Cornell Papers.
42 *NYT* 2 May: 20; 15 May 1949: X1.
43 M. Joseph Costelloe, '*Medea* and the *Birds*,' *Classical Journal* 45.6, Mar 1950: 272–73; *WP* 22 May 1949: L1.

continent to Los Angeles, Anderson sent 'uninhibited hugs and kisses' to her beloved McClintic[44]. She had much to be satisfied with. She had, by sheer determination, managed to bring together a great American poet, a great director and a company made up of some of her closest friends. She had brought 'one good play' to thousands of people across the country and had been hailed as America's greatest tragic actress. And she had personally made well over $60,000 (around $600,000 in 2019 dollars).

---

44 Anderson to McClintic, nd [Sun 5? Jun 1949] from Chicago, Cornell Papers.

ACT V
Anti-climax

Scene Eight
Santa Barbara

I believe the coming Christmas will be the most memorable of my life, for I hope to have my mother, brother, and all his family from England settled with me on my California ranch home. I am older and wise enough to appreciate all the happiness and plenty which surrounds me.

Judith Anderson to *Australian Women's Weekly*, December 1949

The view from 'Rancho Verde,' 2005

Author's collection

Chapter Twenty-seven

Families, Professional and Personal 1950

'Rancho Verde' – a house of my own, built from the ground up, just as I had always dreamed of it

Judith Anderson, unpublished memoir, 1962

In 1949, with the brilliant success of *Medea* just behind her, Judith Anderson appeared to have the world at her feet. She looked forward confidently to further collaboration with her favourite people, Robinson Jeffers and Guthrie McClintic; her marriage, though rocky, was still intact; and she was wealthy for the first time in her life. Accordingly, she set to work to put her private life in order.

Judith Anderson and Luther Greene arrive in Hawaii for the final production of Medea, *June 1949*

Courtesy Luther Greene Jr

During the summer of 1949 Anderson and Luther had rented the rambling old house recently vacated by Isobel Field, Robert Louis Stevenson's step-daughter, on the beach below Santa Barbara, 150 kilometres north of Los Angeles. 'As I sit here,' Luther wrote to his friend Angna Enters, 'on Robert Louis Stevenson's chair and at his desk – I look out to the Pacific, across the garden, the beach and the waves lashing.' Luther's children came to visit; and Anderson suddenly longed for a home and family. Now that she had money she had become consumed by another dream – not of doing a great play, but of recreating 'those family days in Rose Park which, because they were the first I had known, had always seemed the norm.'[1] Her mother

Judith Anderson with Luther 'Spike' Greene and Lenka Greene 1949

Courtesy Luther Greene Jr

had for some years been living in England with Frank, Laura and their family. But, now well into her eighties, she was in declining health. And Frank, his training in morse code no longer needed after the war, was out of work.

Her vivid imagination working overtime, she imagined a house – 'a house of my own, built from the ground up, just as I had always dreamed of it, and land of my own, a ranch, and Frank could run it.'

> *He, mother, Laura, Susan, Judy, David, Jen – their presence could be a bulwark against loneliness. I would be part of something once again. And if not the children of my own that I had always wanted and never had, I would have*

---

1   *NYT* 23 Oct 1949: X3; Greene to Enters, Mon [early Sep 1949] from Serena, Carpinteria, Enters Papers.

around me, watching them grow up, loving them, the children of my favorite brother.

Anderson had always shared what she had with her family. Her mother, to whom she owed so much, had lived with her most of her life. Her first thought, when she began earning $100 a week in 1919, had been to buy insurance policies for her brothers.[2] For many years she had been paying for her sister Did's care. 'I had been the lucky one,' she reasoned: 'hard work had brought me money, and with it the responsibilities that I had always taken for granted.'

Judith Anderson with her beloved mother and two of the series of dachshunds she kept from the 1930s
Courtesy Luther Greene Jr

She found the perfect ranch – 'Rancho Verde' – in nearby Carpinteria. It grew avocados and lemons and had a small house right near the entrance. The school bus passed by the door.

Then the road climbed, precipitous, dizzying, around and between the great palisades of rock and waterfalls, turning on itself, hairpin after hairpin, past wild lilac and scrub oak; a private mountain, very close to heaven, covered with

---

2 Diary 28 Jul 1919, UCSB.

virgin forest. On three sides other mountains rose, fold on fold into the horizon. The ocean sparkled in front, and off-shore lay the Channel Islands.

'I bought it at once,' she wrote 12 years later.[3] She remodelled the existing house for Frank and his family, and built on a room for her mother. At the top of the hill she and Luther built a beautiful Palladian-style villa and set out the flower and vegetable garden that would become her refuge and relaxation.

'I believe the coming Christmas will be the most memorable of my life,' she told the *Australian Women's Weekly* in December 1949, 'for I hope to have my mother, brother, and all his family from England settled with me on my California ranch home. I am older and wise enough to appreciate all the happiness and plenty which surrounds me.'[4]

Judith Anderson with Jenifer, Judy, Susan and David, with their mother Laura behind, soon after they arrived in 1950. Frank followed a few months later.

Courtesy Jenifer McCurry

---

3 See also *LAT* 8 Oct 1949: 15.
4 *AWW* 24 Dec 1949: 17.

As Anderson worked on the re-creation of her family, she and Jeffers began an exciting new project for the spring 1950 season – an adaptation of Friedrich Schiller's 1800 play *Mary Stuart*, about that unhappy Queen's last days.[5] Like *Tower Beyond Tragedy*, the play would provide two major parts (Schiller invents a meeting with Elizabeth I that did not actually happen). Their idea was that Anderson and another equally commanding actress (perhaps Katharine Cornell) would play Elizabeth and Mary on alternate nights.

Jeffers found the play 'powerful and moving' and set to work immediately. He was glad of the diversion. Una, on whom he depended in every way, had been mysteriously ill since January with what would turn out to be a fatal cancer. She became gravely ill during the winter of 1949–50 and Jeffers struggled to finish *Mary Stuart* as he hovered over his dying wife. He managed to visit Anderson and Luther in Carpinteria in March 1950 to discuss the project, but they decided that it could not be finished in time for a fall opening.[6]

Meanwhile Cheryl Crawford, who had wanted to work with Anderson again after their highly successful *Family Portrait* in 1939, approached her to appear in a new subscription series of experimental plays to be staged by the American National Theatre and Academy. ANTA was one of the many

---

5 Greene to Jeffers 22 Oct 1949, RJTH, in James Karman, ed., *The Collected Letters of Robinson Jeffers With Selected Letters of Una Jeffers Volume Three*, 1940–1962, 2015.
6 Una Jeffers to Greene and Anderson, [after 22] Oct 1949; Jeffers to Greene, 8 & 21 Nov 1949, RJTH; Una Jeffers to William Turner Levy, 22 Nov 1949, RJNYPL; Jeffers to Greene & Anderson, 9 Jan 1950; Robin and Una Jeffers to Greene, 25 Jan 1950; Jeffers to Greene, 30 Jan 1950, from San Francisco; Una Jeffers to Anderson, 9 Feb [1950], from Peninsula Community Hospital, Carmel; Jeffers to Greene, 23 Feb 1950, RJTH; to Anderson & Greene, 6 Apr 1950; to Greene, 18 Jun 1950 [18 April 1950], RJTH; Una Jeffers to Greene, 28 Apr 1950, RJTH; Greene to Jeffers, Sat [22 Apr 1950], RJHRC, in Karman, *Collected Letters*; Phoebe Barkan Gilpin, *RJN* Jan 1992: 82.

postwar attempts to create a national theatre in the United States. Established by Congress in 1935, it was envisaged as an alternative to the for-profit Broadway houses. In 1950 it bought the theatre on 52nd Street previously owned by the Theatre Guild and, under the general directorship of its founder, William Breen, and producer, Cheryl Crawford, proceeded to recruit some of America's top actors, to include Judith Anderson, Helen Hayes and Katharine Cornell, to play at basic equity wages in its opening season. Crawford had initially suggested a revival of Molnar's *The Guardsman* with British actor Basil Rathbone – a play that would have provided a lighthearted counterpoint *Medea*'s war between the sexes. But Anderson saw this as a golden opportunity to try out *The Tower Beyond Tragedy* on a New York audience.[7]

Anderson had always wanted to stage *The Tower Beyond Tragedy*, the Jeffers poem whose words she had fallen in love with when she first read his work in 1929. When she had played Clytemnestra in the Forest Theater in Carmel in 1941, it was in an adaptation of the poem written by John Gassner, the drama critic who headed the Theatre Guild's play department. In 1948, with the prospect of McClintic producing the play after *Medea*, with Katharine Cornell and Anderson playing the leading roles, Jeffers had set out to dramatise the poem himself. Despite being gravely ill for several months, he managed to complete the play, and Una had given it to Anderson in October 1948 when she went to San José to see her in *Medea*.[8]

---

7 Michael Kammen, 'Culture and the State in America,' *Journal of American History* 83.3,1996: 814; *NYT* 25 Jan: 20; 6 Sep 6: 48; 10 Sep 1950: 97; *LAT* 8 Oct 1950: D4; *NYHT* 21 Mar 1950, NYPL.
8 Una Jeffers to Anderson, 29 Mar & 7 May; 26 Jun from Eire; 3 Jul, RJTH; [19] Jul; 5 Aug 1948 from Dublin; 22 Jun 1950, RJTH; Jeffers to John Gassner, 10 Jun 1948, RJHRC, in Karman, *Collected Letters*; *Variety* 31 Mar: 57; 4 Aug 1948: 51; *LAT* 10 Aug: 14; 26 Sep 1948: D1; Johnson, 'Interlude With The Calmer Judith Anderson'; *CDT* 3 Oct: f15; 9 Oct 1948.

A few days after Una's death at the beginning of September 1950 Jeffers agreed to work on his adaptation again. In early October he visited Anderson and Luther at their new house to discuss the play. 'Thank you very much – and I am grateful to Luther too – for the pleasant and extremely interesting time I had with you,' he wrote Anderson. 'The place is magnificent, so is the house, and things will soon grow up around it. My love to your mother and to Luther too, and the others of your handsome family.' Sending the second act just before she left for New York, he wrote, 'I love you, Judith, and naturally I wish you good luck on your travels.'[9]

When Anderson opened the ANTA series on 26 November 1950 in *The Tower Beyond Tragedy*, this long-dreamed-of moment was surrounded, however, by sadness. When she left Rancho Verde for New York, her mother was so ill that she feared she would never see her again. When she came home from the final dress rehearsal, on a night battered by a record-breaking blizzard, Frank phoned to tell her that their mother was dead.[10] Calling on all her reserves, Anderson went ahead with the opening. 'I went through it,' she wrote later. 'For her. As she would have wanted me to.'

'The play was played out of love,' Anderson wrote. Although McClintic was unable to direct it and Kit Cornell was not available to play Electra or Cassandra, four friends from *Medea* – Marian Seldes, Don McHenry, Martha Downes and Ludi Claire – joined Anderson in *The Tower*, Seldes in the important role of Electra. 'We and the rest of the cast worked

---

9   Greene to Jeffers, 8 Sep 1950, RJHRC; Jeffers to Greene, 11 Sep 1950, RJTH; Jeffers to Anderson, 10 & 14 Oct 1950, RJTH; to Greene, 25 Oct 1950; to Anderson tel 26 Nov 1950, RJTH, in Karman, *Collected Letters*; *Variety* 19 Oct 1950: 4; *NYT* 26 Oct 1950.
10   *LAT* 26 Nov 1950: 46.

for a fraction of our salaries,' Anderson remembered. 'And if the reality could never quite equal the bright image that had glowed on the horizon of my mind like a beacon, still all of us… felt ourselves in service to the highest reaches of whatever talent we had. "Written in lines of fire," a critic said of the play. It was fire that seared all of us.'

Echoing the sentiments she first expressed as a student of Lawrence Campbell in Sydney, Anderson paid tribute to the role of the playwright in the success of any performance. 'Talent is never enough,' she wrote. 'An actor alone is nothing. Without the vision, the understanding, the heart of the dramatist, without the words that are part music and part painting, an actor is all but powerless.'

Nevertheless, the critics used the word 'genius' when they estimated Anderson's contribution to the success of the play. 'Greek tragedy can be mighty stately if the acting is not tipped with genius,' Brooks Atkinson wrote in the *New York Times*. 'But that is the armor with which Miss Anderson has gone into battle.'[11]

Based on Aeschylus's *Oresteia* and Jeffers's poem on the Electra legend, the play is an unremitting story of inter-familial hatred, jealousy and slaughter, much more bloody than *Medea*, though without the final horror of child-murder.[12] As the 'low-statured, fierce-lipped' Clytemnestra, 'Sinewed with strength… under the purple folds of the queen-cloak,' who kills her hated husband and is in turn murdered by her son, Orestes, Anderson welcomed the competition she had on stage from three other important characters – Orestes, his sister Electra and the prophetess Cassandra.

Clytemnestra, however, is spellbinding as she manipulates

---

11   *NYT* 27 Nov 1950: 38. See also 10 Dec: X5; 17 Dec 1950: X3.
12   *Roan Stallion, Tamar and Other Poems*, 1925; Johnson, 'Interlude With The Calmer Judith Anderson.'

the Grecian crowd, and the audience felt the play was anticlimactic after her spectacular murder. The critics almost unanimously declared it a triumph for Anderson and a failure as a play. Brooks Atkinson declared that 'In all conscience, no one should ever ask to see tragedy acted more magnificently than Judith Anderson plays it in *The Tower Beyond Tragedy*.' 'No one has quite recovered from Miss Anderson's performance in Jeffers' *Medea* three seasons ago,' he wrote, 'But her Clytemnestra overshadows it':

> *Perhaps the part is more congenial, since it is more human and varied. However that may be, her acting has a passion and also a grandeur that make it unforgettable. It is womanly, but it is also savage and horrible. Although Miss Anderson is a small woman, she has incomparable authority on the stage, speaking the lines with terrible ferocity and marching to a tragic doom like a woman possessed.*

'The acting is sculpturally beautiful,' he went on. 'Miss Anderson has not forgotten the physical portraiture… But the qualities that make her acting memorable come from the flaming spirit of a great actress who has dreamed of magnificence and knows how to reach it.' 'No one should ever expect anything finer in the theatre,' he concluded.[13]

Richard P Cooke in the *Wall Street Journal* considered this role even better for Anderson than that of Medea, and characterised the play as 'a theatrical wind as harsh and powerful as the storm which had struck New York the day before.'[14]

Former First Lady Eleanor Roosevelt, always a fan of Judith Anderson, endorsed the play and ANTA in 'My Day.' 'I found this play tense and dramatic the whole way through,' she wrote, 'written and acted in what might be called the

---

13 *NYT* 27 Nov 1950: 38.
14 *WSJ* 29 Nov 1950: 14.

grand manner. There is so little of this on the stage today that I felt proud we had an actress capable of portraying such a tragic figure.'[15]

Buoyed by these outstanding reviews, the play was extended beyond its initial two weeks until 22 December, and Anderson hoped to move the play to a Broadway theatre. But most people agreed with Richard Watts in the *New York Post* and John Chapman in the *Chicago Daily Tribune* that, despite its arresting characters and superb actors, it lacked *Medea*'s dramatic power. Jeffers, called to New York to carry out changes in the script, saw the play twice and agreed. 'Judith is of course tremendous; and carried the whole thing on her shoulders,' he wrote to his future biographer, Melba Berry Bennett. 'To me the play seemed less impressive than the production in the Carmel Forest Theater nine years ago. More polished, of course, but slighter and less interesting… The talk now is of bringing it to California in the spring.' John Gielgud – in town for *The Lady's Not for Burning* and still smarting from the *Medea* experience – wrote cattily to his mother, 'The Jeffers play with Judith Anderson was not much liked despite Brooks Atkinson's rave notice, and failed to transfer after its two weeks at the ANTA Theatre.'[16]

---

15 'My Day,' by Eleanor Roosevelt, 28 Nov 1950.
16 *NYP* 28 Nov1950, NYPL; *CDT* 28 Nov 1950: B4; *Variety* 29 Nov 1950: 50; *WP* 3 Dec 1950: L1; *Billboard* 9 Dec 1950: 37; *NYT* 3 Dec: X1; 8 Dec: 41; Dec 13: 60; 16 Dec: 22; 17 Dec 1950: X3; Jeffers to Greene and Anderson, 10 Dec 1950; to Melba Berry Bennett, 30 Dec 1950, RJHRC, in Karman, *Collected Letters*; Gielgud to mother, 1 Jan 1951, in *Gielgud's Letters*, 2004.

Hirschfeld caught the moment in 1958 when one cohort of First Ladies of the Stage gave way to the next in this mural for the Playbill Restaurant at the Hotel Manhattan. From left: Ethel Merman, Julie Harris, Lynn Fontanne, Helen Hayes, Katharine Cornell, Judy Holliday, Judith Anderson, Ruth Gordon and Shirley Booth

© The Al Hirschfeld Foundation

Chapter Twenty-eight

Changes, Professional and Personal 1951–9

Judith Anderson had always loved *The Tower Beyond Tragedy* much more than *Medea*. When she failed to turn it into a commercial success, she suffered one of her periodic collapses. 'Transfusion. Bed for 2 weeks,' she wrote in her diary early in January 1951. Her shaky marriage to Luther Greene did not survive this disappointment. Their surviving correspondence with Jeffers over the play has Luther's name struck out, suggesting that she blamed him for the play's failures; and he was already falling out with Frank. On 18 January, Anderson's diary recorded cryptically: 'L leaves.'

Her collapse prevented her from accepting an invitation from the Australian government to return for the fiftieth anniversary of the country's federation.[17] By July, however, she was ready to present *Medea* as a US representative at the Festival of Berlin, with her beloved Guthrie McClintic once more directing.[18] While there she persuaded McClintic to help her achieve another of her dreams – to revive *Come*

---

17 *Variety* 6 Dec 1950; 28 Feb 1951; *SMH* 19 Dec: 2; 20 Dec 1950: 2; 13 Feb: 2; 15 Feb: 1; 2 May 1951: 2; *SH* 24 Dec 1950: 2; 6 May 1951 Supplement: 4; *Advertiser* 22 Mar 1951: 11; *News* (Adelaide) 1 May 1951: 3.
18 Diary Feb; 25 Aug to 19 Sep 1951; Anderson to McClintic, [Apr 1951], Cornell Papers; *NYT* 27 May: 58; 9 Jul: 19; 3 Aug: 11; 26 Aug: 11; 6 Sep: 39; 14 Sep: 22; 23 Sep: 111; 14 Oct 1951: 108; *Variety* 25 Jul; 12 & 26 Sep 1951.

of Age, the eccentric musical fantasy by Clemence Dane and Richard Addinsell that she had loved since she performed it in 1934. A well-paid movie role (in *The Furies*, with Barbara Stanwyck and Walter Huston) freed her to once more indulge her passion. McClintic quickly assembled investors eager to see the play revived.[19]

Come of Age was presented, not on Broadway, but at the New York City Center's Civic Playhouse on West 55th Street, where *Medea* had filled the huge auditorium in 1949. Her old friend Maurice Evans had taken over the Playhouse's artistic affairs in September 1949, with his colleague from wartime Hawaii, George Schaefer, as executive producer. In 1951 the 'rotund and enthusiastic' Schaefer, whom Anderson remembered with great affection, replaced Evans as artistic director. *Come of Age* was the last of the 1951–2 winter season's revivals, preceded by Evans and Mildred Dunnock in *The Wild Duck* and Celeste Holm in *Anna Christie*. All actors, including stars, received Equity minimum wages of $80 a week.[20]

'It is one of those sweet mysterious labors of love,' Harry Gilroy wrote in the *New York Times* in answer to his own question: 'Why should this "play in music and words" about a young poet and a worldly woman, which did not go particularly well in 1934, be revived?' 'The light-heartedness of love was all over the place a few night ago,' he continued, 'at a final rehearsal before the *Come of Age* company left to play a week in Hartford.' 'The chief figures of the production smiled over their work and the 14 lesser actors sat in a corner of the stage by a piano heartily approving the Addinsell score and the singing by Muriel Rahn (of *Carmen Jones* fame).' 'I fell in love with the play, I tell you,' Anderson told him. 'Don't writers about the stage ever fall in love?'

---

19   *NYT* 20 Jan 1952: X1, 2–3; 22 Oct 1951: 33.
20   *NYT* 8 Sep 1949: 37; 15 Nov: 33; 16 Dec 1951: 112.

Judith Anderson in Come of Age *1952. From left: Marian Seldes, Judith Anderson, Jacqueline deWit and Muriel Rahn*

Author's collection

Dressed as before in glamorous Valentina gowns, Anderson once more captivated Brooks Atkinson when *Come of Age* opened in New York in January 1952. 'No one needs to be told now that Judith Anderson is a great actress,' he wrote. 'But it is gratifying now and then to have a chance to see her quality proved.'

> *Perhaps she played it as imaginatively in 1934 as she is playing it now. But it is also possible that she did not have then the insight into a part that she has now, nor the abundance of compassion. Isn't this a richer performance than the one she gave originally? At least to one theatregoer, it seems so.*

'It would take John Barrymore to play opposite Miss Anderson,' he wrote. 'When Miss Anderson is off-stage, the magic of *Come of Age* stops… Like a born actress, Miss Anderson draws character in her walk, in her attitudes, in her gestures and glances as well as the lines the author has given her… Miss Anderson brings *Come of Age* alive by being so vital, skilful and imaginative as an actress.'[21]

John Chapman was equally enchanted by Anderson's performance. 'It is easy to see why Judith Anderson has been saying that *Come of Age* is her favourite play,' he wrote, 'for she is magnificent in it and it gives her a wide range thru which to move, showing her feline grace and her ferocious temperament.' Robert P Cooke admired the 'strong gamut' of supercharged emotion as Anderson ran it, 'not a whit less commanding' than that of *Medea* or *The Tower Beyond Tragedy*, although in modern dress.[22]

Come of Age was sold out for its scheduled two weeks before it opened. Anderson remembered in her memoirs that you needed a shoehorn to get into the 2,257-seat theatre. Like *Tower* it was extended for another week to gauge the demand for a move to a Broadway house. Although it was the biggest money draw of the City Center season, it failed, like *Tower*, to find a backer for such a move.[23]

This was the last time for many years that Anderson could indulge herself in plays that she was in love with. Midway through rehearsals of *Come of Age* she received a message that would radically affect her fortunes: her lawyer and financial adviser, T H Canfield, had committed suicide among revelations of large-scale embezzlement. Anderson lost at least $80,000 (about $700,000 in 2019 money) – virtually all her savings.[24] Anderson would now have to take whatever work she was offered.

---

21   Diary 17 Dec 1951 to 21 Jan 1952; *TAM* Apr 1952: 84; Kohle Yohannan, *Valentina: American Couture and the Cult of Celebrity*, 2009, 153; *NYT* 24 Jan 1952: 22.
22   *CDT* 25 Jan 1952: a10; *WSJ* 25 Jan 1952: 4.
23   *NYT* 29 Jan1952: 17; *Variety* 30 Jan: 59; Feb 6: 59; 13 Feb 1952: 69; *NYT* 3 Feb 1952: X1; *CDT* 3 Feb 1952: f4; *WP* 10 Feb 1952: L1.
24   *Santa Barbara Sun* 14 Feb 1952, MHL.

This financial reverse was a clear indication of what she must do. The other reverses she suffered at this time were less clear. Guthrie McClintic, who had rescued her from mediocrity in 1934 and from anger and disappointment in 1948, who had allowed her to burn brightly again in *Come of Age*, had, unknown to her, begun to show signs of illness. Over the next nine years, until his death in 1961, he gradually began to lose his touch. In December 1950 his production of *Captain Carvallo* with Kit Cornell had failed before it was brought to Broadway. During the 1950s Cornell appeared for the first time in 30 years in plays not directed by her husband; and the plays McClintic chose to direct (with or without his wife) were problematic, even though his direction was politely termed 'elegant' and 'fastidious.' Even Brooks Atkinson, the longtime admirer of McClintic and Cornell, declared McClintic's *Four Winds* in 1957 'boring'; and he was hard put to be anything but polite in reviewing the couple's last production together, *Dear Liar*, where Cornell played the great actress Mrs Patrick Campbell at what the more truthful Claudia Cassidy called 'half mast.'[25] In 1955 McClintic directed Anderson one more time in her triumphant performance of *Medea* in Bernhardt's theatre in Paris; but after 1952 she no longer had his sure touch to help move her career beyond that play's golden glow.

Anderson's plans for further triumphs with Jeffers also foundered after *The Tower Beyond Tragedy*. Without Una to care for and encourage him, he had little energy for work outside his own poetry as he moved into his late sixties. In 1952 he helped Anderson prepare the readings from *Medea* and *Tower* that she presented for the nearby Ojai Festival. She and Jeffers were considering Iphigenie, Electra, Phedre, and Maria Stuart, she told Edwin Shallert in the run-up to this presentation.

---

25 John Gielgud to mother, 14 Jan 1951, in *Gielgud's Letters*, 2004; *NYT* 19 Jan 1951: 33; 24 Dec 1950: 36; 18 Mar 1960: 19; *CDT* 14 Jan 1960: c1.

They continued to talk about a translation of Racine's *Phedre*. In 1957, when she visited Jeffers in Carmel, they were still discussing possible collaborations. 'It was so good to see you do you think you might do Electra or Hecuba?' she wrote afterwards. 'If so what should I read to refresh my mind?' A year later, as she was preparing for one of the few modern plays she was offered after *Medea* (*Comes a Day* by Speed Lamkin), she wrote feelingly to Jeffers, 'here trying out play by new young author – and ohg! How I miss you and the glorious music of your poetry.'[26]

By this time, however, it was too late. In August 1961 she saw Jeffers for the last time when she performed the concert version of her readings from *Tower* and *Medea* at the Wharf Theatre in Monterey, near Carmel. Five months later he was dead, aged 75.[27]

Without the genius of McClintic and the poetry of Jeffers, *Come of Age* marked the end of Judith Anderson's career as a sought-after stage actress. This realisation came slowly.

During summer 1952 she played Queen Herodias to Charles Laughton's Herod in the movie *Salome*. Impressed by Anderson's acting, Laughton invited her to join Tyrone Power and Raymond Massey and a chorus of 20 in a dramatic reading of Stephen Vincent Benet's long narrative poem *John*

---

26   Diary 21 & 23 Apr 1952; Jeffers to Anderson, 28 Apr 1952, UCSB; 13, [14?] & 29 May 1952 [tel], RJTH; to John Bauer, 1 May 1952, RJHRC, in James Karman, ed., *The Collected Letters of Robinson Jeffers With Selected Letters of Una Jeffers*, 2015; Anderson to Jeffers, [17 Dec 1957] & 22 Oct [1958], RJHRC; Howard Young, Lewis & Young Productions to Jeffers, 9 May 1952, RJHRC; *NYT* 11 May: X7; 2 Jun 1952: B9; 16 May 1954: X1; *Variety* 25 Jun 1952; *LAT* 18 May 1952: E1, 2; *WP* 18 Dec 1953: 52.
27   For Jeffers' last years see Melba Berry Bennett, *The Stone Mason of Tor House: The Life and Work of Robinson Jeffers*, 1966, 230–38. Jeffers' last message to Anderson was a telegram on 17 May 1961 congratulating her on her Emmy for *Macbeth*, RJTH, in Karman, *Collected Letters*.

Brown's Body that he was directing in the fall. In what Claudia Cassidy called 'Chautauqua with better actors' Anderson played a number of roles, from the 17-year-old swamp girl Medora to the iron-willed Mary Lou Wingate, in a striking gold dress – one of the loveliest she had worn on stage. After a successful tour that took them all over the country, the company played on Broadway for two months until mid-April 1953. Generally hailed as innovative and emotionally intense, *John Brown's Body* maintained Anderson's reputation as 'our greatest tragic actress.'[28]

The following season Anderson was persuaded by rising producer Roger Stevens to star in an unusual new play by Jane Bowles. Stevens had been in 1949 an unknown 'theatre-minded real estate operator' from the mid-west. By 1951 he was a director of ANTA and a non-author member of the influential Playwrights Company. Enormously wealthy (he and his partners bought the Empire State Building in 1951), in 1953 he established, with Robert Whitehead, the City Investing Company and the Playwrights Company, a new, well-funded, corporation to produce plays and operate theatres – the Producers' Theatre. He admired

This beautiful gold dress, worn in John Brown's Body, *is now in the collection of the Performing Arts Centre in Adelaide.*

---

28   *Variety* 29 May; 13 Jun 1952; *LAT* 6 Jun 1952: B9; *NYT* 22 Feb 1953: X1; Diary 8 May to 21 Jul 1952.

Judith Anderson's boldness: in 1950 he had been interested in taking over *The Tower Beyond Tragedy* for a Broadway run; and after *Come of Age* closed in 1952 he was actively involved in finding her a new play.[29]

Jane Bowles was the lesbian wife of the homosexual writer and composer Paul Bowles – an eccentric couple who were part of the expatriate community in Tangier. Now considered an under-appreciated but important feminist writer, Jane had been encouraged by their friend Oliver Smith to use her gift for dialogue to write a play, which he would produce. As Paul Bowles wrote in his memoirs, 'She did and he did.'[30] The play was *In the Summer House*.

With minor-key music by Paul Bowles, *In the Summer House* opened at the end of December 1953, produced by Oliver Smith and the Playwrights Company and directed by José Quintero.[31] Described by one critic as tantalizingly imperfect, it had only a short season – a total of 55 performances – but it drew admiring reviews. Critics likened Bowles's tragi-comedy on loneliness to the work of Chekhov. John Chapman in the *New York Daily News* saw it as 'straight out of *Cherry Orchard*,' while Richard Coe in the *Washington Post* noted that her 'canny' ear for dialogue was 'wrapped in the style of Chekhov, a kind of concise formlessness.' It was, in Coe's opinion, 'the most original and brilliant new play I have seen in some seasons.'

As the flamboyant, vain and commonplace Gertrude Eastman-Cuevas, Judith Anderson brought all of her skill

---

29 NYT 17 Apr 1953: 31; 3 Oct 1949: 13; 27 Apr 1951: 20; 21 Jul 1953: 18; Diary 19 Mar 1952; 16 Jun to 25 Oct 1953.
30 Gena Dagel Caponi, *Paul Bowles: Romantic Savage*, 1994.
31 Diary 6 Oct 1953 to 13 Feb 1954; Jane Bowles, *My Sister's Hand in Mine: The Collected Works of Jane Bowles*, 2005; Millicent Dillon, *A Little Original Sin: The Life and Work of Jane Bowles*, 1998; Paul Bowles, *Without Stopping: An Autobiography*, 1985, 320; Michelle Green, *The Dream at the End of the Word: Paul Bowles and the Literary Renegades in Tangier*, 1991, 105, 139–40.

as an emotional actress to conveying the neediness and desperation below her character's surface gaiety and laughter. 'I shall never forget,' Coe wrote, 'the movement of her arms as she tells her daughter [the shy, unformed Molly] how one should develop personality.' 'Yes,' Coe concluded, '"In the Summer House" is indeed richly original and haunting, a civilized essay in the tragi-comedy style so unfamiliar on our showmanship stages.' Brooks Atkinson considered it 'Very likely… Miss Anderson's most versatile performance… the woman she acts is far from simple – callous, overbearing, adder-tongued, humorous, yet helpless withal, sustained by romantic dreams from the past, unable, despite her strength, to cope with reality.'[32]

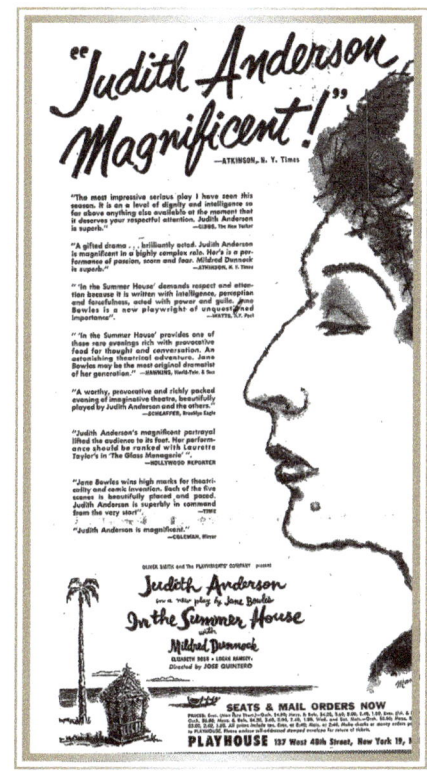

Advertisement for In the Summer House January 1954

In the Summer House was an adventure for Anderson. The character of Gertrude was a challenge that she felt she never adequately conquered, despite the glowing reviews; and she found Jane Bowles captivating and perplexing, possibly because Jane fell in love with her. Richard Coe noted that "Mrs Bowles' respect for Judith Anderson, her star… is something close to reverence'; and *Mademoiselle* editor and gossip

---

32 *LAT* 6 Jun 1954: E2; *WP* 17 Dec 1953: 37; *NYT* 30 Dec 1953: 17.

columnist Leo Lerman noted in his diary of the closing night party, 'Judith Anderson playing Herodias and Jane yearning at her.'[33]

After two failed marriages Anderson was not about to become embroiled in another risky relationship. All of her energies in these years were directed towards even greater achievements in her profession. She had always 'thirsted' to play Joan in Shaw's *Saint Joan*. When *In the Summer House* closed she offered herself to the Theatre Guild, who were about to send it out on tour; but she was told she was too old at 57 for the role. This humiliating rebuff was compounded when 54-year-old former movie comedian Jean Arthur was given the role; and she no doubt felt some satisfaction when the tour ended abruptly with Arthur's nervous breakdown.[34]

Another, more outrageous, dream seemed within reach in summer 1954. Since 1953 Anderson had been talking to Roger Stevens and others about playing Hamlet – not Queen Gertrude as she had before, but Hamlet, the hero. At first she thought the idea preposterous. Then she remembered that Bernhardt and other actresses had been brave enough to do it. 'The project might be dangerous,' she realised; but the more she thought about it, the more she knew she could not live unless she tried it. Remembering an early rehearsal with Gielgud in sweat shirt and slacks, with only a couple of kitchen chairs against the bare brick wall of the stage, she

---

33   Anderson interview with Millicent Dillon, 10 Apr 1978, Dillon Papers; *NYT* 27 Dec 1953: X5; Stephen Pascal, ed., *The Grand Surprise: The Journals of Leo Lerman*, 2007, 155–6. See also Diary 13, 20 & 31 Jan 1954; Bowles to Anderson from Tangier, after 14 Feb 1954, UCSB; Desley Deacon, 'Celebrity Sexuality: Judith Anderson, Mrs Danvers, sexuality and "truthfulness" in biography,' *Australian Historical Studies*, Apr 2012: 45–60; Dorothy Mandel, *Uncommon Eloquence: A Biography of Angna Enters*, 1986, 264–5.
34   *CDT* 20 Jun 1954: e10; *NYT* 15 Nov 1954: 31.

saw how she could stage such a performance: 'a few platforms; uninsistent clothes which would be neither modern nor costume… ; lighting that concentrated on the face and left the rest of the body in semi-darkness; all the emphasis, in short, on the play.' During the 1954 summer she negotiated with a producer about a tour; but it never eventuated. Without a play for the 1954 to 1955 season, she wrote a friend despondently in January 1955 – the fortieth anniversary of her theatrical debut, 'All is well though workless. Talk of a couple of pictures but nothing definite, I do hope something pops soon.'[35]

Anderson appeared only one more time on Broadway until her triumphant return as the Nurse in *Medea* in 1982, when she was 85. Her dream of playing Hamlet almost came to fruition in 1957 but foundered on artistic disagreements; she talked with Roger Stevens about Colette's *Cheri*, but the role was given to the much younger Kim Stanley (who, according to *Time*, was 'about as Gallic as cornflakes and as demimondaine as Betsy Ross')[36]; and he promised her *The Visit*, but that eventually went to the Lunts for their final stage appearance. Meanwhile she played in *Black Chiffon* at the Palm Beach Playhouse and the Coconut Grove Playhouse early in 1956 in the first of many visits to these resorts; and later in the year she made a very successful tour across the continent from California in *The Chalk Garden*.

Desperate for a play on Broadway, she agreed in 1958 to appear in *Comes a Day*, a new work by a relatively untried playwright, Speed Lamkin, produced by her old friend Cheryl

---

35 Diary 15 Feb 1953 to Jan 1955; *WP* 18 Dec 1953: 52; *Times* 8 Mar 1954: 11; *LAT* 5 Jun 1954: A6; *NYT* 4 Jul 1954: X1; *WPTH* 5 Jan 1955: 18; Enters to Anderson, 24 Apr; 15 May; 6 Jul; [Jul?]; 20 Aug; 7 Sep 1954; Eastman Boomer to Anderson, 20 Jul 1954; Anderson to Enters, [Env 3 May]; 12 May; 22 Jul; 13 Aug 1954; 23 Jan1955, Enters Papers.
36 *Time* 26 Oct 1959.

Judith Anderson and George C Scott in Comes a Day *1958*

Author's collection

Crawford with young movie producer Alan Pakula. Despite its brilliant cast (Mary Martin's son Larry Hagman playing 'with wholesome animal magnetism' and the young George C Scott almost stealing Anderson's thunder as a 'suave and unsmiling psychpath'), the play was condemned by critics as an 'uneven, baffling drama' and lasted only 28 performances. Anderson remembered it as a 'shaming' endeavour despite the usual praise her own performance drew.[37]

Anderson's 'joblessness' on Broadway was intensely personal to her, but it was a problem she shared with many others, and had much to do with the changes taking place in American theatre in these years. As commentator Gilbert

---

37 *Variety* 8 Oct 1958: 72; *NYT* 7 Nov 1958: 22. See Diary 8 Jan to 29 Nov 1958; Cheryl Crawford Papers; Anderson to McClintic, 17 Feb 1959, Cornell Papers; Rex Reed, 'The Soft Side of G.C. Scott,' *New York Observer* 4 Oct 1999: 21.

Millstein pointed out in the *New York Times* in 1961, 'In recent years there has been no leading actress of any generation – from Geraldine Page and Maureen Stapleton to Judith Anderson and Katharine Cornell – who has not suffered from a lack of work, inferior plays and short runs in the legitimate theatre.'[38]

The 1950s saw the boom in musicals on Broadway: *Call Me Madam* (1950), *The King and I* (1951), *Pajama Game* (1954), *My Fair Lady* (1956) and *West Side Story* (1957). Costs of theatrical production increased, fewer non-musicals opened and more productions failed. In summing up the 1959–60 season, Brooks Atkinson called it 'calamitous.' 'As a business, Broadway has been bankrupt for 30 years,' he wrote. From a high of 264 new productions in 1927–8, there were now about 50, around 10 of these musicals; and only about one fifth made a profit. There were, therefore, only about 40 plays each season to employ actresses like Anderson, and only eight would succeed. The great mass of those that failed, Atkinson observed, were 'routine merchandise on a low level of intelligence and taste.'[39]

As commercial Broadway declined as a forum for high quality and experimental drama and fine acting, centres of theatrical endeavour diversified. Off-Broadway gradually grew in influence; subsidised organisations such as ANTA and the City Center presented actresses like Anderson, Helen Hayes and Ruth Gordon in brief revivals and new work; the State Department sponsored overseas tours; provincial theatres such as the Royal Poinciana Playhouse in Miami and the Huntington Hartford in Los Angeles featured leading actors for one – or two-week performances; campuses built theatres

---

38 *NYT* 5 Nov 1961: SM28.
39 *NYT* 5 Jun 1960: X1. For figures see *CDT* 8 Jun 1958: g12; *WPTH* 31 May 1959: H9; *Barron's National Business and Financial Weekly* 6 Jun 1960: 1; *NYT* 12 Jun 1960: 115.

and established their own acting companies; and the 'campus circuit' helped revive the road tour, often providing audiences for sole actors giving readings or excerpts from the classics.

In this new environment, the surviving members of Anderson's 1920s cohort suffered similar fates. Alfred Lunt and Lynn Fontanne retired to their farm in Wisconsin in 1959 after their final success in *The Visit*. Katharine Cornell left the theatre after the death of Guthrie McClintic in 1961. But Anderson, Helen Hayes and Ruth Gordon adapted, complaining, to the new order. Ruth Gordon's last big hit was *The Matchmaker* in 1955. She made three more attempts on Broadway over the next few years, one of which lasted only 16 days despite providing what Richard Coe called admiringly an 'acting lesson.'[40] Helen Hayes revived *The Wisteria Trees* at the City Center and *The Skin of Our Teeth* at the ANTA Theatre in 1955 and had her last two Broadway hits for many years in Jean Anouilh's *Time Remembered* in 1957–8 and Eugene O'Neill's *A Touch of the Poet* in 1958–9. She made long overseas tours for the State Department in the 1960s, toured the US with Maurice Evans in excerpts from Shakespeare, and joined the APA (Association of Producing Artists)-Phoenix Repertory Company, which spent half of the year at the Huntington Hartford in Los Angeles, before returning to Broadway in a successful revival of *Harvey* at the ANTA Playhouse in 1970.

Anderson, Hayes and Gordon had always supplemented their theatrical income with movies, Hayes, married to screenwriter Charles MacArthur, more consistently. With her income from the theatre diminishing, in 1956 Anderson played Memnet, the slave-nurse who was present when the baby Moses was found among the bulrushes, in Cecil B De Mille's *The Ten Commandments*, finally appearing in a movie produced

---

40   *WPTH* 18 Oct 1966: B5.

by the man who had rejected her as too plain in 1918. In 1958 she played one of her most admired roles in *Cat on a Hot Tin Roof*, cast against type as the mousy Big Momma; and in the following year she was the Wicked Stepmother in Jerry Lewis's *Cinderfella*. Ruth Gordon, 'rediscovered' in 1965, won an Oscar for her role in *Rosemary's Baby* in 1969 and a permanent place in the hearts of a generation in *Harold and Maude* in 1971. Helen Hayes also won an Oscar in the later part of her career for her role as the little old lady sitting next to a would-be bomber in *Airport* in 1970.

Movies, campus tours, subsidised theatres – all faded into insignificance in this new postwar world compared to

Judith Anderson and Elizabeth Taylor in Cat on a Hot Tin Roof *1958*
Album/ Alamy Stock Photo

the new medium: television. And it was television that gave Judith Anderson and her cohort completely new careers and new heights to scale.

Anderson's family life also had its sorrows in these years. She deeply felt her failure, for the second time, as a wife. Her much loved mother was dead. And Frank – the carefree companion of her youth – was becoming more and more unhappy with his situation as the manager of Anderson's avocado ranch – and as her dependent. She got enormous happiness, however, from her nieces and nephews.

Frank, Laura and family visit Judith Anderson on the set of Salome, *summer 1952*
Courtesy Susan Anderson and Jenifer McCurry

'I had a front row seat at the miracle of the children's growth and the gaiety of their company,' she wrote in her memoirs in 1962. When the Santa Barbara gossip columnist Rosario Curletti captured them in the *Los Angeles Times* in 1958, her pleasure in being 'Aunt Judith, dear, beloved, beautiful Aunt Judith' was obvious. This happiness received a

Judith Anderson with her niece Susan in Paris in 1955

Author's collection

mortal blow, however, when Frank died suddenly in 1960 at 65; and the children, growing up in the sixties, one by one evaded her ambitious plans for their futures.[41]

In the face of her broken marriage, the tensions with her family and the decline of her theatrical career, it was her friends, old and new, who sustained Anderson. She had always had a gift for friendship, and nearby Santa Barbara – 'as agreeable a small city as any in the known world' – proved

---

41   *LAT* 6 Feb 1958: A1; interviews with Susan Anderson, Jenifer McCurry and Judith Valentine, Carpinteria.

especially fruitful in soulmates. She notes visits from two of the most important in her diary on the same day – Sunday 1 June 1951 – 'Lotte Lehman 3 Wright 5.' Lotte Lehmann was the renowned operatic soprano and lieder singer who had recently retired to Santa Barbara, where she shared a home with Frances Holden. Wright was a wealthy art collector and philanthropist, Wright Saltus Ludington, who presided at Val Verde, his extraordinary estate in the Santa Barbara suburb of Montecito, where the garden designed by his school friend Lockwood de Forest provided dramatic settings for his collection of Greek and Roman sculpture, and an art gallery housed his pioneering collection of modern paintings. When Anderson came to know him, he was president of the Santa Barbara Museum of Art, 'the most individual and most beautiful, as well as the most active, small art museum in America,' which he helped to found in 1939 and to which he was a major contributor of money and art.[42]

In 1952 Wright Ludington brought the vibrant young Ala Story to Santa Barbara as director of the museum of art. Blonde, rail-thin, with a caustic wit, a far-ranging mind and alluring manners, Story was accompanied by her partner Margaret Mallory, an upper-class New Englander with interests in art and philanthropy. Together they established their luxurious home in Montecito as a centre of social life.[43]

Lotte Lehmann and Judith Anderson coach Lehmann's most successful student, the soprano, Grace Bumbry, in Lady Macbeth, 1973

---

42 *LAT* 3 Feb 1985: 80; Diary 1 Jun 1951. See Michael H Kater, *Never Sang for Hitler: The life and Times of Lotte Lehmann, 1888–1976*, 2008.
43 See *Two Collections: Margaret Mallory Ala Story*. Catalogue, Santa Barbara Museum of Art and California Palace of the Legion of Honor, 1966.

It is not clear what the relationship was between Wright Ludington and Judith Anderson. He was a handsome man – tall and suntanned in a white linen suit according to an article in *Vogue* in 1960, when he was 60. His 'habit of throwing away better lines than most people repeat' would have appealed to the quick-witted Anderson. They obviously relished each other's company, and in a diary entry in 1956 Anderson drew a heart with an arrow next to his name.[44] But Wright was a known homosexual who had rarely had his name associated romantically with a woman. For many years, however, she and Wright made a foursome with Ala Story and Margaret Mallory, with Story and Mallory blended in her diary as 'Mala.'

A rare photograph of Wright Ludington, in Ludington Court at the opening of the Santa Barbara Museum of Art 1941
Author's collection

The summer of 1951 was also the beginning of two unexpected and rich friendships – with Luther's former wife Ellie Martin, and with Ellie's friend Angna Enters. The friendship with Ellie began when Anderson sent her a slanderous notebook, intended for his children to read 'when they are old enough to understand,' that she had found among Luther's effects. Ellie was grateful, and they became friends. She had

---

44 *Vogue* 1 Aug, 1960: 130; 'Harmony in Diversity: Wright S. Ludington,' in *The Collector in America*, compiled by Jean Lipman and the editors of *Art in America*, 1961; Diary 14 Jul 1956.

remarried – to wealthy Republican Joe Martin – and Anderson enjoyed meeting up with them whenever she was in San Francisco, and she kept up with Luther's children, Spike and Lenka, by then aged 9 and 7, of whom she had grown fond during their marriage. Through Ellie she met the talented mime Angna Enters, who quickly became a firm friend and frequent visitor – and, surprisingly for Anderson, regular correspondent.[45]

Although they never collaborated again on a major project after 1952, Anderson and Jeffers maintained their affectionate friendship during the 1950s, mainly by telephone. In 1951, a year after Una's death, her old friend Mabel Dodge Luhan, who had always had a yen for him, circulated the rumour that he and Anderson were married. But he brusquely repudiated the idea.[46]

Many old friends from New York days now lived in Los Angeles, where she went regularly for work: Anne Morrison Chapin, with whom she had toured in *Dear Brutus* in 1920, was a successful screen and television writer; Mary Servoss, her close friend since *Behold, the Bridegroom*, was a busy movie actress. New friends were former neighbours in Pacific Palisades, producer David Lewis and director James Whale, with whom she often stayed when in LA. (She read the lesson at Whale's funeral after his suicide in 1957.)[47] She

---

45   Ellie [Martin] to Enters, [Env 5 Jul 1951]; Diary 25 & 26 Apr; 22 Aug; 12 Sep; 8, 9, 10 Nov 1952; Anderson to Enters, 12 May; 22 Jul; 13 Aug 1954; Enters to Anderson, 15 May 1954, Enters Papers. Enters made a portrait of Anderson which was sold to her friend the drama critic William Hawkins in 1955; see Enters to Ellie, 2 Feb 1955, Enters Papers.

46   Jeffers to Luhan, 28 Jun 1951, RJYale, in Karman, *Collected Letters*. For Luhan's complex relationship with the Jeffers see Lois Palken Rudnick, *Mabel Dodge Luhan: New Woman, New Worlds*, 1997.

47   Mark Gattis, *James Whale: A Biography*, 1995, 164, 168.

often saw fellow Australian Orry Kelly, who designed many costumes for her; and she caught up with her friend Richard Halliday, his wife Mary Martin and her goddaughter Heller whenever Martin's busy schedule allowed it. In New York she partied with old friends Carl Van Vechten, Helen Menken, Aileen Pringle and Margalo Gillmore, went to the theatre with critic William Hawkins and the opera with 'Mr Met,' the Metropolitan's publicity man Francis Robinson; she kept up with her old lover Nickolas Muray, his wife Peggy and her goddaughter Mimi; she spent weekends in the country with Guthrie McClintic and Kit Cornell; and – most unexpectedly – she dined and wined with Admiral Bill Halsey, her friend and admirer since they met in Hawaii in 1943, then retired in New York.

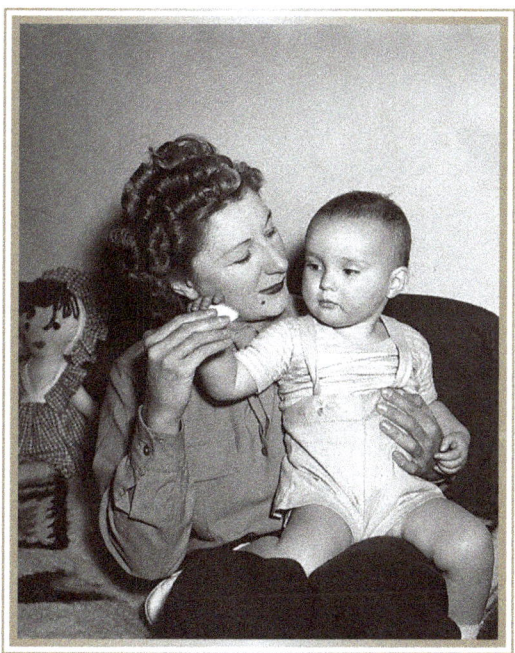

Judith Anderson with her god-daughter Mimi Muray, c 1942

Courtesy Mimi Muray Levitt

Judith Anderson won her first Emmy for Macbeth *in 1955, shown here with fellow-winner Robert Cummings*

Photo by Earl Leaf/ Michael Ochs Archives/ Getty Images

Chapter Twenty-nine

A New Career: Television Star 1950–59

Although I have artistic pretensions, I also have no intention of ending up starving in an attic... if you want to be remembered you have to be in movies or on TV

Maurice Evans 1967

As Judith Anderson gradually realised that her brilliant success in *Medea* had been the climax of her theatrical career – in essence a full stop rather than a doorway to further greatness – she found a new source of livelihood and accomplishment in the flourishing new media of television. Nineteen forty-nine was the beginning of the 'Golden Age of Television' – a period that lasted until about 1960. In a postwar period of increasing affluence when university attendance skyrocketed, a growing middle class formed an eager audience for 'culture' that could be beamed into their suburban living rooms. Beginning with the *Kraft Television Theater* on NBC in 1947, high quality hour-long drama was televised live in prime time by the major networks, which were linked coast to coast by 1951.[48]

Although Anderson claimed to despise the medium,

---

48 See Gary Deeb, 'The '50s. The prime time of television,' *CT* 14 Nov 1976: G37; William Boddy, *Fifties Television: The Industry and Its Critics*, 1993.

television drama, with its emphasis on character and words, actually drew on some of her greatest skills. 'Words are the thing,' a scriptwriter of the period wrote; and the television camera, according to another, could be 'the scalpel with which to lay bare the human heart and spirit' with an immediacy that was not available to the theatre or to film. Commentators advised that 'Emphasis must be on quick character development, on revealing close-ups which make the lift of an eyebrow or the flash of a smile more important than the sweep of an army.' The actor 'must "be" who he represents… The television camera goes inside of an actor's mind and soul, and sends the receiving set exactly what it sees there.' With her mastery of her voice and body, and her ability to convey emotions and character through intimate details, Anderson was a natural for Golden Age television.[49]

Judith Anderson made her debut in November 1950 when she presented a scene from *Macbeth* on the ANTA-produced *Showtime USA*. Sponsored by the Dodge Dealers of America and produced by former ANTA president Vinton Freedley, *Showtime USA* was a short-lived attempt to bring segments of Broadway hits to the television audience.[50]

Her first full-length television play, *The Silver Cord*, was presented in the *Pulitzer Prize Playhouse* series on 26 January 1951, soon after *The Tower Beyond Tragedy* closed. Sidney Howard's 1926 hit, with its charming, domineering mother – as *Variety* put it, 'the psycho mother who refused to relinquish her abnormal hold on her two grown sons' – provided the sort of role Anderson often played in this second half of her career. Her spot on the Ed Sullivan's *Toast of the Town* a few weeks later was the first of many appearances on

---

49 Boddy, *Fifties Television*, 81–4, quoting Edward Barry Roberts, Ann Howard Bailey and William I Kaufman and Robert S Kolodzin.
50 *Variety* 27 Sep: 29; 18 Oct: 31; 1 Nov 1950: 30; *NYY* 29 Oct 1950: 108; *CDT* 1 Oct 1950: n_b13; *WP*, 18 Dec 1950: B9.

celebrity variety shows over the next forty years. The following month she appeared for the first and only time in a Jed Harris production when she played an ageing actress who has lost her nerve in *Farewell Appearance* for the *Billy Rose Playbill*. As Walter Winchell wrote appreciatively of her portrayal of a great actress in this 'teevee drama,' 'Talk about perfect casting.' The *Billboard* reviewer, who praised the brilliant casting and Jed Harris's painstaking supervision, 'had never been so overwhelmed by a performance.' *Farewell Appearance* demonstrated the force of video, he wrote. Switching between medium shots and closeups, the camera 'revealed every twitch of the facial muscles, every studied gesture with the hands, every expression of the eyes' – aspects of acting that Anderson commanded superbly.[51]

As Anderson finished her first season of television with a similar ageing actress role in Somerset Maugham's *Theatre* on the series *Somerset Maugham TV Theatre*, she met up again with her old friend Olga Lee, who was now a theatrical and television agent.[52] She and Olga renewed their friendship and from that time Olga handled her television work.

Although she appeared on many television shows over the next 40 years, Anderson's greatest work was done, starting in 1954, on the *Hallmark Hall of Fame*, under the benign reign of producer George Schaefer. Schaefer had been a 22-year–old 'roly poly sergeant' (actually a private) when Anderson worked with him in Hawaii in 1942 as part of Maurice Evans' Central Pacific Base Command. Since then he had become a leading Broadway producer, most notably with Evans on *The*

---

51   Diary 26 Jan; 11 Feb; 6 Mar 1951; *NYT* 4 Oct 1950: 46; 26 Jan1951: 26; 11 Feb 1951: 104; *WP* 26 Jan: B11; 6 Mar: 33; 11 Mar 1951: L1; *Variety* 31 Jan 1951: 25; *Billboard* 17 Mar 1951: 11.
52   *NYT* 15 Apr 1951: 109.

Teahouse of the August Moon, which ran for three years and won the Pulitzer, Tony and New York Critics prizes in 1953. Anderson had come into contact with him again when he followed Evans as Executive Producer, then Artistic Director, at the City Center, where he supervised her revival of *Come of Age* in 1952.[53]

Hallmark Hall of Fame began quietly in 1951, when the greeting card company agreed to sponsor the made-for-television opera *Amahl and the Night Visitors* on NBC on Christmas Eve. Hallmark's founder, J C Hall, liked the idea of supporting culture for the masses, and began a 50-year collaboration with NBC presenting quality drama on television. Known initially as the *Hallmark Television Playhouse*, it was until 1954 mainly a vehicle for Winston Churchill's actress daughter Sarah Churchill, who hosted the program and acted in most of its offerings.[54]

The program took on its trademark quality when energetic young Mildred Freed Alberg went to NBC with the suggestion that they produce Maurice Evans in his classic vehicle, *Hamlet*. Alberg had become an admirer of Evans when she accompanied her husband, actor Somer Alberg, on his *Devil's Disciple* tour in 1950.[55]

Hamlet was produced as a special two-hour edition of the *Hallmark Playhouse* on 26 April 1953, with Ruth Chatterton as the Queen and Sarah Churchill as Ophelia. Evans produced the play in conjunction with Albert McCleery, the show's regular producer, who also directed, and George Schaefer supervised the overall production. Mildred Alberg made the adaptation.

---

53 See George Schaefer, *From Live Tape to Film: 60 Years of Inconspicuous Directing*, 1996; *NYT* 3 Feb 1952: X1.

54 James Friedman, ed. *UCLA Film and Television Archive presents* Hallmark Hall of Fame, 2001.

55 *NYT* 9 Feb 1958: X13.

Although it had its critics, Evans's television debut was hailed as 'exciting' and its production a 'magnificent' sign of the medium's 'new maturity.'[56] The same team produced *Richard II* for what was now known as the *Hallmark Hall of Fame* on 24 January 1954 with Sarah Churchill as Queen Isabel in an adaptation by Evans, this time directed by George Schaefer.[57]

In July 1954, as Judith Anderson was contemplating her joblessness and dreaming of playing *Hamlet*, Evans began negotiations with her for a repeat for *Hallmark* of their 1941–2 success, *Macbeth*. 'Had a couple of letters from Maurice E and I hope the Macbeth TV goes through… soooooo,' she wrote Angna Enters on 22 July. In mid-August the *New York Times* announced that Evans was preparing *Macbeth* for a colour production in November, and that Anderson would play Lady Macbeth.[58]

Anderson was a reluctant television star. As she wrote to Enters of the filming of Somerset Maugham's *Louise* for the Henry Fonda series *The Star and the Story*, 'It is the dreariest form of making a living, and possibly the hottest, it was last week anyway, wigs, period costume with velvet tight dresses, and petticoats etc. But thank God for it.' It was, she told a reporter in Australia, 'the devil's own work.'[59]

Making a television play was a heart-stopping business in the days when production was live to air. 'Maurice and I spent two terrifying hours dashing from side to side on a set four times as big as the one on which we later did much of the

---

56 *WP* 31 Mar 1953: 1; *CDT* 2 Apr 1953: B2; Evans, 'An Actor Discusses His TV Debut,' *NYT* 26 Apr: X11; 27 Apr 1953: 29; *WP* 10 May: L1–2; 26 May 1953: 35; *LAT* 28 Apr 1953: 24; *CSM* 28 Apr 1953: 6.
57 *NYT* 22 Nov 1953; 25 Jan: 31 Jan 1954; *CDT* 10 Jan 10, 1954: N8; *CSM* 19 Jan 1954: 11; *LAT* 24 Jan 1954: D10.
58 *NYT* 1 Jul; 18 Aug; 22 Aug 1954; Enters to Anderson, [Jul 1954]; 22 Jul [1954], Enters Papers; *CDT* 19 Sep 1954: R3; *LAT* 2 Nov 1954: A3.
59 Anderson to Enters, 22 Jul [1954]; *LAT* 21 Jun 1954: 26; *SMH* 16 Sep 1955: 2.

screen filming of "Macbeth" in Britain,' she told the *Australian Women's Weekly* after she had made a second TV *Macbeth* in 1960. 'And for these two terrifying hours we also seemed to be leaping from costume to costume, in and out of exits.' 'None of the play was cut to make it easier,' she went on, 'and you can imagine what a frightful strain it therefore was to make it live.'[60]

'Those days of live television demanded nerves of iron,' Maurice Evans recollected in his memoirs. In preparation for their new roles as makers of television drama he and George Schaefer had sat down with their chief cameraman in Evans' dining room and learned their craft. 'With large sheets of graph paper before us, and T-squares, triangles, dividers, and pencils at hand, we made the night hideous as we were instructed in the camera capabilities and limitations facing us in our next production.'[61]

Macbeth was filmed at NBC's huge, brand new, state-of-the-art studios on East 14th Street, Brooklyn. 'Accustomed as Judith and I were to performing in a unit setting, we were completely baffled by the totally unrelated television scenery that bore no resemblance whatever to our cosy castle in the theatre's,' Evans recalled. 'The courtyard, the banqueting hall, King Duncan's bedroom, the "blasted heath" were all in separated areas dotted about the studio. At the end of a scene we would find ourselves completely bewildered about what was to follow… At one point, I remember, we met, panic-stricken, in the wilderness between the sets, simultaneously saying to each other, "What the hell comes next?"' 'Although the opening night for a theatrical production is always a nerve-wracking affair, the knowledge that live television was a now-or-never exposure created an unbelievable atmosphere of tension,' he noted. 'It is a cliché, but at the same time

---

60 *AWW* 5 Jul 1961: 39.
61 Evans, *All This… and Evans Too!* 1986, 237.

true, that these unseemly marathons of live television had an immediacy and impact which today's stop-and-go filmed programs seldom achieve.'

These adrenalin-filled performances produced 'a distressing sense of letdown once the final words were spoken,' Evans wrote, ' – no applause, no bravos, no curtain calls. Instead we actors were required to stand stock-still while *Hallmark*'s announcer reminded the viewers that there remained only 40 more days to Christmas.' But, he reminded himself, 'in order to reach a comparable number of spectators in the confines of a modern-sized theatre, appearing eight times a week, the play would have had to run for 49 years, and Judith and I would have been in our late nineties by then.' (When it was screened in November 1954 it was viewed in 6.5 million homes.)[62]

Macbeth was a landmark production, not only for its content, but for its technology. 'Tomorrow I see my first color TV: Judith Anderson in *Macbeth* with Maurice Evans,' photographer Carl Van Vechten wrote a friend. As *Chicago Daily Tribune* TV critic Larry Wolters explained the day after it aired, 'The production was staged in NBC's great new color establishment in Brooklyn. While millions watched it in black and white... a few fortunate thousand saw it on the colored TV sets scattered across the nation.' Watching it alternately in colour and black and white, Wolters decided that 'the impact was immeasurably enhanced by the opulence of full color.' 'This showed to advantage in the royal robes, the blue gold dress of Lady Macbeth, the green of Birnam wood moving on

---

62   Evans, *All This… and Evans Too!* 240–41; *NYT* 16 Jan 1955: X15. For contemporary reactions see *Waco News-Tribune* [Texas] 27 Nov 1954: 11; *Des Moines Register* [Iowa] 28 Nov 1954: 87; *Cincinnati Enquirer* 30 Nov 1954: 11.

Dunsinane, and a dozen other contrasting hues… For the first time on TV we saw the bloody hands of a murderer, the gore upon the daggers.'[63]

Aired on 28 November 1954, *Macbeth* was pronounced the 'high point of the season.' Despite her dislike of the medium, Anderson's performance drew the same high praise from television critics as she had received for her theatrical work. Anderson was always human, Jack Gould wrote in the *New York Times*. Her 'diabolical and earthy persuasiveness as a conspirator and her interpretation of Lady Macbeth's sleep-walking scene are acting treasures that transcend mere media.' 'Have you seen anything of Judith?' her former movie agent Wynn Rocamora wrote to Angna Enters. 'She was magnificent on the *Macbeth* television show – but then she is such a great actress!' 'Yes,' Enters replied. 'We, she and ME, and a few others, had a little party after *Macbeth*. Maurice Evans is giving a big party for her next Wednesday.'[64] Judith Anderson, actress, was back in the spotlight, and was wanted once more.

Anderson's performance as Lady Macbeth won *Hallmark*'s first Emmy – the award presented by the Academy of Television Arts and Sciences – in March 1955. At a nationally broadcast ceremony at Hollywood's Moulin Rouge she was presented with the award for the best actress in a single performance, against such strong rivals as Ethel Barrymore.[65]

This was the first of Anderson's many memorable television performances directed by George Schaefer. For Anderson,

---

63   Carl Van Vechten to Karlo, 27 Nov 1954, Postcard Correspondence from Van Vechten to Priebe, 1946–56, Marquette University Special Collections; *CDT* 29 Nov 1954: c6.
64   *WPTH* 29 Nov: 33; 28 Nov: T3; 29 Nov 1954: 21; *NYT* 29 Nov 1954: 32; Wynn to Enters, 29 Nov 1954; Enters to Wynn, 2 Dec 1954, Enters Papers.
65   Diary 7 Mar 1955; *LAT* 7 Feb: 16; 8 Mar: 2; 9 Mar 1955: 2; *NYT* 8 Mar 1955: 33.

Schaefer *was Hallmark Hall of Fame*. In the wake of their pioneering successes, the series became a major vehicle for Evans, Alberg and Schaefer. In April 1955 Evans signed on as producer of a monthly 90-minute dramatic series on NBC, sponsored by Hallmark, with the proviso that he be given complete artistic autonomy. Mildred Freed Alberg would be his associate producer and George Schaefer his director.[66]

In May 1956 Anderson performed for *Hallmark* as the Abbess in Gregorio and Maria Martinez Sierra's *The Cradle Song*. 'To have missed *The Cradle Song* yesterday afternoon was to have missed one of the most beautiful and deeply stirring programs that television has ever offered,' wrote Jack Gould in the *New York Times*. Anderson was, in his opinion, superlative as the anchor of the drama, playing with authority, humanity and humour. The play earned Evans, Schaefer and writer James Costigan a Christopher award for raising the standard of television.[67]

After two seasons, Maurice Evans handed the *Hallmark Hall of Fame* over to George Schaefer as producer-director, with Mildred Freed Alberg as executive producer. When Schaefer fell out with Alberg, he formed his own production company, Compass Productions in 1959, with Evans' former television secretary Sybil Trubin as Talent Consultant. Compass became Anderson's new theatrical family – what Sybil Trubin called 'the Compatibles.' In June 1959, as Anderson was due to appear in *The Second Happiest Day* for CBS's *Playhouse 90*, Sybil wrote her, in the affectionate tone that characterised their correspondence, that she was looking forward to seeing her performance that evening. *Hallmark* had decided to do a repeat of *Cradle Song* for April 1960 she wrote,

---

66   *LAT* 7 Apr 1955: 34; *CDT* 28 May: D1; 28 Aug 1955: n8.
67   Diary 15 Apr to 6 May 1956; *WPTH* 3 Mar 1956: 8; *NYT* 14 Apr: 37; 7 May: 53; 13 Nov 1956.

and they could not imagine doing it without her. They were also looking out for something for her before then, though their selections so far – *Winterset, The Doll's House* and *The Tempest* – did not have anything suitable.⁶⁸

In September 1959 Compass taped the new production of *The Cradle Song*, with Helen Hayes as the Vicaress. *The Cradle Song* was broadcast on Palm Sunday, 10 April 1960. Scheduled between *NBC Opera*'s 'soaring' $2^1/_2$ hour production of *Don Giovanni* and 'an interesting if rather shallow examination of the career of Andrew Carnegie' on *Our American Heritage* (which also featured Anderson), the 'smooth, effortless' production of *Cradle Song* made *Los Angeles Times* critic Cecil Smith 'rather proud of the big box in the living room.'⁶⁹

Anderson had always appeared in other television programs. In 1958 she starred in a superb production of *The Bridge of San Luis Rey* for the *Dupont Show of the Month* directed by the young Robert Mulligan. Playing the embittered Marquesa de Montemayor in this Thornton Wilder Pulitzer Prize-winning novel, Anderson was praised by the *Saturday Review* for the most illuminating characterisation among a star-studded cast. She was nominated for an Emmy for her performance – her second nomination since her award for *Macbeth* in 1955 – but she lost to Candice Bergen in *The Helen Morgan Story* on *Playhouse 90*.

In October 1959 she reprised *Medea* for television in the opening offering in WTNA's two-year phenomenon *Play of*

---

68   Evans, *All This… and Evans Too!*, 248–51; Trubin to Anderson, 26 Jul 1960; 25 Jun 1959, Schaefer Papers.
69   *NYT* 17 Aug: 47; 18 Aug; 23 Aug 23: X11; 30 Aug 1959: X11; *NYP* 23 Aug 1959, NYPL; Schaefer to Anderson, 5 Oct 1959, Schaefer Papers; *LAT* 12 Apr 1960: A10; *Catholic Preview Of Entertainment* Apr 1960, cover article; *NYT* 11 Apr 1960: 63; Enters to Anderson, 11 Apr 1960, Enters Papers.

Judith Anderson in her Emmy-nominated television performance as the Marquesa in Thornton Wilder's Bridge of San Luis Rey

Author's collection

the Week. This much-praised syndicated series was part of the New Jersey-based station's push for recognition as an innovative new player. The station's president Ely Landau was determined to buck the trend of local stations towards Westerns, crime and situation comedies. 'I don't think any independent station is going to succeed if it just does the... shows that we find everywhere else,' he told a reporter that year.[70]

Anderson was dissatisfied with the production, which was directed by José Quintero, who was new to television. But critics and viewers alike agreed with Jack Gould that her performance was one of 'stunning and enveloping power.' She 'swept all before her in one of those demonstrations of pure artistry that can make acting so exciting,' he wrote in the *New York Times*. 'Her Medea is a veritable symphony of mood, movement, comprehension and projection. She is fiercely dark and evil, lyrical and majestic. A curl of her lip may be the

---

70 *WPTH* Oct 18, 1959: G14.

transition from tenderness of the mother to the mad vengeance of the woman scorned.' The performance 'could have been almost more than [the small screen] could absorb,' he observed, 'but there was a discipline that retained all the fire but avoided the uncontrolled flam.' Fellow actress Helen Hayes wrote her that her television *Medea* showed that she was 'the damndest best actress in the whole world.' All in all, almost 2.5 million viewers saw the program during the seven days it was broadcast.[71]

In February 1960 *Play of the Week* was bought by Los Angeles station KCOP-TV, and by the end of that month the series was offered on eight more stations, giving thousands more the opportunity to see Anderson's 'soaring' *Medea*. When Larry Wolters saw it on Chicago's WGN-TV in May 1960, he voted it 'the play of the year… Or, for that matter, the play of any year.' 'No person who saw her portrayal of the role is ever likely to forget it,' he wrote in the *Chicago Daily Tribune*. 'This was strong stuff and Judith Anderson made it even stronger.'[72]

Television introduced Judith Anderson to a new generation of admirers. In 1956 'two teenage innocents from the Boondocks' came to New York for the first time. 'New York! The Statue of Liberty! The Empire State Building! The Copacobana! Sardi's! *Broadway!!!*' television writer Jim McPherson wrote many years later. 'It was Easter weekend, 1956, that my buddy Paul and I decided it was time we took the Big Apple "on the town".' 'First order to business,' he remembered, 'look up our current celebrity goddess, Judith Anderson, in the phone book (I *said* we were innocent).' (The two boys turned up with roses

---

71   *NYT* 13 Oct: 79; 15 Oct: 78; 1 Nov 1959: X13; Helen [Hayes] to Anderson, [Oct 1959], UCSB.
72   *NYT* 3 Feb: 67; 18 Feb 1960: 67; *WPTH* 27 Feb 1960: B10; *CDT* 9 May 1960: c7.

at the door of another Judith Anderson.) McPherson was still a fan in 1991, when he admitted that he had had her home number for several years but had never used it.[73]

Television not only brought Judith Anderson before a national audience far greater and more diverse than any of her stage performances, but it also introduced her old movies to generations of viewers such as McPherson. In 1950 Val Adams in the *New York Times* remarked that 'The business of distributing and renting feature motion pictures to television stations is growing proportionately as fast as the medium itself. In fact, anyone with a can of old film under his arm today is automatically a television producer.' The major motion picture companies were at this stage reluctant to release their products for television. Independent producers, however, were delighted to find a new market for their movies. In 1951 Republic sold 125 films to television. From 1952 *And Then There Were None* and *Specter of the Rose* were often seen on daytime or late-night television; and from the mid-1950s, when the major Hollywood companies caved in to the demand for movies on television, all of her pre-1948 films were available. In 1961 NBC began showing recent films in prime time, quickly followed by other networks.[74]

The fifties' thirst for culture delivered to the home brought Judith Anderson another source of income – the long-play recording. With what was regarded as the most thrilling voice of her times, and an ability to convey meaning through her readings, she was sought after for this other new medium of the period.

Anderson had always done some radio work. Her first

---

73   Jim McPherson, 'Movies. A Dame named Anderson,' *TV4* 7 Jan 1991. MHL.
74   *NYT* 11 Jun 1950: 105; MPD 21 Aug: 1; 23 Oct 1951: 1; Douglas Gomery, 'Movies on Television,' in *Encyclopedia of Television*, ed. Horace Newcomb, 2004, 1540–43. See Blair Davis, *The Battle for the Bs: 1950s Hollywood and the Rebirth of Low-Budget Cinema*, 2012.

recording, however, was of highlights from *Macbeth*, with music by Lehman Engel, organised by her entrepreneurial co-star Maurice Evans in 1941, with the profits to go to British War Relief. Issued under RCA Victor's prestigious Red Seal label in 1942, *Shakespeare's Macbeth* comprised five 12-inch records that the company marketed in conjunction with the live production, with the two stars often making appearances to sign albums.[75]

In 1949 she made a recording of *Medea* for Decca on four 12-inch discs, with Arnold Moss as Jason, that she considered 'disappointing'; but poetry lovers welcomed it as a valuable alternative to Jeffers' own readings in which his 'meager voice… scratches its way through tightened throat muscles and gives the listener kinaesthetic agonies.' In 1953, as the audience for theatre-on-disc grew, the cast of *John Brown's Body* issued a recording for Columbia.[76]

The previous year, however, two recent college graduates, Barbara Holdridge [later Cohen] and Marianne Mantell, had started up what was to become Caedmon Records with a recording of visiting celebrity poet Dylan Thomas. This was the beginning of a niche business that served the burgeoning demand for mass-produced high culture. As historian Jacob Smith put it, Caedmon was catering to a 'culturally sophisticated audience' who were 'reading paperbacks, listening to FM radio, and patronizing European films.'[77]

---

75   See *WP* 10 Apr 1950: B6; Evans to Anderson, 25 Jul, 8 Aug 1941, Evans Papers; *Variety* 26 Nov 1941; 4 Feb 1942; *NYT* 29 Mar 1942: X8; *CDT* 1 May 1942: 20; *AWW* 10 Oct 1942: 20.

76   Anderson to Robin and Una Jeffers, 1 & 30 Dec 1947, RJHRC; Una Jeffers to Anderson, 24 Dec 1947, RJTH; Diary 26 Jan to 7 May 1948; *NYT* 30 Jan 1949: X6; *Variety* 30 Mar 1949; *Detroit Free Press* 31 Jan 1949: 5; *Poetry* Mar 1952: 353–5; Paul Gregory to Anderson, tel 27 Mar 1953, UCSB; Diary 7 Apr 1953; *Variety* 8 Apr; 23 Sep; 28 Oct 1953; *NYT* 22 Apr 1953: 31.

77   Jacob Smith, *Spoken Word: Postwar American Phonograph Cultures*, 2011, 49–78. See also *CSM* 6 Jun 1962: 10; *NYT* 26 Jul 1959: X12.

The two young women quickly signed up Judith Anderson. Beginning with a reading of the poetry of Edna St Vincent Millay in 1954, Anderson made many recordings for Caedmon over the next 25 years, ranging from excerpts from the Bible to the poems of A A Milne – *When We Were Very Young* and *Now We Are Six*. In 1964 they launched their Theater Recording Society, which included a recording of *Medea* made in England with Anthony Quayle, which, to Anderson's disappointment, used Rex Warner's adaptation rather than that of Jeffers. Nevertheless, Thomas Lask, in the *New York Times*, described the recording admiringly as 'stark and bare, moving like some massive wheel downhill to disaster.' The play's impact was 'as instantaneous as shattered glass,' he wrote, 'the soft voices of the chorus women over the plaintive sounding of flute a fine foil for the imperious, harsh Medea.' 'This is a performance even the Greeks would have enjoyed,' he concluded. In 1970, she recorded *The Poetry of Robinson Jeffers*. In 1955, while in Australia, she recorded a series of five plays for the Australian Broadcasting Commission, including *Fire on the Snow*, *Macbeth* and *Medea*.[78]

Anderson's voice was peculiarly suited to the requirements of recordings. *New York Times* critic Herbert Mitgang attested that 'her voice has shadings and meanings rarely achieved by other narrators and, indeed, by few professional actresses.' 'The fact that famous actresses can create vivid characters on the stage is not an automatic guarantee that they are also good readers of verse,' another *Times* critic wrote. Lynn Fontanne was 'mannered'; Helen Hayes's voice was 'charged, quavery, sometimes coy.' But Judith Anderson, with

---

78 See Caedmon to Anderson, 15 Jul 1957; 20 Jun 1967; contracts, 23 Jun 1967, UCSB; *NYT* 18 Apr 1965: X16; *LAT* 4 Oct 1964: U34; *NYT* 11 Oct 1964: BR3 (full-page ad); Diary 24 Oct, 9 & 15 Nov 1955; *AWW* 2 Nov 1955: 2.

her 'deep, musical voice,' was, in his opinion, 'one actress who can speak verse beautifully.'[79]

These recordings became part of the home culture of many children growing up in the 1950s. Garry Wills, journalist and historian, in high school in the early 1950s, was thrilled by the recorded voices of Judith Anderson, John Barrymore, Fyodor Chaliapin and José Ferrer. Ferrer and Judith Anderson 'first jolted me with a realization of the human voice's range and expressivity,' he wrote in 1992. And Charles Ludlum, the avant-garde actor born in 1943 who created travesties of the classics, including *Medea*, for his Ridiculous Theatrical Company, had been fascinated by Anderson's recording of *Medea* since he was a child. [80]

The 1950s brought enormous disappointments to Judith Anderson, whose dreams of greatness never wavered from the theatrical stage. But her skills as an actress, her ability to convey emotion and character through her voice and her body, transferred readily to the new media of television and audio recordings. And *Medea* continued to fascinate a younger generation of viewers and listeners.

---

79 *NYT* 30 Aug 1959: X16; 21 Aug 1955: X13.
80 Garry Wills, *Outside Looking In: Adventures of an Observer*, 2010, 84; 'Ferrer's Artistry,' *The Sun* [Baltimore] 8 Feb 1992: 9A; *Newsday* 11 Oct 1987: 13.

Interlude
Paris and Canberra

There was something infinitely thrilling to me to dress in the lavish dressing room that had been hers, to walk on the stage where she had walked, to speak in the auditorium that had once vibrated to the whiplash of her voice.

Judith Anderson 1955

Chapter Thirty
International Icon 1955–60

> ... *the cast was lunching at the historic Parisian restaurant Le Grand Vefour when this tall creature got up and started to walk toward our table. It was Jean Cocteau, the self-legendizing poet, playwright and artist, who went straight to Anderson. 'He takes her hand in his,' said Mr Plummer, shifting into the present tense, 'and says, "Ah, Madame Anderson, you make life"'* –
> Ben Brantley interview with Christopher Plummer 1997

Judith Anderson and Guthrie McClintic after she played Medea in Sarah Bernhardt's Theatre in Paris 1955. Alice B Toklas is behind her

UCSB

If producers and audiences did not want their greatest dramatic actress in any modern play in 1955, they still wanted to see her in *Medea* – again and again and again. Brooks Atkinson had written in 1947, 'Perhaps Medea was never fully created until Miss Anderson breathed immortal fire into it.' Now it seemed as if Judith Anderson did not exist if she was not playing Medea. During the 1950s, as she struggled to find other work, her *Medea* took on iconic status as the height of cultural achievement, claimed as such by both her adopted country and that of her birth.

The United States was engaged in these years in what Richard L Coe called 'Diplomacy Via Grease Paint' – a cultural cold war with the Soviet Union. The first shots in this war were fired in 1951 at the Berlin Festival of the Arts, where Anderson in *Medea*, along with the musical *Oklahoma!*, the Juilliard Quartet and the mime artist, Anderson's friend Angna Enters, formed part of the US's 'antidote for Communist propaganda' chosen by the International Exchange Program of ANTA – the semi-official National Theater and Academy that had presented *Tower Beyond Tragedy* the previous year.[81]

By 1955 the US international cultural offensive was 'in big-gun stage,' as Lewis Funke put it in the *New York Times* – this time in the shape of a 'Salute to France' in Paris. Just as Anderson feared that her stage career was over, ANTA again chose her and *Medea* to represent the best of America's high culture.[82] Taking place in Paris's Sarah Bernhardt Theatre where the legendary actress had played many of her greatest roles, this performance, and those that were to follow in this memorable year, restored Anderson's faith in her artistic future.

---

81 *NYT* 27 May: 58; 14 Sep: 22; 14 Oct 1951: 108; *Variety* 12 Sep; 26 Sep 1951: 2.
82 *WPTH* 27 Jan: 54; 17 Feb 1955: 50; *NYT* editorial Jan 30; 28 Feb; 10 Apr 1955: X1.

In her Paris *Medea* Anderson was united for the last time with Guthrie McClintic, whose exuberant vitality gradually faded until his death from cancer six years later. He still had enough energy in 1955 to make sure Anderson had a wonderful time in Paris. His judgment was failing, however, and it was he who was responsible for the choice of 23-year-old Christopher Plummer to play Jason. Plummer had caught the critics' attention in a bit part in McClintic's most recent (failed) production, *The Dark Is Light Enough*. McClintic and Cornell had both seen the potential of this young man, who became one of the world's great actors; and this perception was shared by *Theatre World*, which named him one of the most promising actors of the year in May 1955.[83] Nevertheless, he was a strange choice to play a middle-aged warrior opposite the 58-year-old Anderson.

Nearly 60 years later Plummer recalled a youthful adventure memorable for its highs and lows. The adventure began before the company left New York, when Plummer, trying hard to 'give the impression of masculine power in that improbable, wimpish role Mr Jeffers must have bored himself to death writing,' encountered Anderson pulling out the stops for the first time at the final run-through before 'the cream of Broadway theatrical society (the Lunts, Helen Hayes, George Abbott, Katharine Cornell, Josh Logan, Ruth Gordon and Garson Kanin, Gilbert and Kitty Miller, etc.)' 'She was electrifying!' he remembered:

> *Attired simply in black sweater and black tights she prowled, stalked and slunk about the stage – hissing, spitting, breathing fire like some enraged dragon. She splashed the canvas of her extraordinary voice with every colour in the spectrum: now soothing, seductive – now commanding, tempestuous*

---

83 *NYT* 1 Apr: 23; 12 May 1955: 33; *Hudson Review* Summer 1955: 258–72.

> *– a cadenza of sounds culminating in a finale of frenzy! Truly, we were in the presence that day of a tragedienne of the first order – upon whose shoulders would surely fall the mantle of Rachel or Madame Georges.*

'But, helas!' Plummer wrote. 'Once in Paris all was to change.'

> *... she was to inherit the Divine Sarah's massive dressing rooms with their ornate double doors leading from the ante-chambers into the hallowed sanctum sanctorum still richly reverberating with memories of passion and glory.*
>
> *Judith stood in the midst of her vast new domain staring at the bare walls, the great windows and the high ceilings. Gone were the sumptuous Oriental rugs, the chaise longues, the chandeliers; gone – the majordomo admitting adoring kings... gone – the powdered, liveried footmen... Nothing left now but the empty echoing rooms and far away in a distant corner under a single electric light-bulb, the meanest, most insignificant makeup table imaginable!... and that morning, the tough little sheila from dahn under – lost her voice.*

According to Plummer in an interview in 1997, 'The rasping Medea and her young Jason were roasted in the French press.' But, he remembered, Anderson still had her moment of triumph:

> *Late in their run... the cast was lunching at the historic Parisian restaurant Le Grand Vefour when 'this tall creature got up and started to walk toward our table.' It was Jean Cocteau, the self-legendizing poet, playwright and artist, who went straight to Anderson. 'He takes her hand in his,' said Mr. Plummer, shifting into the present tense, 'and says, "Ah, Madame Anderson, you make life"' — Mr Plummer slapped his hand on a coffee table – 'and left. Well, it made her whole trip.'*[84]

---

84 Christopher Plummer, *In Spite of Myself*, 2012, 135; *NYT* 14 Sep 1997.

Anderson herself remembered the Paris performance with more warmth. 'I was not disappointed in the Theatre Sarah Bernhardt where we played,' she wrote in 1962: 'it was the same Theatre de la Renaissance renamed after the great French actress with whom I had always felt a presumptuous identification.'

There was something infinitely thrilling to me to dress in the lavish dressing room that had been hers, to walk on the stage where she had walked to speak in the auditorium that had once vibrated to the whiplash of her voice.

She also had more nuanced memories of their reception. 'From the Paris audience I felt greater warmth, understanding and intimacy than I had from the one in Berlin,' she wrote. 'Yet the press carried the old complaint: "Perhaps one would have preferred to see the celebrated American tragedienne in some work less saturated with the Greco-Latin essence of classical European culture, in some play more typically, more intrinsically American".' Indeed, the press was much more favourable to the other American dramatic production, Thornton Wilder's rambling, farcical history of the world, *The Skin of Our Teeth*, which at least got the French laughing.[85]

Some critics, she recalled with pleasure, hailed her as 'A new Sarah Bernhardt.' But others dismissed her as 'this beautiful athlete, this irritated sportswoman'; and Britain's Kenneth Tynan memorably described her style as 'armpit rhetoric.' The most hurtful review, which she does not mention, was in the *London Times*. 'The much-heralded Miss Judith Anderson… in *Medea*,' the reviewer wrote, 'turned out to be a grievous disappointment – the more grievous because one felt one was watching the ruins of a great performance, in which mannerisms had taken the place once occupied by style,

---

85   *CSM* 2 Jul 1955: 14.

and hysteria thrust out passion. The voice throbbed still, as if drunk with Jeffers' poetry (some of which is very fine), but all too often the throbbing sounded hollow.'[86]

Nevertheless, Anderson's Paris performance had two happy outcomes. The first was an invitation from the Greek Government to attend a performance by the great Greek actress Katina Paxinou, and her husband Aleko [Alexis] Minotis in the ancient theatre of Epidaurus. In a crowded 48 hours she flew to Athens, clambered over the Acropolis in her high heels (her luggage had been mislaid), took a boat across the Gulf of Aegina to 'an arena stage to beggar the imagination, with fifty-five tiers of seat, fourteen thousand of them, rising like an enormous fan around it.'

After playing in Jeffers' modern adaptation of Euripides' *Medea* for many years, Anderson saw one of the ancient Greek's plays – *Hecuba* – for the first time – and in an ancient Greek theatre. She was overwhelmed – 'not only by Katina and Aleko, both of them tremendous, larger than life, but by the perfectly trained chorus that moved like a great wave; and as if all this were not enough, the transparent daylight darkened and faded, and a full moon rose.' From Epidaurus the *New York Times* reported Paxinou running off the stage at the end of the play crying, 'Judith!' and embracing her before thousands of cheering Greeks. 'Just saw Katina Paxinou play Hecuba in Epidaurus before 20,000 people,' she wrote to Angna Enters from Rome on her way back to Paris, '— superb & incredible experience… back to Paris today London next week, home end of July – It has been a lovely trip… '[87]

---

86   *CSM* 18 Jun 1955: 6; *Observer* 26 Jun 1955: 17; *Times* 22 Jun 1955: 4.
87   *NYT* 5 Jul 1955: 35; Anderson to Enters, 4 Jul 1955, Enters Papers. Anderson remembered the play as *The Trojan Woman*.

Photographs of Anderson at Epidaurus in the Australian press heralded the second fulfilling outcome of her elevation to iconic status – an invitation from the Australian Prime Minister Robert Menzies to inaugurate the first dramatic season of the newly-established Australian Elizabethan Theatre Trust with – of course – *Medea*. Robert Quentin, who had just been appointed general manager of the Trust's new opera company, had sought Anderson out as soon as she arrived in Paris to issue the invitation on the prime minister's behalf. In London two weeks after the Greek trip the Australian High Commissioner held a press conference to announce that Miss Judith Anderson – 'probably the greatest Australian actress abroad' – would open the Elizabethan Theatre Trust's Australian season in Canberra on October 5. She will give two performances in Canberra, he told the press conference, and the play will then be presented in other cities, including Sydney, Brisbane, Melbourne, Hobart and Perth.[88]

The Melbourne *Argus*'s London correspondent reported the next day that 'The Adelaide–born tragedienne is more than just a celebrity in America: she is almost a cult.' 'She belongs to that select coterie of American stage actresses,' he continued, 'who spurn the films except to pick up a little pin money by accepting the occasional small part for a fat fee, who rarely, if ever, appear outside America, yet are accorded more adulation inside the States than all the film stars put together.' 'No one could act less like a tragedy queen,' he noted.

> *Her pale blonde head was bare over a deceptively simple grey dress, and she trailed a mink stole. Her shoes had the highest heels in London. Distance, which hides so much wear and tear in most women, does the reverse for Anderson. From*

---

88 Diary 11 & 18 Jun 1955; *Canberra Times* 21 Jul 1955: 2.

across a room, with her beaked nose and square mouth, she looks a ruthless, dominating female. But peer at her close up and she looks more like 40 than her admitted 57. Her skin is clear and unlined, and her eyes glint with humor.[89]

The Australian Elizabethan Theatre Trust had been established the previous year under the guidance of H C 'Nugget' Coombs, Governor of the Commonwealth Bank, Sir Charles Moses, General Manager of Australian Broadcasting Commission, and John Douglas Pringle, editor of the *Sydney Morning Herald*. Named to commemorate the recent visit of the young Queen Elizabeth to Australia and cleverly announced the day after she departed Australia, the Trust raised £90,000 by public appeal, to which the Commonwealth government added £30,000.[90]

Enthusiasts had been pressing for a national theatre since at least 1935. This movement was given impetus during World War II by the activities of 'Nugget' Coombs, the young Director-General of the Commonwealth Department of Post-War Reconstruction, and Lyndhurst Giblin, chair of the Commonwealth Advisory Committee on Finance and Economic Policy, who argued in 1944 that high culture would redeem Australians from their preoccupation with 'beer, trots and dogs, League matches, the flicks and shops.' After the war the British efforts towards the establishment of a national theatre and the visit of the Old Vic company led by (now 'Sir') Laurence Olivier and Vivien Leigh in 1948 provided added incentive to the Australian movement.[91]

---

89 *Argus* 21 Jul 1955: 2.
90 Australian Elizabethan Theatre Trust, *Annual Report* 1957; *SMH* 10 Aug 1954: 1.
91 Thérèse Radic, 'Johnson, Gertrude Emily (1894–1973)', *ADB*; Lyndhurst Giblin, 'The National Theatre and Leisure,' NAA CPD 20 Sep 1944; Neville Cain, 'Giblin,

In January 1949 the Commonwealth Labor Government invited British theatrical director Tyrone Guthrie to tour Australia and report on the best way to establish a national theatre. After spending a month in Australia talking to theatrical leaders, attending performances and conferring with Prime Minister Chifley, Guthrie decided that Australia was not ready for a national theatre. Meanwhile, Australian talent haemorrhaged abroad, with Peter Finch, Leo McKern, Jane Holland, Frank Thring, Bruce Beeby, Madi Hedd, Keith Michell and Nancye Stewart making careers at the Old Vic, the Stratford Memorial Theatre, the BBC, and other British institutions.[92]

'Nugget' Coombs, now Governor of the Commonwealth Bank and a trusted adviser to Prime Minister Menzies, was the brains and heart behind the Trust. 'Short and sturdy-looking with a face slightly lined with laugh wrinkles,' Coombs was 'courteous, friendly, and rather shy.' Probably the most persuasive man in Australia, and a 'thorough realist,' Coombs obtained the backing of major businessmen for the fundraising project.[93]

By October 1954 the fundraising appeal had reached its target and the 44-year-old British producer-director Hugh Hunt was appointed executive director, no doubt to the disappointment – if not anger – of established Australian producers such as Doris Fitton of Sydney's Independent theatre, John Alden whose Shakespeare company had been lauded as 'the beginning of a true national theatre,' and most important of

---

Lyndhurst Falkiner (1872–1951)', *ADB*; J R Nethercote, 'Unearthing the Seven Dwarfs and the Age of the Mandarins.' In Samuel Furphy, ed. *The Seven Dwarfs and the Age of the Mandarins: Australian Government Administration in the Post-War Reconstruction Era*, 2015; *Observer* 27 Jan 1946: 4; *MG* 10 Jan: 3; 24 Mar 1948: 4; *CSM* 14 Feb 1948: WM7.
92   *SMH* 23 Apr 1949: 4; 16 Nov 1950: 3; 5 Jan 1952: 6; *The Sphere* 24 Apr 1954: 148; 27 Aug 1955: 314; *Times Pictorial* 4 Sep 1954: A1; *Picture Show* 9 Jan 1954: 4.
93   *Mail (Adelaide)* 8 May 1954: 2; *SH* 4 Apr 1954: 18; *SMH* 2 Apr 1954: 6.

all, the young John Sumner, who had, in the past three years, turned the Melbourne Union Theatre Repertory Company into a fulltime profitmaking organisation.[94]

Described by the *New York Times* as 'a modest, pleasant, youngish man with ruddy hair and an affable manner,' Hunt was welcomed for his wide directing and administrative experience and his familiarity with national theatre during some years at the Abbey Theatre, Dublin. He was, however, a cultural conservative who preferred moral and aesthetic uplift over the vernacular. In a period of increasing nationalism, when Australians were breaking their ties to Britain, therefore, he was, in what he called his 'Five Years Hard' in Australia, swimming against the tide that swept in the *Summer of the Seventeenth Doll* a year later. Perhaps to help balance Hunt's conservatism, John Sumner was appointed the Trust's Sydney manager in April 1955.[95]

This is the context in which Judith Anderson was invited in June 1955 to bring *Medea* to Australia. *Medea* was high culture; and Anderson's performance had the seal of approval of the greatest critics and most discerning audiences in the US and Europe.

Lauded as 'the greatest Australian actress abroad,' Anderson felt a certain falsity in her position. 'I was Australian by birth and nationality,' she remembered several years later, 'but American through long residence.' 'The press, writing of my arrival at the airport,' she went on, 'mentioned my "slight American accent".' (Which was ridiculous – no impure vowel or rolled 'r' ever touched that perfect British accent, even when she was playing a Western pioneer woman.) Her hosts in Canberra, she recalled, were the

---

94 *SMH* 26 Oct 1954: 2; Ailsa McPherson, 'Fitton, Dame Doris Alice (1897–1985)'; John Rickard, 'Alden, John (1908–1962)'; Richard Waterhouse, 'Hunt, Hugh Sydney (1911–1993)', *ADB*.
95 *Argus* 23 Apr 1955: 13.

American Ambassador and his wife, while her invitation had come from the Prime Minister of Australia, and the company she performed with was Australian.[96] And, she could have added, the director, Hugh Hunt was British.

Nevertheless, she was determined to revel in her return to her homeland, as she put it, 'as a personage, entrusted to the care of two governments'; and to present to her fellow Australians what she considered the height of cultural achievement, a play written by one of the greatest American poets, based on the work of one of the greatest classical Greek playwrights, played by an actress who had been called one of the greatest tragediennes of the American stage. She was going to expunge from memory that failed return in 1927 and those despised sex plays her Melbourne and Adelaide audiences had spurned.

This determination to give the Australian audiences the very best was clear from the beginning. 'Move down there. Look at me. Keep your head down. Further back,' Zoe Caldwell remembered her instructing the cast autocratically on the first day of rehearsals after her arrival. 'We practically curtsied,' Caldwell recalled many years later, after she herself was a world-renowned star who had played Medea, with an 85-year-old Anderson as the Nurse. Caldwell, at 21, was one of three young actors who had been chosen from the Melbourne Union Theatre to tour with the ETT company. Caldwell would play Second Woman of Corinth, Marie Tomasetti one of the two women attendants, and Malcolm Robertson one of the four solders. Doris Fitton, veteran of 25 years as director of Sydney's Independent Theatre, played the Nurse. Anderson's old friend from her Julius Knight days, Ailsa Graham, who had since made her name in Britain with the Old Vic and the Royal Shakespeare Company at

---

96 See Dorothy I. Peaslee to Anderson, 30 Sep [1955], UCSB; *AWW* Nov 1955: 14–15.

Stratford-upon-Avon, played the First Woman of Corinth. Visiting British actor Clement McCallin took the important part of Jason, while John Alden played Creon. A 25-year-old Peter Kenna, later a major playwright of Australian life, had a bit part as a slave.[97]

This disparate and partly mutinous company had been rehearsing for some time before Anderson's arrival, directed by Hugh Hunt from the stage manager's script from Gielgud's original New York production. Hunt did not like Jeffers' star-centred script (British and Australian actors and audiences were wedded to the earlier translation by Australian classicist Gilbert Murray) and had probably encouraged the cast to find their own marks. One of Anderson's conditions for accepting the Trust's invitation was that she would have full control over the production, and no one was going to ruin what she regarded as 'her' play. When Robert Quentin wrote to Hugh Hunt two days after her arrival that she was 'more than living up to her reputation as being the most troublesome actress in the world,' she was already indicating that no one and nothing was going to get in the way of her giving the Australian public the best *Medea* that was possible.[98]

There were many obstacles in the way of this goal. Apart from what was apparently an instant dislike between Hunt and Anderson, and the hurt feelings of Doris Fitton and John Alden, the theatres in which she was called upon to perform were woefully inadequate. The premiere was to take place in what was essentially a country hall, the Albert Hall in the capital Canberra, itself at that time a small town of about

---

97 Zoe Caldwell, *I Will Be Cleopatra: An Actress's Journey*; *Age* 13 Aug 1955; *Argus* 16 Aug 1955: 9; Richard Waterhouse, 'Kenna, Peter Joseph (1930–1987),' *ADB*.
98 Robert Quentin to Hugh Hunt, 6 Sep 1955, AETT. Fiona Gregory, 'High-Cultural Histrionics: Judith Anderson's 1955 tour of Australia,' *Australasian Drama Studies*, Apr 2006: 6–7 provides an excellent account of this visit.

Judith Anderson as Medea, Sydney 1955, with Peter Cohen and Robert Rosen as her sons
Author's collection

30,000 people. After eight days of rehearsal the company set off for Canberra, where the inadequacies of the venue were revealed. To make it worse, the organisers had not ensured that the hall was free for the dress rehearsal the day before, and the company had to begin their rehearsal at 10 o'clock at

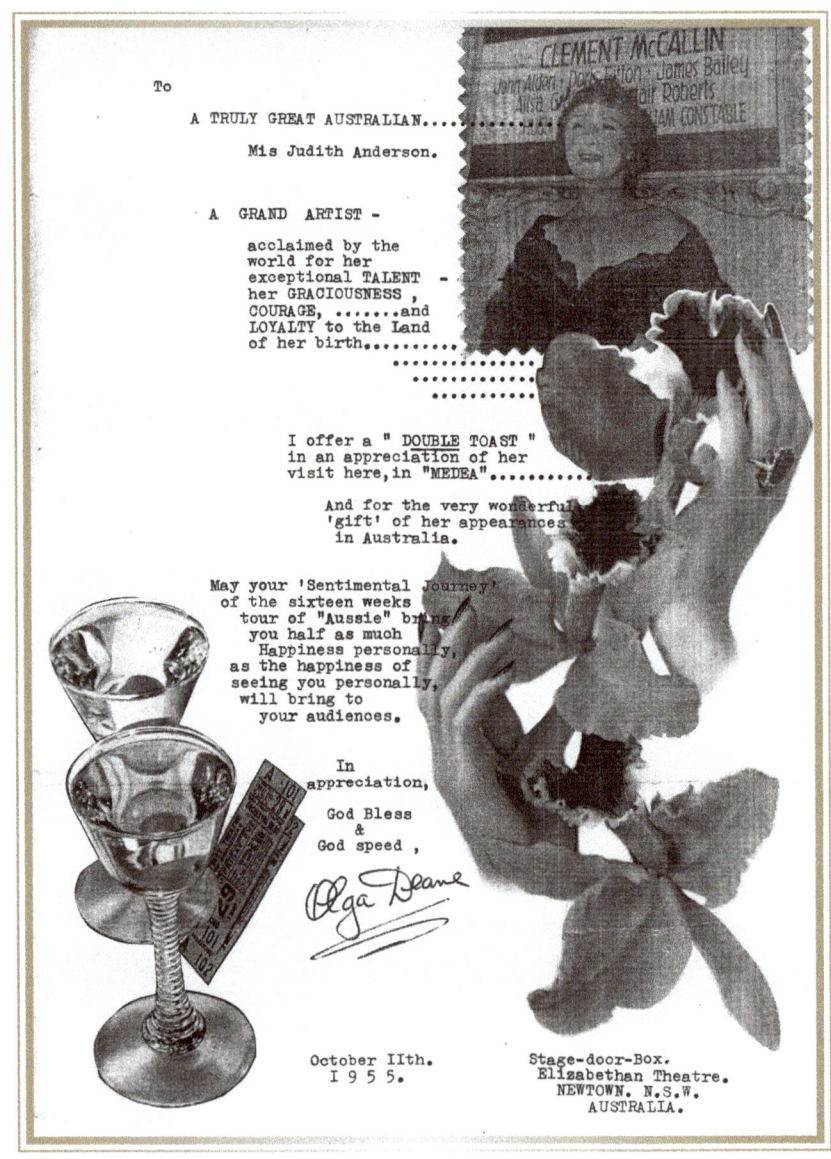

A tribute from fan Olga Deane, October 1955

night. And their star, Judith Anderson, had a throat infection.[99] But ever the consummate professional, Anderson lunched with Prime Minister Menzies at Parliament House the next day before opening that evening, Wednesday 5 October, in *Medea*.

The Sydney theatre also had its limitations. Hurriedly renamed the Elizabethan, the former Majestic Theatre in suburban Newtown had been a popular venue for variety shows and melodramas before becoming a movie theatre in 1928. During the war it had been a military showroom. The Trust had refurbished the theatre when they leased it, but its 1,642-seat auditorium was still poorly ventilated. Nevertheless, Anderson rose above all this to provide what the usually trenchant Josephine O'Neill proclaimed in the *Daily Telegraph* a 'Magnificent Medea' when she opened in Sydney on 11 October. Critics and letters to the editor did not all agree with O'Neill's assessment; but everyone agreed it was a triumphant opening night.[100]

No matter what the critics said, Anderson loved every minute of her Australian tour. As the company completed its three-week season in Sydney and embarked on to a 16-week tour of Brisbane, Adelaide, Hobart, Melbourne and Perth, she enjoyed everything – the Lord Mayors' receptions, her Guest of Honour spot on the ABC, opening art exhibition, making a series of radio plays for the ABC. *The Australian Women's Weekly* featured her in multi-page coloured spreads. She met up with old friends – and made new ones. She had an

---

99   *SMH* 5 Oct 1955: 4:5.
100   *Farmer and Settler* 25 Mar 1955: 21; 8 Jul 1955: 22; *DT* 12 Oct 1955: 7; *SMH* 12 Oct: 6; Barbara Knox [Bellevue Hill] & G.P. Stokell [West Pymble], Letters to editor 17 Oct 1955: 2; *Daily Mirror* 12 Oct 1955: 19; *AWW* 26 Oct 1955: 18; *Argus* 15 Oct 1955 Weekender: 5.

affectionate reunion with her brother Jack and his wife Kathleen and her three nieces, and met their husbands and small children. As she wrote to Angna Enters from Brisbane, 'It is really very thrilling… the country is really beautiful & Sunday I will go with friends up the shore line to Paradise beach' (presumably Surfers Paradise). 'Heavenly day,' she wrote in her diary after that day at the beach.[101]

Anderson's return to Adelaide was a much happier one than it had been in 1927. 'Treated no longer as an actress but as a personage,' as she put it, she was given a reception by the Lord Mayor, lunched at Government House, dined at the Adelaide Club and made new friends of Bill and Ursula Hayward at Carrick Hill, with whom she shared her love of gardening. This was also an occasion to remember her humble beginnings in Adelaide with a curtain speech in memory of her mother. A committee of former classmates invited her to a reception at Rose Park School, where she was greeted by her old teacher, 'Biddy' Nation; and she returned to the shop, which was unchanged

Judith Anderson enjoying her return to Australia 1955

Author's collection

---

101   *SMH* 20 Sep: 13:2; 2 Oct: E15; 3 Oct: 6; 19 Oct 1955: 3; *Age* 3 Oct 1955; Diary 19 Sep; 1, 19 & 20 Oct 1955; *AWW* 28 Sep 1955: 24; *Woman's Day* 5 Sep 1955: 11; Anderson to Enters, 11 Nov 1955, Enters Papers; Diary 13 Nov 1955.

The Australian press was always interested in Judith Anderson's wardrobe, especially when it was designed by fellow-Australian Orry-Kelly

Adelaide News, November 1955

from her days of delivering orders on Dolly. She made a sentimental visit of gratitude to her old elocution teacher Mabel Kerr, long since retired; had a reunion with her former unofficial fiancé Greg Bruer; and saw members of her mother's family.[102]

---

102   Diary 24 Nov to 11 Dec 1955; *Advertiser* 25 Nov: 1; 26 Nov: 1; 30 Nov 1955; *News* 25 Nov: 1; 29 Nov 1955; *Mail* 26 Nov 1955. Lionel Gregory Bruer married Hilary Heath in 1924 soon after he graduated as an architect.

Her reception from Adelaide audiences was, however, less warm than that of the city elite and her old friends and relatives.[103] Again she (or her managers) seemed to have misread the Australian tastes. Perhaps audiences were put off by the publicity campaign that portrayed Anderson and *Medea* as representing 'high culture,' accessible only to 'culture vultures.' But as Anderson told local critic C B de Boehme, probably remembering Lady Kitty's rebuke of many years ago, she was 'determined that she would appear before her own people only in a great play.'[104] Fanny Anderson still wanted to be 'best, and never bested.'

Medea's final gift to Judith Anderson came in December 1959, when, away from home, she had a message to call the Australian Ambassador. When she returned the call she received the astounding news: 'Her Majesty, Queen Elizabeth, has bestowed upon you, Frances Margaret Anderson, the title of Dame Commander of the British Empire. Will you accept this title?' Trembling, alone in her hotel room, her first thoughts were of her younger self, pulling out of Sydney harbour on the *Sonoma*, determined to make a career for herself, and of her mother – how pleased she would have been, and how sure that the Queen had been right in recognising her daughter's achievements.

This honour was momentous, not only for Anderson herself, but also for the profession to which she had devoted her life. She was the first Australian to be made a Commander of the British Empire for service to the performing arts. Dame Nellie Melba's honour in 1918 had been for patriotic work during the war and in 1927 she had been elevated to Dame

---

103   *SMH* 1 Dec 1955: 5; *Argus* 10 Jan 1956: 10.
104   *News* 28 Nov; 15 Dec 1955; *Advertiser* 28 Nov 1955.

Grand Cross for services to Australia. Sir Robert Helpmann, knighted in 1968, was the first Australian man to be so honoured.

Americans were never quite sure what this honour meant and how to address the new dame. As columnist and friend Whitney Bolton put it, 'Your Queen has honoured you with a title, which I respect, yet how can I, when next we meet, bow rigidly and intone "Dame Judith"?' The *Los Angeles Herald-Examiner* settled for calling her 'Dame Anderson,' while others riffed endlessly on 'There's nothing like a dame.' Charles Champlin, in the *Los Angeles Times*, could not resist the headline: NOTHING LIKE A DAME; the *Hollywood Reporter* later dubbed her character in the movie *A Man Called Horse* 'Dame Buffalo Cow Head'; Jim McPherson, in *TV4*, headed his memories of the great actress 'A Dame named Anderson'; and anecdotes such as the following, true or false, circulated, playing on the incongruity between the 'British' and the 'American' actress:

> *Dame Judith Anderson is standing on the edge of the movie set between takes while the cameras and lighting equipment are being reset. An electrician on a ladder yells down to her: "Hey, Judy, baby, move over a few feet!"*
>
> *The great dramatic actress slowly swivels her head upward and in her deep resonant voice says, 'It's Dame Judy Baby!'*[105]

Judith Anderson herself played down the significance of the honour for her American audience. 'Having been made a Dame (by the Queen) has made a slight difference in my life,' she told *Performing Arts* in 1969. 'I find myself wearing gloves more often.' To her close friends, however, she revealed how

---

[105] *Cumberland Evening Times* [Maryland] 13 Jan 1960: 8; *LAHE* 25 Jul 1970, MHL; *LAT* 10 Oct 1965: B19; *HR* 23 Dec 1968, MHL; *The Writer* Oct 1993: 18.

much this recognition meant to her. 'It is mine my very own,' she wrote to fellow hard-working actor Lillian Gish, '– not via a husband's title.'[106]

Equally important, however, was that it was 'from my beloved native land.' 'My country, which I had never thought cared much about me,' she wrote two years later in her memoirs, 'had recognized me at last. The unwanted child was wanted after all.'

This brilliant moment in Anderson's life was, however, shadowed by tragedy. Relations with Frank had deteriorated in the past couple of years, culminating in a violent quarrel. Before they could mend their differences, Frank had a heart attack. As she celebrated her New Year honour Frank lay in hospital; a few weeks later he was dead. As Anderson wrote in her memoirs two years later, 'Happiness and despair, those Siamese twins, were still walking by my side.'

---

106   *Performing Arts* Mar 1969, MHL; Anderson to Gish, 19 Jan 1960, Gish Papers.

Scene Nine
Grande Dame

Judith Anderson outside Buckingham Palace after being made a Dame Commander of the British Empire July 1960

Everett Collection Inc/ Alamy Stock Photo

Chapter Thirty-one
Dear Darling Dame 1960–63

Dear Darling Dame Judith, I feel somewhat the way I did that first night I saw you do Come of Age. You are absolutely staggering in this, Judith, and I congratulate you.

Sybil Trubin to Dame Judith Anderson after seeing rough cut of *Macbeth* 1960

George Schaeffer directing Maurice Evans and Judith Anderson in Macbeth 1960
Everett Collection Inc/ Alamy Stock Photo

Early in 1960 George Schaefer and Sybil Trubin proposed *Hallmark*'s most ambitious production and what was to become Judith Anderson's most admired television performance – a two-hour *Macbeth* to be filmed in colour in London and on location in Scotland with Anderson reprising her prize-winning role and Maurice Evans once more playing Macbeth. It was to be a joint television-movie production, to be premiered on television in the United States, but shown in movie theatres in the rest of the world.[107]

Evans spent the spring scouting locations. On Rhodes he found a Crusader castle, The Palace of the Grand Master, whose interior he had copied at MGM's Elstree studio in London. In Scotland he decided on the Hermitage Castle, a sinister semi-ruin in a bleak valley near the Scottish border. Leslie Howard's sister Irene was responsible for casting the mainly British actors (who included the Australian-born Trader Faulkner), and one of England's foremost cinematographers, Freddie Young, was director of photography.[108]

By mid-May 1960 Anderson was in Scotland to film *Macbeth*. Despite the sorrow of Frank's death, this was a happy time among friends. In July she was to be honoured by the Queen at Buckingham Palace. In August she would appear as Madame Arkadina in *The Seagull* at the Edinburgh Festival and then at the Old Vic for five weeks. In mid-June, when Sybil Trubin left for New York after shooting had begun in London, she wrote to her 'Dear Darling Dame,' who had shared her Mayfair apartment with her: 'I can't thank you enough for taking me out of the Bury Court Hotel [and] sharing your happy home… Thank you, thank you, thank you!' 'With the best Lady Macbeth ever I don't see

---

107 *NYT* 26 Apr 1960: 75; *LAT* 7 Jun 1960: 25. See Cayton Hutton, *Macbeth: The Making of the Film*, 1960. The movie was initiated by Sidney Kaufman and Grand Prize Films Ltd. See 'Sidney Kaufman, A Figure In Film Production,' *NYT* 1 Aug 1983.
108 Maurice Evans, *All This… and Evans Too!* 1986, 264–5.

how we can miss,' she ended. 'Much love.'[109]

On 12 July 1960, in a simple tan dress by Victor Stiebel (who had just designed Princess Margaret's going-away dress for her marriage to Anthony Armstrong-Jones), Judith Anderson went to Buckingham Palace to be presented with the insignia of the Most Excellent Order of the British Empire. She was accompanied by her friend Maie [Lady] Casey, who gave a party to teach her how to curtsey, and Lady Harrison, the wife of the Australian High Commissioner.[110] After the two-hour ceremony, which Anderson described as worse than any first night, Richard Addinsell (from *Come of Age*, now a famous composer) gave a celebratory lunch for her, and George Schaefer, Maurice Evans, and others gave her a dinner that evening in the Elizabethan Room of the Gore Hotel.

The next day, when Anderson arrived at the studio to film the sleepwalking scene, she was greeted by bagpipes and a procession with blazing torches. When the castle doors opened, Evans and an official from Hallmark gave speeches in her honour and presented her with the portrait of herself in a red gown as Lady Macbeth that hung for the rest of her life in her homes at Carpinteria and Montecito. In reply she spoke warmly of her gratitude to the people of the United States who had 'opened their hearts, their arms and their stage doors' to her.[111]

As filming was completed at the end of July, George Schaefer hosted a farewell dinner for 50 at the River Club and Anderson was left to start rehearsals for *The Seagull*. 'The American contingent miss you,' Sybil Trubin wrote from New York. 'Much love to you from me and the rest of the Compatibles.'[112]

---

109   *NYT* 29 May 1960: X11; Michael Benthall to Anderson, tel 3 May 1960 from London, UCSB; *AWW* 1 Jun 1960: 2; Trubin to Anderson, 15 Jun 1960, UCSB.
110   Lord Casey, formerly Richard Casey, was in London to take up his recent peerage.
111   Evans, *All This... and Evans Too!* 265–6: *Variety* 20 Jul 1960: 2.
112   *NYT* 31 Jul 1960: X5; Trubin to Anderson, 26 Jul 1960, Schaefer Papers.

Cecil Smith in the *Los Angeles Times* had written gloomily in August 1960 that 'the tube as a dramatic proscenium is in the worst shape it has been in during its short decade as America's foremost mass entertainment medium.' But Compass knew they had a winner in *Macbeth*. 'Dear Darling Dame Judith,' Sybil Trubin wrote to Anderson after she saw the rough cut. 'I feel somewhat the way I did that first night I saw you do *Come of Age*.' 'You are absolutely staggering in this, Judith,' she continued, 'and I congratulate you.'[113]

Critics felt the same way when it debuted on NBC television on 20 November. Cecil Smith expected it to be good. 'The one steady light that has beamed through the years from television's flickering, faltering tube,' he wrote at the beginning of the season, 'is the annual series of six plays in color that arrive spasmodically under the banner of the Hallmark Hall of Fame.' He was not disappointed. 'Miss Anderson once more proves herself one of the greatest actresses of our time,' he wrote, praising every aspect of this 'magnificent' production. Jack Gould and John P Shanley in the *New York Times* agreed. 'The Lady Macbeth of Miss Anderson was nothing short of a masterpiece,' they wrote. 'She was alternately vibrant, calculating, cruel, regal and pitiful; the intricacy of the characterization was knitted so faultlessly that it had a chilling power.' Critics vied with each other to find the language to describe Anderson's performance. For Melvin Maddocks in the *Christian Science Monitor* it was 'a volatile mix of fire and dry ice'; *Time* magazine thrilled to her 'blood-red hair and blood-red voice.'[114]

Laurence Laurent, in the *Washington Post and Times Herald*, considered the production among the finest in *Hallmark*'s

---

113 *LAT* 14 Aug 1960: L3; Trubin to Anderson, 29 Aug 1960, Schaefer Papers.
114 *LAT* 23 Oct; A10; 21 Nov 1960: A14; *NYT* 21 Nov 1960: 59; *CSM* 22 Nov 1960: 6; *Time* 28 Nov 1960.

series of memorable productions. Viewer Gordon R Wynne wrote from Texas that 'The reaction to Macbeth in our area has been startling… for the first time Macbeth has come alive.' Larry Wolters in the *Chicago Daily Tribune* thought the Scottish setting lent the production authenticity. Melvin Maddocks put most clearly the qualities that made this production so powerful. 'The decisive, impelling factor behind this production, filmed on locations in Scotland and in a London studio, was not the personnel but the medium,' he wrote. 'The dominating presence was that technological star, the camera: spectacle; light and continuous action; cross-cutting; perspective; sound track; sudden close-up of murderer.'[115]

It was no surprise, therefore, when *Macbeth* scooped the pool at the 13th Annual TV Awards in May 1961, winning five Emmys: for outstanding drama; for program of the year; for best director; for best actor; and for best actress – the second award Anderson had received for that role. Even its sponsor, Joyce C Hall, president of Hallmark Cards, was given an honorary Emmy for his 'uplifting of TV standards with the Hallmark Hall of Fame.' As Jack Gould put it in the *New York Times*, 'The television industry was saved from embarrassment last week by Shakespeare.' Newspapers across the US and Australia featured photos of Anderson hugging her Emmy or stills of her and Evans in the movie. At the Moulin Rouge in Hollywood, she received a thunderous ovation for what was, at age 64, a second pinnacle of her long and brilliant career.[116]

The Hallmark *Macbeth* had its movie premiere in London early in December 1960, in a gala charity event at the Royal Festival Hall attended by Princess Alexandra. The *Guardian*'s

---

115 *WPHT* 21 Nov 1960: A17; Gordon R Wynne to George Schaefer, 22 Nov 1960, Schaefer Papers; *CDT* 21 Nov 1960: C17; *CSM* 22 Nov 1960: 6.
116 *NYT* 17 May: 75; 21 May1961; *LAT* 17 May 1961: 75; *SMH* 18 May 1961: 3; *AWW* 5 Jul 1961: 39.

Judith Anderson receiving her second Emmy for her performance as Lady Macbeth 1961
Author's collection

film critic was cool ('This film of *Macbeth* is not great, but it will serve.') and seemed surprised that 'Australian' Judith Anderson's Lady Macbeth was 'really good – truly a study of steely ruthlessness betrayed by a woman's sensibility and frailty of physique.' When it was released in the UK in May 1961, the same critic again damned it with faint praise and again reserved praise for Dame Judith Anderson's 'forceful, even melodramatic exception to the general tameness.' The *Times* reviewer, however, felt that Anderson was 'inclined to push what is legitimately theatrical a little beyond its natural bounds.' And Penelope Gilliatt in the *Observer* was dismissive, likening the experience of viewing *Macbeth* to watching a hit from Irving's Lyceum. When it opened in Australia, however, the *Women's Weekly* greeted it as 'Powerful… Shakespeare to remember.'[117]

When it was finally released in North America by arrangement with Capri Films, *Macbeth* was premiered in Hallmark headquarters in Kansas City on 20 October 1963 to little notice. It enjoyed a long life, however, in art houses, Shakespeare Festivals and schools for many years.[118]

In the early 1960s Judith Anderson's name was associated with the very best of television. Delivering his verdict on the current state of television in January 1961, Larry Wolters in the *Chicago Daily Tribune* lamented that 'What looked so much like a great new medium for education, illumination, and information 14 years ago is dedicated today too largely to trash and rubbish.' Fred Danzig in the *Los Angeles Times* made

---

117   *Guardian* 12 Dec 1960: 7; 27 May 1961: 5; *Times* 24 May 1961: 16; *Observer* 28 May 1961: 29; *AWW* 16 Aug 1961: 19.
118   Schaefer to Anderson, 27 May 1963; Trubin to Anderson, 5 & 24 Sep 1963; Anderson to Trubin, 9 Oct [1963], Schaefer Papers; *WPHT* 14 Nov 1963: C10; *Variety* 29 Oct 1963: 3; *NYT* 16 Jan 1964: 89; *LAT* 8 Feb 1974: E23; *Variety* 18 Jan 1978.

the same point. 'My computer tells me that my 1960 TV viewing time will total 1,364 hours 15 minutes,' he wrote. Only 105 hours 15 minutes were, in his opinion, outstanding. Along with Richard Burton in *The Tempest*, Harry Belafonte, Perry Como's season finale, he included Anderson in *Macbeth*. In similar vein, Cecil Smith, the *Los Angeles Times* entertainment editor, recalled Anderson's 'miracle of Medea' and *Macbeth* as *Hallmark Hall of Fame's* noblest effort of the year.[119]

That same month Anderson's *Play of the Week* performance of *Medea* won the prize awarded by the first International Television Festival in Monaco for the best single program in dramatic form. Laurence Olivier was named the best single performance by an actor for *The Moon and Sixpence*, in which Anderson had played.[120]

Over the next few months, *Macbeth* was showered with honours. As well as running away with the Emmy awards, it was named program of the year in the polls conducted by *Radio-TV Daily* and *TV Guide*. In February George Schaefer was acclaimed by the Directors Guild of America for the most outstanding directorial achievement in television for *Macbeth*. 'The award to George Schaefer was richly deserved,' Cecil Smith wrote. 'He is to television as the giants Ford, Huston and Wyler are to movies. His Hall of Fame productions are lofty islands in the sea of television mediocrity. In July *Macbeth* was chosen as the British entry in the Berlin Film Festival. Later that year, in October, *Hallmark Hall of Fame* repeated *Macbeth* as the beginning of its 1961–2 season.[121]

---

119 *CDT* 1 Jan 1961: nwB; *LAT* 2 Jan: A15; 3 Jan 1961: D39.
120 *Variety* 23 Jan 1961, 12; *LAT* 24 Jan 1961: A6.
121 *LAT* 23 Feb: A8; 14 Jun: 2; 7 Feb: A10; 20 Oct 1961: A12; *Guardian* 3 Jul 1961: 7. For profile of Schaefer see Eugene Nest, 'The Taskmaster,' *Pittsburgh Press* 27 Dec 1964: 109.

Despite all this adulation, Anderson had 'neither picture, play nor television' offered her during the first part of 1961. In May, as this acclaim reached its peak, a literary representative approached her suggesting she write her autobiography, and over the next few months she worked with her old friend from *The Old Maid* and New Guinea, former actor Robert Wallsten, dictating her memoirs. In late summer Tom Brock of the Monterey Wharf Theater asked her to read condensed versions of *Medea* and *Tower Beyond Tragedy* as part of a proposed television series of Jeffers' poems read against the background of Tor House and scenes in 'Jeffers country.' This would be her final tribute to Jeffers, who had been too ill to leave home for the past three years. When she opened the performance on 14 August, she had her final glimpse of the poet, who died less than six months later.[122]

With nothing better offering, Anderson agreed when San Francisco concert manager Spencer Barefoot suggested that she tour the college circuit in a similar set of readings, with some added excerpts from *Macbeth*. Bill Roerick, a Hollywood actor and playwright who had played Jason in the Monterey *Medea* (and who had appeared with Anderson in Gielgud's *Hamlet*), would accompany her. 'I had no play and one must work,' she told Cecil Smith. At 64 she was setting out, admittedly in costumes by Valentina and Jean Louis, on a three-month series of one-night stands. 'Start 20th Seattle,' she wrote Angna Enters on 16 September, '– a one night tour so will be strenuous.'[123]

---

122 Shirley Burke, literary representative, to Anderson, 11, 12 & 17 May 1961; [May 1961]; R. Wallsten, Letter, *SMH* 26 Jul 1961: 2; Anderson to Enters, 16 Sep 1961, Enters Papers.
123 *Variety* 22 Aug: 5; 6 Sep 1961: 58; *WPHT* 27 Aug 1961: G1; *LAT* 12 Nov: A16; 27 Oct 1961: B9; Anderson to Enters, 16 Sep 1961, Enters Papers.

As *Macbeth* returned triumphant to the television screens on 20 October, Anderson was wending her way from campus to campus until she reached Los Angeles, where she appeared for two weeks at the Huntington Hartford in mid-November, and then onwards until mid-December. The performance consisted of five scenes from *Macbeth*, one from *Tower Beyond Tragedy* and two from *Medea* that made up two-thirds of the evening, the reviewer in *Variety* wrote. One simple set provided the backdrop for all three dramas, and William Roerick ably undertook a variety of supporting roles. 'Here is a rare opportunity for serious students and practitioners of the drama to observe one of the most gifted members of the acting fraternity in a novel display of her artistry,' he noted. 'But, as commercial theatre, it is a dubious presentation of limited appeal.'

> *To offer, out of context, isolated passages from three heavy, depressing works that, even intact, are challenging to the intellect and the endurance, creates severe demands on both artist and audience. That the program comes off as well as it does is a tribute to the skills of this renowned actress, whose range of emotion, richness and clarity of vocal expression and intensity performance in spite of the terrible handicaps of a la carte theatre is quite a histrionic achievement.*[124]

There was much to upset Anderson during this arduous tour. Her beloved Guthrie McClintic, who had been ill since April, died of cancer on 29 October. Her hero, Robinson Jeffers, was dying. More immediately, as she wrote to Angna Enters, her tour was 'being stupendously mishandled.' 'Don't ask me how Judith got involved with Barefoot,' Ellie Martin wrote to Enters from San Francisco, 'the story is loud, vituperative

---

124   *LAT* 29 Oct 1961: A12; Sybil [Trubin] to Anderson, 20 Oct 1961, Schaefer Papers; *Variety* 15 Nov 1961: 3; see also 22 Nov: 3, 57; but see also *LAT* 15 Nov: D9.

and unintelligible, as you can imagine.' 'Everything was utter chaos when she played here, and just a little improved when I last saw her in LA,' she continued. 'Also, she lost money hand over fist, just to make matters worse.'[125]

There was no sign of this bitter disappointment, however, in the profile Cecil Smith wrote for the *Los Angeles Times* in mid-December, rather ambiguously titled 'Curtain Call for Dame Judith.' 'On a mountaintop near Carpinteria stands a pink palace in solitary glory,' Smith wrote in an article illustrated by striking photographs of Anderson in her beautiful home.

> *From its great windows, the land sweeps away down a massive corridor lined with lemon and avocado groves to where a fiery sunset smears the sky with orange and gold. The Channel Islands hunch their massive slate-grey shoulders against the gaudy sunset sky and the fretful sea swirls in foaming anger around them.*
>
> *This a place of incredible peace and quietude – bordered always by the turbulent restlessness of the sea. It is almost a perfect reflection of the woman who built this palace and who lives here alone – Dame Judith Anderson.*

'As with any actress, the future for Dame Judith is an unknown quantity,' Smith ended his admiring portrait. 'She's never given up the idea that she'd one day like to play Hamlet… She will be 64 in February [actually 65] and she knows the strain of great roles can tire her now. She waits in the quietude of the pink palace on this mountain knowing, as always, the turbulent, pulsing passion of the nearby sea.'[126]

The immediate future, however, held only repetitions

---

125   Anderson to Enters, [Env 4 Nov 1961]; Ellie Martin to Enters, 12 Dec 1961, Enters Papers.
126   *LAT* 18 Dec 1961: Family Part II: 1, 8.

of *Medea* and *Macbeth*. Grieving for Jeffers, who had died on 21 January, Anderson was on the road again in February 1962, this time with just two roles, Lady Macbeth and Medea, produced by Monterey's Tom Brock and Robert Carson and supported by Roerick, her friend, acting coach Lilyan Chauvin, and Monterey actor Fred Forsman. The tour was absolutely exhausting, she wrote Angna Enters from Dallas.[127]

In Chicago Anderson's most fervent admirer since she was a young stranger from Australia, Claudia Cassidy, was scathing. 'Instead of a black panther this Medea was rather a fishwife, and the play cut to shreds by more than one blue pencil, was sometimes absurd enough to suggest going straight back to Euripides… Lady Macbeth listed no director, which makes sense. Medea '62 said it was "based on the original interpretation of Guthrie McClintic." Not really. In fact, not at all.'[128]

After a 'fraught' summer, with domestic disasters and family illnesses, Anderson resumed her punishing tour in September, starting in Minneapolis, and ending in Brooklyn in early December. Writing to Ellie Martin from New York on 2 December, Angna Enters was concerned:

> *Have just come from seeing Judith who is in town for a few days before going home for Christmas and then she starts out on another tour! She seems to be enjoying it – says so – but I think she looks dreadful and am worried! Of course this may be due to a bad cold and cough – hope it is only that. She seems to think that bashing around from town to town in a station wagon is trouping but I think she must ask for a more comfortable car!*'[129]

---

127 For Roerick see obituary, *Indianapolis Star* 6 Dec 1995: 51; Anderson to Enters, 10 Feb [1962], Enters Papers.
128 *CDT* 26 Mar 1962: B7.
129 Anderson to Enters, 8 Oct [1962]; Enters to Ellie Martin, 2 Dec 1962, Enters Papers.

Judith Anderson was not the only great star 'trouping' in 1962. Helen Hayes at 61, and Maurice Evans at 62 were touring in a collection of scenes from Shakespeare they called *A Program for Two Players*. Starting in Detroit in October, they expected to cover 19,000 miles, 69 cities and 135 performances by the time they finished the tour in March 1963. An article in the *New York Times* called them 'part of a burgeoning movement back to the old days of trouping.' Hayes and Evans travelled in some comfort, however – by a specially fitted-out bus, which they preferred to the train travel of earlier days; and each had a secretary-maid/valet-companion.

Claudia Cassidy was no less blistering about Hayes and Evans than she had been about Anderson. 'This is minor circuit Shakespeare in which the play's not the thing, but the players,' she wrote in November 1962. 'They indulge in a kind of complacent barnstorming that delights the groundlings and embarrasses everyone else.' 'Mr Evans' Hamlet today is a clearly spoken robot,' she went on. 'His Macbeth is elocution.' And Helen Hayes got worse:

> *Miss Hayes, who has no ear for Shakespeare, is painfully coy… Her Lady Macbeth is a misfortune, her death of Cleopatra makes you cringe.*

'A Program for Two Players' is the kind of inexcusable makeshift that misleads the uninformed audience, dismays the initiated, and cheats two players worth better treatment of their theater birthright,' Cassidy concluded testily.[130]

Judith Anderson's long tour, undertaken primarily to make money, ended badly. ANDERSON CANCELED a headline in the Oregon *Medford Mail Tribune* of 21 April 1963 declared,

---

130   *CDT* 20 Nov 1962: a1.

reporting that she had been hospitalised with nervous exhaustion. 'No word! How are you ???????' Angna Enters wrote her in early June. 'Olga [Lee] told me – and Bill [Hawkins], too, the horrid news as to the financial contretemps of the tour.' Anderson replied with a sad story of bounced checks. 'They, Brock and Carson have vanished completely,' she wrote, 'and I am sure that I will never get a penny, so that is that.' 'Oh well,' she ended, uncharacteristically defeated, 'that's a woman alone's life.'[131]

To top off that year's miseries, Knopf decided not to publish Anderson's memoirs. 'The book is off,' she wrote Enters in August, 'Knopf wont publish Bob Wallsten's script and I don't know just what, if anything I will do try to work again with him or get another writer. It is a mess, and I am very sorry for him, so I am going to sleep on it for the time being.'[132]

---

131   *Medford Mail Tribune* (Oregon) 21 Apr 1963: 16; *CDT* 20 Nov 1962: a1; Enters to Anderson, 9 Jun 1963; Anderson to Enters, 20 Jun [1963], Enters Papers. See also *Variety* 8 May 1963: 219.
132   Anderson to Enters, 25 Aug [1963], Enters Papers.

Hirchfeld's view of Anderson's Oresteia, *Ypsilanti, 1966, with Jacqueline Brookes, Donald Davis, Ruth Volner, John Michael King, Frederic Warriner, Karen Ludwig, and Ruby Dee (far right) as Cassandra. Behind the cloud: Jack Fletcher and Bert Lahr in* The Birds.

© The Al Hirschfeld Foundation

Chapter Thirty-two

Dame Judith the Great, in Tennis Shoes 1963–9

As the Clytemnestra, this festival is blessed with Judith Anderson. There are very few living actresses who could, from the first moment, encompass the immensity of this role and this play. In stature and voice, Dame Judith is magnificent... her performance is possible only to a large talent used by a large spirit.

Stanley Kauffmann, New York Times 1966

'Have not heard from Judith since she left here last September,' Angna Enters wrote to Ellie Martin in April 1964. 'Not even a card at Christmas although I've written to ask how she was.' Anderson must, indeed, have felt that her career was over. 'I don't understand the American theater anymore,' her old friend Vincent Price complained. 'Take a star of the brilliance and magnitude of Judith Anderson... she doesn't work as frequently as she should, because there are not enough star parts for her.' Her family life had also disintegrated: her brother was dead; her nieces had gone their own ways, none of them following her into the theatre as she had hoped; and the ranch she had bought with such high hopes 14 years ago was failing. Putting that dream behind her, she decided to sell. By October 1965 she had moved to an 'English style cottage' with a magnificent view of the mountains at 808 San Ysidro Lane in the up-market Santa Barbara suburb, Montecito. Harking back to her father's Scottish home town, she called it 'Arbroath.'[133]

Judith Anderson, Grande Dame, had not, however, done with the theatre that was her life. Throughout this fallow period, from her 67th to her 69th year, she did everything she could to keep her name before the public, accepting invitations from campus 'celebrity series' and regional theatres to perform, and delighting in the occasional honorary doctorates that were bestowed on her – the unschooled little girl who had become a major exponent of Shakespeare and the Greeks.[134]

Late in 1964 she made a highly regarded recording of *Medea* with Anthony Quayle; and she took part in a pilot for a CBS TV series to be called *The Haunted*, with young actress Diane Baker, who became a lifelong friend. The newspapers remembered her from time to time: in November 1964, Dorothy Kilgallen in the *Washington Post, Times Herald* announced, 'Judith Anderson May Do Musical'; and in April 1966 the *Pittsburgh Post-Gazette* was sure that she was set for a summer theater tour in *Little Foxes*, the play she had declined in 1945; but neither of these ever materialised.[135]

In 1965, as she got her affairs into order, new opportunities opened up for her. Since 1963 a group of determined townspeople in the small town of Ypsilanti in Michigan had

---

133 Enters to Ellie Martin, 6 Apr 1964, Enters Papers; *Detroit Free Press* 10 Feb 1966: 39; *PP* 10 Jan 1965: 39; *Des Moines Register* 25 Dec 1965: 9.

134 *Republic* 26 Jan 1964: 29; *Variety* 31 Jan 31, 1964: 8; *LAT* 27 Sep: R3; 15 Oct 1964: F6; 5 Jun 1968: F3. Anderson was given an honorary degree from Fairfield University 16 May 1964 in celebration of Shakespeare Day. See *Variety* 20 May 1964: 62; *Bridgeport Post* (Conn) 26 Apr: 4; 17 May 1964: 1; *NYT* 16 May 1964: 12.

135 *RJN* 8 Sep 1964; *Variety* 30 Sep: 51; 22 Dec 22 1964: 8; *LAT* 4 Oct 1964: U34; *NYT* 11 Oct 1964: BR31; *WPHT* 15 Nov 1964: G4. This musical, an adaptation of Paul Osborn's 1939 Broadway play *Morning's at Seven*, was never heard of again.

been planning a Greek Theatre. Anderson had given them her support from the beginning, appearing at their first fund-raising dinner in May 1964. In mid-1965 an executive director and an architect were appointed, and Alexis Solomos, director of the Greek National Theatre, agreed to become artistic director for their first season the following summer. In September Solomos announced that Anderson would appear in their first production. At the same time another old friend, Bill [Sir Edward] Hayward, invited her to appear in her hometown at the Adelaide Festival of the Arts the following March.[136]

Meanwhile, a new 2,685-seat theatre – the Valley Music Theater – had opened in Woodland Hills, Los Angeles. Primarily a venue for musicals, its creators, producer Nick Mayo and his partners, wanted to present one drama with a 'star' attraction every season. Dame Judith tried to persuade them to take a chance on *Come of Age*; but they decided that the drama for fall 1965 should be *Medea*, and that she would again be its star. Charles Champlin in the *Los Angeles Times* considered this 'a bold and chancy gesture' in a town that did not have a regular theatre habit. Advertised as 'The Greatest Performance of the Century!' the three-week run, with Henry Brandon once more as Jason '(the best Jason I ever had') and Marian Seldes as the Nurse, also featured fellow-Australian Michael Pate, with his son Christopher playing one of Medea's children.[137]

After Anderson opened in *Medea*, Champlin applauded 'a classic performance by one of the world's greatest actresses, a landmark in the histrionic arts which no one who cares

---

136   *CT* 2 Jun 1965: b2; *NYT* 9 Sep 1965: 36; Hayward to Anderson, 24 Aug & 8 Sep 1965; Max Lamshed, Administrator, Adelaide Festival, to Anderson, 9 Sep 1965; Robert Campbell to Anderson, 9 & 12 Nov; 14 Dec 1965, UCSB; *Advertiser* 6 Oct 1965; *Variety* 27 Oct 1965: 74.
137   *LAT* 11 Jul: A2; 18 Aug: D12; 6 Sep: D11; 10 Oct: B19; advertisement 5 Oct 1965: D12; *RJN* Aug 1965; *Variety* 23 Aug 1965: 2.

Judith Anderson with 'the best Jason I ever had,' Henry Brandon, in Medea *1965*
Author's collection

for theater can think of missing.' '"Medea" is a jolt, and no mistake,' he conceded. 'In a time of neon, smog, situation comedy and comfort symbols, it thrusts us back 2800 years to high tragedy in the grand manner… It is, from start to finish, a fantastic performance, fantastic in its energy and in its range.' Echoing Brooks Atkinson nearly 20 years before, he stated flatly, 'She *is* Medea.'[138]

Hollywood's elite, including Judy Garland and Mark Herron, Eve Arden, Juliet Prowse and Lee Marvin, flocked to Anderson's dressing room on opening night; and Maurice Evans and young Australian star Diane Cilento with husband Sean Connery, arrived in town in time to catch one of her final

---

138 *LAT* 14 Oct 1965: D19. See also *RJN* Nov 1965; *Variety* 14 Oct 1965: 10.

performances. But Los Angeles' appetite for the classics was not as great as the producers had hoped, and *Medea* made a profit only because its three-week season was supported by the California Teachers Association, whose members had sent their students to see this classic play. The city's hunger for the theatre in general did not meet the Valley Music Theater's expectations, and, despite a number of successful musicals, the theatre closed the following September and its owners filed for bankruptcy, putting an end to any further plans involving Anderson.[139]

In February 1966 Anderson set off once again for Australia to appear in Adelaide's Festival of the Arts, knowing that she would be returning to take part in one of the great Greek tragedies, Aeschylus' *The Oresteia*, in Ypsilanti's new Greek Theatre. 'Judith called last week en route to Australia,' Ellie Martin wrote Angna Enters, 'she is to play bits of Medea & McBeth there with an Australian cast which is already in rehearsal under an unknown director. They await Dame Judith – OH DEAR!'[140]

But as in 1955 Anderson seemed to enjoy every minute of the visit, even though the public was more interested in the young Russian poet, Yevgeny Yevtushenko, who was the undeniable star of the Festival. Accompanied by her 20-year-old niece Jenifer, Anderson stayed in Adelaide with her friends, Sir Edward and Lady Ursula Hayward, at their extensive property, Carrick Hill. They socialised with Adelaide's

---

139   *Variety* 14 Oct: 2; 19 Oct: 3; 2 Nov 1965: 2; 12 Jan 1966: 76; *LAT* 31 Oct 1965: B39; 30 Sep 1966: 3; 1 Jan 1967: C17. Mark Herron, who married Judy Garland the following month, was later Henry Brandon's long-term partner. For Anderson's impassioned plea to re-open the theatre see *Variety* 2 Mar 1967: 3; *LAT* 2 Mar 1967: SF1; Diary 1 Mar 1967.
140   Ellie to Enters, 2 Mar [1966], Enters Papers.

leading citizens, swam at the beach, attended the races and caught up with friends and relatives. Richard Casey, now Baron Casey, had become Australia's governor-general, and Anderson and Jenifer visited him and Maie at Government House, Canberra, where they lunched with 'Nugget' Coombs. They drove to Griffith to visit her brother Jack and his family.[141]

She was also warmly greeted by the critics. Saluted as a 'munificent gesture to the city of her birth' (she donated her services to the Festival), her performance was 'a warm and exciting occasion, a superb co-ordination of voice and movement and whatever else it is that makes an artist great,' Mary Armitage wrote in the Adelaide Advertiser. Variety's critic, calling her 'probably Australia's greatest export,' described Anderson in royal blue robes in Macbeth and a loose yellow gown in Medea, accompanied by the handsome Australian actor James Condon. 'There has been no performance in Australia in years to equal this,' he concluded. John Healey in the Sunday Mail was less effusive, blaming the unsuitable Elder Hall for problems of hearing and visibility.[142]

Soon after she arrived, she had agreed to read translations of the poems that Yevgeny Yevtushenko would recite in Russian in his performances at the accompanying Writers Festival and in Sydney. This charismatic and arrogant young man was, according to his host, Geoffrey Dutton, not happy to have his poetry read by 'that old crow.' 'I would prefer the daughter,' he told Dutton. But the arrangement went ahead, and there is no record of how Anderson felt about playing second fiddle to the 'rebellious young poet' that Australia fell in love with, especially when he had the advantage

---

141   Diary 24 Feb to 6 Apr 1966; Rose Wilson, 'Hayward, Sir Edward Waterfield (Bill) (1903–1983)', ADB; Richard Heathcote, Carrick Hill: A Portrait, 2012.
142   Stan, Variety 30 Mar 1966: 88; Advertiser 12 Mar 1966; Sunday Mail 12 Mar 1966. Anderson played on 11, 14 & 16 Mar in Elder Hall.

of the magnificent Regent Theatre for his recital. In the *Advertiser*, John Satterley rhapsodised about his 'remarkable performance':

> *Yevgeny Yevtushenko last night drenched his first Festival audience with all the fire and passion that a rebellious young poet can muster. And they loved it.*

Acknowledging the poet's 'assistants' (Anderson in a 'stunning long gown' and actor Peter O'Shaughnessy) for 'giving of their best,' Satterley noted that 'it was to the poet himself that the audience really addressed itself.' 'The lithe 6-footer,' he wrote, 'knows how to get the most out of his rich, showmanlike baritone. The English readings were subdued in comparison... Mr Yevtushenko might not be understood, but he can never be ignored.'[143]

Anderson returned from Australia to one of the most audacious – and costly – attempts to bring Greek theatre to the American mid-West. Ypsilanti, population 27,000, was a declining industrial town a few kilometres from the university town of Ann Arbor and 58 kilometres from Detroit. The home of Eastern Michigan University, a group of locals had decided that a Greek Theatre on the grand scale might turn this automobile-manufacturing town into a centre of culture. Hoping to attract the private and government funds increasingly available for regional theatre, they bravely appointed Alexis Solomos as artistic director and announced a 10-week season for their first productions, Aeschylus' *The Oresteia* and Aristophanes' *The Birds*, to be presented in new translations by

---

143 *SMH* 7 Mar 1966: 7; *Advertiser* 18 & 23 Mar 1966; Geoffrey Dutton, *Out in the Open*, 1995, 317–23. See also *SMH* 19 Mar: 9; 24 Mar 1966: 32; *Canberra Times* 22 Mar 1966: 13; Dutton, 'The Poet as Public Figure: Yevtushenko and the Adelaide Establishment,' *Bulletin* 12 Mar 1966: 24–5.

Robert Lowell and Walter Kerr respectively, in the theatre that was to be built in time for them to open in June 1966. Experimental composer Iannis Xenakis would provide the music. Anderson would once more play Clytemnestra – the part she had played in Jeffers' *Tower Beyond Tragedy*, and Bert Lahr, of *Wizard of Oz* fame, would star in *The Birds*.[144]

As the opening of this grand project drew near, it was clear that the $2.5million classical Greek theatre would not be ready in time. (In fact it was never built.) Instead they would open in a baseball stadium – the Walter O Briggs Stadium on the university campus – which would be converted to seat 1,900. The company opened gamely for previews on 14 June 1966, with Ruby Dee playing a 'savage and frenzied' Cassandra, Canadian actor-director Donald Davis 'immensely impressive' in the twin roles of Agamemnon and Apollo, and Jacqueline Brookes as Athene and Leader of the 16-member female Chorus. The adaptation was not that of poet Robert Lowell, but of Richard Lattimore – 'straight-forward but rarely lyrical' according to critic Cecil Smith.[145]

When the play opened formally on 28 June, it was a national event, with every major critic attending. William Leonard of the *Chicago Tribune* captured their combined wonder and admiration when he wrote:

> *A group of plucky small town people, who would not quit, wrote a chapter in American theater's history here tonight. The Ypsilanti Greek theater scored a coup simply by opening, when the odds against them had been so great. Then they scored another coup by putting on a powerful production of an extremely trying classic.*

---

144   *NYT* 9 Sep1965: 36; *SMH* 11 May 1966: 13:9; Laura C. Bird, *The Ypsilanti Greek Theatre*, 1999, 11–15. See Jim O'Quin, 'Going National: How America's Regional Theatre Movement Changed the Game,' *American Theatre* 16 Jun 2015.
145   *LAT* 30 Jun 1966: A9.

> *In a converted baseball stadium on the campus of Eastern Michigan university, they presented the first professional offering in America of one of the oldest dramas still in existence, Aeschylus' The Oresteia, and they did it in high style, with a company that obviously had been drilled intensively but just as obviously has not lost its enthusiasm.*

Like the other critics who attended that performance, Leonard placed Judith Anderson at the centre of the play's success. 'Judith Anderson, possibly the greatest classic tragedienne of our time, draws a vividly gripping portrait of Clytemnestra, the unhappy heroine,' he wrote, 'yet her performance, despite its strength, does not overpower the rest of a highly professional cast.'

'The lighting is beautiful,' Leonard continued, 'the choreography of the women's chorus is striking in its simplicity, and the music by Iannis Xenakis is a weird and wonderful obligato, full of strange whistling and clattering and scratching that fits well into the uncomfortable story.'

'The Ypsilanti Greek theater has a long, tough road ahead of it,' he concluded, 'and its prospects are not rosy, but it need not apologize for its first production.'[146]

'I hope the festival continues,' Alexis Solomos told Stanley Kauffmann early in July. 'I should like to do Euripides's *Hecuba* with Judith Anderson.' 'I have admired her ever since I saw her in *Medea*,' he went on. 'Here she was wonderful – she was the youngest in the company. She has the ideal offstage personality for a great actress.' Anderson had found a successor to Guthrie McClintic. But the Ypsilanti Greek theater was too frail a reed to allow them to work together again. Despite the brilliance of their productions, they could not fill the stadium night after night. By early August, the *New York Times*

---

146   *CT* 29 Jun 1966.

was reporting that 'Ypsilanti Theater Fights to Complete Lean Season.' When the season ended on 4 September, the theatre was $233,000 in debt. By March 1967 the dream of a Greek theatre in small-town America was dead.[147]

As Cecil Smith put it in the *Los Angeles Times*, it was miraculous that it had happened at all.[148]

This adventure – and the stimulating direction of Alexis Solomos – revived Anderson's fighting spirit; and it reminded producers that she was still a player. Soon after she opened in *The Oresteia*, Anderson had a telegram from Jean Dalrymple at the City Center: 'Should love to talk with you as have definite offer for television special.' The City Center had produced only musicals since the 1956–7 season. Now Dalrymple was proposing a season of drama, including a revival of Maxwell Anderson's 1930 verse play *Elizabeth the Queen*, directed by Margaret Webster. Judith Anderson had always wanted to play the English queen, though she had hoped it would be in a play written by Robinson Jeffers; but she readily agreed when Dalrymple offered her the part – and she would be working again with Peggy Webster, who had directed her in *Family Portrait* and *Macbeth*. Donald Davis, who was playing so successfully with her in *The Oresteia*, would play her young ambitious lover, the Earl of Essex. Although this is not clear, it seems from the wording of the telegram that an arrangement had been made with George Schaefer and Compass for the television production that followed in 1967.[149]

'*Elizabeth the Queen* Panned and Praised' – Associated Press critic William Glover's headline – summed up the play's

---

147 *NYT* 5 Jul: 39; 9 Aug 1966: 28; *LAT* 17 Sep 1966: 16.
148 *LAT* 6 Jul 1966: c8.
149 Dalrymple to Anderson, [?] Jun 1966, UCSB; *NYT* 3 Jul: 39; 17 Jul: 73; 3 Aug 1966: 42; Diary 4 Jul to 13 Nov 1966.

reception when it opened in November 1966. Anderson was suffering from the flu and remembered her performance with chagrin. 'The production was not only not good, it was bad,' she declared bluntly two years later. The main problem seemed to be the play, which, with its tendency to try to out-Shakespeare Shakespeare, had not weathered well; and it seemed, to *New York Times* reviewer Walter Kerr, under-rehearsed. Directed at the last minute, not by Peggy Webster but by Herbert Machiz, Judith Anderson seemed, to Kerr, 'to be remembering an effect instead of creating one.' Richard P Cooke in the *Wall Street Journal*, however, considered that it was Miss Anderson's performance that gave the evening what dramatic validity it possessed.

> *For the first few minutes of Elizabeth the Queen... there is a routine costume drama. But soon along comes a figure in the stiffest of gowns and spangles of jewels. It's Judith Anderson and she looks so much like the portraits of Elizabeth I that it's uncanny.*

Cooke conceded that 'through much of the play there is talk of love, honor and ambition without much substance in the enacting of these human conditions.' 'Nevertheless,' he concludes, 'it is a pleasure to watch a fine actress in a strong role as Miss Anderson fulfills our hopes that she could bring a great queen once more to life.'[150]

Anderson was able to make up for her sense of failure when she made her last major performance for *Hallmark Hall of Fame* in the play the following year, with Charlton Heston as her co-star. At 71, Anderson was an almost exact counterpart of the 67-year-old Elizabeth and Charlton Heston 45 as compared to the 35-year-old Essex. Heston is best known for

---

150   *Courier-Journal* [Louisville, Ky] 4 Nov 1966: 17; *NYT* 28 Jan 1968: D27; 4 Nov 1966: 30; *WSJ* 7 Nov 1966: 18. See also *NYT* 5 May 1967: 77.

his epic film roles, such as *Ben Hur* and *The Ten Commandments*, but he had begun on Broadway in *Antony and Cleopatra* with Katharine Cornell and appeared often on television and in regional productions of Shakespeare. He had just played Sir Thomas More in *A Man for All Seasons*.

Elizabeth the Queen was taped in Hollywood during October 1967. As *Variety* put it, 'Judith Anderson "Liz" On Hallmark Tee-Off.' Anticipating the broadcast of this 'Tiffany of the dramatic shows,' the *TV Guide* critic described how Anderson, this tiny, soft-spoken, unassuming woman, 'like someone's sparkly maiden aunt,' was 'an actress to her bone

Judith Anderson and Charlton Heston in the television production of Elizabeth the Queen 1968

Author's collection

marrow,' who 'skillfully suspends belief and brings Elizabeth richly, vibrantly, sensually to life.' 'Hallmark *is* George Schaefer, his taste, his know-how,' she told the reporter, explaining how they had met in the Pacific many years before, '– a most meticulous man, I like that.'[151]

Angna Enters considered Anderson 'magnificent as always' when she saw *Elizabeth the Queen* on 31 January 1968. Critics agreed wholeheartedly, although Jack Gould in the *New York Times* thought the play outdated and Cecil Smith in the *Los Angeles Times* found it 'slick and pat and pretentious,' its poetry now seeming 'piddling stuff.' Despite the limitations of the play, however, Gould stated forcefully the universal opinion that 'it was Miss Anderson who single-handedly illuminated the screen with her portrayal of the Queen's fatal struggle with Lord Essex in matters of state and heart.' 'In the preliminary sparring with the young nobleman who poses a threat to her own reign,' he wrote, 'Miss Anderson vividly underscored a mastery of court intrigue [and] in the climatic scene, when Elizabeth grows old before one's eyes after Essex prefers the executioner to the perils of a shared throne, Miss Anderson was a figure of tragic and touching stature.'[152]

Judith Anderson's portrayal of Elizabeth I earned her a final Emmy nomination in April 1969. The other nominations for Best Actress were Canadian Genevieve Bujold for her performance in *Saint Joan*, another *Hallmark* production, Colleen Dewhurst in *The Crucible*, Anne Jackson in *Dear Friends*, and Maureen Stapleton in Truman Capote's *Among the Paths to Eden*. At the awards at the Palladium in Los Angeles presided over by Frank Sinatra, and the Americana Hotel in

---

151   Diary 4 to 26 Oct 1967; *LAT* 17 Oct: C15; 4 Nov: B1; 22 Nov 1967: C11; 28 Jan 1968: C3; *Variety* 25 May 1967: 9; *TV Guide* 26 Jan 1968, MHL.
152   Enters to Anderson, 8 Feb 1968, Enters Papers; *NYT* 1 Feb 1968: 75. See also *LAT* 2 Feb 1968: c16; *WPTH* 2 Feb 1968: C7; *SMH* 3 Feb 1968: 10:3; *CSM* 5 Feb 1968: 6; *Variety* 7 Feb 1968: 38.

New York hosted by Dick Van Dyke, on 19 May, Anderson lost to Maureen Stapleton; but *Elizabeth the Queen* won the Emmy for Outstanding Drama of the Year – an unpopular decision with some critics.[153]

After Anderson completed *Elizabeth the Queen* in October 1967, she was restless as usual. 'I am doing nothing,' she wrote Angna Enters, 'little nibbles, but no job, and it is such a waste of time, as I haven't much left for activity, theatre wise.' 'I am well, and happy and love my house and garden,' she added, 'have a room for you anytime you will come here, I wish that you would.'[154]

It was not a play, however, but a movie – and another powerful woman – that brought her work. 'Dame Buffalo Cow Head,' the *Hollywood Reporter* dubbed her as she set off for Durango, Mexico, to portray the Sioux matriarch who enslaves Richard Harris in *A Man Called Horse*. 'Imperious Judith, a perfectionist in diction… will play a tough old Indian,' the *Hollywood Citizen-News* reported, in a part that 'will have little or no words.' Although she made a new friend of her co-star Corinna Tsopei, 72-year-old Anderson found the three months on location outside Durango from October 1968 to January 1969, a 'horrendous' experience. The contact lens required to change her blue eyes to brown caused a frightening inflammation; and she returned with an injured back. 'Judith called on her return from Mexico, miserable,' Ellie Martin wrote Angna Enters, 'she had to wear brown contact lenses… scratched her eye balls raw. The location was awful etc – The film is finished at last.'[155]

---

153   *LAT* 17 Apr: D1, 241; 20 May 1968: 3; *NYT* 21 Apr: 74; 19 May: D23; 26 May 1968: D29; *CT* 20 May 1968: 21; *CSM* 22 May 1968: 4; *Variety* 24 May 1968: 19.
154   Anderson to Enters, [July? 1968], Enters Papers.
155   *HR* 23 Dec 1968; *HCN* 22 Oct 1968; 28 Jan 1969, MHL; *Desert Sun* 8 May 1970;

As an exciting new theatrical venture developed quietly behind the scenes, Anderson made one final performance for *Hallmark Hall of Fame* and George Schaefer in *The File on Devlin*, a Catherine Gaskin spy story that opened *Hallmark*'s fall 1969 season. 'We love you and know you'll be divine as Elizabeth [Devlin],' Sybil Trubin wrote Anderson in May 1969 as she negotiated over her billing after the young stars of the play, David McCallum and Elizabeth Ashley. Shot over four days in August, it was broadcast on 21 November 1969. The first work presented by *Hallmark Hall of Fame* under its new policy of presenting new plays, *The File of Devlin* was dismissed by George Gent in the *New York Times* as 'claptrap'; and Cecil Smith in the *Los Angeles Times* mourned the tarnishing of the great series by this 'sluggish and tedious' melodrama.

Judith Anderson as 'Dame Buffalo Cow Head' in A Man Called Horse *1968*
Author's collection

In *The File on Devlin*, Anderson was, in fact, presiding over the beginning of the end for the program and the television era that had given her an illustrious new middle-age career. This end was presaged by the retrospective of George Schaefer's television shows at the New York Cultural Center, held from 18 to 23 November, in which *The File on Devlin* was the opening show, followed by *Macbeth*, *Blithe Spirit*, *Saint Joan*,

---

Diary 28 Oct 1968; 29 & 30 Jan 1969; *Variety* 3 Feb: 28; 12 Feb 1969: 61; *SMH* 9 Feb 1969: 11; *LAT* 1 Sep 1969.

The Magnificent Yankee, Anastasia, Green Pastures, Little Moon of Alban, and *Do Not Go Gentle Into That Good Night*. This was not the end of Schaefer's long career. He continued to direct theatrical productions and diversified into movies. After directing five movies and returning to television to produce and direct *Truman at Potsdam* for *Hallmark* in 1976, he was, in 1985, appointed Chairman and later Associate Dean at the School of Theater, Film and Television at the University of California, Los Angeles. He retired in 1991, but continued to direct television movies until his death in 1997.

As one chapter ended another re-opened. Throughout her years in thrall to Medea and Lady Macbeth, Judith Anderson had not stopped dreaming of one further great role. In October 1969, at 72 years of age, she startled the theatrical world by announcing that she was at last going to take on the ultimate challenge – Hamlet.

Dame Judith Anderson as Hamlet 1970

Author's collection

Chapter Thirty-three
Hamlet 1969–71

*There is nothing like a Dame Judith Anderson.
But as Hamlet?*

Dan Knapp, Los Angeles Times, 1969

Judith Anderson had a long history with *Hamlet*. Her first appearance on the professional stage had been as a page in Walter Bentley's *Hamlet* in Sydney in March 1913. In her first months in New York in 1919 she had seen Walter Hampden as Hamlet and criticised his reading as 'intelligent… but by no means inspired.' 'I think one must be to play Hamlet,' she noted in her diary. She had seen the greatest Hamlets of her era – John Barrymore, produced by Arthur Hopkins, in 1922; and in 1936 she had played Gertrude, Hamlet's seductive mother, with John Gielgud in the role that had made his name at the Old Vic a few years earlier. 'It is natural for an actress to want to play Shakespeare,' she had told the *New York Herald Tribune* as she prepared for what had been her first major Shakespearean role, produced by Guthrie McClintic.[156]

During the 1950s, when she was still full of confidence that she could move on to even greater heights than

---

156   Clyde Packer, 'Dame Judith Anderson.' In *No Return Ticket: Clyde Packer Interviews Nine Famous Australian Expatriates*, 1984, 59; Diary 24 Feb 1919; NYHT 20 Sep 1936: 5:1.

Medea, admirers had begun to talk to her about playing Shakespeare's most challenging emotional role – Hamlet himself, as her heroine Sarah Bernhardt had done. Although none of these plans had eventuated, Anderson never forgot her ambition. In January 1968, she had told Australian journalist Judy Stone that she regretted never having played that great role. 'In the theater, I want to think, to laugh, be enraptured, dream, cry,' she explained. A few months later Paul Gregory, the impresario who had masterminded *John Brown's Body* in 1953, called her – and her long-postponed dream was set in motion. *Hamlet* 'encompasses every emotional note on the scale,' she told the *Los Angeles Times* when their plans for a 26-week tour were announced in November 1969.[157]

Paul Gregory's best days as a producer were behind him in 1969. Although he was then only 49, he had married former movie star Janet Gaynor five years earlier and retired to Palm Springs. His last Broadway production had been in 1962, and since then he had toured Joseph Cotton and his wife Patricia Medina in a two-person theatrical anthology and co-produced a dramatisation of a Thomas Wolfe novel at the Actors Theater in Beverly Hills. He still had theatrical clout, however, and had interested the young, flamboyant San Francisco director, William Ball, in including Anderson's *Hamlet* in his 1970–71 offerings.

William Ball was 38 years old in 1969. In a meteoric rise from Pittsburgh, where he founded the American Conservatory Theatre in 1965, he brought his organisation to San Francisco in 1967. Backed by the wealthy San Francisco Theater Foundation, Ball quickly established a reputation for exciting adventurous productions. Early in his tenure in San

---

157 *NYT* 28 Jan 1968: D27; *Variety* 29 Oct 1969: 1; *NYT* 19 Nov 1969: 44; *LAT* 20 Nov 1969. See also *Bulletin* 27 Dec 1969: 53–4. For an excellent account of Anderson's Hamlet by a theatre historian see Fiona Gregory, 'Crossing Genre, Age and Gender: Judith Anderson as Hamlet,' *Journal of American Drama and Theatre* 26.2, 2014.

Francisco he announced a *'Hamlet* Tetralogy': four versions of the play – one experimental, one traditional, *Rosencranz and Guildenstern Are Dead*, and a contemporary, fragmented, absurd production.[158]

The first of these productions was staged in May 1968, to a mixed critical reception to its 'antic, frantic affectation' and a Hamlet that did not stir the emotions. It was probably about this time that Paul Gregory approached William Ball with the suggestion of a *Hamlet* starring Judith Anderson. This would have appealed to Ball for many reasons. First of all, this was, as Howard Taubman put it in the *New York Times*, a 'Theater with Pluck.' Moreover, Ball insisted that his actors move well (for this he used the Alexander Technique) and that they should speak with clarity – characteristics for which Anderson was considered the model.[159]

When William Ball announced his tetralogy, he described his first *Hamlet* as 'a directorial experiment in sound.' He wanted to 'explore the resources of the actors' verbal expressivity and achieve dramatic impact in an assault on the emotions through the ear of the audience.' The emphasis would be on the text, with limited movement, spectacle, colour, lighting and composition. The experience would be spare and classical – more Greek than Renaissance in quality. These were the ideas he poured into Anderson's *Hamlet*. 'From the beginning, William Ball's staging of Judith Anderson's *Hamlet* is aimed in a single direction,' *Los Angeles Times* critic, Dan Sullivan, wrote after her appearance at Royce Hall, UCLA. 'It is intended to set her apart to set her off like a priceless jewel to be admired from afar.'

---

158   *NYT* 8 Sep 1966: 43; *WPTH* 16 Apr 1967: L1; *LAT* 27 Sep 1967: d12; obituary, *Guardian* 6 Aug 1991: 29; William Ball, *A Sense of Direction: Some Observations On The Art Of Directing*, 1984.
159   *NYT* 10 Jun 1968: 59; 18 Feb 1969: 34; *LAT* 13 May 1968: C24.

> *Much as a concert artist will make a guest appearance with the local symphony, Dame Judith is served up, not as a member of a cast of players, but as the star attraction – a solitary figure in traditional black against velvet surroundings of a deep and rich wine color: designer Robert Fletcher's low, asymetrical platforms, jagged screens and uniformed performers (boots, pants, tunics and gowns of the same cut and cloth, blending with the background and each other).*
>
> *No furniture. No props...* [160]

From the announcement of the production in October 1969, it had attracted incredulity and a certain degree of mockery. Dan Knapp in the *Los Angeles Times* could not resist the temptation to have fun with the concept: 'Lady Hamlet. There is nothing like a Dame Judith Anderson,' he wrote. 'But as Hamlet?' 'Poor Yorick Will Flip His Skull Over This Hamlet,' Michael Kernan wrote in the *Washington Post and Times Herald*. 'Should an Actress attempt to play Hamlet?' Margaret Harford asked in the *Los Angeles Times*.[161]

Anderson was still much in the public eye at the end of 1969: her 1960 *Macbeth* was re-run at 19 Los Angeles theaters that October; her recent movie, *A Man Called Horse*, was being widely publicised; and she was about to make another *Hallmark Hall of Fame* appearance in *File on Devlin*. In New York to attend the retrospective of George Schaefer's television productions, she told Louis Calta of the *New York Times* that she wanted to play *Hamlet* because it 'encompasses every emotional note on the scale.' 'He's just a human being in torment,' she told another interviewer. To another she emphasised that 'the music of his words is all-important.'[162]

---

160 *LAT* 27 Sep 1967: d12. For a good description of the staging see Morlin Bell, Review, *Educational Theatre Journal* 1 May 1971: 197.
161 *LAT* 29 Oct 1969: G1; 13 Sep 1970: P41; *WPTH* 3 May 1970: G1.
162 *LAT* 10 Oct 1969: h13; 16 Nov 1969: n79d; *Variety* 28 Oct 1969: 114 [full-page];

In Judith Anderson's mind, therefore, and in the mind of director William Ball, the success of this *Hamlet* lay in her rendition of a 'tortured, humiliated, agonized soul' – a human being whose gender was immaterial – through a voice that conveyed 'the magic and music of Shakespeare's language.' By 'ripping the traditional skin off the play' and 'shaping the ingredients in the form of a modern sculpture,' the production asked more of this 73-year-old actress (and her audience) than had ever been asked before.[163]

Anderson's *Hamlet* opened in preview with three performances from 24 to 26 September 1970 in her hometown of Santa Barbara. The following week she opened a three-week engagement at the American Conservatory Theatre's home theatre, the Geary in San Francisco. The *Los Angeles Times* critic, Dan Sullivan, who was often critical of William Ball's more extravagant ventures, was appalled: he found the performance 'so far off the mark in conception and execution that it is hard to know where to start.' Anderson's 'heavy haunted voice belongs in the National Archives as a permanent treasure,' he conceded ('nobody hovers on the edge of tears so thrillingly'); and her reinterpretations of emotional moments were often brilliant. But she was, in his opinion, the victim of three obdurate facts: 'She is a woman. She is a rather a short woman. She is Judith Anderson.' 'Alone, in the soliloquies, she is Judith Anderson reading Shakespeare – beautifully, too'; but every interaction with another actor brought 'a distracting and sometimes ludicrous ghost-image' – of Lady Macbeth, of Miss Jean Brodie, of Norma Desmond buying Joe a suit. 'Dame Judith is not Hamlet, nor was meant to be,' he concluded. 'One is sorry, with so many challenging classical roles still at her disposal, that she had to try this

---

NYT 19 Nov 1969: 44; *CSM* 25 Sep 1970: 4; *LAHE* 19 Sep 1970, MHL.
163   *LAT* 27 Sep 1970: 30, 40.

one.' Four years later he still recalled his discomfort when he described a play that 'gave this reviewer the worst time he has had since Judith Anderson played Hamlet.'[164]

For *Oakland Tribune* critic Robert Taylor the voice and the emotion were enough to take the performance beyond a curiosity. 'What a voice!' he wrote. 'Miss Anderson is not like an aging opera singer whose range has grown narrower.'

She growls and spits out her vengeance at Claudius… and when she cries, we can hear the heart break.

The *San Francisco Examiner*, however, saw only 'a matronly cry baby who is neither commanding nor moving.' The *National Observer* was more cruel, with its headline 'Hamlet's Mother Plays Him'; and the *Daily Pioneer* flatly called it 'a fiasco.' Nathan Cohen, Canada's leading critic, hated everything about the production. Under the headline 'Female Hamlet Never Satisfying,' he described 'a meagerly-attended, apathetically received performance' that lacked colour and was poorly directed and staged.[165]

These reviews must have pierced Anderson's heart. But, as William Ball told an interviewer, she was 'as tough as a set of claws'; and she was convinced that the national audience in schools and colleges and small towns across the country were hungry for the 'greatness' she could bring them. On 19 October 1970 she set off on a 26-week national tour of 123 theatres. The Shakespeare Society of America produced a special edition of their magazine to honour the Hamlets of the century, including Dame Judith's. When she appeared in Palm Springs (the home town of her producer Paul Gregory), the women's committee of the Palm Springs Desert Museum

---

164   *This Week in Santa Barbara,* Theatre Issue, 24–26 Sep 1970: 21, Prompt, NLA; *LAT* 1 Oct 1970: G1; 9 Sep 1974: G1.
165   *OT; SFE; WPTH* 2 Oct 1970: D8; *National Observer* 5 Oct 1970: 17; [St Paul?] *Daily Pioneer* 6 Oct 1970; *Toronto Daily Star* 27 Oct 1970, UCSB.

chartered three buses to take pre-curtain diners to the performance at the local high school. The *La Crosse Tribune* wrote warmly that 'Dame Judith Triumphs.' But Chicago, which had always loved Judith Anderson, regretfully admitted that they were 'Rooting in Vain for Dame Judith.' 'We all have learned to love and respect and admire Dame Judith,' William Leonard wrote in the *Chicago Tribune*, 'and she certainly has brought the rich experience of half a century's career to the production.'

> *Seldom has there been a Hamlet who enunciated the immortal lines with more feeling, or more sincerity. The cadences, the emphasis, the timing, the ringing of each vowel – all are beautiful and affecting.*
>
> *But the trouble is, it doesn't work.*
>
> *Judith Anderson is no more Hamlet, Prince of Denmark, than Joe Namath is Cleopatra, Queen of Egypt.*
>
> *If all those lovely utterances of hers were in a baritone, this might be one of the finest Hamlets of our generation. But the credibility just isn't there.*

'Devotee of Shakespeare owe it to themselves to see Dame Judith Anderson as the young prince of Denmark – strictly as a collector's item,' he concludes. 'Others had better wait for something else.'[166]

In mid-January 1971, 'bloodied but unbowed by rapier sharp notices,' as Dan Knapp put it, Anderson moved off the college circuit to give two performances at New York's Carnegie Hall. Mel Gussow, the new young reviewer at the *New York Times*, was merciless. He attacked, not only the 'absurdity' of her attempt, but also her acting. 'She has no concept, no consistent approach,' he wrote. 'This is a

---

166   *CSM* 25 Sep 1970: 4; *Variety* 11 Nov 1970: 1; *LAT* 6 Nov 1970: I3; *La Crosse Tribune*, [17? Dec 1970], UCSB; *CT* 29 Dec 1970: a4.

bloodless production, with no power, poetry, or humor.' 'Mostly she plays with a pained expression, fixed gestures… and many sighs and suspirations,' he continued relentlessly. 'One hates to be inhospitable, but this play is not even vanity – more like arrant knavery.'[167]

William Glover at the *Los Angeles Times* was more forgiving. The Anderson Hamlet has 'an odd, disturbing quality,' he wrote, but you have to ignore its peculiarity and concentrate on the majestic lines, which she handles with technical brilliance. 'This Hamlet is an experience you may admire or spurn,' he concludes, 'but won't easily forget.' John Beaufort, in the *Christian Science Monitor*, was ready to judge it for what it was – 'a somewhat stylized concert reading rather than a full-scale performance.' 'Since the idea of a woman's playing Hamlet goes all the way back to Mrs Siddons,' he wrote, 'it does not deserve to be classified as a stunt, however unusual.' He praises Anderson's attempts to solve the inherent problems posed by such an attempt and the warmth and simplicity of its staging. Her old friend Lillian Gish told an interviewer, 'No, I certainly have *not* ever played Hamlet, and I didn't go to see Judith in it – I knew I couldn't go back to my friend and say I liked it'; and Helen Hayes incurred her anger by saying that she had stubbed her toe on *Hamlet*.[168]

Bob Mondello, on Public Broadcasting's *All Things Considered* some years later, gave a welcome personal account of Anderson's power and versatility in her much maligned *Hamlet*:

> *She was 67 when I caught her on a college tour performing 'Hamlet.' Not performing in 'Hamlet,' you understand. She'd done that more than 30 years earlier, playing Sir*

---

167 *LAT* 6 Jan 1971: H7; *NYT* 15 Jan 1971: 18.
168 *LAT* 16 Jan 1971: C7; *CSM* 18 Jan 1971: 4; *WPTH* 1 Dec 1973: F1, 2; *NYDN* 2 Dec 1973: 13, 16, NYPL.

John Gielgud's mother on Broadway. No, at 67 she was performing all of 'Hamlet' — Gertrude to grave digger, every word and every character in a student lounge for an audience of about 50. We were all transfixed by something many of us had expected to be high camp, an aging theatrical legend past her prime. Dame Judith was clearly in her prime. Though she never spoke loudly, her deep voice must have resonated all the way out into the quad because people kept peering in and then staying. After just a moment or two, they had no trouble believing her as Hamlet. I remember being more surprised that her teen-age Ophelia was so delicate and feminine because audiences had always loved her in take-charge roles, especially ones that allowed her to run a gamut of emotions, like the sinister housekeeper in Hitchcock's **Rebecca** *who tries to convince Joan Fontaine to abandon Laurence Olivier and throw herself into the ocean.*[169]

As the tour moved on through Syracuse, Binghamton, Ithaca, Rochester and Bethlehem, Pennsylvania, it is somehow sad to see this 74-year-old's notation in her diary as they travel from Buffalo to Fredonia, 'Birthday Party in Bus.'[170] Her Washington reception would not have gladdened her weary spirit, as veteran critic Richard Coe lamented that the performance was 'gallant, but not Hamlet.'[171] When she finally wrote 'Finis' in her diary on 2 March 1971, marking the end of the Hamlet tour, Dame Judith Anderson probably felt that is was the end of her stage career as well.

---

169   Bob Mondello, *All Things Considered*, NPR, 1992.
170   Diary 10 Feb 1971.
171   *WPTH* 19 Feb 1971: B1, 2.

Dame Judith, now playing the nurse, will break your heart
Glenne Currie, United Press International 1982

Chapter Thirty-four
Medea Recidiva 1982–92

> *Time has not eroded the gravity of Anderson's voice nor the dignity of her presence. She gives a touching performance as the befuddled witness to Medea's horrible acts.*
>
> James Lardner, *Washington Post*, 1982

In 1979, when Judith Anderson was 82, it seemed that she was finally retired, basking in the pleasures of family, friends and garden. As British actor Emlyn Williams wrote after enjoying her hospitality that year, 'You exude such vitality and fun – no wonder your family loves you, and Santa Barbara seems to appreciate your presence too!'[172]

Since she had written 'Finis' to her *Hamlet* tour, Anderson had returned to Australia to make her penultimate – and most bizarre – movie, *The Inn of the Damned*, a pioneering attempt by Australian New Wave filmmakers to capture the US market with an 'Aussie/Western variation on the *Psycho* formula.' She had made several well-received television movies, including Enid Bagnold's *The Chinese Prime Minister*, in a performance that Cecil Smith in the *Los Angeles Times* described as 'so completely realised and deeply felt that you would like to hang it in a closet so you could take it out every once in a while simply to admire its perfection.' Always dreaming

---
172 Emlyn Williams to Anderson, 1 Nov 1979, UCSB.

of bringing greatness to her audience, she contemplated a one-woman show playing her heroine Sarah Bernhardt.[173]

As she prepared for a rare public performance at the Jeffers Festival, however, in May 1979, there was a strong note of loss when she told an interviewer flatly, 'I'm not in demand.' Anderson's old friends and colleagues were fading away. Alfred Lunt died in 1977, Jed Harris in November 1979 and Olga Lee in August 1980. Some, however, were still going strong. Maurice Evans and Helen Hayes were performing on board luxury liners in 1977; Bette Davis was travelling with a one-woman show; and Cathleen Nesbitt, at 88, was thanking God that she was still getting roles.[174]

Dame Judith was also not ready to fade into obscurity. In 1977 she had seen Zoe Caldwell in a 'superlative' television production of *Sarah*, on the life of Bernhardt. Here, she thought, was the ideal new Medea. Two years later, when her former producer Robert Whitehead, now a distinguished theatrical figure, was in California to try out his latest production, she called him, their old feud forgotten, urging him to revive *Medea* with this marvellous actress. She herself, she told Whitehead in her deep resonant voice, would play the Nurse.[175]

Anderson had not recognised Caldwell as the young Australian who had played one of the chorus during her Australian tour of *Medea* in 1955. Nor had she realised that this superb actress was now married to Robert Whitehead. In suggesting this revival of her great play, she was, in fact, courting new theatrical royalty.

Born in 1933, Zoe Caldwell was the daughter of a Melbourne plumber and a stage-struck mother who enrolled

---

173 Diary 13 Nov 1973; *SMH* 14 Nov 1973: 2; 18 Nov 1975: 7; *Variety* 8 May 1974: 229; *LAT* 23 Oct 1974: F1; Williams to Anderson, 19 Nov 1972, UCSB.
174 *LAT* 3 May 1979: SE_A1; WP 16 Jan 1977: F11; *NYT* 19 Jan: 59; 17 Aug 1977: 60.
175 *NYT* 30 Nov 1977: 76; *LAT* 18 Jan 1981: x52; *HR* 13 Jul 1981, MHL.

her in elocution lessons at age seven. Like Anderson, she came up through elocution competitions and amateur theatricals. Like Anderson, she was never a beauty, but had a vivid presence. And she had enormous talent, which was nurtured in Melbourne's Union Theatre Repertory Company, along with Noel Ferrier and Barry Humphries.

In 1955 she was one of three actors from the Union Theatre chosen to appear with Anderson when she inaugurated the Elizabethan Theatre Trust with a national tour of *Medea*. Considered Australia's finest young actress, Caldwell went to England when she was 24 on a three-year scholarship to the Shakespeare Memorial Theatre at Stratford-upon-Avon. In 1963 she joined the Minneapolis repertory company of Tyrone Guthrie, with whom she had worked in Stratford. Critic Claudia Cassidy of the *Chicago Tribune*, who had always been a great supporter of Judith Anderson, was equally admiring of this young Australian, who had, like her predecessor, 'voice, manner and style.' Three years later, at the age of 33, she was discovered by Broadway, where she immediately won a Tony award for her role in Tennessee Williams' *Slapstick Tragedy*. Within another two years – a 'sexy dame' with red hair and freckles who 'talks a blue streak' – she had won an Emmy for *The Prime of Miss Jean Brodie*. The same year, 1968, she married her producer, Robert Whitehead, who had made his debut 21 years before with Anderson's *Medea*.[176]

Over the next few years Caldwell combined motherhood (the couple had two sons, born in 1969 and 1972) with appearances in London's West End as Lady Hamilton in *Bequest to the Nation*, as Colette off-Broadway, as Eve in Arthur Miller's *The Creation of the World and Other Business*, as Alice

---

[176] *Argus* 18 May: 9; 16 Aug 1955: 9; *CT* 9 May 1963: c9; *Canberra Times* 17 Jun 1966: 13; *LAT* 12 Nov 1967: P20; *NYT* 22 Apr: 58; 18 Jan: 46; 28 Jan: D1; 4 Feb: D1, 2; 10 May 1968: 55.

in Strindberg's *Dance Of Death*, and as Mary Tyrone in *Long Day's Journey Into Night*.[177]

Since 1947, when Robert Whitehead began his career with *Medea*, he had become one of the country's most successful and admired producers, often in collaboration with wealthy businessman Roger Stevens. The 'New Power Behind Broadway' by the mid-1950s, Stevens had pursued a number of daring projects with Anderson at that time, none of which had come to fruition. By 1979, when Whitehead approached him with the idea of the *Medea* revival, he was one of America's most powerful political and theatrical figures. The first Chairman of the National Council on the Arts (later the National Endowment for the Arts) in 1965, he was Chairman of the Board and 'Master Money-Raiser' for what became the Kennedy Center for the Performing Arts, which opened in Washington DC in 1971. The Eisenhower Theater at the Kennedy Center was a frequent venue for Whitehead and Stevens productions during the 1970s, and became the logical place to stage the *Medea* revival.[178]

The Kennedy Center celebrated its tenth birthday in 1981 with a disappointing season in which Sir Ralph Richardson played to half and two-thirds houses and Roger Stevens had two heart attacks. He was glad, therefore, to add *Medea* to the 1981–2 season, along with revivals of Durrenmatt's *The Physicists*, *The Late Christopher Bean*, *The Imaginary Invalid* and *Ghosts*. The critics did not like the 'sadly feeble' *Physicists*, nor the 'weary revival' of *Christopher Bean*; so they were electrified by 'The Magic of *Medea*' when it opened at the Kennedy Center on 6 March 1982.[179]

---

177 *Canberra Times* 8 Jul 1969: 4; *AWW* 30 Aug 1972: 24; *NYT* 25 Sep: 36; 7 May 1970: 59; 25 Oct 1972: 42; 5 Apr 1974: 24; 23 Oct 1977: D6; *WP* 28 Aug 1975: B14.
178 *LAT* 5 Nov 1955: 15; 24 Feb 1965: 4; *WPTH* 11 Mar 1969: B1; 7 Sep 1971: B1; 29 Oct: L3; 29 Feb 1972: C1; *NYT* 8 Sep 1971: 52; *WP* 3 Oct 1980: C1.
179 *WP* 28 Jun: K1; 30 Sep: B1, 2; 18 Dec 1981: W9; 26 Jan: C1; 8 Mar 1982: B1–2; *NYT*

The new *Medea* had opened early in February at the Clarence Brown Theatre at the University of Tennessee, Knoxville, for a two-week run. To mark the passing on of the role, Anderson presented Caldwell onstage after the first performance with the Mucha poster of Bernhardt as Medea that she had received when she first played Jason's vengeful wife. On opening night at the Kennedy Center, David Richards of the *Washington Post* found Caldwell 'mesmerising.' Against the background of Ben Edwards' classical set, with its massive pillared doorway 'rising into the chill of a starry night,' Caldwell accentuated Medea's foreignness – her exoticism and her sexuality.[180]

The *Post*'s music critic Joseph McLellan was old enough to remember Anderson in the role, and felt that Anderson's 'relatively understated' (!!) performance had had more impact than Caldwell's operatic, Tosca-like approach. But Caldwell's interpretation of the role fitted well with the 1980s' fascination with 'difference.' Richard L Coe, the *Post*'s veteran drama critic, hailed Caldwell's 'awesome daring and ingenuity' in a performance he would remember, he wrote, for a lifetime. 'She gives us a blazingly barbaric Medea,' he wrote, 'someone far beyond the horizon of the Greeks, fully capable of the magic with which Jason could obtain the Golden Fleece. She is not a Greek and, ill at ease in their terrain, expresses natural force against the serene civility of her husband's people.' 'The concept is wholly unlike Anderson's,' he continued:

> *Her Medea had tried to assimilate a civilization she respected. She was an outsider who had made it into the inside. Caldwell's Medea remains the outsider, battles for*

---

30 Sep: C27; 2 Oct 1981: C15.
180   *WT* 1 Sep 1996: 4; *WP* 8 Mar 1982: B1–2.

her individuality and scorns what to her are the new mores. Africa looking at the rest of the world? The Uzbeks scorning directions from Moscow?

Choosing this image, the actress goes at it with no holds barred. She writhes, undulates, caresses her thighs. Her voice never hits the same tone twice in succession. Blazing from within, her eyes see only a vengeance invisible to others. Her passion is both exotic and believable, and mainly because of her, so, too, is the production.[181]

Commentators were intrigued by 'the strange sequence of chance encounters, bizarre parallels, hard words and shared memories' that led to this *Medea* – the fact that Robert Whitehead had produced the original 1947 performance by Anderson; that the young Zoe Caldwell had played the second Corinthian woman when Anderson had taken the play to Australia in 1955; that Anderson had seen Caldwell's television performance as Bernhardt and had told Whitehead she must play Medea, not knowing that the two were married. Most of all they loved the fact that the 85-year-old Anderson was now playing the Nurse to Caldwell's Medea. As Anderson put it, 'If anything ever came full circle, this is it.'

Whitehead and Caldwell were initially terrified at the thought of doing the play with its former star in the production. But it turned out to be a triumph, artistically and personally. 'I think it's terribly important for actors to have a chance to work with other actors who have become part of their traditions,' Caldwell told one reporter. 'It's like life, death and rebirth'; and Whitehead was grateful that he and Anderson had achieved a friendship that made him aware of all he had lost during the 30 years they had been estranged.[182]

Critics praised the decision to cast Anderson as the Nurse

---

181   *WP* 12 Mar: W5; 4 Apr 1982: G1.
182   *WP* Feb 28, 1982: H1, 3; *NYT* 16 Jan 1982: 15.

and were full of admiration for her performance. 'Time has not eroded the gravity of Anderson's voice nor the dignity of her presence,' James Lardner wrote in the *Washington Post*. 'She gives a touching performance as the befuddled witness to Medea's horrible acts.' But, he added, 'above and beyond the particular distinctions of this revival,' there is the sense of a torch being passed along. Unlike European theater, he pointed out, the American theater is more cavalier about such matters of tradition.[183]

When the play opened on Broadway on 2 May, Frank Rich at the *New York Times* was enthralled by the 'special flame' that Caldwell brought to the character of Medea. 'Euripides demands an intense psychological realism from actors,' he wrote. 'and that is what Miss Caldwell has bestowed on her marathon role.'

> *This actress makes us believe in the warped logic by which Medea murders her two sons to wreak vengeance on Jason, the ambitious husband who has betrayed her for a Greek princess. And because she does, we are, by evening's end, brought right into the thunderclap of Euripides' tragedy.*

Equally the heroine of the hour was Dame Judith, greeted affectionately from the welcome-back ovation at the theatre to the 'hands reaching out to make contact with the tiny, 81-year-old actress' at the opening night party at Sardi's, which 'hummed with reminiscence… as aging theatregoers boasted, with a certain rueful bravado, of having seen the 1947 production starring Judith Anderson.' Glenne Currie of United Press International stated simply, 'Dame Judith, now playing the nurse, will break your heart.' Jack Kroll, in *Newsweek*, noted that 84-year-old Anderson 'plays the nurse with an eloquent simplicity that's beautiful to behold.' Edwin Wilson,

---

183   *NYT* 2 May 1982: D1; *NYSN* 2 May 1982, Leisure: 3, 15.

reviewing what he called 'A Strong Play About the Agonies of Apartheid' in the *Wall Street Journal,* praised her for 'the poise and power of an actress half her age.' Clive Barnes, in the *New York Post,* admired her 'magnificently gnarled dignity.' *Variety,* more cynically, called it 'an impressive performance from a venerable legit star, and incidentally a shrewd bit of casting.'[184]

Both Zoe Caldwell and Judith Anderson were nominated for Tonys for their performances in *Medea.* Caldwell, pitted against Katharine Hepburn in *The West Side Waltz*, Geraldine Page in *Agnes of God* and Amanda Plummer in *A Taste of Honey*, was the winner of the Best Actress award; Anderson, competing with Mia Dillon and Mary Beth Hurt in *Crimes of the Heart* and Amanda Plummer in *Agnes of God*, lost to up-and-coming young Plummer in the Best Featured Actress category. She had, after all, won a Tony for her original performance in *Medea* in 1947.

The new *Medea* reached a huge audience when a 90-minute television version was shown on PBS in April 1983 as part of *Kennedy Center Tonight.* Filmed in Canada in November 1982 and skilfully directed by the BBC's Mark Cullingham, it was hailed as 'a lesson in classical acting which will remain as unforgettable for viewers as the tragic theme itself.' 'Dame Judith counterpoints the shrill harshness of Medea with a calm melancholy,' Arthur Unger wrote in the *Christian Science Monitor.* 'To miss *Medea* would be tragedy,' the *Chicago Tribune* headlined. In a masterly discussion of the differences between the stage and the television productions, John Corry of the *New York Times* called it 'a triumph of nuance.' 'The camera changes the focus,' he wrote. 'Other things swim into view.'

---

184   *NYT* 5 May 1982: C19 & 23; *Newsweek* 17 May 1982, MHL; *WSJ* 7 May 1982: 27; *Variety* 5 May 1982: 152.

Judith Anderson's nurse, for one, is more imposing on television, more full of presence. Miss Anderson looks, she listens, she scarcely seems to be acting at all. When the nurse tells Medea that she has seen Creon and his daughter burning alive, the flesh falling from their bones, Miss Anderson speaks quietly, but it is certain that even as she speaks she sees the flames. The camera, forcing us to look squarely at Miss Anderson, Miss Caldwell huddled against her, narrows our vision. We see with a different mind's eye.[185]

Medea marked the beginning of a final resurgence in Judith Anderson's career. At 85 she was once more a celebrity. She was interviewed by her old friend Mary Martin on PBS program on ageing, *Over Easy*; she was the subject of a long article by Cecil Smith in the *Los Angeles Times*; and the Directors Guild presented her with the Lifetime Achievement Award of the Academy of Television Arts and Sciences, where she expressed her eternal gratitude to her 'stage and TV and film family' and especially 'to dear George Schaefer.'[186]

But there was more to come in that career. In August 1983 she was encouraged by her grand-nephew to accept the part of the Vulcan Princess in *Star Trek III*. In June 1984 the Lion Theatre on West 42nd Street was renamed the Judith Anderson Theatre, as *Star Trek III* premiered and Anderson announced that she would join the cast of the television soap *Santa Barbara* as the matriarch Birdie Lockwood. To friends and fans who criticised her, she replied that there was no indignity in earning $5,000 a week. As she told *New York Times*' Peter Kaplan, 'Bernhardt would have accepted it.' To

---

185 *Monessen Valley Independent* [Penn], 16 Sep 1982; *Time* 20 Sep 1982: 72; *Variety* 12 Nov 1982; *CSM* 19 Apr 1983: 18; *CT* 20 Apr 1983: d9; *NYT* 20 Apr 1983: C.27.
186 *LAT* 20 Apr 1983: G1; *New Castle News* [Penn] 10 Dec 1982; *HR* 1 Jun 1983, MHL.

Judith Anderson as the Vulcan High Priestess in Star Trek III: The Search for Spock *1984*
Author's collection

Jill Evans, in the *Weekend Australian*, she confessed how much she wanted to work again. It was an 'awful thing to rot away,' she added.[187]

Anderson's friends and colleagues continued to drop away. Her dear friend Wright Ludington was confined to his final beautiful home, October Hill, and would see no one. Her long-forgotten husband, Luther Greene, and her late-life friend, Emlyn Williams, died in 1987. Angna Enters, Maurice Evans, Laurence Olivier, Aileen Pringle and Valentina, who had designed those beautiful dresses for her 50 years before, all died in 1989. In 1990, the friend of her early days in Hollywood, Mary Martin, and Henry Brandon, who had so often played Jason to her Medea, died.

But she still made new friends. In 1985 the playwright

---

187 *LAT* 16 Sep 1984: S5; *Doylestown Intelligencer* (Penn) 26 Sep 1984; *NYT* 11 Jun 1984; *Weekend Australian* 22–23 Sep 1984: 5.

James Prideaux was looking for the right person to play an elderly actress in his new play *Bread*. George Schaefer was to direct the television production and suggested her for the part. 'She could no longer remember lines and the filming was difficult,' Prideaux recalled, 'but her performance was exquisite. She acted with a clarity that astonished and delighted me.' This began a friendship that lasted until her death. 'There was never a friend more loyal,' Prideaux wrote. 'She was also a passionate supporter of one's work and full of ideas for projects. Had I sent my new play to Robert Whitehead? Had I talked with Toby Rowland in London? How about tackling a new play on Mary Stuart? Why didn't I write something about Sarah Bernhardt that Zoe Caldwell could do on the stage? It was just this interest that I think kept her young.'[188]

Bread was Anderson's last television play, but she continued in *Santa Barbara* until June 1987, a few months after her 90th birthday. Her beautiful voice was still heard as The Sister of Purgatory in the television film *Impure Thoughts* (1986) and on recordings, where she read from the Bible with 'commanding clarity, dignity and unforced eloquence.' She continued to read Robinson Jeffers' poetry at commemorative occasions.[189]

In April 1985 she made 'a brief, classy appearance' as guest of honour at the annual Los Angeles Drama Critics Circle awards. In November, she was part of 'the largest reunion ever of film stars from Hollywood's golden era.' In March 1986 she travelled to San Diego to receive a Women's International Center Living Legacy Award for dedicating 'time, money and God-given talent' to humanity. The following year she offered a tribute to her friend from the twenties, the sculptor, poet and art historian, Agnes Yarnell.[190]

---

188 *Variety* 30 Sep 1985: 24; *WP* 6 Oct 1985: TV3: 3; *LAT* Jan 6, 1992: 5.
189 *LAT* 15 Jul 1986: 4; 19 Apr 1987: 4; *RJN* Dec 1986 & Spr 1994.
190 *Variety* 27 Nov 1985: 4; *Tribune* (San Diego) 10 Mar 1986: D-2; *LAT* 9 Mar 1987: 1.

Dame Judith, still elegant at 89, attends the premiere of Just Between Friends *Santa Monica 1986*

Ron Galella/Getty Images

Increasingly Santa Barbara was the focus of her life. A 1985 *Los Angeles Times* article depicted 'Dame Jude' in the beautiful Blue Room of her Montecito house, enjoying the companionship of the latest in her long line of dachshunds, Bozo, given her by Robert Whitehead and Zoe Caldwell, and named for them. Surprisingly, in view of her lack of interests in her own movies, she agreed to act as chairman of the honorary board of directors of the Santa Barbara Film Festival and appeared with other movie veterans at its inauguration in 1985 and every other year until her final illness. In 1989 she returned to the stage, introduced by fellow Santa Barbara resident Robert Mitchum, in 'Poems of a Silent Man,' a recitation of about 20 short poems of Robinson Jeffers. In 1990 George Schaefer, now professor of theater and associate dean of the UCLA School of Theater, Film and Television, dedicated an acting award to his former star.[191]

In August 1991 Judith Anderson suffered what was first thought to be a stroke, but was later diagnosed as a tumor on the brain. For a while she was able to return home, where she received visitors in her elegant bedroom, surrounded by exquisite furniture and golden cherubs dancing on the walls. 'Bozo reclined at her feet – one eye always on her,' James Prideaux remembered, 'and across the room French doors were open to provide a view of the magnificent mountains.' The previous June, Anderson's name had appeared on the Queen's Birthday List as the recipient of a Companion of the Order of Australia, the highest honour an Australian can receive. In September, her friends gathered in her garden to see the Australian Consul General present her with the medal. 'I'd thought we'd have the ceremony around her bed,' Prideaux wrote of the occasion, 'but there she was suddenly in the garden, dressed, helped into a high-backed chair. Behind it the Australian flag fluttered on a standard. Oh, how old she was and how ill and gallant!'

'We stood as the Australian national anthem was played,' Prideaux continued, 'even Judith attempting, futilely, to rise. Nevertheless, as the Consul General read out the proclamation and gently pinned the medal on her chest, she sat as straight as a ramrod, proud, humble, deeply moved.'[192]

Three months later she was dead, a month before her 95th birthday.

---

191   *LAT* 20 Oct 1985: y10; 11 Oct 1985: 1; 5 Nov 1989: 53; *Variety* 17 & 25 Feb 1987; 8 Mar 1990; *HR* 9 Feb 1990, MHL; *RJN* 77, 1989; *LAT* 31 May: 2; 8 Jun 1990: 2; *UCLA Daily Bruin* 7 Jun 1990: 38, MHL.
192   *SMH* 10 Jun 1991: 4; *LAT*, Jan 6, 1992: 5.; *HR* 20 Sep 1991, MHL.

ACT VI
Finis

Plaque commemorating Dame Judith Anderson in the wall of the Adelaide Festival Centre. It is currently in storage during the redevelopment of the Centre.
Performing Arts Collection, Adelaide Festival Centre

Chapter Thirty-five

The (Almost) Last First Lady

> *For years she was one of the first ladies of the American theater, repeatedly portraying women gripped by powerful emotions... Her fiery portrait of a barbarian woman who takes revenge on Jason, the unfaithful father of her two sons by murdering them won the actress an honored niche in theater history.*
>
> Eric Pace, New York Times January 1992

James Prideaux's first reaction to the news of Anderson's death was to go home and watch her *Medea*.

'It was, as always, like an electric shock to see such power in a performance,' he wrote a few days later. 'There was not another actress on the face of the globe who could ascend such dazzling heights of drama. No voice would ever again match the beauty of Dame Judith's. No soul would ever be bared so nakedly. No cries would issue so terrifyingly from the human heart.'

'But,' he mused, 'that was only a small part of her remarkable career. Who can forget the wicked Mrs. Danvers in *Rebecca*? Who doesn't remember those lovely, muted scenes – so beautifully underplayed – with Vincent Price in *Laura*? And, going back, the glamorous nightclub owner in *Blood Money*? Or the disfigured gun moll in *Lady Scarface*?

'Or,' he went on, ' – the list seems endless – her vicious Lady Macbeth opposite Maurice Evans in *Macbeth*? Her motherly Gertrude with Sir John Gielgud in *Hamlet*? Her frustrated sister with Katherine Cornell and Ruth Gordon in *The Three Sisters*? Her very small Big Mama in *Cat on a Hot Tin Roof*?'[1]

Anderson's obituaries tended not to remember so variously. The *New York Times* and the *Washington Post* set the tone for how she would be recollected. As Eric Pace of the *Times* wrote:

> *Dame Judith Anderson, who electrified Broadway audiences in 1947 with her savage performance of the title role in Medea and was a memorably sinister housekeeper in the 1940 film Rebecca, died yesterday at her home in Santa Barbara, Calif… For years she was one of the first ladies of the American theater, repeatedly portraying women gripped by powerful emotions… Her fiery portrait of a barbarian woman who takes revenge on Jason, the unfaithful father of her two sons by murdering them won the actress an honored niche in theater history.*[2]

Martin Weil of the *Post* emphasised the darkness of her portrayals even more:

> *As Lady Macbeth on Broadway in 1941, she was described as 'almost too frightening to be watched.' In the title role of Medea in 1947 she was, in the words of another critic, 'pure evil, dark, dangerous, cruel, raging, ruthless.'*
>
> *In the film version of* **Rebecca***, her Mrs Danvers was a malignant presence that, film observers said, embedded itself in the minds of audiences as the personification of evil.*

---

1 James Prideaux, 'An Appreciation. Remembering a Terrific Dame,' *LAT* 6 Jan, 1992: 5, F6.
2 Eric Pace, 'Dame Judith Anderson Dies at 93; An Actress of Powerful Portrayals,' *NYT* 4 Jan 1992: 27.

He also provided some personal touches that aligned her personality with her roles:

Through her devotion to her art, the fiery intensity of her presence, and even the touches of off-stage temperament for which she was known, she became for generations the embodiment of theatrical stardom…

Described as both light-hearted and taciturn, she once hinted at the sources of her onstage thunder. 'I have not myself a very serene temperament,' she said.[3]

Bob Mondello, in his personal account on Public Broadcasting's *All Things Considered* of Anderson's power and versatility in *Hamlet*, also remembered her last theatrical role, the Nurse in *Medea* 10 years before:

I remember the moment Anderson strode on stage. Regal at 84, I realized she was still a star and that this was a generous gesture. I also remember that her voice sent a chill up my spine.[4]

Other obituaries made passing reference to the fact that Anderson had not always played sinister roles. A widely-reprinted article quoted a 1961 interview in which she had complained: '"People always think of me as playing these terrible, terrible women… but no one remembers the pleasant people I've played – Mary, the mother of Jesus, and so many others. I haven't always been an ogre."'[5]

The most thoughtful review of Anderson's career was written by W J Weatherby, the longtime correspondent for the British *Guardian*, who was to die himself a few months later.

---

[3] Martin Weil, 'Obituaries. Actress Judith Anderson Dies at 93,' *WP* 4 Jan 1992: D4.
[4] 'In Memoriam. Actress Judith Anderson Dies,' *All Things Considered*: 1. Washington, D.C.: National Public Radio, Jan 4, 1992.
[5] 'Dame Judith Anderson, Broadway star and screen villain, dies at 93,' *Austin American Statesman* 4 Jan 1992: A18.

With the reservations British critics had always held about Anderson's over-the-top performances, he described her as 'a grande dame of the English-speaking theatre who was born in the wrong period to be fully appreciated.' 'Often at odds with current realistic styles and low key private lives,' he wrote, 'she was more suited to the times of Mrs Patrick Campbell or Sarah Bernhardt, outsize personalities who reduced plays to vehicles and life to a glorified stage.'

> Dame Judith often seemed uncomfortable in modern realistic roles and at home only in Shakespearean or Greek tragedy or the few modern equivalents such as the Greek-influenced plays of Eugene O'Neill. When she did squeeze her awesome tragic presence into some modest contemporary character, she often appeared like a visitor from another play that was more serious and more grandly histrionic. In life, too, she gave much the same impression, seeming to exist on a mundane level with difficulty but with immense panache while she awaited the arrival of her deus ex machina...
>
> Although her outsized personality and classical appearance were unsuitable for most films, she will be remembered for Laura and King's Row, but especially as the formidable housekeeper, Mrs Danvers, in Hitchcock's Rebecca, whom she made the personification of evil. While making Star Trek III, the crew persuaded her to sing 'There Is Nothing Like A Dame'. She loved it.
>
> In her eighties, angry with old age for slowing her down and putting most stage roles beyond her physical powers, she began a new career in American TV soap operas like a grande dame slumming – and thoroughly enjoying it. Playing the matriarch of a once wealthy family with a wastrel son in Santa Barbara, a new daytime drama, she commented: 'I think Bernhardt, whom I worshipped, would have accepted a daytime drama if they'd offered one to her.

Except for the immorality, of which I heartily disapprove, I love the soaps. No matter what you do, if you care about it, if you're passionate about it, it becomes great. You strike a great chord, and after that, it's all music.'

Made a Dame in 1960, the year she played in The Seagull at the Edinburgh Festival and at the Old Vic, she was twice divorced and gave gardening as her 'recreation'. But even her gardens, magnificent displays of her favourite flowers, seemed to reflect a larger-than-life personality who charged even routine moments with dramatic importance.[6]

Later appreciations of Anderson's career fought against what *Boston Herald* critic Arthur Friedman called the 'Mrs Danvers syndrome.' 'The Australian-born Anderson, who died last week at 93, had a wider range,' he wrote: 'witness her lovely Caedmon recording of Hans Christian Anderson's fairy tales and her portrayals of the yearning Olga in Chekhov's *Three Sisters* (opposite Katharine Cornell and Ruth Gordon), Maxwell Anderson's *Elizabeth the Queen*, Shakespeare's Gertrude (with John Gielgud as Hamlet), Lavinia in Eugene O'Neill's epic *Mourning Becomes Electra*, and mysterious Miss Madrigal in Enid Bagnold's *The Chalk Garden*.'[7] At the *Washington Post* Michael Kernan recalled 'A Fragile Grande Dame' preparing to play her ill-fated *Hamlet*.[8] Historian Garry Wills testified to how, as a young man, a recording of Anderson in *Medea* 'first jolted [him] with a realization of the human voice's range and expressivity.'[9]

In a letter to the editor, audience member Diane Ney

---

6 'Dame Judith Anderson, Broadway star and screen villain, dies at 93,' *Austin American Statesman* 4 Jan 1992: A18.
7 Arthur Friedman, 'Theater. Dame Judith Anderson's career a labor of love,' *Boston Herald* 10 Jan 1992: S18.
8 Michael Kernan, 'The Face Of Judith Anderson. A Sinister Guise, a Fragile Grande Dame,' *WP* 12 Jan 1992: G1.
9 Garry Wills, 'Ferrer's Artistry,' *The Sun* (Baltimore) 8 Feb 1992: 9A.

remembered seeing her in *Hamlet*. 'Sitting in the back of the house, I saw a lithe figure dressed in black moving about the stage like a graceful young man,' she recalled. 'I heard a clear, strong voice echoing humanity's confusions. The fineness of her acting made me forget who she was and see only the character she had become.' 'Such chance-taking by established actors is not something we see a lot of anymore,' she concluded. 'Judith Anderson will be missed.'[10]

Judith Anderson's final farewell came in October 1992, when the Robinson Jeffers Festival devoted the afternoon to 'A Tribute to Dame Judith Anderson.' Actress Lili Bita gave dramatic readings from *Medea* and *Tower Beyond Tragedy*; Robert Zaller spoke on 'The Actress as Playwright'; and James Karman on 'Dame Judith and Robinson Jeffers: The Letters.' The evening concluded with a banquet with Marsha Hovick reading from Anderson's favourite Jeffers lyrics.[11]

In December 1992 James Prideaux, sitting opposite a French antique mirror left to him by Judith Anderson, declared the end of the era of leading ladies. Announcing the appearance of the 85-year-old Katharine Hepburn in his television play *The Man Upstairs,* he saw it as her last, marking the moment when the 'leading ladies of this world' (including Anderson) 'dissolve and in their place… the emergence of the Madonna Era.'[12]

---

10   Diane Ney, 'Judith Anderson as Hamlet,' *WP* 19 Jan 1992: C6.
11   *Jeffers Newsletter* 84, Autumn 1992.
12   Robert Epstein, 'Prideaux May Signal End to Leading Lady Era,' *LAT* 4 Dec 1992: OCF17. Hepburn made four more movies before she died in 2003.

ACT VII
Afterlife

Judith Anderson as Mrs Danvers fondles her former mistress's fur in the boudoir scene with the new Mrs De Winter

Author's collection

Chapter Thirty-six

Popular Culture Icon

Film is the chosen hiding place of sexual fantasy... Stars are alluringly indefinite creatures whose appeal must spill over the strict boundaries of gender. No wonder that the objects of our pining affection are so ambiguous.
Peter Conrad, The Observer 1998

The great actor David Garrick is said to have remarked ruefully that 'an actor's name is writ in water.' Judith Anderson's theatrical triumphs – even the 'unforgettable' *Medea* – live on in the memory of a few who may have seen her on stage or television in her later years. Her glorious voice has been preserved on recordings that brought her younger admirers. And thanks to YouTube and video we can still enjoy Anderson's 1959 televised *Medea* and her movies, while the arts of her contemporary, rival and friend, Katharine Cornell, are lost to us because she eschewed movies and television.

But this was the Madonna Era, and Judith Anderson, great tragedienne, is indelibly impressed on the twenty-first century collective memory in one role in a medium she despised – as Mrs Danvers, the mesmerising, menacing housekeeper in *Rebecca*, the 1940 Academy Award-winning movie produced by David Selznick and directed by Alfred Hitchcock. And in that collective memory she has been cast, firstly, as a lesbian poster girl, part of Hollywood's 'Sewing Circle' of gay movie stars, despite her two marriages and numerous flirtations, and second, as the epitome of spine-tingling movie dread.

Variety, reviewing *Rebecca* in March 1940, had been doubtful of its appeal to the public. It was an artistic success, they conceded, but its 'b.o. [box office] lure' would be limited.[1] They were wrong, and *Rebecca* became one of the great box office successes of all time. Although commentators recognised Mrs Danvers' sexuality from the beginning, it did not become an object of widespread analysis until the 1970s, when popular and academic work influenced by the feminist and gay movements turned the spotlight onto Hitchcock's ambiguous creation.[2]

After Laura Mulvey published her path-breaking article 'Visual Pleasure and Narrative Cinema' in 1975, applying feminist psychoanalytic theory to Hitchcock's movies, an avalanche of articles and books made images from *Rebecca* iconic of the Hollywood lesbian.[3] At a more popular level, Gay Activists Alliance member Vito Russo travelled throughout the US from 1972 to 1982 delivering a lecture with film clips on Hollywood's treatment of gay, lesbian, bisexual and transgender characters. In 1981 he published *The Celluloid Closet: Homosexuality in the Movies*, including *Rebecca* in his list of films with gay characters.[4] The HBO documentary of the same name narrated by Lily Tomlin and released in 1996,

---

1   *Variety* 26 Mar 1940.
2   Robin Wood, *Hitchcock's Films Revisited*, 1989. For a comprehensive account of writings on Hitchcock see Jane Sloan, *Alfred Hitchcock: A Filmography and Bibliography*, 1995. Hans Lucas (Jean-Luc Godard), Maurice Scherer (Eric Rohmer) and others began major critical discussion of Hitchcock's work in the French journal *Cahiers du Cinema* from its first issue in 1951. The British journal *Movie*, which began in 1962, brought scholarly debate on Hitchcock to the English-speaking world.
3   Laura Mulvey, 'Visual Pleasure and Narrative Cinema,' *Screen* 16:3, 1975: 6–18.
4   Vita Russo, *The Celluloid Closet: Homosexuality in the Movies*, 1981, rev 1987. See Robin Wood, *Canadian Forum* Feb 1982: 35–6.

placed *Rebecca* and Mrs Danvers at centre stage and made the boudoir scene an important part of the general public's image of the lesbian on film.[5] *Rebecca* itself was brought out in a deluxe edition DVD by Criterion in 2001, with Anderson menacing Fontaine on the cover.

Left: Cover of Criterion DVD of Rebecca *2001. Right: Cover of Criterion Blu-ray of* Rebecca *2017*

When Criterion issued a Blu-ray version in 2017 the cover featured Anderson alone, exhibiting the 'sinister menace' that seemed to act as a codeword for 'lesbian' when the movie was made.[6]

Judith Anderson (or Mrs Danvers) has, since 1975, become

---

5   *The Celluloid Closet* (1995) produced and directed by Rob Epstein and Jeffrey Friedman. See *NYT* 13 Oct 1995. The DVD Special Edition (Sony 2001) includes an audio commentary with the late Russo, a 1990 interview and some deleted interviews making up a second documentary, *Rescued From the Closet*.

6   *Alfred Hitchcock's Rebecca*, Criterion Collection, 2001. See *LAT* 29 Nov 2001: F13. *Rebecca*, Criterion Collection, 2017. See Rhona J. Berenstein, 'Adaptation, Censorship, and Audiences of Questionable Type: Lesbian Sightings in *Rebecca* (1940) and *The Uninvited* (1944),' *Cinema Journal* 37:3, 1998: 16–37.

the poster girl for scholarly analyses of lesbian sexuality in film. As Patricia White points out, '*Rebecca* figures as insistently in feminist film theory as does Rebecca in the second Mrs de Winter's psyche.'[7] Two major academic books, *The Women Who Knew Too Much* published in 1988 and *Uninvited* published in 1999, have iconic pictures of Anderson and Fontaine on their covers – the scholarly counter-point to the Garbo, Stanwyck and Deitrich trio on the covers or in the photographic pages of the more popular *Sewing Circle: Sappho's Leading Ladies* (1995) by celebrity biographer, Axel Madsen, critic David Ehrenstein's *Open Secret: Gay Hollywood 1928–98* (1998) and journalist Diana McLellan's *The Girls: Sappho Goes to Hollywood* (2001).

Mrs Danvers demonstrates the transparency of Rebecca's nightgown in the movie's boudoir scene

Author's collection

---

7   Patricia White, *Uninvited: Classical Hollywood Cinema and Lesbian Representability*, 1999, 27.

These popular books unquestioningly identify Anderson as a lesbian, usually without any attribution, following Boze Hadleigh's dubious 'outing' in *Hollywood Lesbians* (1994). Peter Conrad, reviewing *Open Secret* in the London *Observer*, described the boudoir scene in *Rebecca* as 'the most candid account of a lesbian seduction ever filmed.' He accused the 'bullish' Anderson of hypocrisy for denying knowledge that 'such monstrous and unnatural females existed.' (*Bullish* is a common word used to describe Anderson, who was actually tiny and considered by her contemporaries as the epitome of glamour.) An article in the *Glasgow Herald* accompanying the screening of highlights of the 14th London Lesbian and Gay Film Festival in 2000 is typical in its identification of Mrs Danvers' sexuality and that of Judith Anderson: 'The archetypal Hollywood lesbian,' it read, 'is arguably… Mrs Danvers, in Rebecca… Judith Anderson, who played her, is said to have belonged to the legendary Hollywood "sewing circle" of actresses who were lesbian.'

'The archetypical Hollywood lesbian' – an ironic fate for one who struggled all her life against typecasting in her life and in her work. From the age of eight she had refused to settle for the ordinary life of a dependent woman. In 1924, when she had her first taste of success, she told *Theatre Magazine* that she wanted to play all sorts of women on the stage – 'A whimsical creature, a capricious one, a woman of many contradictory moods, a cruel one, a malevolent one, a tender one, a woman broken on the wheels of her own emotions. Feline creatures, subtle, tricky, clever, selfish. All of them.'[8] And at the end of her life, when gossip writer Boze Hadleigh had tried to pin her down to a sexual identity, she sent him packing with the defiant words, 'I do not associate myself with anyone – group or individual… I won't join up with anything. Ever.'[9]

---

8   Judith Anderson, 'A Stage Vamp on Women,' *Theatre Magazine* Oct 1924: 22, 26, 63.
9   Hadleigh, *Hollywood Lesbians*, 176.

Mrs Danvers as pop culture icon, by Alejandro Mogollo

Courtesy of artist

Anderson's portrayal of the ambiguous, passive-aggressive character of Mrs Danvers has moved beyond academic and lesbian and gay politics in recent years into the larger popular culture as a well recognised – and even loved – symbol of quiet menace. Her image is on mugs and t-shirts, and there is even a Mrs Danvers doll ('everybody's favourite unhinged housekeeper'). There was until recently a Mrs Danvers Café

Coffee cup from Mrs Danvers Café, Liverpool

in the lovely Port of Liverpool Building in Liverpool.

The grey filly, Mrs Danvers, had an unbeaten two-year-old season on English racetracks in 2016. The all-girl band 'Mrs Danvers' headlined at the Boston Dyke in Boston in 2009. The Return to Mandalay collection of nail varnish includes a shiny black colour named Mrs Danvers.

Mrs Danvers has also inspired sculpture and public architecture. A spiky dark confection of 'Pine, wire, linen thread, acrylic paint, high-density polyethylene, fabric, and hand-cut paper' by Jade Yumang of the School of the Art Institute of Chicago is part of his collection focussing on the concept of the queer form. And at the entrance to the Leytonstone tube station in London is a mosaic of the well-known scene of Mrs Danvers menacing the second Mrs De Winter, one of 17 murals that commemorate Hitchcock's birth.

Mrs Danvers (Rebecca), *2015, by Jade Yumang*

Courtesy of artist

Judith Anderson may have been dismayed to find her work and her personality reduced to one role and one identity; but she would have been gratified to be remembered. Who now remembers Katharine Cornell in *The Barretts of Wimpole Street* or Helen Hayes in *Victoria Regina*? But everyone

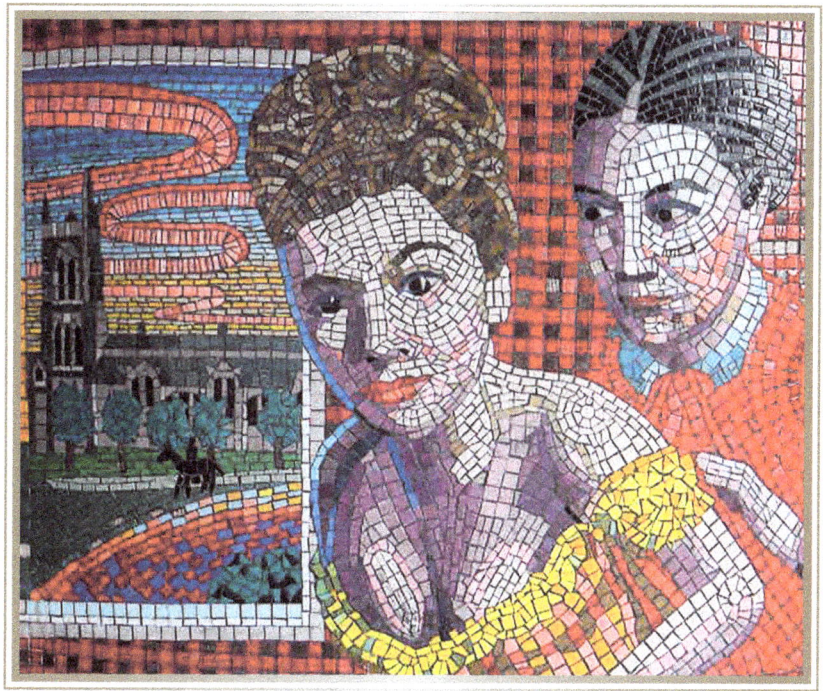

Mosaic at the entrance to the Leytonstone tube station in London

Author's collection

recognises *Rebecca* and Mrs Danvers, and many are surprised to discover that her creator, Judith Anderson, had another, more important life, as one of the great dramatic actresses of the twentieth century.

Judith Anderson Performances

1915

26 May to 27 September Julius Knight's Farewell Tour
  A Royal Divorce: Stephanie de Beauharnais
  The Lady of Lyons: Madame des Chapelles
  The Sacrament of Judas: Jeffik

30 October to 26 November Modern Amusements Ltd Julius Knight Dramatic Company
  Adelaide
  The Silver King: Susy, a Waitress
  The Third Degree: Maid at Brewsters
  Paid in Full: Beth Brooks

11 December to 22 January 1916 Modern Amusements Ltd Julius Knight Dramatic Company
  Melbourne
  The Three Musketeers: Constance
  The Lady of Lyons: Madame des Chapelles
  The Christian: Polly Love

1916

10 June to 1 December Julius Knight Company by arrangement with J C Williamson Ltd
  10 June to 21 July Sydney
  22 to 27 July Newcastle
  31 July Toowoomba
  5 to 23 August Brisbane
  28 August Geelong
  29 to 30 August Ballarat
  2 to 15 September Adelaide
  23 September to 13 October Perth
  21 October to 1 December Melbourne
  The Lion and the Mouse: Miss Nesbitt
  A Royal Divorce: Stephanie de Beauharnais
  The Sign of the Cross: Ancaria
  Under Fire: Jeanne
  The Silver King: Susy, a Waitress
  Monsieur Beaucaire; Mrs Mabsley

1917

24 February 1917 to 4 January 1918 J and N Tait's New Comedy Company
  24 February to 19 April Melbourne
  21 April to 30 June Sydney

3 to 18 July Brisbane
21 to 27 July Newcastle
28 to 8 August Hobart
9 to 10 August Launceston
18 August to 7 September Adelaide
10 to 11 September Ballarat
22 December to 4 January 1918 Sydney
Turn to the Right: Katie; from 9 August Jessie Strong
The New Henrietta: Hattie, a strange young woman

1918

30 December to 28 April 1919 Emma Bunting Stock Company, 14th Street Theatre, New York City
    Within the Law: Mary Turner
    Up Stairs and Down: Betty
    Sinners Polly
    Under Cover
    In Old Kentucky: Barbara
    Bought & Paid For: Fanny Blaine
    The Two Orphans: Henriette
    Officer 666: Sadie
    Paid in Full: Beth
    St. Elmo: Agnes Powell
    The Kerry Gow: Nora Drew [?]
    Common Clay: Anne
    Seven Keys to Baldpate: Myra

1919

12 May Clancy Stock Company, Waterbury
    When The Boys Come Home: Mary
    The *Lion and the Mouse* Shirley Rossmore
    Fatal Wedding: Child
    Mrs Dane's Defense: Mrs Dane
    One Day: Opal
    Bought and Paid For: Eugenia

25 August to 4 October 14th St Theatre, New York City
    Third Degree: Annie Sands [?]
    Dr Jekyll and Mr Hyde: Agnes Carew
    Alias Jimmy Valentine: Rose
    The Common Law: Valerie West [?]
    The Deep Purple: Doris Moore [?]
    One Day: Opal

13 October to 31 December *Dear Brutus* Touring Company with William Gillette: Joanna Trout
    Stamford to Philadelphia

1920

1 January to 17 April *Dear Brutus* Touring Company with William Gillette Philadelphia to Chicago to Newark

26 April to 17 May Schenectady Stock Company
Please Get Married: Muriel
Heart of Wetona: Wetona
Divorce Question: Mamie
The Naughty Wife: Eloise

21 June to 24 July The Armory Players, Binghamton
The Crowded Hour: Peggy Lawrence
Baby Mine: Aggie
The Country Cousin: Nancy Price
Daddy Long Legs: Judy
The ? Wife: Mrs Bevington

13 August to 22 October Colonial Players, Albany
Pollyanna: Pollyanna
Forever After: Jennie
She Walked in Sleep: Daphne
Grumpy: Virginia
Civilian Clothes: Florence Lasham
Paula Bedscan? Angelica
Johnny & Gerty Are ? Jordan
Woman in Room 13: Laura

1 November to 31 December Arlington Players, Boston
Please Get Married: Muriel Ashley
Peg O' My Heart: Peg
A Pair of Queens: Polly Webb
Way Down East: Anna
Lombardi, Ltd: Norah Blake
Cappy Ricks: Florrie Ricks
The Rosary: Alice and Tania [dual role]
Dawn and the Mountain: Dawn
The Girl from Out Yonder: Flotsam

1921

10 January to 25 March Arlington Players, Boston
Peg O' My Heart: Peg
Way Down East: Anna
A Tailor-Made Man: Tanya Huber [?]
Daddy Long Legs: Judy
Civilian Clothes: Florence Lasham
Uncle Tom's Cabin:
Freckles: Angel
St Elmo: Edna Earl

1922 [as Frances Anderson]

25 September to 4 December *On the Stairs* Broadway: Mrs Bellmore

1923 [as Judith Anderson]

16 April to 22 June *Peter Weston* Company, with Frank Keenan: Jessie Weston
    16 to 18 April Dayton, Ohio
    19 to 21 April Toledo, Ohio
    25 February to 22 June Chicago

2 to 16 July George Marshall Stock Company Washington, DC
    After the Rain
    Why Men Leave Home

10 September to 6 October *Peter Weston* Company, with Frank Keenan: Jessie Weston
    10 to 14 September Atlantic City
    18 September to 6 October Broadway

12 October to 26 November the *Crooked Square* Company Broadway: Barbara Kirkwood

1924

2 to 24 March the *Patches* Company Chicago: Mrs Warren Brown

15 April to 28 November the *Cobra* Company, with Louis Calhern: Elise van Zile
    15 to 18 April Brooklyn
    22 April to 15 November Broadway
    17 November Philadelphia
    22 to 28 November Chicago

1925

26 January 1925 to 1 May 1926 *The Dove* Produced by David Belasco, with Holbrook Blinn: Dolores
    26 January Baltimore
    2 February Washington DC
    11 February to 27 June; 24 Aug to 3 Oct Broadway
    25 October Cleveland
    3 November Pittsburgh
    9 November to 3 April 1926 Chicago

1926

5 Apr to 1 May Boston

7 June to 15 July *Thieves* Keith-Albee Circuit

7 June Chicago
11 July New York
15 July Washington DC

1927

8 January to 27 June J C Williamson Ltd
    Sydney
    8 January to 18 February *Cobra*: Elise van Zile
    19 February to 31 March *Tea for Three*: The Wife
    Melbourne
    2 to 27 April *Tea for Three*: The Wife
    30 April to 25 May *The Green Hat* Iris
    Adelaide
    28 May to 3 June *The Green Hat*: Iris
    Sydney
    9 to 22 June [matinees only] *The Green Hat*: Iris
    23 to 27 June [evening also] *The Green Hat*: Iris

30 November to 26 February 1928 *Behold the Bridegroom* Produced by Rosalie Stewart: Antoinette Lyle
    30 November Atlantic City
    5 December Bronx
    11 December Jamaica
    3 December Brooklyn
    26 December to 26 February 1928 Broadway

1928

27 February to 31 March *Behold the Bridegroom* Produced by Lee & J J Shubert
    27 February to 10 March Broadway
    12 March Brooklyn
    19 to 31 March Boston

9 May to mid-June *The Young Truth* [*Anna*] Produced by Samuel Samrach: Anna
    9 to 12 May Great Neck, Mamaroneck, Springvale, Conn
    15 May to mid-June Broadway

30 June to 24 May 1930 *Strange Interlude* Produced by the Theatre Guild: Nina
    30 June to 16 December Broadway
    24 December to early February 1929 Broadway

1929

    18 February to mid-April Broadway
    23 to 30 April Los Angeles

1 to 3 May Santa Barbara
4 to 5 May San Diego
6 to 18 May Hollywood
20 May to 19 June San Francisco
30 September to 26 October Quincy, Mass
27 October Rochester, NY
12 November Cleveland, Ohio
25 November to 18 January 1930 Chicago

1930

24 February to 25 April Philadelphia
28 April to 9 May Baltimore
12 to 24 May Newark

Madame of the Jury 8 Mins. Warners New York Vitaphone No. 1121 November

22 November to 30 May 1931 *As You Desire Me* Produced by Lee Shubert: The Unknown One
22 November Princeton
24 to 29 November Washington DC
1 to 27 December Philadelphia
29 December to 24 January 1931 Chicago

1931

28 January to 30 May Broadway

6 July *Cobra* Chamberlain Brown Players Westchester Theatre, Mount Vernon

20 July *Strange Interlude* Cape Playhouse, Dennis, Cape Cod

17 September to 31 October *As You Desire Me* Produced by Lee Shubert
17 to 19 September Rochester
21 to 26 September Toronto
28 September to 3 October Montreal
5 to 31 October Boston

1932

4 January to 21 May *Mourning Becomes Electra* Produced by the Theatre Guild: Lavinia
4 to 9 January Baltimore
11 to 16 January Washington DC
18 to 30 January Pittsburgh
1 to 6 February Cincinnati
8 to 13 February Buffalo
15 February to 5 March Chicago

7 to 24 March Detroit
5 to 9 April Columbus
11 to 16 April Kansas City
4 to 7 May Milwaukee
9 to 21 May Broadway

21 November to 31 December *Firebird* Produced by Gilbert Miller Broadway: Carola

1933

18 February to 5 March *Conquest* Produced by Arthur Hopkins Broadway: Helen Nolte

1 May to 10 June *The Mask and the Face* Produced by the Theatre Guild: Countess Savina Grazia
    1 to 6 May Boston
    8 May to 10 June Broadway

3 to 8 July *Reunion in Vienna* Castle Theatre, Long Beach: Elena

Blood Money (Twentieth Century) 17 November Produced by Darryl F. Zanuck. Directed by Rowland Brown: Ruby Darling

24 November to 2 December *The Drums Begin* Produced by George Abbott and Philip Dunning Broadway: Valerie Latour

1934

12 January to 10 February *Come of Age* Produced by Delos Chappell Broadway: A Woman

23 to 28 July *The Shining Hour* Castle Theatre Long Beach: Mariella Linden

13 to 18 August *Female of the Species* Pittsburgh Civic Playhouse

27 September to 27 October *Divided by Three* Produced by Guthrie McClintic: Lila
    27 September New Haven
    2 to 27 October Broadway

31 December 1934 to 29 April 1936 *The Old Maid* Produced by Harry Moses. Staged by Guthrie McClintic: Delia Lovell
    31 December 1934 to 5 January 1935 Baltimore

1935

7 January to 17 September Broadway
6 May Pulitzer Prize
Coast to coast tour: 30 September to 29 April 1936 Philadelphia; Boston; Springfield; Utica; Rochester; Buffalo; Pittsburgh; Lexington; Wheeling; Youngstown; Akron; Cleveland; Detroit; Toledo; Cincinnati; Dayton; Lexington; Louisville; St Louis; Chicago.

1936

Minneapolis; Rochester; Des Moines; Omaha; Wichita; Lincoln; San Francisco; Santa Barbara; Los Angeles; Fresno; Long Beach; San Diego; Phoenix; Tucson; El Paso; San Antonio; Austin; Houston; College Station; Waco; Dallas; Denton; Wichita Falls; Oklahoma City; Tulsa; Little Rock; Memphis; Kansas City; Jackson; Hattiesburg; Mobile; New Orleans; Montgomery; Birmingham; Nashville; Chattanooga; Knoxville; Atlanta; Charlotte; Greensboro; Hershey; Reading; Wilmington.

30 September to 20 February 1937 *Hamlet* Produced and Staged by Guthrie McClintic: Gertrude
30 September to 3 October Toronto
5 to 6 October Rochester
8 October to 30 January 1937 Broadway

1937

1 to 6 February Washington DC
8 to 13 February Boston
15 to 20 February Philadelphia

27 November to 15 January 1938 *Macbeth* Produced by Old Vic Directed by Michal Saint-Denis London: Lady Macbeth

1939

8 March to 17 June *Family Portrait* Produced by Cheryl Crawford in association with Day Tuttle and Richard Skinner Broadway: Mary

1940

Rebecca (MGM) 27 March Produced by David O. Selznick. Directed by Alfred Hitchcock.

Academy Award Nomination for Best Supporting Actress

Forty Little Mothers (MGM) 10 April. Produced by Harry Rapf. Directed by Busby Berkeley

12 to 31 August *Hands Across the Sea* Produced by Theatre Guild of Southern California Los Angeles

1941

Free and Easy (MGM) 28 February. Produced by Milton H Bren. Directed by George Sidney: Lady Joan Culver

18 to 27 June *Family Portrait* Directed by Bernard Szold Del Monte Summer Theatre: Mary

2 to 5 July *The Tower Beyond Tragedy* Directed by Moroni Olsen Forest Theatre, Carmel: Clytemnestra

Lady Scarface (RKO) 4 August. Produced by Cliff Reid. Directed by Frank Woodruff: Slade

23 October to 28 February 1942 *Macbeth* Produced by Maurice Evans and Judith Anderson in association with John Haggott. Directed by Margaret Webster: Lady Macbeth
    23 to 25 October New Haven
    27 October to 1 November Boston
    11 November to 28 February 1942 Broadway

1942

All Through the Night (Warner Bros.) 10 January. Produced by Hal B Wallis. Directed by Vincent Sherman: Madame

Kings Row (Warner Bros.) 2 February. Produced by David Lewis. Directed by Sam Wood: Mrs. Harriet Gordon

Macbeth tour: 2 March to 4 June Buffalo [replaced by Margaret Webster]; Rochester; Hartford; Philadelphia; Baltimore; Washington DC; April Pittsburgh; Detroit; Indianapolis; Cincinnati; St Louis; Chicago; St Paul; Minneapolis; Milwaukee; Columbus; Cleveland; Philadelphia; Fort Meade

30 November to 30 March 1943 *The Three Sisters* Produced by Katharine Cornell. Staged by Guthrie McClintic: Olga
    30 November to 6 December Washington DC; Baltimore; Fort Meade; Philadelphia
    21 December to 30 March 1943 Broadway

1943

5 April to 12 June *The Three Sisters* tour: Boston; Cleveland; Fort Meade; Detroit; Toronto; Pittsburgh; Chicago

Edge of Darkness (Warner Bros.) 9 April Produced by Jack L Warner. Directed by Lewis Milestone: Gerd Bjarnesen

Stage Door Canteen (UA) 24 June. Produced and Directed by Frank Borzage: self

8 August to 25 October *Macbeth* Produced and directed by Maurice Evans Hawaii: Lady Macbeth

1944

16 August to 16 September USO Camp Show New Guinea: MC and sketches including from *Macbeth*

Laura (Twentieth Century Fox) 11 October Produced and Directed by Otto

Preminger: Ann Treadwell

8 November to 19 December USO Camp Show Panama Canal and Caribbean

1945

And Then There Were None (Twentieth Century Fox) 31 October. Produced and Directed by Rene Clair: Emily Brent

1946

The Diary of a Chambermaid (United Artists) 15 February. Produced by Benedict Bogeaus. Directed by Jean Renoir: Madame Lanlaire

The Specter of the Rose (Republic) 5 July. Produced and Directed by Ben Hecht: Madame La Sylph

The Strange Love of Martha Ivers (Paramount) 25 July. Produced by Hal B Wallis. Directed by Lewis Milestone: Mrs Ivers

1947

Pursued (Warner Bros.) 5 March. Produced by Milton Sperling. Directed by Raoul Walsh: Mrs Callum

The Red House (United Artists) 16 March. Produced by Sol Lesser. Directed by Delmer Daves: Ellen Morgan

3 October to 15 May 1948 *Medea* Produced by Robert Whitehead and Oliver Rea. Directed by John Gielgud: Medea
    3 to 4 October Princeton
    6 to 18 October Philadelphia
    20 October to 15 May 1948 Broadway

Tycoon (RKO) 27 December. Produced by Stephen Ames. Directed by Richard Wallace: Miss Braithwaite

1948

3 September to 2 July 1949 *Medea* Produced and Directed by Guthrie McClintic: Medea
    Santa Barbara; San Francisco; Los Angeles; Pasadena; Fresno; San José; Portland; Seattle; Salt Lake City; Des Moines; Columbia; St Louis; Chicago

1949

Medea tour: St Paul; Minneapolis; Columbus; Toledo; Detroit; Cincinnati; Cleveland; Erie; Ithaca; Syracuse; Rochester; Pittsburgh; Philadelphia; Baltimore; Reading; Allentown; Wilmington; Hartford; Northampton; Springfield; New Haven; Boston

2 to 14 May City Center New York

16 May to 2 July University of Virginia; Hershey; Sylvan Theater [outdoors] Washington DC; Honolulu

1950

The Furies (Paramount) 16 August. Produced by Hal B. Wallis. Directed by Anthony Mann: Flo Burnett

26 November to 22 December *The Tower Beyond Tragedy* Produced by Luther Greene and ANTA. Staged by Robert Ross: Clytemnestra

1951

26 January *The Silver Cord, Pulitzer Prize Playhouse*: Mrs Phelps

6 March *Farewell Appearance* Produced by Jed Harris Directed by Daniel Petrie, *The Billy Rose Show*

16 April *Theatre* Directed by Martin Ritt, *Somerset Maugham TV Theatre*: Julia Lambert

13 to 17 September *Medea* Produced by State Department and American National Theatre & Academy. Staged by Guthrie McClintic: Medea. Berlin Arts Festival

1952

15 January to 10 February *Come of Age* Produced by George Schaefer. Directed by Guthrie McClintic. New York City Center Theater Company
    15 to 19 January Hartford
    23 January to 10 February New York City

30 May to 1 June Excerpts from *Tower Beyond Tragedy* and *Medea* Ojai Festival
    7 June Lobero Theatre Foundation Santa Barbara

1 November to 11 April 1953 *John Brown's Body* Produced by Paul Gregory. Directed by Charles Laughton: Medora
    Santa Barbara; Pasadena; Bakersfield; Fresno; Sacramento; Stockland; San Francisco; Salt Lake City; Wichita; Kansas City; Sioux City; Omaha; Chicago; Minneapolis; December Duluth; Beloit; East Lansing; Hormel; Menasha; Detroit; Toronto; Rochester; Syracuse; Buffalo; White Plains; Hartford; Boston; Philadelphia; Brooklyn

1953

    John Brown's Body: Wilmington; Newark; Washington DC; Baltimore; Norfolk; Richmond; Chapel Hill; Huntington; Pittsburgh; Cincinnati; Louisville; Decatur; Springfield; Chicago; Bloomington; Peoria; Columbus; Tulsa; Oklahoma City; Dallas; Austin; Houston; El Paso;

February Phoenix; Tucson; Beverly Hills; San Diego; Occidental
14 February to 11 April Broadway

Salome (Columbia) 13 February Produced by Buddy Adler and Rita Hayworth. Directed by William Dieterle: Queen Herodias

10 to 15 August *Family Portrait* Produced by Robert Porterfield Barter Theatre, Abingdon: Mary

25 to 30 August *Family Portrait* Produced by Marshall Migatz Salt Creek Summer Theatre Hinsdale: Mary

26 November to 13 February 1954 *In the Summer House* Produced by The Playwright's Company and Oliver Smith. Directed by José Quintero: Gertrude Eastman Cuevas
    26 to 28 November Hartford
    30 to 12 December Boston
    15 to 26 December Washington DC
    29 December to 13 February 1954 Broadway

1954

20 April *Black Chiffon, The Motorola Television Hour*: Alicia

24 October *Light's Diamond Jubilee* TV Special Produced by David O Selznick

28 November *Macbeth, Hallmark Hall of Fame* Produced by Maurice Evans Directed by Hudson Faussett and George Schaefer: Lady Macbeth. Emmy for Best Actress in a Single Portrayal

24 December *Yesterday's Magic, The Elgin Hour* Directed by Donald Richardson: Evaline Morly

1955

19 February *Louise, The Star & the Story Hosted by Henry Fonda* Produced by Warren Lewis Directed by Robert Stevenson: Louise

30 April *Virtue, The Star & the Story Hosted by Henry Fonda* Produced by Warren Lewis Directed by Peter Godfrey: Margaret Bishop

14 to 18 June *Medea*, Salute to France, Paris International Drama Festival Produced by State Department, American National Theatre and Academy and Roger Stevens Directed by Guthrie McClintic: Medea

5 October to 28 January 1956 *Medea*, Produced by Australian Elizabethan Theatre Trust and J C Williamson Ltd. Directed by Hugh Hunt: Medea
    5 to 6 October Canberra
    11 to 5 November Sydney
    8 to 23 November Brisbane
    25 November to 10 December Adelaide
    12 to 17 December Hobart
    20 to 14 January Melbourne

3 December *The Creative Impulse, The Star & the Story Hosted by Henry Fonda* Produced by Warren Lewis Directed by Robert Florey: Mrs Albert Forrester

1956

17 to 28 January *Medea* Perth

5 March *Caesar and Cleopatra, Producers' Showcase* Supervisors Donald Davis and Dorothy Mathews Directed by Kirk Browning: Flatateeta

19 to 24 March *Black Chiffon*, Palm Beach Playhouse: Alicia

2 to 7 April *Black Chiffon*, Coconut Grove Playhouse, Miami: Alicia

14 April *The Senora, The Star & the Story Hosted by Henry Fonda* Produced by Warren Lewis Directed by Roy Kellino: The Senora

6 May Gregorio and Maria Martinez Sierra's *The Cradle Song, Hallmark Hall of Fame* Produced by Phil C Samuel Directed by George Schaefer: The Prioress

14 to 19 May *Black Chiffon*, Spring Drama Festival, Ann Arbor: Alicia

4 to 9 June *Black Chiffon*, Finneytown Tent Theater-in-the-round: Alicia

21 June *The Circular Staircase, Climax!* Produced by Edgar Peterson Directed by Ralph Nelson: Rachel

6 September to 5 January 1957 *The Chalk Garden* Produced by Edward Choate and Albert H. Rosen Directed by Albert Marre: Miss Madrigal
    Santa Barbara; Los Angeles; San Francisco; Sacramento; Stockton; San José; St Louis; Minneapolis; Madison; Milwaukee; Cleveland; Pittsburgh; Louisville; Columbus; Cleveland; Cincinnati

The Ten Commandments (Paramount) 5 October Produced and Directed by Cecil B De Mille: Memnet

1957

7 January to 16 February *The Chalk Garden*: Miss Madrigal Baltimore; Washington DC; Toronto; Montreal; Hershey; Princeton

7 November *The Clouded Image, Playhouse 90* Produced by Peter Kortner Directed by Franklin J Schaffner: Aunt Bee

1958

7 January *Abby, Julia and the 7 Pet Cows, Telephone Time* Produced by Jerry Stagg. Directed by Arthur Hiller

21 January *The Bridge of San Luis Rey, The DuPont Show of the Month* Produced by David Susskind Directed by Robert Mulligan: Marquesa de Montemayor. Nominated for Emmy for Best Single Performance by an Actress.

17 February to 1 March *The Chalk Garden* Coconut Grove Playhouse, Miami: Miss Madrigal

Cat on a Hot Tin Roof (MGM) 18 September. Produced by Lawrence Weingarten Directed by Richard Brooks: Big Mama

1 October to 29 November *Comes a Day* Produced by Cheryl Crawford and Alan Pakula Directed by Robert Mulligan: Isabel Lawton
    1 to 4 October Wilmington
    6 to 18 October Philadelphia
    20 October to 1 November Boston
    6 to 29 November Broadway

1959

25 June *The Second Happiest Day, Playhouse 90* Produced by Peter Kortner Directed by Ralph Nelson: Ava Norris

12 October *Medea, Play of the Week* Produced by David Susskind Directed by H Wesley Kenney and José Quintero: Medea

30 October *The Moon and Sixpence* Produced by David Susskind Directed by Robert Mulligan: Tiare

18 November *The Felizia Kingdom Story, Wagon Train* Produced by Howard Christie Directed by Joseph Pevney: Felizia Kingdom

13 December *A Christmas Festival, Hallmark Hall of Fame* Produced and Directed by George Schaefer: Narrator

1960

10 February *To the Sound of Trumpets, Playhouse 90* Produced by Herbert Brodkin Directed by Buzz Kulil: Mme Duvier

22 to 27 February *The Madwoman of Chaillot*, Royal Poinciana Playhouse, Palm Beach Directed by Warren Enters: Countess Aurelia

10 April *Millionaire's Mite, Our American Heritage* Produced by Mildred Freed Alberg Directed by Jack Smight: Margaret Morrison Carnegie

10 April *Cradle Song, Hallmark Hall of Fame* Produced by George Schaefer and Mildred Freed Alberg Directed by George Schaefer: The Prioress

22 August to 1 October *The Seagull* Produced by Old Vic Directed by John Fernald: Mme Arkadian
    22 to 27 August Edinburgh Festival
    1 September to 1 October Old Vic, London

20 November *Macbeth, Hallmark Hall of Fame* and Grand Prize Films Produced by Sidney Kaufman, Phil C Samuel and George Schaefer Directed by George Schaefer: Lady Macbeth.

Emmy for Best Single Performance by an Actress

Cinderfella (Paramount) 18 December Produced by Jerry Lewis Directed by Frank Tashlin: Wicked Stepmother

1961

Why Bother To Knock (*Don't Bother To Knock*) (Haileywood and Associated British) 29 May. Produced by Frank Godwin Directed by Cyril Frankel: Maggie Shoemaker

14 to 19 August *An Evening with Judith Anderson* [*Medea* and *Tower*] Wharf Theater and Opera House, Monterey

20 September to 1 December *Dame Judith Anderson* [*Medea, Tower, Macbeth*] Seattle; [colleges]; San Francisco; Los Angeles; [colleges]; La Jolla; Santa Barbara

1962

10 February [?] to c.14 April *Medea '62* and *Lady Macbeth* Produced by Thomas Brock and Robert Carson Directed by Jacques Gross
    Included Dallas; Washington DC; Westport; Hartford; Staunton; Chicago; Farminstead; Michigan; Detroit; Pittsburgh; Hillsville

8 October [?] to 1 December *Dame Judith Anderson and Company* [*Medea '62* and *Lady Macbeth*] Produced by Thomas Brock and Robert Carson Directed by Jacques Gross
    Included Minneapolis; Columbia; Chicago; St Louis; Athens; Tallahassee; Savannah; Montgomery; Huntington; New Wilmington; Columbus; Norfolk; Westchester; Princeton; Allentown; Philadelphia; Cortland; Brooklyn

1963

6 January to ca 21 April *Dame Judith Anderson and Company* [*Medea '62* and *Lady Macbeth*]
    Included New Orleans; Albuquerque; El Paso; Salt Lake City; Washington DC; New York; Bethlehem

1964

28 January to 8 February *Black Chiffon* Produced by Richard Charlton Sombrero Playhouse, Phoenix, Arizona

August *The Ghost of Sierra de Cobre, The Haunted* Produced by Joseph Stefano Directed by Joseph Stefano and Robert Stevens: Paulina

18 October Scenes from *Medea*, *Macbeth* and *Merchant of Venice* Chapman College, Orange, California

1965

12 to 30 October *Medea* Valley Music Theater, Woodland Hills Produced by Nick Mayo, Randolph Hale and Art Linkletter Directed by Christopher Cary: Medea

1966

11, 16, 21, 22 March *Night of Drama and Fiesta* [*Medea* and *Macbeth*] Staged by Jean Marshall Adelaide Arts Festival

17 March Yevgeny Yevtushenko recital, read in English by Anderson and Peter O'Shaughnessy Adelaide Arts Festival

24 to 28 March Yevgeny Yevtushenko recital, read in English by Anderson and Peter O'Shaughnessy
    24 March Sydney University
    26 March University of New South Wales
    28 March Trocadero

28 to 29 April *Medea* Mississippi Arts Festival, Jackson

14 June to 4 September *Oresteia* Ypsilanti Greek Theatre Produced and Directed by Alexis Solomos: Clytemnestra
    14 to 26 June previews
    28 June to 4 September

4 to 16 October *Medea* Houston Arts Festival: Medea

3 to 13 November *Elizabeth the Queen* Directed by Herbert Machiz Presented by the New York City Center Drama Company, Director Jean Dalrymple: Elizabeth

1967

11 April *A Celebration of Robinson Jeffers* Veterans' Auditorium, San Francisco Presented by the San Francisco State College Poetry Center

11 April *Give Your Heart to the Hawks* (Jeffers documentary) produced for National Education Television by David Myers and Mark Linenthal: self

1968

31 January *Elizabeth the Queen*, Hallmark Hall of Fame Produced and Directed by George Schaefer. Nominated for an Emmy for Best Single Performance by a Dramatic Actress in a Lead Role

1969

21 November *File on Devlin*, Hallmark Hall of Fame Produced by Robert Hartung Directed by George Schaefer: Elizabeth Devlin

1970

A Man Called Horse (National General) 23 April. Produced by Sandy Howard Directed by Elliot Silverstein: Buffalo Cow Head

24 September to 27 March 1971 *Hamlet* Produced by Paul Gregory in association with the American Conservatory Theatre Directed by William Ball
    Previews: 24 to 26 September Santa Barbara; 27 San Francisco
    Tour: San Francisco; Sacramento; Fresno; Los Angeles; San Diego; El Camino; Claremont; Palm Springs; Phoenix; Denver; Emporia; Norman; Wichita; Denton; Fort Worth; Dallas; Houston; New Orleans; Jackson; Starkville; Memphis; Jackson; Birmingham; Cleveland; Albion; Columbus; Champaign; Stockyards; Kansas City; Indianapolis; Carbondale; Evansville; Omaha; Ames; La Crosse; Milwaukee; Chicago

1971

    Hamlet: Gary; Detroit; Toledo; New York; Newark; Baltimore; Brunswick; Boston; Syracuse; Binghamton; Buffalo; Fredonia; Ithaca; Bethesda; Rochester; Carlisle; Bethlehem; Washington DC; Philadelphia; Thomasville; Tallahassee; Macon; Jacksonville; St Petersburg; Palm Beach; Milledgeville; Troy; Mobile; Montgomery; Atlanta; Columbia; Fayetteville; Durham; College Park; Louisville; St Louis

1973

31 May *A Special Place*, *Matlock Police* Produced by Rod Hardy and Rita Tanno Directed by John Jacob: Lee McDonald

14 December *The Borrowers*, *Hallmark Hall of Fame* Produced by Warren Lockhart and Walt DeFaria Directed by Walter C Miller: Aunt Sophy. Nomination for Emmy for Performer, Outstanding Individual Achievement in Children's Programming

1974

Dramatic readings from Jeffers and Shakespeare, International Poetry Forum
    29 March Pittsburgh
    26 April Berkeley

6 May *The Underground Man* Produced by Philip L Parslow Directed by Paul Wendkos: Mrs Snow

29 September *The Chinese Prime Minister*, *Hollywood Theater* Produced by George Turpin Directed by Brian Murray: She

1975

Inn of the Damned (Roadshow) 23 October. Produced by Terry Bourke and Rod Hay Directed by Terry Bourke: Caroline Straulle

1981

Tor House: Lines from Robinson Jeffers Produced by James Eddy Hatch: Self

1982

10 February to 27 June *Medea* Produced by Robert Whitehead and The Kennedy Center Directed by Robert Whitehead: The Nurse. Nominated for a Tony for Outstanding Performance by An Actress in a Featured Role in a Play
    10 February Preview: Produced in association with the University of Tennessee's Clarence Brown Theatre Knoxville
    6 March to 10 April Kennedy Center Washington DC
    21 to 24 April Preview Boston
    7 to 30 April Preview Broadway
    2 May to 27 June Broadway Produced by Barry and Fran Weissler under arrangement with Kennedy Center for the Performing Arts and Bunny Austin and Warren Austin.

10 December *Over Easy*: Self

1983

20 April *Medea, Kennedy Center Tonight* Produced by Mary Rawson Directed by Mark Cullingham: The Nurse. Nominated for Primetime Emmy Award for Outstanding Supporting Actress in a Limited Series or Movie

20 April *Reflections on Medea* PBS: Self

1984

Star Trek III: The Search for Spock (Paramount) 1 June. Produced by Harve Bennett Directed by Leonard Nimoy: Vulcan High Priestess

30 July 1984 to 10 June 1987 *Santa Barbara*: Minx Lockridge. Nominated for a Daytime Emmy for Supporting Actress in a Drama Series 1986

1985

9 October *Bread, The Booth* Produced by Schaefer/Karpf Directed by George Schaefer

Hitchcock, Il Brivido Del Genio (*The Thrill of Genius*) (Italian-Docu-Color-16m) Directed by Francesco Bortolini and Claudio Masenza: Self

1986

30 November *Impure Thoughts* Produced by Michael J Malloy, Michael A Simpson and William VanDerKloot Directed by Michael A Simpson: The Sister of Purgatory

1990

18 February *Dame Judith Anderson: Performs Shakespeare* Santa Barbara

Recordings

Shakespeare's Macbeth, with Maurice Evans and Judith Anderson, 1942. RCA Victor Red Seal DM 878: 5 X 12".

Judith Anderson, *Dramatic Sketches: Lincoln's Letter To Mrs. Bixby / Sermon on the Mount / The Fog / The Statue of Liberty*. RCA Victor Red Seal DM 960: 3 X 12".

Medea, with Judith Anderson, 1949: 4 X 12". Decca DLP 9000.

Stephen Vincent Benet's John Brown's Body, with Raymond Massey, Judith Anderson, Tyrone Power, 1953. Columbia SL 181: 2 X 12".

Judith Anderson, The *Poetry of Edna St. Vincent Millay*, 1954. Caedmon TC 1024.

Arias Sung and Acted – final scene from *Carmen* sung by Rise Stevens and Jan Peerce and acted by Judith Anderson and Shepperd Strudwick. RCA Victor: 45rpm.

Judith Anderson Reading the Book of Judith / Claire Bloom Reading the Book of Ruth, 1956. Caedmon TC 1052.

Judith Anderson Reading the Psalms and The Tale of David, 1957. Caedmon TC 1053. Psalm 23 / The Annointing Of David / Psalm 88 / Psalm 84 / David And Goliath / Psalm 61 / Psalm 8 / / The Lament of David / Psalm 123 / David And Bathsheba / Psalm 130 / Psalm 121 / The Bringing-Up Of The Ark / Psalm 100 / Psalm 149 / Psalm 150

Judith Anderson, *Stevenson's* A *Child's Garden of Verses*, Vol. 1, 1957. Caedmon TC 1077.

Judith Anderson, *A Child's Garden of Verses*, Vol. 2, 1958. Caedmon TC 1077.

Judith Anderson, *Genesis: The Creation to Noah*, 1958. Caedmon TC 1096.

Euripides Medea, with Judith Anderson and Anthony Quayle, 1964. Caedmon TRS 302: 2 X LP.

George Bernard Shaw's Caesar And Cleopatra, with Judith Anderson, Max Adrian, Claire Bloom, 1965. Caedmon TRS-M 304.

Henry James, *The Turn of the Screw* (Abridged) Read By Judith Anderson,

1969. Caedmon TC 2045: 2 x LP.

The Poetry of Robinson Jeffers Read by Judith Anderson, 1970. Caedmon TC 1297.

Frank R. Stockton, The Lady Or The Tiger Read by Judith Anderson, 1970. Caedmon TC 1313.

The Poems of A. A. Milne – When We Were Very Young & Now We Are Six Read by Judith Anderson, 1971. Caedmon TC 1356.

Charles Tazewell: The Littlest Angel Read by Judith Anderson, 1973. Caedmon TC 1384.

The Book of Dragons Read by Judith Anderson. Caedmon TC 1427.

Silas Marner, with Judith Anderson, Basil Rathbone, Cathleen Nesbitt, 1968. Caedmon TC 2024.

Emily Brontë (Abridged), with Judith Anderson, Claire Bloom, James Mason, 1978. Caedmon TC 2086: 2 X LP.

Sources

The most extensive collection of Anderson Papers is held in the Special Research Collections of the University of California Santa Barbara Library [UCSB]. Her unpublished memoir, written with Robert Wallsten, is in the Robert Wallsten Papers, UCSB. Her sister Elizabeth Anderson ['Did'] wrote a series of autobiographical memoirs held by the family, who allowed me to have a copy. I have not provided footnotes for either of these where it is clear that they are the source. Anderson also kept small appointments diaries from 1919 to 1973 [UCSB]. The Billy Rose Theatre Division of The New York Public Library [NYPL] has many clippings on microfilm and photographs from most of her performances. Anderson material at the Performing Arts Collection of the Adelaide Festival Centre [PAC] includes some of her costumes. The PROMPT collection at the National Library of Australia [NLA] has material on her stage career.

Other collections used in this book are:

AETT	Australian Elizabethan Theatre Trust Records, National Library of Australia
AWM	Australian War Memorial
Browne Papers	Ellen Van Volkenburg and Maurice Browne Papers, Special Collections Research Center, University of Michigan Library
Cornell Papers	Katharine Cornell Papers, Billy Rose Theatre Division of The New York Public Library
Crawford Papers	Cheryl Crawford Papers, Billy Rose Theatre Division of The New York Public Library

DOS	The David O. Selznick Collection, Harry Ransom Center, The University of Texas at Austin
Enters Papers	Angna Enters Papers, New York Public Library
Evans Papers	Maurice Evans Papers, Billy Rose Theatre Division of The New York Public Library
Gish Papers	Lillian Gish Papers, Billy Rose Theatre Division of The New York Public Library
JCW	Williamson Collection, Manuscript Collection, National Library of Australia
McKelvie Papers	Martha Groves McKelvie Papers, Nebraska State Historical Society, Lincoln, Nebraska
Dillon Papers	Millicent Dillon Papers, Harry Ransom Center, The University of Texas at Austin
MHL	Margaret Herrick Library, Beverly Hills
Muray Papers	Nickolas Muray Papers, Archives of American Art
PAC	Performing Arts Centre, Adelaide Festival Centre
RJBerk	Robinson Jeffers Collection, The Bancroft Library, University of California, Berkeley
RJHRC	Robinson Jeffers Collection, Harry Ransom Center, The University of Texas at Austin
RJOC	Robinson Jeffers Collection, Special Collections Department, Occidental College, Los Angeles, California
RJSF	Robinson Jeffers Collection, Donohue Rare Book Room, University of San Francisco
RJTH	Robinson Jeffers Collection, Robinson Jeffers Tor House Foundation, Carmel, California
RJYale	Robinson Jeffers Collection, Beinecke Rare Book and Manuscript Library, Yale University
Schaefer Papers	George Schaefer Papers, UCLA Library Special Collections
Sullivan Papers	Noël Sullivan Papers, Bancroft Library, University of California, Berkeley
USC	Pressbooks, Performing Arts Archives, University of Southern California
WB	Warner Bros. Archives, University of Southern California

Reference

Australian Dictionary of Biography [ADB]. Melbourne University Press and online.

An Encyclopaedia of New Zealand, ed. A.H. McLintock, originally published 1966, *Te Ara – The Encyclopedia of New Zealand*, updated 18 September 2007

Internet Broadway Database [IBDB]

Internet Movie Database [IMDB]

Frequently Consulted Newspapers and Journals

Age (Melbourne)
American Mercury
Argus (Melbourne)
Arrow (Sydney)
Australian Women's Weekly [AWW]
Australasian Drama Studies [ADS]
Billboard
Boston Globe [BG]
Boston Herald [BH]
Boston Post [BP]
Boston Transcript [BT]
Brisbane Courier
Brooklyn Daily Eagle [BDE]
Bulletin (Sydney)
Canberra Times
Chicago Daily Tribune [CDT]
Chicago Journal of Commerce
Chicago Tribune [CT]
Christian Science Monitor [CSM]
Chronicle (Adelaide)
Courier-Mail (Brisbane)
Daily Telegraph (London) [DT]
Educational Theatre Journal (USA)
Evening News (Sydney) [EN]
Guardian (United Kingdom)
Hollywood Citizen-News [HCN]
Hollywood Reporter [HR]
Hollywood Times [HT]
Lone Hand (Sydney) [LH]
Los Angeles Examiner LAE]
Los Angeles Herald-Examiner [LAHE]

Los Angeles Times [LAT]
Mail (Perth)
Manchester Guardian [MG]
Melbourne Herald [MH]
Mercury (Hobart)
Midweek Pictorial
Motion Picture Daily [MPD]
Motion Picture Herald [MPH]
National Observer (Melbourne)
News (Adelaide)
Newsweek
New York Daily Mirror [NYDM]
New York Daily News [NYDN]
New Yorker
New York Evening Post [NYEP]
New York Herald Tribune [NYHT]
New York Journal [NYJ]
New York Morning Telegraph [NYMT]
New York Post [NYP]
New York Sunday News [NYSN]
New York Telegram [NYTel]
New York Times [NYT]
New York World [NYW]
New York World-Telegram [NYWT]
Oakland Tribune [OT]
Observer (London)
Picture Show (London)
Pittsburgh Post-Gazette [PPG]
Pittsburgh Press [PP]
PM (New York)
Queenslander (Brisbane)
Queensland Figaro (Brisbane)
Queensland Times (Ipswich)
Referee (Sydney)
Robinson Jeffers Newsletter [RJN]
San Francisco Chronicle [SFC]
San Francisco *Examiner* [SFE]
Santa Barbara Sun
Saturday Morning Post
Saturday Review of Politics, Literature, Science And Art (London) [SR]
South Australian Advertiser [SAA]
South Australian Register [SAR]
Sport (Adelaide)
Sunday Herald (Sydney) [SH]
Sydney Morning Herald [SMH]
Sunday Times (Sydney) [ST]

Table Talk (Melbourne) [TT]
Telegraph (Brisbane)
Theatre (Sydney)
Theatre Arts Monthly (USA) [TAM]
Theatre Magazine (New York) [TM]
Theatre, Society and Home (Sydney) [TSH]
The Classical Journal (USA)
The Hudson Review (USA)
The Newsletter: an Australian Paper for Australian People (Sydney)
The Sphere (London)
The Stage (London)
The Sun (Baltimore)
The World's News (Sydney) [TWN]
This Week in Santa Barbara
Time
Times (London)
Town Topics (New York) [TT]
UCLA *Daily Bruin* (Los Angeles, California)
Vanity Fair [VF]
Variety
Vogue (New York)
Washington Post [WP]
Washington Post and Times Herald [WPTH]
Weekend Australian
West Australian (Perth)
Winner (Melbourne)

Published Material

Judith Anderson, 'A Stage Vamp on Women,' *Theatre Magazine* Oct 1924: 22, 26, 63

Judith Anderson, 'Interview with Joanne Hodgen,' *Coasting* [Carmel, CA], 1 Oct. 1986: 33

Janice Arkatov, 'Judith Anderson Remembers Jeffers,' *Los Angeles Times*, 5 November 1989: I53

Alan Atkinson, 'Speech, Children and the Federation Movement,' in J. Damousi & D. Deacon (eds), *Talking and Listening in the Age of Modernity: Essays on the History of Sound*. Canberra: ANU Press, 2007, 35–47

Alec Bagot, *Coppin the Great: Father of the Australian Theatre*. Melbourne University Press, 1965

Jane Baldwin, 'The Rediscovery of Michal Saint-Denis.' Introduction to Baldwin, ed., *Theatre: The Rediscovery of Style and Other Writings*. Routledge, 2008

William Ball, *A Sense of Direction: Some Observations on The Art of Directing*. Hollywood: Drama Publishers, 1984

Milly S Barranger, *Margaret Webster: A Life in the Theater*. University of Michigan Press, 2004

Doris G Bazzini, William D McIntosh, Stephen M Smith, Sabrina Cook & Caleigh Harris, 'The aging woman in popular film: Underrepresented, unattractive, unfriendly, and unintelligent,' *Sex Roles* 36:7–8, April, 1997: 531–43

Philip D Beidler, 'Remembering the Best Years of Our Lives,' *Virginia Quarterly Review*, Autumn 1996: 591–604

Melba Berry Bennett, *The Stone Mason of Tor House: The Life and Work of Robinson Jeffers*. Foreword by Lawrence Clark Powell. Menlo Park, CA: The Ward Ritchie Press, 1966

Rhona J Berenstein, 'Adaptation, Censorship, and Audiences of Questionable Type: Lesbian Sightings in Rebecca (1940) and The Uninvited (1944),' *Cinema Journal* 37.3, Spring 1998: 16–37

Matthew Bernstein, *Walter Wanger, Hollywood Independent*. University of Minnesota Press, 2000

Ina Bertrand & William Routt, 'The Big Bad Combine: Some Aspects of National Aspirations and International Constraints in the Australian Cinema, 1896–1929.' In A. Moran & T. O'Regan, eds, *The Australian Screen*. Ringwood, Vic: Penguin, 1989, 23–27

Laura C Bird, *The Ypsilanti Greek Theatre*. Michigan State University, 1999

Geoffrey Blainey, *The Rise of Broken Hill*. Sydney: Macmillan, 1968

William Boddy, *Fifties Television: The Industry and Its Critics*. University of Illinois Press, 1993 [1990]

Stella Bowen, *Drawn from Life: A Memoir*. Sydney: Picador, 1940; Pan Macmillan, 1999

Jane Bowles, *My Sister's Hand in Mine: The Collected Works of Jane Bowles*. Preface by Joy Williams. Introduction by Truman Capote. New York: Farrar, Straus and Giroux, 2005 [1966]

Out in the World: Selected Letters of Jane Bowles 1935–1970. Millicent Dillon, ed. Santa Rosa: Black Sparrow Press, 1990

Paul Bowles, *Without Stopping: An Autobiography*. New York: Ecco Press, 1985 [1972]

In Touch: The Letters of Paul Bowles, ed. by Jeffrey Miller. New York: Farrar, Straus and Giroux, 2014

Robert Brophy, 'Judith Anderson Letters and Memorabilia, Tor House Foundation,' *RJN* 56, June 1980: 45–47

Robert. Brophy, 'Jeffers Scholarly Resources: Tor House Foundation, Carmel,' *RJN* 65, Dec. 1984: 31–32

Una Jeffers, 'Una Jeffers Correspondent: Letters to Judith Anderson, 1941–50,' *RJN* 65, Dec. 1984: 8–31

Julie Burchill, 'Saturday Review: Books: Screen Sapphos: Julie Burchill on love among the leading ladies,' *Guardian* 31 March 2001: 9

Neville Cain, 'Giblin, Lyndhurst Falkiner (1872–1951)', *Australian Dictionary of Biography*, National Centre of Biography, Australian National University, 1981

Zoe Caldwell, *I Will Be Cleopatra: An Actress's Journey*. New York: W W Norton, 2002.

Gena Dagel Caponi, *Paul Bowles: Romantic Savage*. Southern Illinois University Press, 1994

Ilka Chase, *Past Imperfect*. New York: Doubleday, Doran and Company, 1942

'Cinema Club 9 Program Notes,' WTOP-TV 9, Washington DC (Stephen F. Zito), ca 1970s, MHL

Mimi Colligan, 'Lemmone, John (1861–1949),' *Australian Dictionary of Biography*, National Centre of Biography, Australian National University, 1986

Mimi Colligan, *Circus and Stage: The Theatrical Adventures of Rose Edouin and G. B. W. Lewis*. Monash University Press, 2013

Diane Collins, 'The Movie Octupus.' In Peter Spearritt & David Walker, eds, *Australian Popular Culture*. Sydney: Allen & Unwin, 1979

Peter Conrad, 'Out and about in Beverly Hills: Hollywood has still never had an openly gay leading man. What are the studios so afraid of?' *Observer* (London) 15 Nov 1998: 3

Andrew Cook, 'Edward Reeves, Lionel Logue and King George VI,' http://blogs.adelaide.edu.au/uni-archives/2011/04/04/edward-reeves-lionel-logue-and-king-george-vi/

Bertram Cox, *The First Hundred Years: History of SA Tattersalls Club*. Adelaide: Brolga Books, 1980

Cheryl Crawford, *One Naked Individual: My Fifty Years in the Theatre*. New York: Bobbs-Merrill, 1977

Jonathan Croall, *Gielgud: A Theatrical Life, 1904–2000*. London: Continuum, 2000

Joy Damousi, *Colonial Voices: a Cultural History of English in Australia, 1840–1940*. Cambridge University Press, 2010

Blair Davis, *The Battle for the Bs: 1950s Hollywood and the Rebirth of Low-Budget Cinema*. Rutgers University Press, 2012

Fitzroy Davis, *Quicksilver*. New York: Harcourt, Brace & Company, 1942

Desley Deacon, '"Films as foreign offices": Transnationalism at Paramount in the Twenties and Early Thirties.' In *Connected Worlds: History in Transnational Perspective*, ed. Ann Curthoys and Marilyn Lake. Canberra: ANU Press, 2006

Desley Deacon, 'World English? How an Australian invented "Good American Speech".' In *Talking and Listening in the Age of Modernity.* Joy Damousi and Desley Deacon, eds. Canberra: ANU Press, 2007, 73–82

Desley Deacon, 'Cosmopolitan at Home.' *Meanjin* 66.4 & 67.1, 2007–08: 190–99

Desley Deacon, 'Cosmopolitans at Home: Judith Anderson and the American Aspirations of JC Williamson Stock Company Members, 1897–1918.' In Robert Dixon and Veronica Kelly, eds. *Impact of the Modern: Vernacular Modernities in Australia 1870s-1960s.* Sydney University Press, 2008, 202–22

Desley Deacon, 'Location! Location! Location: Mind Maps in Australian Transnational History.' Presidential Address, Biennial Conference of the Australian Historical Association, July 2008. *History Australia* 4.3, Dec 2008: 1–16

Desley Deacon, 'Shallow Roots? Judith Anderson and Her Transnational Families,' History Program Seminar, Research School of Social Sciences, Australian National University, 2009

Desley Deacon, 'Becoming Cosmopolitan: Judith Anderson in Sydney, 1913 to 1918.' In *Transnational Lives: Biographies of Global Modernity, 1700-present.* Ed. with Penny Russell and Angela Woollacott. Basingstoke, UK: Palgrave Macmillan, 2009

Desley Deacon, 'Celebrity Sexuality: Judith Anderson, Mrs Danvers, Sexuality and "Truthfulness" in Biography,' *Australian Historical Studies*, Apr 2012: 45–60

Desley Deacon, 'Outlaw Fan: Judith Anderson, International Star, Grows up in Adelaide,' *Journal of the Historical Association of South Australia* 40, 2012: 66–80

Desley Deacon, 'From Victorian Accomplishment to Modern Profession: Elocution Takes Judith Anderson, Sylvia Bremer and Dorothy Cumming to Hollywood, 1912–1918,' *Australasian Journal of Victorian Studies*. Special Issue on Colonial Girlhood 18.1, 2013: 40–65

Ray Denton, compiler, *The Day Dream Silver Mining Company. A History of the Mine, Consisting of a Collection of Reports from the Silver Age Newspaper 1884–1891.* Broken Hill, NSW: R. Denton, 2008

Digby Diehl, 'With A Song,' *Los Angeles Times,* Dec 31, 1970: C15

Ann Douglas, *Terrible Honesty: Mongrel Manhattan in the 1920s*. New York: Farrar, Straus and Giroux, 1995

Martin Duberman, *The Worlds of Lincoln Kirstein*. New York: Alfred A Knopf, 2007

Geoffrey Dutton, 'The Poet as Public Figure: Yevtushenko and the Adelaide Establishment,' *Bulletin* 12 Mar 1966: 24–5

Geoffrey Dutton, *Out in the Open*. St Lucia: University of Queensland Press, 1995

Robin Eakin, *Aunts Up the Cross*. Ringwood, Vic: Penguin, 1997

Robert Eichelberger, *Dear Miss Em: General Eichelberger's War in the Pacific 1942–1945*. ABC-CLIO, 1972

The Australia Elizabethan Theatre Trust, *Annual Report* 1957

Suzanne Edgar, 'Logue, Lionel George (1880–1953),' *Australian Dictionary of Biography*, National Centre of Biography, Australian National University, 2000.

David Ehrenstein, *Open Secret: Gay Hollywood 1928–2000*. New York: Perennial, 2000 [1998]

David Ehrenstein, 'Out of Hollywood's Closet. *Behind the Screen How Gays and Lesbians Shaped Hollywood*, 1910–1969 By William J. Mann. Viking: 432 pp., $29.95,' *Los Angeles Times*, 30 Dec 2001: R.2

Lehman Engel, *Words with Music: Creating the Broadway Musical Libretto*. Updated and Revised by Howard Kissel. New York: Applause, 2006

Peter Entwisle, *Behold the Moon: The European Occupation of the Dunedin District 1770–1848*. Dunedin, NZ: Port Daniel Press, 1998

Euripides, *Medea, adapted by Robinson Jeffers*. New York: Random House, 1946

Maurice Evans, *All This… and Evans Too! A Memoir*. University of South Carolina Press, 1986

Gerald Fischer, 'The Professional Theatre in Adelaide 1838–1922,' *Australian Letters* 2, 1960: 79–97

Kathleen Fitzpatrick, *Solid Bluestone Foundations and Other Memories of a Melbourne Girlhood 1908–1928*. Melbourne University Press, 1998 [1983]

James Forsyth, *Tyrone Guthrie: The Authorised Biography*. London: Hamish Hamilton, 1976

James Friedman, ed., *UCLA Film and Television Archive presents* Hallmark Hall of Fame: *The First Fifty Years*. Los Angeles: Regents of the University of California, 2001

Mark Gattis, *James Whale: A Biography*. London: Cassell, 1995

S Gaunson, 'Australian International Cinema: The Royal Commission on the Moving Picture Industry in Australia, 1926–1928, Australasian Films Ltd. and the American monopoly,' *Studies in Australasian Cinema* 6.3, 2012: 291–300

Leyla Georgie, *The Establishment of Madame Antonia*. Paris: The Vendôme Press, 1938.

Gielgud's Letters: John Gielgud in His Own Words. Introduced and edited by Richard Mangan. London: Weidenfeld & Nicolson, 2004

Lyndhurst Giblin, 'The National Theatre and Leisure,' NAA CPD 20 September 1944

Phoebe Barkan Gilpin, *Jeffers Newsletter* 81, January 1992: 82

Dagmar Godowsky, *First Person Plural: The Lives of Dagmar Godwosky by Herself*. New York: Viking Press, 1958

Isaac Goldberg, *George Gershwin: A Study in American Music*. New York: Frederick Ungar, 1958

Ruth Gordon, *My Side: The Autobiography of Ruth Gordon*. New York: Harper & Row, 1976

Michelle Green, *The Dream at the End of the Word: Paul Bowles and the Literary Renegades in Tangier*. New York: Harper Collins, 1991

Martin Gottfried, *Jed Harris, the Curse of Genius*. Boston: Little, Brown, 1984

Fiona Gregory, 'High-Cultural Histrionics: Judith Anderson's 1955 tour of Australia,' *Australian Drama Studies*, Apr 2006: 91–114

Fiona Gregory, 'Crossing Genre, Age and Gender: Judith Anderson as Hamlet,' *Journal of American Drama and Theatre* 26.2, 2014

Boze Hadleigh, *Hollywood Lesbians*. New York: Barricade Books, 1994

Jed Harris, *A Dance on the High Wire: A Unique Memoir of the Theatre*. New York: Crown Publishers, 1979

Christopher Hassall, *The Timeless Quest: Stephen Haggard*. London: Arthur Barker, 1948

Richard Heathcote, ed., *Carrick Hill: A Portrait*. Kent Town, SA: Wakefield Press, 2011

H Heron, *History of the Forest Theater* foresttheaterfoundation.org

Cayton Hutton, *Macbeth: The Making of the Film*. London: Max Parrish, 1960

Charles Higham, 'Dame Judith: "Ugly! Dirty!"' *Bulletin*, 12 March 1966: 38

'J A Hogue,' in Heather Radi, Peter Spearritt and Elizabeth Hinton, *Biographical Register of the New South Wales Parliament 1901–1970*. Canberra: Australian National University Press, 1979

Tony Howard, *Women as Hamlet: Performance and Interpretation in Theatre, Film and Fiction*. Cambridge University Press, 2007

Frances Holden and David E. Russell, 'Lotte Lehmann: The Santa Barbara Years,' Davidson Library Oral History Program, University of California, Santa Barbara

Jane Hunt, '"Unrelaxing Fortitude": Susannah Franklin,' *Australian Literary Studies*, Oct 2002: 379–88

Robinson Jeffers, *Roan Stallion, Tamar and Other Poems*. New York: Boni and Liveright, 1925

John Jenkin, 'Brose, Henry Herman Leopold Adolph (1890–1965),' *Australian Dictionary of Biography*, National Centre of Biography, Melbourne University Press, 1993

Gary Johansen, 'Judith Anderson: Grand Dame of the Theater,' *Sunday World-Herald Magazine of the Midlands,* 1 June 1969: 14–15

Robert Kafka & Michael Mooney. "Jeffers Scholarly Materials: Small and Minor Holdings," *RJN* 56 (June 1980): 47–55

Michael Kammen, 'Culture and the State in America,' *Journal of American History* 83.3, 1996: 814

James Karman, ed., *The Collected Letters of Robinson Jeffers With Selected Letters of Una Jeffers. Volume One, 1890–1930*. Stanford University Press, 2009

James Karman, ed., *The Collected Letters of Robinson Jeffers With Selected Letters of Una Jeffers Volume Two, 1931–1939*. Stanford University Press, 2011

James Karman, ed., *The Collected Letters of Robinson Jeffers With Selected Letters of Una Jeffers Volume Three, 1940–1962*. Stanford University Press, 2015

Michael H Kater, *Never Sang for Hitler: The life and Times of Lotte Lehmann, 1888–1976*. Cambridge University Press, 2008

RHB Kearns, 'A Pioneer Pastoralist of the West Darling District: H.B. Hughes of Kinchega' (unpublished paper, 1970, Broken Hill Historical Society, 21 pages, copy held in ADB file)

RHB Kearns, *Broken Hill*, Volume I: 1883–1893: Discovery and Development. Broken Hill, NSW: Broken Hill Historical Society, 1987, c1973

Orry Kelly, *Women I've Undressed; The Fabulous Life and Times of a Legendary Hollywood Designer and a Genuine Australian Original*. Foreword by Catherine Martin. Afterword by Gillian Armstrong. North Sydney: Ebury Press, 2015

Veronica Kelly, 'Julius Knight, Australian matinee idol: costume drama as historical re-presentation,' *Australasian Victorian Studies Journal* 9, 2003: 128–44

Veronica Kelly, 'A Complementary Economy? National Markets and International Product in Early Australian Theatre Managements,' *New Theatre Quarterly* 21.1, 2005: 77–95

Veronica Kelly, 'Minnie Tittell Brune and the Gallery Girls: an Australian Idol of Modernist Consumerism,' *Theatre Research International* 31.1, 2006: 17–36

Veronica Kelly, *The Empire Actors: Stars of Australasian Costume Drama 1890s-1920s*. Strawberry Hills, NSW: Currency House, 2009

Veronica Kelly, 'Australia's Svengali: Gaston Mervale in Theatre and Film,' *Australasian Drama Studies* 5, 2011: 107–25

Veronica Kelly, 'Australia's First Belgian Day (1915): History of Stage and Street.' In *A World of Popular Entertainments: An Edited Volume of Critical Essays*, ed. Gillian Arrighi & Victor Emeljanow. Newscstle upon Tyne: Cambridge Scholars Publishing, 2012, 137–49

Veronica Kelly, 'Australasia: mapping a theatrical "region" in peace and war,' *Journal of Global Theatre History* 1.1, 2016: 62–77

Kay Koenig, *Broken Hill: 100 Years of Mining*. New South Wales: Department of Mineral Resources, 1983

Phil A Koury, *Yes, Mr DeMille*. New York: G.P. Putnam's Sons, 1959

Nancy Kuhl, *Extravagant Crowd: Carl Van Vechten's Portraits of Women*. Yale University Press, 2007

Lawrence Langer, *The Magic Curtain*. New York: E P Dutton, 1951

Marilyn Lake, 'Sounds of History: Oratory and the Fantasy of Male Power.' In *Talking and Listening in the Age of Modernity*. Joy Damousi & Desley Deacon, eds. Canberra: ANU Press, 2007, 49–58

Benjamin Lehman, 'Recollections and Reminiscences,' *RJN* 63, June 1983: 12–18.

Roy Liebman, *Vitaphone Films: A Catalog of the Features and Shorts*. Jefferson, North Carolina: McFarland, 2003

Norman Lindsay, *Bohemians of the Bulletin*. Sydney: Angus and Robertson, 1965

'Harmony in Diversity: Wright S. Ludington.' In *The Collector in America*, compiled by Jean Lipman and the editors of *Art in America*. New York: Viking Press, 1961

Mabel Dodge Luhan, *Lorenzo in Taos*. Santa Fe, NM: Sunstone Press, 2007; facsimile of original 1932 edition

Guthrie McClintic, *Me And Kit*. Boston: Little, Brown, 1955

Diana McLellan, *The Girls: Sappho Goes to Hollywood*. Robson Books, 2001

Ailsa McPherson, 'Fitton, Dame Doris Alice (1897–1985)', *Australian Dictionary of Biography*, National Centre of Biography, Australian National University, 2007

Jim McPherson, 'Movies. A Dame named Anderson,' *TV4*, 27 January 1991

Guy Madden, 'Blood Money,' *Film Comment* 43.3, May 2007: 8

Axel Madsen, *The Sewing Circle; Sappho's Leading Ladies*. New York: Kensington Books, 2002

Two Collections: Margaret Mallory Ala Story. Catalogue, Santa Barbara Museum of Art and California Palace of the Legion of Honor, 1966

Dorothy Mandel, *Uncommon Eloquence: A Biography of Angna Enters: Writer, Dance-Mime, Artist*. Denver, Colorado: Arden Press, 1986

William J. Mann, *Behind the Screen: How Gays and Lesbians Shaped Hollywood, 1910–1969*. New York: Viking, 2001

David Marr, *Patrick White, a Life*. New York: Vintage, 1991

Barth Carpenter Marshall, 'The Jeffers Family: A Reminiscence,' *RJN* 69, Apr. 1987: 17–19

Hugh Massingberd, 'Sapphic stars of the silver screen,' *The Mail on Sunday* (London) 1 April 2001: 66

Jill Matthews, 'Education for Femininity: domestic arts education in South Australia,' *Labour History*, Nov 1983: 30–53

P. Monaghan, 'Medea in Australia: responses to Greek tragedy in contemporary Australian theatre,' *Didaskalia* 6.3, 2006

Sheridan Morley, *John Gielgud: The Authorized Biography*. New York: Simon & Schuster, 2010

Bernadine Morris, 'Valentina, a Designer of Clothes For Stars in the Theater, Dies at 90,' *New York Times* 15 Sep 1989

Michael A. Morrison, *John Barrymore, Shakespearean Actor*. Cambridge University Press, 1999

Tad Mosel with Gertrude Macy, *Leading Lady: The World and Theatre of Katharine Cornell*. Boston: Atlantic-Little, Brown, 1978

Laura Mulvey, 'Visual Pleasure and Narrative Cinema,' *Screen* 16:3, 1975: 6–18

Nickolas Muray and Paul Gallico, *Revealing Eye: Personalities of the 1920s*, in photographs by Nikolas Muray and words by Paul Gallico. New York: Atheneum, 1967

George Jean Nathan, *The Theatre Book of the Year, 1947–1948: A Record and an Interpretation*. Madison, NJ: Fairleigh Dickinson University Press, 1975 [1947]

J. R. Nethercote, 'Unearthing the Seven Dwarfs and the Age of the Mandarins.' In Samuel Furphy, ed., *The Seven Dwarfs and the Age of the Mandarins: Australian Government Administration in the Post-War Reconstruction Era*. Canberra: ANU Press, 2015

Stuart Oderman, 'Lillian Gish: A Friend Remembered,' *Journal of Popular Film and Television*, 22:2, Summer 1994: 52–7

Stuart Oderman, *Lillian Gish, A Life on Stage and Screen*. Jefferson, NC: McFarland & Company, 2000

Laurence Olivier, *The Autobiography: Confessions of an Actor*, London: Orion Books, 1994 [1982]

Sally O'Neill, 'Coppin, George Selth (1819–1906),' *Australian Dictionary of Biography*, National Centre of Biography, Australian National University, Melbourne University Press, 1969.

Sally O'Neill, 'Hughes, John Bristow (1817 – 1881),' *Australian Dictionary of Biography*, National Centre of Biography, Australian National University, Melbourne University Press, 1972

Jim O'Quin, 'Going National: How America's Regional Theatre Movement Changed the Game,' *American Theatre*, 16 Jun 2015

Clyde Packer, 'Dame Judith Anderson.' In *No Return Ticket: Clyde Packer Interviews Nine Famous Australian Expatriates*. North Ryde, NSW: Angus & Robertson, 1984

Philip Parsons, ed., *A Companion to Theatre in Australia*. Cambridge University Press, 1995

Stephen Pascal, ed., *The Grand Surprise: The Journals of Leo Lerman*. New York: Knopf, 2007

John R. Payne, 'Robinson Jeffers: Humanities Research Center, Austin,' *RJN* 60, June 1982: 222–3.

Danny Peary, 'The Hollywood Gangster, 1927–1933,' in *Cult Movies 2: Fifty More of the Classics, the Sleepers, the Weird and the Wonderful*. New York: Dell, 1983

Bruce Pennay, 'McCulloch, George (1848 – 1907),' *Australian Dictionary of Biography*, National Centre of Biography, Australian National University, Melbourne University Press, 1974

Joel Pfister, *Staging Depth: Eugene O'Neill and the Politics of Psychological Discourse*. Chapel Hill: University of North Carolina Press, 1995

Andrew Pike and Ross Cooper, *Australian Film 1900–1977: A Guide to Feature Film Production*. Melbourne: Oxford University Press, 1998

Christopher Plummer, *In Spite of Myself*. New York: Vintage, 2012 [2008]

Howard Pollack, *George Gershwin: His Life and Work*. Berkeley: University of California Press, 2006

Hal Porter, *Stars of Australian Stage and Screen*. London: Angus & Robertson, 1965

James Prideaux, *Knowing Hepburn and Other Curious Experiences*. Faber & Faber, 1996

Thérèse Radic, 'Johnson, Gertrude Emily (1894–1973)', *Australian Dictionary of Biography*, National Centre of Biography, Australian National University, Melbourne University Press, 1996

Eric Reade, *Australian Silent Films: A Pictorial History of Silent Films from 1896 to 1926*. Melbourne: Lansdowne Press, 1970

Edmund Richardson, 'Re-living the apocalypse: Robinson Jeffers' Medea,' *International Journal of the Classical Tradition* 11.3, December 2005: 369–82

John Rickard, 'Alden, John (1908–1962)', *Australian Dictionary of Biography*, National Centre of Biography, Australian National University, Melbourne University Press, 1993

Ann N Ridgeway, ed., *The Selected Letters of Robinson Jeffers 1997–1962*. Baltimore: John Hopkins Press, 1968

Major James Robertson, *With the Cameliers In Palestine*. Naval & Military Press, 2006 [1938]

Emily A Rollie, Review of Gay Smith, *Lady Macbeth in America: From the Stage to the White House, Theatre Survey* 53.2, Sept 2012: 334–6

Eleanor Roosevelt, 'My Day.' The Eleanor Roosevelt Papers, Digital Edition, Columbian College of Arts & Sciences, George Washington University www.gwu.edu/~erpapers/myday/

Lois Palken Rudnick, *Mabel Dodge Luhan: New Woman, New Worlds*. Albuquerque: University of New Mexico Press, 1997 [1984]

Vita Russo, *The Celluloid Closet: Homosexuality in the Movies*. New York: Harper and Row, 1981, rev 1987

Martha Rutledge, 'J A Hogue and Oliver Hogue,' *Australian Dictionary of Biography*, National Centre of Biography, Australian National University, Melbourne University Press, 1983

Andrew Sarris, 'Big Funerals,' *Film Comment* 13.3, May/Jun 1977: 6–9, 64

George Schaefer, *From Live Tape to Film: 60 Years of Inconspicuous Directing*. Los Angeles: A Directors Guild of America Publication, 1996

Tom Shales, '"Celluloid Closet": HBO's Breath Of Fresh Air,' *Washington Post* 30 Jan 1996: D1

Jack Shulimson, 'Maurice Evans, Shakespeare and the U.S. Army,' *Journal of Popular Culture* 10.2, Fall 1976: 255

Jane Sloan, *Alfred Hitchcock: A Filmography and Bibliography*. Berkeley: University of California Press, 1995

Jacob Smith, *Spoken Word: Postwar American Phonograph Cultures*. Berkeley: University of California Press, 2011

Jane E Southcott, 'Changing the Voices of Teachers and Children: singing and elocution in South Australia in the nineteenth and early-twentieth century,' *Journal of Historical Research in Music Education*, Oct 2006: 53–70

Peter Spearritt, 'Willis, Henry (1860–1950),' *Australian Dictionary of Biography*, National Centre of Biography, Australian National University, Melbourne University Press, 1990

A M Sperber and Eric Lax, *Bogart*. London: Weidenfeld and Nicolson, 1997

Elliott Stein, 'Fox Before the Code: Film Forum, December 1–21,' *Village Voice*, 29 November 2006

David Stratton, *The Avocado Plantation: Boom and Bust in the Australian Film Industry*. Sydney: Pan MacMillan, 1990

Viola Tait, *A Family of Brothers: The Taits and J C Williamson*. Heinemann, 1971

Kevin Thomas, 'Screening Room,' *Los Angeles Times*, 22 May 2003

Kenneth Turan, 'Pre-Code Films: Sex and Lies but no Videotape. In the '30s, before morality became an issue, Hollywood took up with tawdry women and brutal men. UCLA screens some examples,' *Los Angeles Times*, 17 May 2003: E.1

Decherd Turner, 'Robinson Jeffers at Texas,' *Library Chronicles of the University of Texas at Austin* 40, 1987: 21–23

Phoebe Vincent, *My Darling Mick: The Life of Granville Ryrie, 1865–1937*, Canberra: National Library Australia, 1997

Frederic Wakeman, *The Saxon Charm*. New York: Rinehart & Company, 1947

Michael Walsh, 'Building a New Wave: Australian Films and the American Market,' *Film Criticism* 25.2, Winter 2001: 21–39

Stephen Walsh, *Stravinsky: The Second Exile: France and America, 1934–1971*. New York: Alfred A Knopf, 2006

Richard Waterhouse, *Private Pleasures, Public Leisure: A History of Australian Popular Culture since 1788*. Melbourne: Longman, 1995

Richard Waterhouse, 'Kenna, Peter Joseph (1930–1987)', *Australian Dictionary of Biography*, National Centre of Biography, Australian National University, Melbourne University Press, 2007

Margaret Webster, *The Same Only Different: Five Generations of a Great Theatre Family*. New York: Knopf, 1969

John West, 'Nellie Bramley,' *Companion to Theatre in Australia*, ed. Philip Parsons. Cambridge University Press, 1995, 96–7

Patricia White, *Uninvited: Classical Hollywood Cinema and Lesbian Representability*. Bloomington: Indiana University Press, 1999

Paul Whiteman and Mary Margaret McBride, *Jazz*. New York: J H Sears, 1926

Garry Wills, *Outside Looking In: Adventures of an Observer*. New York: Viking, 2010

Rose Wilson, 'Hayward, Sir Edward Waterfield (Bill) (1903–1983)', *Australian Dictionary of Biography*, National Centre of Biography, Australian National University, Melbourne University Press, 2007

Robin Wood, *Hitchcock's Films*. New York: A S Barnes and Co, 1965

Robin Wood, *Hitchcock's Films Revisited*. New York: Columbia University Press, 1989

Lindy Woodhead, *War Paint: Madame Helena Rubinstein and Miss Elizabeth Arden*. New York: Wiley, 2010 [2004]

The Letters of Alexander Woollcott. New York: The Viking Press, 1944

'Writing great leads,' *The Writer* 106.10, Oct 1993: 18

Kohle Yohannan, *Valentina: American Couture and the Cult of Celebrity*. New York: Rizzoli, 2009

William C Young, *Famous Actors And Actresses On The American Stage Books*. New Providence, NJ: R.R. Bowker, 1975

Jeff Zorn, 'The Robinson Jeffers *Medea*,' *Jeffers Newsletter* 90, Spring 1994; from *Laetaberis: The Journal of the California Classical Association*, New Series No. IX, 1992–93: 18–24

Unpublished Theses

Fiona Gregory, Enduring Transformations: Landmark Performance in the Careers of Mrs Patrick Campbell and Judith Anderson. PhD thesis, ANU, 2003

Jane Hunt, Cultivating the arts: Sydney women culturists 1900–1950, PhD thesis, Macquarie University, 2001

Angela Macdonald, Hollywood Bound: A History of Australians in Hollywood to 1970. PhD thesis, University of Sydney, 2001

Documentary

The Celluloid Closet (1995) produced and directed by Rob Epstein and Jeffrey Friedman

Acknowledgements

This book has taken almost as long as my dear friend Jill Roe's biography of Miles Franklin. I wish she were here to read the finished product of what had been the subject of many lively conversations. I have been supported and encouraged for many years by my feminist colleagues and friends, Cath Bishop, Larry Boyd, Barbara Caine, Ann Curthoys, John Docker, Ann McGrath, Marilyn Lake, Susan Magarey, Jill Matthews, Carroll Pursell, Yves Rees, Sue Sheridan, Carolyn Strange, Anne Whitehead and Angela Woollacott, several of whom were part of our stimulating discussion group, the Modernistas, in the early days of this project. I am also grateful to John Muller for his forensic research on the Anderson homes in Adelaide.

This was a transnational undertaking, and the travel involved could not have been attempted without the support of an Australian Research Council Discovery Grant (DP0558626). I have to thank numerous archivists and librarians for their assistance, especially at the University of California, Santa Barbara Special Collections, the Margaret Herrick Library Special Collections, Academy of Motion Picture Arts and Sciences, Los Angeles, the UCLA Special Collections, the Warner Bros Archives and the Cinematic Arts Library at the University of Southern California (what wonderful places to have to work in), the New York Public Library, who opened the Katharine Cornell papers to me when they were in the process of recataloguing them, the Harry Ransom Centre at the University of Texas at Austin, the Nebraska State Historical Society, Lincoln, Nebraska, the Australian Performing Arts Collection at the Arts Centre Melbourne, the National Library of Australia PROMPT Collection, the Performing Arts Collection at the Adelaide Festival Centre and the Mitchell Library at the State Library of New South Wales. I was also lucky enough to meet three of Judith Anderson's nieces, Susan, Jenifer and Judith, and to correspond by email with her step-children, Lenka Myers and Luther Greene, Jr, all of whom generously provided family photographs for use in the book; and to speak by telephone with her grand-niece, Jan Read and her niece, Jess Horder. Her god-daughter Mimi Muray Levitt generously provided copies of correspondence between Anderson and her father, Nickolas Muray, and access to the photograph by Muray on the cover of this book. In Los Angeles, actor Diane Baker talked about her late life friendship with Anderson; and in New York Marian Seldes spoke about her long association with her. Archival work can be very lonely, and I appreciated the hospitality I received from old and new friends, Eileen Boris, Patricia Cohen, Lois Banner, Emily and Tom Cutrer, George Wolf and John Taylor, Margaret Jacobs, Rosalind Rosenberg, Alice Kessler-Harris, Jane and Michael Marcus, Sylvia and Tony Francis, and in Austin, John Higley, Christine Williams and Martin Button and other old friends and colleagues.

No book such as this could be researched so thoroughly without the extraordinary riches provided by online resources such as our own wonderful Trove, the numerous international newspapers, magazines and journals available through the State Library of New South Wales and the Australian National University, by *Variety* online and the many US provincial newspapers accessible through newspapers.com.

Progress on the book was slowed down delightfully by my two lively grandchildren, Inez and Raphy, who spent many hours with me before school claimed them. My family as always keeps me entertained and grounded, and my many new friends at Waterbrook spurred me on by regularly asking 'Have you finished your book yet?'

List of Illustrations

View from Mount Lofty, looking towards the Port, across the Adelaide Plains ca 1846 by George French Angas and J W Giles.	2
My Pretty Maid. Fanny Anderson and Nancy Sack. Winners of the Humorous Duet at the Recent Unley Competitions.	8
Picnickers at Watson's Bay, Looking Towards North Head	20
Fanny Anderson at 15	21
Julius Knight as Napoleon	30
Francee Anderson at 18	42
Broadway 1918	53
Francee Anderson in America aged 21	54
Anderson's co-star Louis Calhern was one of her brief flirtations of this period.	73
The pylons of the Harbour Bridge had just been completed when Judith Anderson returned to Sydney in 1927.	92
Truth's view of Judith Anderson's 'sex play,' 16 January 1927	93
The Cobra Woman	97
McCrae in The World's News caricatures Judith Anderson's sexual magnetism in Cobra, 5 February 1927	98
Los Angeles, 1929, looking from La Brea towards Hollywood	118
Judith Anderson, by Nickolas Muray 1927	119
Although she starred in a number of failures from 1927 to 1934, Judith Anderson was a 'class draw' admired by critics and featured often in magazines	123
Robinson Jeffers 1930s	128
Jed Harris on the cover of Time 3 September 1928	130
... moulded in the most exquisite gown of the theater season... Judith Anderson in As You Desire Me, Vogue 1931	138
Judith Anderson and José Rubin in As You Desire Me, by Hirschfeld	141
Judith Anderson in The Mask and the Face as Countess Savina Grazia, with Humphrey Bogart as her would-be lover	146
Judith Anderson and George Bancroft in Blood Money 1933	148
Blood Money featured cross-dressing women and elegant clothes, as well as the usual gangster violence and vice	151
The Old Vic where Judith Anderson performed Macbeth with Laurence Olivier in 1937	158
Judith Anderson dressed by Valentina in Come of Age 1934	159
Judith Anderson and Helen Menken in The Old Maid 1935	164
Judith Anderson and Guthrie McClintic in his garden discussing Divided by Three September 1934	167

Judith Anderson and John Gielgud in Hamlet 1936	176
Judith Anderson and Laurence Olivier in Macbeth at the Old Vic 1937	186
Berkeley from the hills 1940, by Don Kingman	196
Judith Anderson and Ben 'Peter' Lehman September 1937, by Carl Van Vechten	197
Judith Anderson as Mary, mother of Jesus, in Family Portrait 1939	208
Telegram to Judith Anderson from Cecil B De Mille, 3 May 1939. UCSB. He later bought the film rights to Family Portrait	212
Pacific Coast Highway looking north to Santa Monica, Pacific Palisades and Malibu 1940	216
Judith Anderson menacing Joan Fontaine in Rebecca 1940	217
Judith Anderson and Joan Fontaine in Rebecca 1940	222
'Judith Anderson, in the plum role of Mrs Danvers, is quite unforgettable:… significantly modified from du Maurier to make her younger and more clearly a coded lesbian.' Tim Robey 2009	223
'Mr Hitchcock is a very tolerant director and a very kindly man.' Judith Anderson 1940	225
The quality of living danger and waiting disaster	226
David O Selznick, Joan Fontaine, Alfred Hitchcock and Judith Anderson, Academy Awards Dinner February 1941	227
Maurice Evans and Judith Anderson in Macbeth 1941	234
Katharine Cornell, Judith Anderson and Ruth Gordon, Time, December 1942	240
Judith Anderson in New Guinea 1944	248
Judith Anderson in Hawaii with future television producer and director George Schaefer 1943	252
An elegant Judith Anderson with Vincent Price in Laura 1944	254
Judith Anderson and Shirley Cornell entertained by RAAF officers after a wartime show at Aitape, Northeast New Guinea, 1944	259
Judith Anderson, Teresa Wright and Robert Mitchum with the prone figure of John Rodney in Pursued 1947	262
The moody lighting of Pursued casting shadows over its protagonists and their secrets.	268
Jeb (Robert Mitchum) sings the Londonderry Air while Adam (John Rodney) can't bring himself to join in	270
Judith Anderson as Ma Callum saves Robert Mitchum from a lynching	271
Judith Anderson as Medea 1947. Photographer unknown	278
Anderson 'plots the doom of her enemies with the intelligence of a priestess of black magic.' Brooks Atkinson, 1947	279
Judith Anderson with Robin and Una Jeffers outside Tor House. Donnan Jeffers and his wife Lee are on the left, 1947	282

List of Illustrations

Anderson's vision of Medea, captured by Freuh	284
Toscanini's telegram to Judith Anderson before opening night of Medea *1947*	290
Judith Anderson as Medea, by Richard Avedon	292
Playbill for Medea II	299
The view from 'Rancho Verde,' 2005	308
'Rancho Verde' – a house of my own, built from the ground up, just as I had always dreamed of it	309
Judith Anderson and Luther Greene arrive in Hawaii for the final production of Medea, *June 1949*	310
Judith Anderson with Luther 'Spike' Greene and Lenka Greene 1949	311
Judith Anderson with her beloved mother and two of the series of dachshunds she kept from the 1930s	312
Judith Anderson with Jenifer, Judy, Susan and David, with their mother Laura behind, soon after they arrived in 1950. Frank followed a few months later.	313
Hirschfeld caught the moment in 1958 when one cohort of First Ladies of the Stage gave way to the next in this mural for the Playbill Restaurant at the Hotel Manhattan. From left: Ethel Merman, Julie Harris, Lynn Fontanne, Helen Hayes, Katharine Cornell, Judy Holliday, Judith Anderson, Ruth Gordon and Shirley Booth	320
Judith Anderson in Come of Age *1952. From left: Marian Seldes, Judith Anderson, Jacqueline deWit and Muriel Rahn*	323
This beautiful gold dress, worn in John Brown's Body, *is now in the collection of the Performing Arts Centre in Adelaide.*	327
Advertisement for In the Summer House *January 1954*	329
Judith Anderson and George C Scott in Comes a Day *1958*	332
Judith Anderson and Elizabeth Taylor in Cat on a Hot Tin Roof *1958*	335
Frank, Laura and family visit Judith Anderson on the set of Salome, *summer 1952*	336
Judith Anderson with her niece Susan in Paris in 1955	337
Lotte Lehmann and Judith Anderson coach Lehmann's most successful student, the soprano, Grace Bumbry, in Lady Macbeth, *1973*	338
A rare photograph of Wright Ludington, in Ludington Court at the opening of the Santa Barbara Museum of Art 1941	339
Judith Anderson with her god-daughter Mimi Muray, c 1942	341
Judith Anderson won her first Emmy for Macbeth *in 1955, shown here with fellow-winner Robert Cummings*	342
Judith Anderson in her Emmy-nominated television performance as the Marquesa in Thornton Wilder's Bridge of San Luis Rey	353
Judith Anderson and Guthrie McClintic after she played Medea in Sarah Bernhardt's Theatre in Paris 1955. Alice B Toklas is behind her	361

Judith Anderson as Medea, Sydney 1955, with Peter Cohen and Robert Rosen as her sons	373
A tribute from fan Olga Deane, October 1955	374
Judith Anderson enjoying her return to Australia 1955	376
The Australian press was always interested in Judith Anderson's wardrobe, especially when it was designed by fellow-Australian Orry-Kelly	377
Judith Anderson outside Buckingham Palace after being made a Dame Commander of the British Empire July 1960	382
George Schaeffer directing Maurice Evans and Judith Anderson in Macbeth *1960*	383
Judith Anderson receiving her second Emmy for her performance as Lady Macbeth 1961	388
Hirchfeld's view of Anderson's Oresteia, *Ypsilanti, 1966, with Jacqueline Brookes, Donald Davis, Ruth Volner, John Michael King, Frederic Warriner, Karen Ludwig, and Ruby Dee (far right) as Cassandra. Behind the cloud: Jack Fletcher and Bert Lahr in* The Birds.	398
Judith Anderson with 'the best Jason I ever had,' Henry Brandon, in Medea *1965*	402
Judith Anderson and Charlton Heston in the television production of Elizabeth the Queen *1968*	410
Judith Anderson as 'Dame Buffalo Cow Head' in A Man Called Horse *1968*	413
Dame Judith Anderson as Hamlet 1970	416
Dame Judith, now playing the nurse, will break your heart	426
Judith Anderson as the Vulcan High Priestess in Star Trek III: The Search for Spock *1984*	436
Dame Judith, still elegant at 89, attends the premiere of Just Between Friends *Santa Monica 1986*	438
Plaque commemorating Dame Judith Anderson in the wall of the Adelaide Festival Centre. It is currently in storage during the redevelopment of the Centre.	442
Judith Anderson as Mrs Danvers fondles her former mistress's fur in the boudoir scene with the new Mrs De Winter	452
Left: Cover of Criterion DVD of Rebecca *2001. Right: Cover of Criterion Blu-ray of* Rebecca *2017*	455
Mrs Danvers demonstrates the transparency of Rebecca's nightgown in the movie's boudoir scene	456
Mrs Danvers as pop culture icon, by Alejandro Mogollo	458
Coffee cup from Mrs Danvers Café, Liverpool	459
Mrs Danvers (Rebecca), 2015, by Jade Yumang	460
Mosaic at the entrance to the Leytonstone tube station in London	461

Index

Page references in **bold** denote illustration

Abbott, George 131, 363, 469
ABC (Australian Broadcasting Commission) 256, 375
Abel, Walter 142
Academy of Motion Picture Arts and Sciences 242, 468, 499, 502: Academy Award (Oscar) **227**, 227-30, 250, 253, 272, 274
Academy of Television Arts and Sciences: Emmy 326n27, **342**, 350, 352, **353**, 387, **388**, 390, 411-12, 429, 474-5, 477-80; Lifetime Achievement Award 435
Actors union (Australia) 33
Addinsell, Richard 160, 322, 385
Adelaide **2**, 2-18, 23, 43-4, 48, 50, 58, 62, 65, 68n22, 100-05, 108, 111, 256, 327, 367, 371, 375-8, 463-4, 467, 474, 478; Festival Centre **442**, 482, 499; Festival of the Arts 401, 403-5; Jockey Club 9; Kent Town 6; Norwood District High School 15, 18; Port Adelaide Racing Club 6; racecourses 5-6; Rose Park, 6, 9, 311: Primary School 9-12; Tattersalls Club 6, 9
Aeschylus 142-3, 317, 403, 405-7
Akins, Zoe 168
Alberg, Mildred Freed 346, 351, 476
Alden, John 371-2
American Academy and National Institute of Arts and Letters award 296
American Conservatory Theatre (ACT) 418-25
American National Theatre and Academy (ANTA) 314-9, 327, 333-4, 344, 362, 473-4
American theatre 57, 58-9, 69-70, 83-4.123-6, 130-32
American Theatre Wing 241: Tony Award 296, 429
Americanisation 109-14: 'Yankee twang' 108
Anderson, Frances Margaret (Fanny, Francee, Frantic, Judith, Peg, Meg, Judy)
  As an Australian 2-51, 73-4, 82, 91, 92, 114, 255-61, 370-71, 379
  And United States of America: 50-51, 53, 100, 370-71, 379, 385
  As an actor: Emotional 26, 44-45, 67-69, 74, 99, 101-3, 121, 125, 143-4, 161, 167, 181, 194, 210-211, 237, 246, 291, 300-01, 324, 329, 358, 392, 418-22, 444; character 27, 40, 74, 103, 121, 127, 153, 169, 224-5, 228-9, 232, 238; 246, 255, 266-74, 288, 303, 323, 329, 344, 386, 425, 448; voice (singing) 13, 18; voice (speaking) 11, 22, 27, 74, 83, 99 101-2, 121, 139, 147, 159, 225, 246, 283, 290, 303, 344, 355, 357-8, 363-4, 366, 386, 404, 421-2, 425, 433, 437, 443, 445, 447-8, 453; face and body 22, 27, 68, 74, 83, 99, 122; **138**; 141, 147, 159, 225-6, 283, 290, 344, 404; personality 40, 44, 72, 103, 153; sexuality 154, 181, 454; fashion icon 69, 71-21, 39, 89, **138**, 141, 145-6, **146**, **148**, 150, 152-3, **159**, 160, 167, 180-82, 253, 286, **323**, **327**, 367, **385**, **438**; modernity 84-5; illness 102, 127, 155, 214, 294-5; 321; depression 120, 143, 153, 156-7, 170; 'genius' 101, 106, 161, 317; greatness 161, 211, 235, 238, 273, 289, 290-91, 300, 304, 318, 323, 345, 350, 367, 386, 401, 404, 407, 422, 436; jobless 65, 91, 253, 331, 332, 347, 362, 391, 399, 412, 436; lesbian poster girl 455-7
  Awards and accolades: see Woman's Christian Temperance Union; Ballarat South Street Eisteddfod; Academy of Motion Picture Arts and Sciences; American Theatre Wing, Tony Award; Academy of Television Arts and Sciences: Emmy; Lifetime Achievement Award; First Lady of the American Stage; Donaldson Award; American Academy and National Institute of Arts and Letters; Drama League of New York Most Distinguished Performance; New York Drama Critics; Women's International Center Living Legacy Award; Dame Commander of the British Empire; Companion of the Order of Australia
  Family: David, grandfather 3; David, nephew 311, **313**, **336**; Elizabeth Jessie 'Did', sister 5,17, 21, 25, 62, 75, 170, 173, 199, 298, 312: memoir 5n2, 7n19, 482; Frank Batchelor, brother 5, 21, 199, 222, 311-12, **336**; George Batchelor, uncle 3; Jack, brother 5, 21, 47, 376; James, father rise and fall 3-7: from Arbroath, Scotland 3, 179, 400; refuses contact 47, 143; death 143, 221-2; Jenifer McCurry, niece 311, **312**, **313**, **336**, 500; Jessie Margaret, nee Saltmarsh, mother 4-23, 47, 51, 96, 100, 143, 173, 183, 185,199, 201, 232-3, 311, 312; Judith Valentine, niece 311, **313**, **336**, 500; Kathleen, wife of Jack 376, wife of Frank 222, **313**, **336**; Susan, niece 311,
313, **336,** 337n41, **337**, 500; see also Saltmarsh
  Education: truant 12, 17-18; poor spelling, grammar 172; lack of education 190-91
  Elocution see Mabel Kerr; Lawrence Campbell
  Homes: Adelaide 6, 9-12; Sydney 22-3; New York 58, 59-60, 183; Pacific Palisades, Los Angeles 231; Berkeley 200; see also 'Villa Vallambrosa'; 'Rancho Verde'; 'Arbroath'
  Names: Fanny 9; Frantic 22, 24-5; Francee 24, 26, 31; Judith 67; Peg 157, 172-3, 184, 188, 198-9, 205, 213; Judy 136, 142, 252, 295, 379
  Physical description 22, 26, 55-6, 67-8, 183, 367-8; moderne 72-5, 83, 89; glamorous 26, **138**, 140-41; profile 140, **141**; 188, 194; nude pictures 199; lithe 448
  Relationships, romantic: see Oliver Hogue; Greg Bruer; 'Doug'; Daniel Joseph Mahoney; Louis Calhern; Nickolas Muray; Charlie Chaplin; Philip Merivale; Benjamin 'Peter' Lehman (husband); Ian Keith; Luther Greene (husband)
  Temperament: temper 11, 153, 189-91, 221, 283; individuality 11-12; performer 12; love of music 18, 70, 85-6; determination 22, 114; impetuous 22; ambitious 22, 129, 131; gift for friendship 22, 24; charm 96, 200-01; temperamental 200; 'good sport' 251-2, 255-61; compassionate 252-3, 255-61; magnetism 245; 'ideal offstage personality' 417
Antheil, George 267
Arbroath, Scotland 3, 179
'Arbroath,' Montecito, Santa Barbara 400
Arlen, Michael 87, 101-5
Arlington Players, Boston 65, 465
Armitage, Mary 404
Armory Players, Binghamton 64, 465
Atkinson, Brooks 121, 124, 139, 144, 145, 160, 167, 169, 180, 210, 236, 237, 278-9, 287, 317-99, 323, 325, 329, 333, 362, 402
Australian Elizabethan Theatre Trust 367-78
Australian theatre 17
Australians, on Broadway 48-50; 72, 80; see Jean Robertson, O P Heggie, Leon Errol, Zoe Caldwell; in Hollywood see Annette Kellerman, Enid Bennett; Sylvia Bremer (Breamer); Dorothy Cumming; Errol Flynn; Orry Kelly; Arthur Shirley; Ronald Byram, Eily Malyon, Plumpton Wilson, Michael Pate
Avedon, Richard **292**, 299

Baker, Diane 400, 500
Ball, William 418-9
Ballarat South Street Eisteddfod 14, 15
Bancroft, George **148**
Bankhead, Tallulah 59
Barefoot, Spencer 391-3
Barnes, George 228
Barnes, Howard 255, 273
Barrett, Franklyn 25n22
Barrymore, Ethel 60, 170, 300, 350; John 61, 233, 323, 358, 417
Batchelor, Elizabeth Anderson, mother of James Anderson 3n1
Baylis, Lilian 193, 194
Behrman, Sam 70, 85, 86, 126
Belasco, David 18, 57-8, 79-80, 83-4, 87-91, 95-6, 99, 101, 108, 114, 120-21, 124-6, 166, 466
Bell, Nelson B 142-3, 245, 273
Bellamy, Madge 63
Bennett, Enid 34, 48, 49
Bennett, Richard 110
Bentley, Walter 17, 362, 365, 390, 417
Berlin Arts Festival 321, 362, 365, 473; Film Festival 390
Bernhardt, Sarah 121, 291, 325, 331, **361**, 362, 364-5, 428, 431-2, 435, 437, 446-7
Best, Mabel see Mrs S D Kerr 13
Blinn, Holbrook 79-80, 87, 131-2, 466
Bogart, Humphrey 145, **146**, 168
Booth, Shirley 145, **320**
Boucicault, Dion Jr. 94
Bowles, Jane 327-30; Paul 328
Brady, Alice 142
Bramley, Nellie 31, 34-5
Brandon, Henry 298, 302-3, 401, **402**, 403n139, 432, 436
Breen, William 315

Bremer (Breamer), Sylvia 34, 48, 49
Bridges, Roy 98
Britain: Empire 3, 108; rivalry with USA 108; film industry 108-9; imperial preference 108-9; theatre 110
British War Relief 241, 356
Broadway 18, 31, **53**, 57, 60, 65, 70-72, 126, 130-31, 202, 255, 289, 315, 331-5, 363, 429-30, 466-72, 474, 476, 480
Brock, Tom 391, 394, 396, 477
Broken Hill 4, 6; Cosmopolitan claim 4; Broken Hill Proprietary Limited 4
Brooks, Eileen, nee Robinson 256
Brookes, Jacqueline **398**, 406
Brough and Boucicault Company 33
Brown, Katherine 'Kay' 218-20
Brown, Rowland 151, 469
Browne, Irene 33-4
Bruer, Greg 48, 56, 57, 61, 62, 77
Bunting, Emma 464, 59-60
Burton, Richard 390
Butler, Sheppard 68
Byram, Ronald 35

Caedmon Records 356-7, 447, 481-2
Caldwell, Zoe 295, 371, 428-9, 431-5, 437-8
Calhern, Louis 73, 91, 95, 289, 466
Camel Corps (Cameliers) 47-8, 57; see also Oliver Hogue
Campbell, Lawrence 23-7, 34, 317
Carlyle, Pom 23
Carmel, California 132-3, 200, 205, 232-3, 263, 281, 295, 315, 319, 326, 471
Carpinteria, California 311n1, 312-13, 314. 337n41, 385, 393
Casey, Maie (Lady) 385, 404; Lord (former Richard Casey) 385n110, 404
Cashin, Bonnie 253
Cassidy, Claudia 139, 295-6, 301-2, 325, 327, 394, 395, 429
Castillo, Antonio 285-7, 300
Celebrity 75, 82, 83, 139, 344-5, 354, 367, 400, 435
Censorship 108-14, 153-4, 454-5; see also 'Sex plays'; Royal Commission into the Moving Picture Industry in Australia; Pre-Code movies; Motion Picture Production Code; Rebecca
Champlin, Charles 379, 401-2
Chapin, Anne, nee Morrison 64, 340
Chaplin, Charlie 88
Chapman, John 264, 319, 324, 328
character actors 219, 232, 255, 266-74
Chase, Edna Woolman 88; Ilka 88, 95
Chatterton, Ruth 149, 150, 346
Chekhov, Anton 132, 135, 243-6, 328, 447
Chiarelli, Luigi 145
Chicago 64, 66-71, 82, 85-7, 139, 142-3, 171, 228, 246-7, 301-2, 394, 423, 429, 465-9, 471-3, 477, 479
Cilento, Diane 402-3
City Center; see New York City Center Civic Playhouse
Clair, Rene 266, 472
Claire, Ludi 316
Cocteau, Jean 364
Coe, Richard L 303, 362, 431
Coffey, Vera 15
Cohen, Barbara, nee Holdridge 356-7
Peter Cohen **373**
Coleman, Robert 83, 139-40
Colman, Ronald 219, 243
Columbia Records 356, 481
Come of Age **159**, 160-62, 165-6, 170, 177, 179, 185, 188-9, 193, 199, 213, 265, 266, **323**, 321-6, 328, 346, 385, 386, 401, 469, 473
Compass Productions 351-2, 386, 408; see also George Schaefer
Condon, James 404
Connery, Sean 402-3
Conrad, Peter 453, 457
Cook, Katherine 13
Cooke, Richard P 318, 324, 409
Coombs, H.C. (Nugget) 368-9, 404
Coppin, George 17
Cornell, Katharine (Kit) 69-70, 75, 84, 89, 94, 96, 124-5, 160, 165-6, 170-71, 173-4, 188, 235, **240**, 242, 243-6, 284, 289, 296, 302, 314, 315, 316, **320**, 325, 333-4, 341, 363, 410, 444, 447, 453, 460, 471

Corry, John 434-5
Coulouris, George 284
Coward, Noël 86-7, 94, 126, 181, 184, 192-3, 203, 206, 289
Craig, Ailsa see Ailsa Graham
Crawford, Cheryl 204, 206, 209-11, 314-5, 331-2, 470, 476
Cullingham, Mark 434, 480
Cumming, Dorothy 34, 49, 58
Currie, Glenne 426, 433

D'Acosta, Mercedes 231
Dalrymple, Jean 478
Daly, Arnold 65
d'Ana, Paolo 250
Dane, Clemence 70, 84, 160, 162, 165, 177, 178, 188, 322
Darwell, Jane 227-8
David, Hal 250
Davis, Bette 149, 242-3, 247, 428
Davis, Donald **398**, 406, 408, 475
de Boehme, C B 378
De Mille, Cecil B 55-6, **212**, 230, 334, 475
Deane, Olga **374**
Decca Records 356, 481
Dee, Ruby **398**, 406
Dennis, C J 99
Directors Guild of America 390: Lifetime Achievement Award, Academy of Television Arts and Sciences 435
Donaldson Award for Best Actress 296
'Doug' 64-76
Douglas, Kirk 245
Douglas, Melvyn 243
Downes, Martha (stage name of Millie Rowland) 298-9, 316
Drama League of New York Most Distinguished Performance 296
Duse, Eleonora 76, 166, 183
Dutton, Geoffrey 404

Eagels, Jeanne 87, 96
Eakin, Robin 23
Ebert, Roger 255
Edinburgh Festival 384, 447, 476
Edwards, Ben 288, 296, 300, 431
Ehrenstein, David 456
Eichelberger, Lieutenant General Robert 258-9, 300
Emery, John 284, 298, 301
Emmy Award see Academy of Television Arts and Sciences
Engel, Lehman 356
Enters, Angna 264n223, 280, 310, 331n35, 339-40, 347, 350, 362, 366, 376, 391-4, 396, 411-12, 436
Evans, Maurice 135, 161, 209, 233, **234**, 235-9, 241, 243-4, 247, 249-51, **251**, 260, 293, 322, 334, 343, 345-52, 356, **383**, 384-95, 402, 428, 436, 444, 471, 474, 481
Ewell, Tom 211

Famous Players Film Company (Famous Players-Lasky; Paramount Pictures) 49, 87
Faulkner, Trader 384
Feminist scholarship 454-6
Ffolkes, David 285
Finch, Peter 369
'The Firm'; see J C Williamson Ltd
First Lady of the American Stage 125-6, 165, 244; Anderson as 144, **320**, 444
Fitton, Doris 369-71
Flynn, Errol 244
Fonda, Henry 228, 347, 374-5
Fontaine, Joan **217**, 219, 222-8, **222**, **223**, **226**, **227**, 425, 455-6, **456**
Fontanne, Lynn 59, 83, 124-7, 288-9, **320**, 334, 357
Forest Theater, Carmel **232**, 232-3, 319, 471
Francis, Kay 150
Franklin, Sydney 230
Freedley, Vinton 340
Funke, Lewis (LF) 302, 362

Gallery Girls 16n16, 35
Gallipoli 40, 48, 61, 261; see also Oliver Hogue
Garbo, Greta 140, 150, 155, 230, 456
Garland, Judy 402, 403n139

Index

Garland, Robert 140, 144, 161, 167
Garmes, Lee 266
Gassner. John 202, 204-6, 315
Gay Activists Alliance 454
Geary Theatre, San Francisco 300, 421
Gershwin, George 84-6
Geva, Tamara 301
Giblin, Lyndhurst 368
Gielgud, John 122, 174, **176**, 177-85, 188, 192-5, 205, 235-7, 281, 283-95, 303, 319, 330, 372, 417, 425, 444, 447, 472
Gilkey, Stanley 166, 202
Gillette, William 63, 464-5
Gilliatt, Penelope 389
Gillmore, Margalo 59, 75, 84, 341
Gish, Dorothy 136; Lillian 127, 131, 135, 180, 184, 188, 193, 195, 380, 424
Godowsky, Dagmar 70-71, 85-6
Gordon, Leon 94, 97-9, 111
Gordon, Max 203, 289
Gordon, Ruth 58-9, 83, 124, 126, 132, 134, 231, 236, **240**, 243-7, **320**, 333-5, 363, 444, 447
Gould, Jack 350-53, 386-7, 411
Graham, Ailsa, nee Craig 35, 371-2
Greene, Ellie; *see also* Ellie Martin 264, 266, 298; Lenka *later* Myers 264, 266, 298, **311**, 340, 500; Luther 264-6, 280-81, 298-304, **310**, 310-21, 340, 436, 473; Luther Jr (Spike) 264, 266, 298, **311**, 340, 500
Gregory, Paul 418-25, 473, 479
Gussow, Mel 423
Guthrie, Tyrone 192, 369, 429

Hadleigh, Boze 457
Haggard, Stephen 160, 199
Hagman, Larry 332
Halliday, Heller 340; Richard 340
Halsey, Admiral Bill 252, 341
Hamlet 61, 174, **176**, 177, 184, 192-3, 209, 235-7, 274, 284, 295, 330-31, 336-7, 391, 393, 395, 414, **416**, 417-25, 444-5, 447-8, 470, 479
Hammond, Percy 127, 144-5
Hampden, Walter 61, 417
Hanna, Len 203-6
Harcourt Beatty-Madge McIntosh Company 17
Harris, Jed 124-56, 129-37, **130**, 141-3, 155, 247, 263-4, 345, 428, 473
Harris, Julie **320**
Harris, Radie 288-9
Harris, Richard 412
Harry Clay's Vaudeville Company 36
Hart, Moss 131
Hawkins, William 233, 340n45
Hayes, Helen 58, 62-3, 76, 83, 124-6, 137, 149-50, 184, 236, 289, 295, 315, **320**, 333-5, 352, 354, 357, 362, 395, 424, 428, 460
Hays, Will 154; see also Censorship
Hayward, Sir Edward 'Bill' & Ursula 376, 401, 403,
Healey, John 404
Hecht, Albert 284
Hecht, Ben 267, 472
Heggie, O P 58, 80
Heifetz, Jascha 70, 85-6, 107, 162
Helpmann, Robert 282, 379
Henderson, Ray 125, 166
Hepburn, Katharine 203, 434, 448
Heston, Charlton 409-11, **410**
Heyward, Leland 220
Hirschfeld, Albert 140, **141**, **320**, 398
Hitchcock, Alfred 218-28, **225**, **227**, 425, 446, 453-9, 470, 480
Hogue, Gwen 57; James Alexander 24; John Roland 24, 57, 61; Oliver 22, 24-5, 27-8, 40, 47-8, 48n42, 50-51, 57, 61-2 (death), 64, 261; Tien (Anne Christine) 24-5, 25n22, 27, 35
Holdridge, Barbara; *see* Barbara Cohen
Hollywood 25n22, 48-9, 55-7, 87, **118**, 140, 148-54, 171, 185, 201, 219-21, 227-31, 237, 247, 253, 256, 266-74, 274n238, 281, 289, 298, 301, 350, 355, 387, 402, 410, 436-7, 468; Canteen 241-2; Victory Committee 242; lesbians 453-7; 'Sewing Circle' 454
Hopkins, Arthur 145, 417, 469
Hopper, Hedda 167, 230-31, 281

Howard, Leslie 75, 384
Howe, James Wong 270
Hughes, Henry 6
Humphries, Barry 429
Hunt, Hugh 369-72, 474
Hurst, Fannie 162, 184
Huston, Walter 322

Ibsen, Henrik 247
Independent Theatre, Sydney 369, 371
International Exchange Program (ANTA) 362
International Television Festival, Monaco 390

J & N Tait 46, 463
J C Williamson Ltd 'The Firm' 16-17, 24, 32-3, 35-6, 46, 91, 94-5, 98, 104, 463, 467, 474
Jeffers, Donnan **282**; Garth 252, 253; Lee **282**; Robinson **128**, 129, 132-3, 167-8, 202, 205-6, 212, 232, 243, 247, 263-5, 280-304, **282**, 309, 314-9, 321, 325-6, 326n27, 340, 340n46, 356-7, 363, 366, 391, 392, 394, 406, 408, 437-8, 478-82; Una 200, 253, 263-5, **282**, 316; Festival 428: Tribute to Dame Judith Anderson 448-9
Johnsrud, Harold 137

Kalgoorlie, Western Australia 3, 221
Kanin, Garson 231, 363
Kaufman, Beatrice 166
Keenan, Frank **66**, 67-71, 466
Keith, Ian 154-6
Kelly, George 121-3
Kelly, Gregory 59
Kelly, Orry 230, 232, 341, **377**
Kenna, Peter 372
Kennedy Center for the Performing Arts, 430-34, 480
King, Dennis 243, 294
Kellerman, Annette 73
Kerr, Mrs S D (Mabel), nee Best 13-18, 23, 377
Kerr, Walter 406, 409
Kingsley, Grace 110
Knapp, Dan 420, 423
Knight, Julius 14, 17, **30**, 31-45, 47, 48, 49, 55, 241, 371, 463
Knopf, Alfred & Blanche; *see also* Alfred A. Knopf, Inc. 88
Kronenberger, Louis 290-91

'Lady Kitty' (*Adelaide Register*) 104
Lamkin, Speed 326, 331-2
Landau, Ely 353
Langner, Lawrence 202-6, 289
Laughton, Charles 161, 193, 326-7, 473
Lawrence Campbell School of Public Speaking and Dramatic Art 23, 26-7, 34, 317
Lawrence, Gertrude 86, 107, 289
Lee, Olga, nee Hammerslough 62, 64-5, 96-8, 345, 396, 428
Lehman, Benjamin 'Peter' 129, 132-6, 140-43, 150-57, 160, 162-3, 167-74, 177-85, 187-95, **197**, 198-206, 209-14, 221, 221n61, 236
Lehmann, Lotte 300, 338, **338**
Leigh, Vivien 193, 204, 218, 368
Lemmone, Jack 16
Leonard, William 406-7, 423
Lerman, Leo 329-30
Levitt, Mimi, nee Muray
Lewis, David 231-2, 340, 471
Lewis, Jerry 335, 477
Light Horse Brigade 27, 47; *see also* Oliver Hogue
Litvinoff, Ivy 245
Lobero Theatre, Santa Barbara 300, 473
Lockwood, Billie 107
Logue, Lionel 13
Longford, Raymond 25n22
Lord, Pauline 69, 84, 110, 127, 245
Los Angeles Drama Critics Circle awards 437
Lubitch, Ernst 149-50
Ludington, Wright Saltus 338-9, **339**, 436
Ludlum, Charles 358
Luhan, Mabel Dodge 200, 340, 340n46
'Lulworth,' Potts Point 23; *see* Patrick White
Lunt, Alfred 59, 83-4, 126, 203, 205, 289, 331, 334, 363, 428

Lupino, Ida 227
Lyell, Lottie 25n22

MacArthur, Charles 125, 149
McCleery, Albert 346
McClintic, Guthrie 59, 70, 82, 84, 124-5, 162, 165-74, **167**, 177-88, 201-2, 206, 235, 243-6, 265, 284, 297-304, 309, 315-6, 321-6, 332n37, 334, 341, **361**, 361-6, 392, 394, 407, 417, 469-74
McIntosh, Hugh 43-4, 95
McKelvie, Martha 'Gloria' 55-7
McKern, Leo 369
McLachlan, Lena 35
McLellan, Diana 456
McMahon, Aline 284, 286
McPherson, Jim 354-5
Machiz, Herbert 409, 478
Mack, Willard 79-80
Macy, Gertrude 166, 202, 244
Maddocks, Melvin 386-7
Madsen, Axel 456
Mahoney, Daniel Joseph 70, 163n67, 168n71
Mallory, Margaret 338-9
Malyon, Eily 219
Mann, Thomas 211
Mantell, Marianne 356-7
Mantle, Burns 121, 125, 166, 169
'Maramanah,' Potts Point 23
Marinoff, Fania 188, 200, 203
Marsh, Leo 80-81
Martin, Ellie; *see also* Ellie Greene 339-40, 392-4, 399, 403, 412; Joe 339-40
Martin, Mary 332, 341, 435, 436; *see also* Richard & Heller Halliday
Massey, Raymond 204, 242, 289, 326-7, 481
Maugham, Somerset 106, 124, 145, 345, 347, 473
Mayo, Nick 401-2, 478
Medea 129, 132, 134, 136, 139, 141-2, 167-8, 263-6, **278**, **279**, **284**, **290**, 278-91, **293**, **299**, 293-304, 309-10, 315-9, 321-2, 324-6, 331, 343, 352-4, 356-8, **373**, **374**, 360-78, 390-4, 400-04, 407, 414, 418, **426**, 427-35, 436, 443-5, 447-8, 453, 472-8, 480-81
Mencken, H L 88
Menken, Helen 75, 84, 91, 111, 144, **164**, 168-71, 188, 203-4, 241, 298, 341
Melba, Dame Nellie 16, 18, 36-7, 50, 378
Melbourne Union Theatre Repertory Company 370-71, 429
Meredith, Burgess 242, 266
Merivale, Philip 89, 111
Merrill, Beth 83, 96
Mervale, Gaston 17, 47
MGM 149, 150, 227, 229, 232, 253, 384, 470, 476
Michell, Keith 369
Mielziner, Jo 177-8
Milgrim, Sally **71**, 71-2
Miller, Gilbert 144, 469
Miner, Worthington (Tony) 202, 205
Minotis, Aleko (Alexis) 366
Mitchum, Robert **262**, **270**, **271**, 268-71, 438
Modern Amusements Limited 43-4, 463
Moffitt, Jack 270, 273
Molnar, Ference 120, 124, 315
Mondello, Bob 424-5, 445
Montalvo ('Villa Montalvo'), Saratoga, California 214
Montecito, California 338, 385, 400, 438
Monterey Wharf Theater 326, 391, 394, 477
Moore, Grace 87, 89n53, 135
Moore, Maggie 17
Moran, Harold 35
Morgan, Charles 194
Morris, Howard 250
Morris, Roger 250
Morrison, Anne; *see* Anne Morrison Chapin
Moscovitch, Maurice 110, 112
Moses, Sir Charles 368
Moss, Arnold 356
Motion Picture Production Code 150, 154; *see also* Censorship
Mucha, Alphonse Maria **360**, 431
Mulvey, Laura 454

Muray, Mimi; *later* Levitt 83n40, 89n51, 341, **341**, 500; Nickolas 82-3, 88-9, **119**, 121, 203, 204, 341, 500
Murray, Gilbert 372
Musgrove, George 32, 35

Naldi, Nita 87
Nathan, George Jean 254, 267
Nation, Lona 'Biddy' 10, 12, 376
National Board of Review of Motion Pictures 226; *see also* Censorship
Nazimova, Alla 142, 219-20, 230
Nesbitt, Cathleen 428, 482
New Guinea: Aitape 257, **259**; Biak Island, 257, 260; Dobodura 258-9; Finschhafen 256-7; Nadzab 356-7; Hollandia, Dutch New Guinea 257-60
New York City Center Civic Playhouse 303, 322-4, 332, 334, 346, 408-9, 473, 478
New York Drama Critics prize 221
Niblo, Fred 34-5, 49, 108
'Norma' (*Border Watch*) 104

Ojai Festival, California 325, 473
Old Vic, London **158**, 178, **186**, 189, 192-5, 235, 268-9, 371, 384, 417, 447, 470, 476
Olivier, Laurence 155, **158**, **186**, 194, 203-4, 219, 228, 274, 289, 295, 368, 390, 425-6
Olsen, Moroni 232, 471
O'Neal, Charles 432; Ryan 432
O'Neill, Eugene 69, 124, 126-7, 142-3, 156, 334, 446-7
O'Neill, Josephine 375
Oscar *see* Academy of Motion Picture Arts and Sciences

Packer, Clyde 51-3, 475, 477, 480
Pakula, Alan 332, 476
Paramount Pictures 150, 229, 230, 250, 472
Parker, Dorothy 204
Parkes, Lizette 34, 44, 47-50
Parsons, Louella 221, 266
Pate, Christopher; Michael 401
Paul Scott agency 59, 64
Paxinou, Katina 366
Philip Lytton's Dramatic Company 36
Pirandello, Luigi 137-42
Playwrights Company 326-8
Plummer, Amanda 434; Christopher 363-4
Pollock, Arthur 161, 210,
Porter, Hal 58
Potts Point, Sydney 22-3, 96
Power, Tyrone 243, 326-7, 481
Pre-Code movies 150-53; *see also* Censorship
Preminger, Otto 254-5, 471-2
Price, Ellis; Maurice 25
Price, Vincent 253-5, **254**, 399, 443
Prideaux, James 436-7, 439-44, 448
Pringle, Aileen 87-8, 185, 341, 436
Pulitzer Prize 110, 121, 124, 126, 170, 346, 352, 469

Quayle, Anthony 357, 400, 481
Quentin, Robert 367, 372
Quintero, José 328, 353, 474, 476

Radio 96, 201, 203, 206, 241, 355, 356, 375
Rahn, Muriel 322, **323**
'Rancho Verde,' Carpinteria **308**, **309**, 312-6
Rathbone, Basil 111, 120, 243, 314, 482
Rea, Oliver 281-4, 294-7, 472
Rebecca **217**, **222**, **223**, **226**, **227**, 217-29, 231, 272-3, 425, 443-4, 446, **452**, **454**, **456**, **458**, **459**, **460**, **461**, 453-61, 470; sexual perversion 223 *see* Censorship
Redgrave, Roy 17
Reed, Florence 142, 188, 286, 288, 296
Reeves, Edward 13-14
Renoir, Jean 266-7, 472
Republic Studios 267, 355, 472
Reynolds, James 160
Rialto, New York City 60
Rich, Frank 433

Index 509

Road, the 38, 170-71, 231, 334, 394-5,
Robertson, Jean, *later* Brose 14, 21, 62
Robertson, Malcolm 371
Robey, Tim 225
Robinson, Edward G. 230, 266
Robinson, Eileen, *later* Brooks 256
Robinson, Francis 341
Robson, Flora 219-20
Roerick, William 391-2, 394
Rogers, Mary (Pickford) & Buddy 281
Roosevelt, Eleanor 184, 245, 252, 318
Rowland, Millie (stage name Martha Downes) 298-9; Toby 280, 298, 437
Royal Commission into the Moving Picture Industry in Australia 109, 112
Rubin, José **141**, 206
Russo, Vito 454

Saint-Denis, Michel 189, 192-5, 470
Saltmarsh, Fanny (aunt) 12-13, 22; Jessie Margaret: see Jessie Margaret Anderson; William (uncle) 13; William Henry (grandfather) 12
'Salute to France' 362, 474 *see also* State Department
Santa Barbara, California 264, 300, 310, 336-9, 400, 421, 427-8, 468, 470, 472-3, 475, 477, 479, 481; Film Festival 438; Museum of Art **339**
Sarah Bernhardt Theatre, Paris 362-6
Sarris, Andrew 154
Satterley, John 409
Schaefer, George 249-50, 252, 322, 345-8, 350, 384-7, 390, 408, 411-14, 420, 435, 437, 438-9, 473-80
Schallert, Edwin 220, 227-9, 242-3, 255, 272-3,
Schenck, Joseph 150, 154
Schlee, Valentina **159**, 160, 287, 323, 391, 436
Scotland 3, 32, 143, 178-9, 384, 387, 400
Scott, George C **332**, 332
Seldes, Marian 285, 299, **299**, 316, **323**, 401, 500
Selznick, David O 218-28, **227**, 453, 470, 474
Servoss, Mary 122, 185, 199-200, 202, 204, 237, 298, 340
'Sex plays' 113-14, 371; *see also* Censorship; Royal Commission into the Moving Picture Industry in Australia
Sexual fantasy 453
Shakespeare, William 15, 178, 180, 192, 194, 233, 235-9, 239-41, 249, 334, 356, 369, 371, 387-9, 395, 400, 400n134, 410, 417-25, 446-7, 479, 481; Shakespeare Society of America 422
Shaw, George Bernard 84, 242, 293, 330
Shearer, Norma 140, 150
Sherwin, Amy 18
Shirley, Arthur 25n22
Shubert Organization 122, 137-42, 243, 467-8
Smith, Cecil 246, 352, 386, 390-91, 393, 406, 408, 411, 413, 427, 435
Smith, Oliver 328, 474
Solomos, Alexis 401, 405-8, 478
South Street Competitions *see* Ballarat South Street Eisteddfod
Sperling, Milton 268, 270, 472
Stage Women's War Relief Society 241
Stanwyck, Barbara 149, 267, 322, 456
Stapleton, Maureen 333, 411-12
Starr, Frances 58, 90
State Department (US) 333, 473-4 *see also* International Exchange Program
Steichen, Edward 82, 181, 203
Stevens, Roger 327, 330-31, 430, 474, 477
Stewart, James 'Jimmy' 166, 228, 229
Stewart, Nancye 47, 50-51, 62, 369; Nellie 17, 47, 50, 98-9,
Stewart, Rosalie 120-22, 467
Stone, Dr Hannah 199
Stone, Judy 121, 418
Story, Ala 338-9
Stover, Harry F. 'Freddy' 250
Stravinsky, Igor 265
Studio system 274, 274n238
Sullivan, Dan 419-22
Sullivan, Ed 344
Sullivan, Noël 132, 154, 172-3, 177, 182-5, 188-221, 297
Sumner, John 369
Sydney Permanent First Nights Club 96

Tait, E J 'Ted' 46-8, 70, 95; Dorothy 95; Jessie 95; John 46; Nevin 46
Tallis, George 94
Talmadge, Norma 87
Taylor, Elizabeth 353, **335**,
Taylor, Laurette 57, 289
Temple, Emma 33
Theater Recording Society 357
Tony Award; *see* American Theatre Wing
Tittell Brune, Minnie 16-17, 34
Toklas, Alice B **361**
Tomasetti, Marie 371
'Tor House,' Carmel 185, **282**, 391
Toscanini, Arturo 203, 210-11, 289, **290**
Triangle Film Corporation 49
'Trooper Bluegum' (Oliver Hogue) 48n42
Trubin, Sybil 351-2, 384-6, 413
Tynan, Kenneth 365
Twentieth Century Pictures 151, 469
Twentieth Century Fox 253, 471-2

Ulric, Lenore 57, 80, 83, 90-91, 95, 120, 125
'Uncle James' (*Sunday Times*) 106-8
United Services Organization (USO) 242, 255-6
United States Film Registry 255

'Val Verde,' Montecito 338; *see also* Noël Sullivan
Valentina; see Valentina Schlee
Valentino, Rudolph 87
Valley Music Theater 401-3, 478
Van Vechten, Carl 86, 184, 188, **197**, 199-200, 203, 230, 341, 349
Vaughn, Hilda 232, 298-9, 302
Vert, Bernice 70
Victor, Leslie 97
'Villa Vallambrosa,' Whitley Heights, Los Angeles 298
Vitaphone 150, 468

Whale, James 231, 340
Wallis, Hal B 232, 471-3
Wallsten, Robert 6n3, 258, 391, 396
Walsh, Raoul 268, 472
Ward, Hugh 35
Warner Bros 149-51, 229, 232, 471-2
Watson, Dr John B 65, 199; Rosalie 65, 170, 199
Watts, Richard 237-8, 319
Webster, Margaret (Peggy) 203, 209, 231, 236-7, 408-9, 471
White, Patrick 23 *see also* 'Lulworth,' Potts Point
Whitehead, Robert 281-97, 327, 428-34, 437, 438, 472, 480
Wilder, Thornton 352, **353**
William Anderson Dramatic Company 17
Williams, Emlyn 427, 436
Williamson, J C 17, 32, 35-6
Willis, Hon. Henry 24
Wills, Garry 358, 447
Wilson, Plumpton 33
Winchell, Walter 345
Winter, Keith 161, 193
Wittber, August 12
Wolters, Larry 349-50, 354, 387, 389
Woman's Christian Temperance Union (WCTU) 14, 15-16
Women's International Center Living Legacy Award 436
Wong, Anna May 231
Woollcott, Alex 122, 140, 184

Xenakis, Iannis 406-7

Yarnell, Agnes 214, 437
Yevtushenko, Yevgeny 403-5
Ypsilanti Greek Theatre **398**, 400-01, 405-8

Zanuck, Darryl F 469, 150-51, 153

www.ingramcontent.com/pod-product-compliance
Lightning Source LLC
Chambersburg PA
CBHW041436300426
44114CB00025B/2897